THE LANGUAGES OF
CHINA

S. ROBERT RAMSEY

The Languages of China

PRINCETON UNIVERSITY
PRESS

Copyright © 1987 by Princeton University Press
Published by Princeton University Press, 41 William Street,
Princeton, New Jersey 08540
In the United Kingdom: Princeton University Press,
Chichester, West Sussex

Library of Congress Cataloging in Publication Data will be found on the last
printed page of this book

ISBN   0-691-06694-9
ISBN 0-691-01468-X (pbk.)

Second printing, with revisions, and
first Princeton Paperback printing, 1989

Publication of this book has been aided by grants from the
Harold W. McGraw, Jr., Fund of Princeton University Press
and the University of Maryland

This book has been composed in Linotron Sabon

Princeton University Press books are printed on acid-free paper and
meet the guidelines for permanence and durability of the Committee on
Production Guidelines for Book Longevity of the Council on Library Resources

Printed in the United States of America

10   9   8   7   6   5   4

CONTENTS

LIST OF ILLUSTRATIONS

LIST OF TABLES

PREFACE

Although it seems rather obvious now, I remember being exhilirated one day a few years ago by the discovery that linguistic information could be woven into a narrative about other themes. For example, I had long struggled to explain what was meant by "the Chinese language": Were the "dialects" really dialects of a single language, or were they in fact separate languages, each an entity in its own right? My usual explanation in those days was to say, in a very straightforward manner, that it depended on what was meant by the term "language," and that the definition of the term derived from a variety of "extralinguistic factors," including the social, cultural, and political contexts, and so on. The explanation was certainly valid, but it was unbearably dry and, somehow, something was missing. Finally it occurred to me that, if those extralinguistic factors were so important to understanding the problem, then would it not make sense to discuss the language in terms of those factors from the beginning?

Out of this idea eventually came the first chapter in this volume. The essay can be read on one level as a simple narrative about the National Language Movement, but it is also meant to be something more. Showing how the Chinese themselves have tried to cope with the linguistic diversity of their country is a practical way, I believe, of introducing the themes of standardization and variation. The story is really about what should be called the Chinese language.

Later, in order to broach the topic of Chinese grammar and structure, I found that it was useful to discuss how, for reasons peculiar to our own Western history, we have created what might be called "the myth of the primitive language." And, in a similar fashion, the question "Is Chinese monosyllabic?" can be talked about by looking first at the concept of the word in our own culture.

These are examples of the approaches I take in this volume. In various ways—in lists, charts, notes, and in text set in smaller type—I have made room for reference information; but the essays that form the backbone of the work were written first and foremost with the educated general reader in mind. They are my attempts at building bridges.

There is another aspect of this work that should perhaps be explained to the reader. The picture of China presented here is a study not just of one language but of many. Along with a description of what we in the

West conventionally call "Chinese," it also contains descriptions of the dozens of other languages spoken within China's international borders, the languages of the so-called national minorities. In contrast with its widely held image, China is not an ethnic and cultural monolith. The people who speak Mandarin share their country with an extremely large variety of other groups who continue to flourish under the overarching umbrella of Chinese civilization. Throughout the long history of East Asia, these groups have played an important role in the composition of the Chinese state and they are still, in a number of subtle ways, affecting what goes on today. It is my conviction that China, the Chinese, and especially the Chinese language can all be seen in sharper focus against this varied background.

The viewpoints expressed in this work have been shaped by the ideas, counsel, and encouragement of others. Sam Martin's eclectic brand of linguistics and his unfailing good sense have for me always been a model of responsible scholarship. In almost daily conversations over the better part of a decade, Gari Ledyard shared with me his thoughts on the widest possible variety of topics. I also remember discussions with many other Columbia colleagues during those years, and to all of these people I owe a debt of gratitude. No one, however, has had more to do with this work and with my own thinking about language than Robert Austerlitz. It was he who first suggested that I teach a survey course on these languages; it was he with whom I discussed every topic in this volume and who read and commented on every draft; and it was he who showed me what humanism and humanity are really about. If this book were to carry a dedication, it would be to him.

I shall mention some of the other people who helped me to complete this work, either through discussion, or through correspondence, or by reading and suggesting changes in the various drafts: Paul Anderer, Paul Benedict, Hans Bielenstein, David Bradley, Kun Chang, Cheng Yumin, Myron Cohen, John DeFrancis, June Dreyer, William Hannas, Ann Hashimoto, Mantaro Hashimoto, C. T. Hsia, Robert Hymes, Jack Jacoby, David Johnson, Eugene Liu, Irene Liu, Victor Mair, James Matisoff, Jerry Norman, Loretta Pan, Shi Ziqiang, Ting Yen, Galal Walker, Ronald Walton, Eddie Wang, P. Y. Wu, and Paul Yang. The research and the collection of materials upon which the study is based were supported, in part, by the National Endowment for the Humanities and by the Columbia University Council for Research in the Humanities. The maps of China were drawn by Roy Ashley, Cartographic Services Laboratory, University of Maryland, and subsidized by an award from the General Research Board of the

Graduate School, University of Maryland. These maps have won the Out-standing Achievement award in the category of thematic maps in the American Congress on Surveying and Mapping 13th Annual Map Design Competition.

TRANSCRIPTIONS AND SYMBOLS

Standard Chinese forms are Romanized in Pinyin. Chinese proper nouns are also given in Pinyin, but there are a few exceptions. Cities such as Canton, Hong Kong, Amoy, Chungking, and Nanking already have well-known English names, and to normalize these spellings into Guangzhou, Xianggang, Xiamen, Chongqing, and Nanjing would serve only to make them sound less familiar. I vacillated considerably before choosing to spell the capital of China Peking instead of Beijing, since both forms are by now in common use; however, in the end, I decided to keep the traditional English spelling. (In English we normally write Moscow, Vienna, and Havana instead of Moskva, Wien, and La Habana.) For somewhat arbitrary stylistic reasons, I have retained a few of the old Postal Code spellings, such as Soochow and Hangchow, yet normalized others, such as Foochow, which is here written Fuzhou; in cases where confusion might result, I have included the alternative spelling in parentheses. It would not be appropriate to change the spellings of the names Sun Yat-sen, Chiang Kai-shek, Taipei, or Hu Shih; but Lu Xun, Chen Duxiu, Mao Zedong, and Zhou Enlai have now become the usual English forms.

The system of phonetic transcription adopted in this work was designed to minimize diacritics and exotic symbols. Many consonants are transcribed as digraphs or trigraphs (that is, as sequences of letters), but most of these complex symbols are already familiar conventions in English-language writing. Vowels cannot be handled in this way because of the particular structure of the Chinese syllable, and so for these sounds unitary symbols were adopted. Two dots over a vowel—often called an umlaut—indicate rounding; a Spanish tilde indicates nasalization; a (raised) *r* after a vowel shows that the vowel is pronounced with the tip of the tongue retracted or retroflexed; a colon indicates a long vowel. Numerical superscripts are used to transcribe tones; the convention used to assign the numbers is explained in the section "From Middle Chinese to Peking Mandarin" at the end of Chapter 7. The arrangement of the charts displaying consonant systems is shown in the accompanying table.

Consonant Systems

	Labial	Denti-labial	Dental	Retro-flex	Alveo-lar	Palatal	Velar	Post-velar	Glottal
Voiceless stop	p		t			ty	k	K	q
Aspirated stop	p'		t'			t'y	k'	K'	
Voiced stop	b		d			dy	g	G	
Voiceless affricate			ts	chr	ch	chy			
Aspirated affricate			ts'	ch'r	ch'	ch'y			
Voiced affricate			dz	jr	j	jy			
Voiceless fricative	F	f	s	shr	sh	sy	x	X	h
Voiced fricative	V	v	z	zhr	zh	zy	gh	GH	ɦ
Nasal	m		n			ny	ng		
Voiceless nasal	mh		nh				ngh		
Lateral			l						
Voiceless lateral			lh						
Flap or trill			ŕ	r					
Voiceless flap			ŕh						
Semivowels	w, wy					y			

PART I THE CHINESE LANGUAGE

1 A LANGUAGE FOR
ALL OF CHINA

In the early years of the Republic, a Chinese intellectual named Qian Xuantong published an open letter to Chen Duxiu, the leader of the attack on Confucianism.

> Dear Mr. Chen:
>
> In an earlier essay of yours, you strongly advocated the abolition of Confucianism. Concerning this proposal of yours, I think that it is now the only way to save China. But, upon reading it, I have thought of one thing more: If you want to abolish Confucianism, then you must first abolish the Chinese language; if you want to get rid of the average person's childish, uncivilized, obstinate way of thinking, then it is all the more essential that you first abolish the Chinese language.

To keep China from perishing and to make the Chinese people into a civilized, twentieth-century people, argued Qian, the Chinese language had to be replaced by Esperanto.

After the overthrow of the Manchu dynasty in 1911, many of the new leaders of China planned to create a totally different kind of Chinese state. The collapse of the dynastic system, they thought, had at last given them the opportunity to build a free and independent nation. Often foreign-educated themselves, these young idealists believed that the hope for the future lay in abandoning Chinese tradition and creating a modern, completely Westernized culture. What was left of the old China had to be done away with and reconstruction begun on a new foundation. They were divided among themselves as to how the reforms were actually to be carried out, and in what direction. But they shared a determination for a sharp departure from the past, an admiration for Western science and materialism, and—most important of all for a people who had long suffered foreign domination—they shared a dedication to Chinese nationalism.

One of the first orders of the day was to give China a national language. Few of the would-be reformers were willing to go as far as Qian Xuantong and advocate the substitution of some artificial language in place of Chinese. But they were all in agreement that whatever form the national language took, it would be an indispensable element in the functioning of the modern nation-state. This connection had been made clear by the model that Western countries had provided. Those colonial powers that had occupied China had established national languages as an integral and vital part of nationalism in their own states. France, England, Germany, and Russia all had well-defined national languages. Language standardization obviously brought with it national strength. Then there was also the enviable and perhaps more appropriate model provided by Japan. Far more Chinese students had studied there than in Europe or America, and the seeming speed and ease with which the Japanese had established their national language had made a deep impression upon these students. Here was an East Asian neighbor with a writing system much like their own that had nevertheless modernized with enough success to rival the greatest of the Western powers. When they returned to "old" and "backward" China, these students were determined to imitate the Japanese success.

It was not that China had no linguistic standards—far from it. In fact China had unified standards for language use that had been established for over two thousand years. No other country East or West could compare with that. But it was this very tradition that the new leaders found most oppressive. For the linguistic standards then in use in China applied only to the written, classical language and had not the slightest thing to do with the modern vernacular, the form of the language upon which they believed a modern state had to be founded.

This ancient written language, the only real language in the minds of many, had for most of Chinese history been the main linguistic standard. In the early days of this century, the standard national language (if it can be called that) was still Classical Chinese. Every literate person had to be able to write precisely the correct forms of the characters and to form sentences following the style of the ancient writers. But the way the texts were read depended upon what part of the country one came from. A common tradition of recitation had been established in the Tang period, but over a thousand years had passed since then, and in the meantime the pronunciations in each part of the country had changed and become very different from each other. The readings now used in Canton were totally incomprehensible in Peking. Those used in Fuzhou could not be understood in Canton. And beyond these texts there were no national standards, for almost no one had given a thought as to how people should speak. To be sure, it was sometimes useful to know modern Mandarin, Guānhuà, since this "language of the officials" had served as an informal lingua franca since the fifteenth century, especially for administrative purposes. But Mandarin, which was based on the educated speech of the Peking capital, was by no means the standard language in late imperial times. Southerners were not ashamed of having Southern accents, and some, in fact, even tended to look down on Northern speech because it had not preserved many of the older, Tang-period distinctions that could still be found in the South. It would not be easy to agree on national colloquial standards.

Within a few months after the founding of the Chinese Republic in 1912, the reformers got the chance they had been waiting for. The new Ministry of Education announced plans to hold a Conference on Unification of Pronunciation, the avowed purpose of which was to create national standards for language use, both written and spoken. Interested parties from a variety of fields and regions of the country were invited to attend, and in Peking on 15 February, 1913, the first meetings began.

The conference had several specific tasks set before it: "to establish a standard national pronunciation for the characters, to analyze the national pronunciation in terms of its basic sounds, and to adopt a set of phonetic symbols to represent these basic sounds." These were ambitious plans, and to the new government it seemed that everything could be accomplished in short order. But in organizing the conference, the Ministry of Education had hardly laid the groundwork for the kinds of results that they expected. The objectives of the conference required a group of "wise experts," selflessly dedicated to what they had to do. But the motley assemblage of delegates at this conference were not those wise experts. Invitations had been passed out more on the basis of political considerations than linguistic expertise, and the partisan groups that attended could scarcely be expected to find workable solutions to the many practical problems with which they were faced.

The most fundamental decision that had to be made was just which sounds would be adopted as standard. On this question the delegates were divided into two seemingly irreconcilable factions: delegates from the North, who thus spoke "Mandarin" dialects, and delegates from the southern coastal area, around Shanghai, who spoke non-Mandarin dialects. The Northerners argued for the adoption of Mandarin pronunciation, which, they pointed out, had long served as a lingua franca throughout China and, in fact, was serving the same purpose at these very meetings. But the Southerners countered that this Northern dialect was not acceptable because it had not preserved many distinctions that were indispensable to people from the South. Since the two factions were about equal in strength, progress ground to a halt. The conference had reached a deadlock.

The problem was serious. A decision had to be made that would affect the lives of the Chinese people for many years to come, but political bickering had obscured what was really at stake. Regionalism had masked a linguistic dilemma. Here, in China, the issue of standardization was not like that of many other countries because what was called "the Chinese language" was extremely diverse, far more so than any other single language in the world. The person born and bred in Peking could not understand conversations he might happen to overhear on the streets of Shanghai, because to him the local "dialect" was incomprehensible. As far as he was concerned, it was merely part of the backdrop of regional color, much as the local fish dishes were. When it came to important matters, he had to find people who knew how to speak Mandarin in order to conduct his business. In the far South, in Canton, speech was again different, and there the local dialect was incomprehensible to anyone from either Peking or Shanghai. The "dialects" were not mutually intelligible.

To be sure, the fact that some Chinese speakers could not talk to each other did not make Chinese unique. No language, after all, is completely uniform. Romans understand little of the Italian spoken in Sicily, and the kind of Japanese heard in Southern Kyushu is almost totally impenetrable to anyone from Tokyo. Even English, which is relatively less varied than most widely spoken languages, has some dialects that are not understood everywhere in the English-speaking world. Few Americans understand Cockney, for example. People who "speak the same language" are not necessarily able to talk to each other; even if people cannot communicate with each other directly, they can still be said to speak the same language if their speech is nevertheless close enough to be linked by an intermediate variety of the language. The American and the Cockney might have difficulty conversing with each other, but both can get along fairly easily with a speaker of upper-class British. On the periphery of any language there are usually a few dialects that have to be linked in this way. English has such dialects, Japanese has some, too, and so do the languages of all the other countries that were major powers.

What makes Chinese different is the number and complexity of such dialects. In order to classify this enormous linguistic body as a single language, a very large number of links are required to connect all of its many varieties of speech—more, probably, than for any other single language on earth. The interconnections between its dialects are in fact as complicated as those which connect a family of languages. Romance languages, such as French, Spanish, Portuguese, and Italian, are linked to each other just about as closely as the Chinese dialects are. French, for example, is not sharply separated from Italian, but rather changes into its sister language gradually, from village to village across the French-Italian border. Its peripheral dialects merge into those of Italian. The people living in one French village can talk to their neighbors in the next village to the southeast, and they to those in the next, and so on, so that the chain of intelligibility continues unbroken into Italy. Peking Mandarin is linked to Shanghainese with about the same degree of complexity. From a linguistic point of view, the Chinese "dialects" could be considered different languages, just as French and Italian are.

In other words, the scale of China's language standardization problem could hardly be compared to that of a single European nation. Rather, the observation of a romantic historian that China was "another Europe lying just beyond Europe" was in some ways more apt. Fully one-quarter of humanity lived in China. It was a nation of another order of magnitude when compared to France, England, or Germany. The problem of choosing a standard language was, with a slight stretch of the imagination, a little like choosing one of the vernacular Romance tongues to replace Latin in a Europe just emerging from the Middle Ages. Yet, that analogy was not quite appropriate either. China was not just a kind of united Europe; the Chinese people felt themselves to be part of the same nation in ways that no European alliance could begin to approximate. Then, too, the European analogy was misleading because China was not a patchwork of linguistic groups more or less equal in size, such as was found in Europe. Its long national unity and the political domination by the North had produced a much more lopsided distribution in favor of the Northern, or "Mandarin" dialects. The Mandarin-speaking area was larger in both area and population than all the rest of the "dialect" areas combined. Yet in the immensity of China, many of these non-Mandarin "dialects" still had more speakers than most European languages. There simply was no comparison that could be made to give a sense of the language problem the new Chinese Republic had to face.

Few of the delegates at the 1913 conference on pronunciation seem to have had any idea of what they were up against. The negotiations were marked by frustratingly naive arguments. "Germany is strong," it was said, "because its language contains many voiced sounds and China is weak because Mandarin lacks them." But if linguistic knowledge was in short supply, commitment to position was not. Passions were hot, and frustrations grew. Finally, after months of no progress, Wang Zhao, the leader of the Mandarin faction, called for a new system of voting in which each province would have one and only one vote, knowing full well that the numerically superior Mandarin-speaking area would then automatically dominate. Delegates in other areas were incensed. The situation became explosive. Then, as tempers flared, Wang Rongbao, one of the leaders of the Southern faction, happened to use the colloquial Shanghai expression for 'ricksha,' *wangbo ts'o*. Wang Zhao misheard it for the Mandarin curse *wángba dàn* 'son of a bitch [literally, turtle's egg],' and flew into a rage. He bared his arms and attacked Wang Rongbao, chasing him out of the assembly hall. Wang Rongbao never returned to the meetings. Wang Zhao's suggestion to change the voting procedure was adopted, and after three months of bitter struggling, the Mandarin faction had its way. The conference adopted a resolution recommending that the sounds of Mandarin become the national standard.

These sounds were to be defined by indicating the pronunciations of some 6,500 characters in a *Dictionary of National Pronunciation* (*Guóyīn cídiǎn*). The pronunciations were to be marked by using a system of thirty-nine phonetic letters (*zhùyīn zìmǔ*, later to be known as *zhùyīn fúhào* 'phonetic symbols'), which had been made up by modifying and simplifying characters.

The conference ended with the submission of a resolution to the Ministry of Education recommending that this National Language be taught in all primary, middle, and normal schools. Thus the word Guóyǔ 'National Language'—a term that had ultimately been borrowed from the Japanese word for their national language—came into the official Chinese vocabulary.

But in 1913, the sounds of Mandarin were still far from becoming the national standard. Power had changed hands in the Ministry of Education, and more conservative forces were in charge of the Republican government now. Interest in effecting the kind of revolution that this new approach to language and letters represented had cooled. It was 1919 before the Ministry of Education could be persuaded to establish a National Language Unification Commission and to publish the Guoyin dictionary that the 1913 conference had recommended.

Moreover, the publication of the Guoyin dictionary in 1919 did not settle the controversy of the "dialects," as it was supposed to do, but in many ways actually set back the advancement of Mandarin as the standard. For although the Mandarin faction had emerged victorious from the 1913 conference, its adherents did not have the resolve or the linguistic expertise to set down actual Mandarin pronunciations. Instead, the Mandarin-speaking delegates seems to have been swayed by the argument of the Southern faction that Mandarin had lost too many of the traditional distinctions recognized by Chinese philologists. Therefore, instead of representing the actual sounds of Mandarin (as, for example, it was spoken in Peking), the phonetic symbols the delegates adopted to represent the standard pronunciations in fact reflected many ancient features and distinctions not preserved in Mandarin. The so-called "fifth" or "entering" tone, for example, was marked in this dictionary even though it had been lost throughout almost the entire Mandarin-speaking area. In short, the dictionary represented not Mandarin as it was spoken but Mandarin as a few scholars thought it should be spoken. The official national language of China was an abstract ideal that not a single person in the country spoke as his native idiom. Yet, in spite of this fact, these artificial pronunciations were subsequently designated as those to be taught in the schools throughout China. But of course no teacher could be found to teach them. Finally, a Peking scholar named Wang Pu, who was a member of the newly formed National Language Commission, was given the task of making a set of phonograph records that could be used as a model. But with his native Peking dialect, this scholar was unable to capture all of the distinctions of the official "language." He could not pronounce the "fifth" tone, for example, since it had long ago disappeared from Peking speech, and instead gave all the character readings marked in the dictionary with this tone the falling pitch of the Peking fourth tone.

The National Language had to be salvaged from this embarrassment. Finally, after some deliberation, the task of producing passable recordings of the standard pronunciations was given over to Yuen Ren Chao (Zhào Yuánrèn), another member of the commission. Chao was a young American-trained linguist who had already gained a reputation in China, and in the West as well, as a phenomenally skilled phonetician, and it was felt that if anyone could do the job, it would certainly be Chao. Chao dutifully made a set of records to accompany a textbook of the National Language, and he himself proceeded to teach them in his Chinese courses at Harvard. But the existence of Chao's records, which sounded like Chinese no one had ever heard before, only underscored the futility of asking each citizen to imitate such a model. The Guoyin pronunciations remained the standard for another thirteen years, but no one except Chao was able to teach them. The supporters of the National Language

Movement were thrown into disarray. No one was quite sure what the standard was, and a growing number of people began to doubt whether there should be—or could be—standard pronunciations at all.

Meanwhile, though pronunciation standards remained at a standstill, writing in a colloquial style was moving rapidly ahead. Literary reformers, principally the American-trained philosopher and literary critic Hu Shih, had campaigned effectively for a vernacular style of writing based upon Mandarin. Such writing, know as *báihuà*, had been in use for many centuries as the medium of popular novels such as *The Dream of the Red Chamber*; but as long as Classical Chinese had been the only standard, *baihua* literature had remained on the fringes of the Chinese literary tradition. Drama and fiction had never been taken seriously by educated Chinese, and the style, *baihua*, was considered prolix and vulgar—quite the opposite of the tersely elegant phrasing of Classical Chinese. Now, however, Hu Shih and others had begun to win for this long-neglected mode of writing a new respectability, and this change did much to advance the cause of the spoken standard as well.

Gradually, as authors began writing more and more in *baihua*, the members of the National Language Unification Commission came to realize that the natural speech of some single, uniform dialect had to be selected as the standard, and the obvious choice was the dialect spoken in Peking. One of the most influential advocates of this uniform standard was Chao himself, and he and a number of other knowledgeable spokesmen began to win support for the new scheme. At last, in 1932, without a formal announcement, the commission published the *Vocabulary of National Pronunciation for Everyday Use* (*Guóyīn chángyòng zìhuì*). This new dictionary was much the same as the old Guoyin dictionary, but with one major difference: The pronunciations marked for each of the characters had all been normalized to those that actually existed in the Peking dialect. Thus, with no fanfare and without official notification of any change, the standard language for all of China become the variety of Mandarin spoken in Peking.

It may seem incredible that it took more than two decades after the fall of the Manchu dynasty for this dialect to be recognized as the standard language. It had, after all, been serving for centuries as an informal means of spoken communication. But China's fledgling government ought not to be blamed too much. The idea that a popular form of speech might be raised to the position of an official language was a revolutionary concept that could not be assimilated overnight. It was one thing to talk about a national language and quite another to pick those colloquial forms that actually filled the bill. We should also remember that speaking a language does not make the user consciously aware of its sounds. Language is like the air we breathe. We go about our daily lives articulating thousands of words without once thinking about what we are doing or how we do it. If asked to record on paper the actual sounds that we speak, and not those that we customarily write, how many of us would be able to do so? How many Americans, for example, know that they usually pronounce the words *where* and *wear* exactly the same way? Like the rest of us, the Chinese were seldom more conscious of speaking than of breathing. What they were aware of was what they wrote, and what they wrote was very far removed from the sounds of the Peking dialect. It took linguistic sophistication to analyze the living word and commit its distinctions to paper with the accuracy that Chao and his colleagues had done. The publication of the *Vocabulary of National Pronunciation for Everyday Use* in 1932 was an important step along China's road to modernization.

But fixing standards by legislation did not mean that everyone accepted them. It was not that Southerners still doubted the wisdom of choosing the Peking dialect out of the many varieties of speech in China—Chao and the coterie of intellectuals who had pushed most for its adoption were themselves mostly from the southern coastal area around Shanghai. The question was the role that this National Language would and should play in the parts of China that were not Mandarin-speaking. Many people found the idea of an inflexible standard threatening, because they realized that speakers of other "dialects" would automatically become handicapped in a state that permitted communication only in this Mandarin Guoyu. In a society that had supposedly committed itself to the democratic principle of "the people's rights and powers" (*mínquán*), it seemed unfair to condemn millions of good Chinese citizens to a permanent linguistic handicap. Fears had been raised by integralist slogans such as, "Force the South to follow the North," and proponents of linguistic unification were obliged to assuage apprehensions of linguistic authoritarianism. They argued that "everyone *may* speak the National Language, but everyone doesn't *have* to speak it." The "dialects" would not be "abolished," they promised. The arguments were for the most part persuasive. Chinese intellectuals of both the Right and the Left began to see an urgent need for some kind of common language if China was ever to modernize and become strong.

But one part of the problem could not be dismissed by the integralists, because by now almost everyone had come to realize that it would take a very long time before this National Language could be taught to all the Chinese people. Opponents argued that it would take a thousand years to unify China linguistically. The integralists responded, as best they could, by saying that it did not have to take that long. If only compulsory education in the National Language could be started immediately, they pleaded, then everyone could be a literate user within a hundred years. By the year 2030, they predicted, all China would be linguistically one, provided a consistent educational policy be put into effect at once. But this rather utopian appeal to the welfare of China in the future only hardened the resolve of those who were already suspicious of government intentions. What about the millions of Chinese living right now? Was this as well as the next few generations of non-Mandarin speakers to be simply thrown under the wheels of progress in the hope that their grandchildren would fare better? The attitude of the integralists, largely unstated, was yes, it was just this kind of sacrifice to the cause of Chinese nationalism that was necessary. They saw no alternative way to progress.

In this intellectual climate China began to be further polarized by events that were taking place in Europe. The kind of linguistic assimilation the Guoyu proponents seemed to be advocating was just at that time being carried to its utter extreme in Europe by the National Socialist and Fascist movements. But against the integral nationalism of Hitler's Germany or Mussolini's Italy had emerged in Soviet Russia the ideal of a different kind of nationalism, namely, that of "federal nationalism."

Federal nationalism, as it was interpreted by the Soviets, meant local autonomy, and under such a system each region of a country was "free"—and indeed obliged—to use and develop its own local language and culture. In non-Russian Soviet republics Russian was officially the "second" language. This regional autonomy in the matter of language did not lead to disunity, the Soviets claimed, but was, rather, a "factor for strength and unity."

Stalin's famous slogan "Nationalist in form, socialist in content" had an understandable appeal among those Chinese who found the attitudes of the Guoyu proponents unbearably elitist. Never mind the inherent contradictions of Soviet theory, and never mind that Stalin himself had already embarked on a policy of ruthless suppression of minorities. The important thing was that the Soviet ideal offered China's left-leaning intellectuals a romantic alternative to the National Language policies being advocated by those erstwhile liberals who were increasingly gravitating to the Right.

The most vociferous exponent of the Soviet approach was a self-styled language expert named Qu Qiubai. Qu, a reporter who was converted to communism while on assignment in Moscow, had participated in the Soviet projects to develop systems of Romanization for the languages of the Soviet minorities. Qu advocated the Romanization of Chinese and argued that local standards for speaking and writing had to be recognized in each of the various dialect areas. "The dialects cannot be forcibly unified," he said; all the Chinese people had to be allowed to become literate, each group in its own local form of speech. He dismissed the problem of the mutual unintelligibility between these groups by claiming that China already had a "common language" (*pǔtōnghuà*) that could serve as a general standard. Although the idea of a "common language" was to have a long-lasting effect on China, Qu never got around to explaining just what this meant. From his scheme of Romanization it can be deduced that Qu must have been vaguely thinking of some form of generalized Mandarin. Qu knew virtually nothing about linguistics or the systematic study of language; his forte was fiery political rhetoric and intuitive leaps rather than rational argument. Nevertheless, his proposals excited China's Left and drew support away from the government-sponsored National Language. Qu himself was shot by one of Chiang Kai-shek's Kuomintang firing squads in 1935, a few short years after he had slipped back into China from the Soviet Union. But others took up his cause of separate standards, including such influential intellectuals as Mao Dun, Guo Moruo, and—perhaps most important of all—Lu Xun (Lu Hsun), a man even then almost worshipped as China's greatest modern writer.

China's language problem thus became in the 1930s part of the political battleground between the Right and the Left. On the Right were arrayed the dedicated advocates of Guoyu, the National Language, who resisted any plan to create separate standards, even temporarily. They believed that such a plan could only serve to fragment China. Opposed to them were intellectuals on the Left, who believed that separate standards for each "dialect" area were morally unavoidable. The "dialects" were so different from each other, the Leftists maintained, a single Mandarin standard for the whole country would doom non-Mandarin speakers to illiteracy and, effectively, to second-class citizenship. A single standard, they believed, would work only to the advantage of the bourgeoisie. Moreover, Guoyu, the government-approved standard, was to be identified with Guanhua—Mandarin—and that smelled of Qing officialdom and all the bureaucratic excesses that that implied. The Guoyu advocates, who had begun in liberal reaction against Qing institutions, were stung by this accusation. One offered the memorable counterargument that the *guān* in *Guānhuà* did not mean 'official,' as was commonly assumed, but rather 'public,' as in *guān-cèsuǒ* 'public toilet.' If opponents refused to use Guanhua because of this *guan*, he argued, then by the same logic they would not be able to use the public toilets, either. Whatever they wanted to call it, the Leftists had no real alternative to Guanhua or Guoyu. Insofar as they recognized the need at all for some kind of speech that could be understood by all Chinese, they spoke only of the vague "common language" mentioned by Qu Qiubai. Just what this "common language" was, none of them were willing, or able, to say. In any case the issue was unimportant to intellectuals like Lu Xun or Mao Dun, who rejected out of hand any concept of a national standard, whether it be called "common language" or "National Language." For them the only essential thing was to give each of the many mutually unintelligible varieties of Chinese equal recognition.

This leftist alternative to a single national standard was an idea never to be tried. The Kuomintang government was hostile toward it, confiscating its literature and arresting its advocates, and that opposition never let up, continuing throughout the war years. Sponsorship fell by default to the Communist movement, but in the period following the Communist Revolution, the idea of separate standards was diluted, transformed, and, in the final analysis, rejected. Five years of study, planning, and debate led in 1955 to two national conferences on language reform, and early the following year, in February of 1956, a document was published that made clear the official language policy of the People's Republic of China. This document, which was called "Directions with Respect to the Promotion of the Common Language," read, in part, as follows:

> The foundation for the unification of the Chinese [*Hàn*] language is already in existence. It is the Common Language [*Pǔtōnghuà*], which has as its standard pronunciation the Peking pronunciation, as its basic dialect the Northern dialect, and as its grammatical model the exemplary literary works written in the modern colloquial. The principal method of achieving the complete unification of the Chinese language is to promote the use of the Common Language in the cultural and educational systems and in all phases of the daily life of the people.

In other words, the National Language Movement under a different name had weathered the Communist Revolution. The Communist goal was now stated to be the "unification of the Chinese language," and this was the very program that had been advocated by supporters of the National Language, pursued by the Kuomintang government, and bitterly opposed by the Left. Ignored or forgotten were the suggestions of Lu Xun or Mao Dun that Canton, Fuzhou, Shanghai be given equal status with Peking. The Chinese people were to be unified by a single set of standards for language use, and these standards were still to be based upon the speech of the capital. It seems that when it came time to put words into action, the new government had decided to be as practical in such matters as its predecessor had been.

To be sure, the ideological commitment to Soviet-style federalism was not completely forgotten. It survived quite well in the official policy toward the "non-Han" minorities. Whereas the Kuomintang government had openly vowed to assimilate minority groups such as the Tibetans and the Mongols into the great Han Chinese race, the People's Republic has articulated a policy in which these groups and their languages are given official recognition.

A trace of federalism can also be found in the new name for the national language, Putonghua 'the Common Language.' In elevating Qu Qiubai's term for a rather minor part of his proposed program to the centerpiece of language policy, the Communist leaders meant to play down the inherent exclusiveness of a standard language. They have stressed that Putonghua is not to be "pure" Peking dialect, but rather something more broadly based. It should, they say, absorb the most "viable and potent" elements from other dialects and the speech of workers and peasants. To the extent that this contrasts with earlier declarations that dialects should not be allowed to "contaminate" the National Language, Putonghua is indeed, at least in theory, different from Guoyu. (One latter-day supporter of the National Language has described Putonghua as a "debased" form of Mandarin.) But in actual practice, the changing of the name Guoyu to Putonghua has mostly been cosmetic—certainly, what passes for Mandarin or Guoyu these days in Taiwan is virtually indistinguishable from the Putonghua spoken on the Mainland. There is today only one standard language for all the Chinese people, and it is based, however loosely, on the variety of speech heard in Peking. Language education continues apace, but for the masses of non-Mandarin speakers, the standard is as far removed from their own idiom as it ever was.

But let us not be too cynical about the leaders of China after 1950. The leftists of the 1930s were fond of attacking Guoyu as a bourgeois conspiracy, but how serious were they really about creating multiple standards? It is perhaps significant that even the most iconoclastic of them continued to refer to all non-Mandarin varieties of Chinese as "dialects" and never as "languages." It would in any case be unrealistic to expect the practical men who had managed to consolidate control of the entire country to turn around and Balkanize China by recognizing the status of these dialects as separate languages.

There is also the serious question as to how far these dialects should be thought of as separate languages at all. It is true that they are as different from each other as French from Italian and, when taken together, are probably more complex than the whole Romance family. But should we really begin saying the "Chinese languages," in the plural, just as we say the "Romance languages"?

The Chinese themselves would unhesitatingly answer, no; for few of them have ever thought of their country as multilingual. The practical demands of communication mean that many must learn different "dialects," but these are never studied as foreign languages, the way a person from Italy, say, might study French. Educated Chinese from all parts of the country generally learn to speak enough Mandarin, or Putonghua, to get by, today more than ever before. But they still do so not so much through formal study as through contact with others and by informally learning a few general rules relating the pronunciations of their own idiom to those of Mandarin. This is not thought of as learning another language; it is just "picking up" pronunciations different from one's own "dialect." Such learning strategies are commonly used to pick up other varieties of Chinese as well, and in parts of South China that are particularly complex linguistically, many people end up knowing not just one, but two or three, or even more, different "dialects." These casual solutions to the problems of communicating usually work up to a point, given the common base of vocabulary from the written language. But they are far from perfect, and real cases of confusion are by no means rare. Anecdotes about "dialect" problems abound. In one such incident reported in a Chinese newspaper, telegraph service to a particular dialect-speaking area was said to have been interrupted because a verbal order from Peking to examine the telegraph lines was interpreted in this area as an order to tear the lines down! Yet, no matter how different from Peking Mandarin the sounds of that dialect may have been, no one would have ever suggested that it might have been another language.

The Chinese believe that they speak dialects of a single language not because they are unaware of the objective linguistic facts, but because of certain cultural considerations. Unlike the peoples who speak Romance,

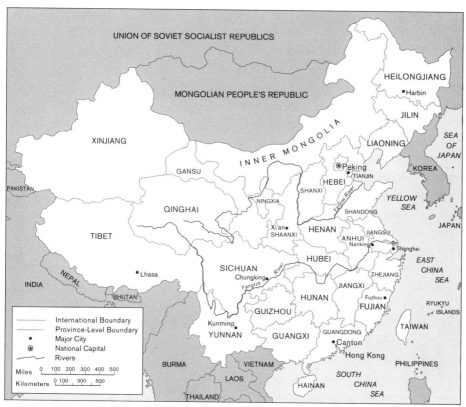

Figure 1. Political Divisions of China

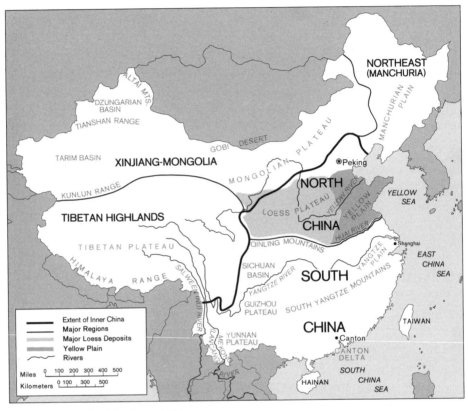

Figure 2. Geographical Regions of China

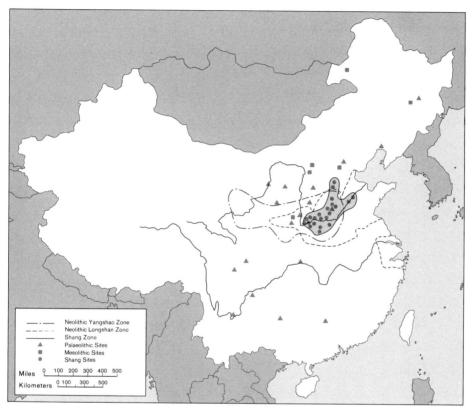

Figure 3. Pre-History and the Shang Period (ca. 1600-1100 B.C.)

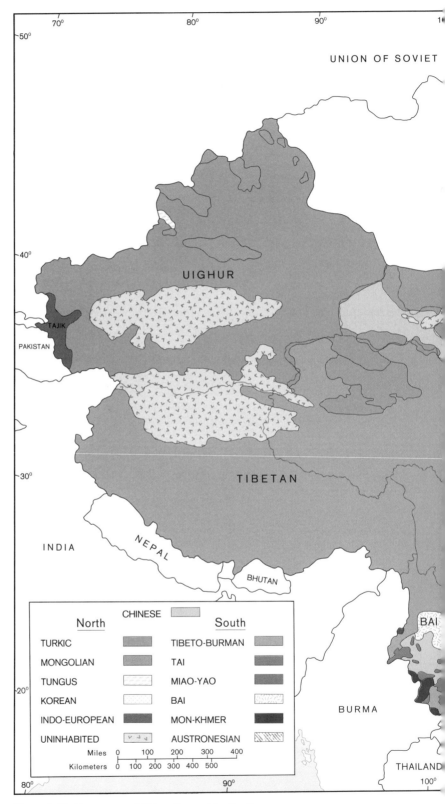

Figure 4. The Languages of China Grouped by Family

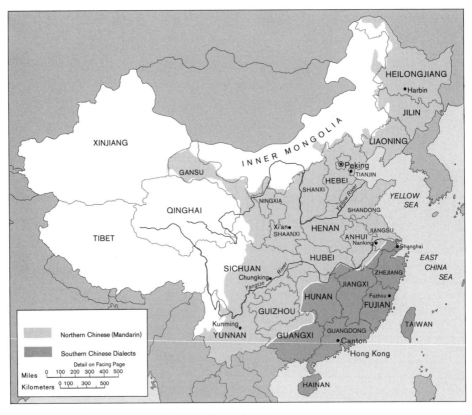

Figure 5. The Chinese Language: Basic North–South Division

Figure 6. The Chinese Dialects

the Chinese are not divided into a number of national units corresponding roughly to the several groups of closely allied dialects. Rather, the
Chinese language is spoken by a single group of people with a common
cultural heritage. China is not only the most populous country on earth,
it is also the oldest social institution, and the Chinese people belong to
and follow cultural and national traditions that have continued since the
days of the Han Empire and before. They feel themselves to be part of the
same language community in ways that the Romance peoples, with their
separate histories, cultures, and language norms, could never do. In the
definition of what Chinese is, these are not insignificant considerations.
The Han people coalesce as a nation and therefore speak one language;
the Romance peoples are several nations and therefore speak several
languages.

This difference is not only a matter of one's point of view. There is a
linguistic aspect as well. Regardless of its size, a group of people who
share a single, well-defined culture usually has a single set of standards
for language use. The villagers on either side of the French-Italian border
may be able to talk to each other, but there is more to their total linguistic
behavior than casual chats with the neighbors. They also talk to visitors
and social superiors. They go to school, attend Mass, read books and
newspaper, write letters, and, these days, watch television. The language
for all such social uses is not just the local vernacular dialect, but is, in
varying degrees, something shaped by the national standard. By virtue of
this fact, the people on the French side of the border are pulled in a
different direction from those on the Italian side, and in some respects,
therefore, share more linguistic bonds with Parisians than they do with
their Italian neighbors. A French farmer may be able to talk to an Italian
farmer, but could he write him a letter? The division of the Romance-
speaking area into several national units has real linguistic significance.
French is a different language from Italian in a very deep sense.

In China, however, groups of dialects are not separated from each
other in this way. They do not have different national standards. On the
contrary, the speakers of all dialects look toward a common model. Just
as a single European country such as France has established conventions
for linguistic behavior, so China, too, has linguistic standards that are
accepted throughout the country by all the Chinese people. These standards may be much farther removed from actual speech than is the case
with French. It is also true that when most Chinese think of a language
that unites them as a people, the "common language" they have in mind
is still fundamentally their written language. But in the sense that many

of the uses of language are guided and focused by the same norms, it is impossible to ignore the essential unity of China. The power of unification exerted within Chinese culture by Chinese writing should not be underestimated; even the illiterate have always felt its influence. For these reasons, we usually do not speak of Chinese in the plural, even though in other, less cohesive contexts, the dialects would unquestionably be considered different languages. The same factors that help divide Romance into several languages serve to unite Chinese into a single language.

2 CHINA, NORTH AND SOUTH

Today, in the last decades of the twentieth century, Chinese is spoken by about one billion people. No other language is remotely comparable. English, the next most widely spoken language, has fewer than half that many speakers.

Almost all of the Chinese people live in the densely populated eastern half of China, an area geographically about the size of the United States east of the Mississippi. Relatively few live outside this region. In modern times the Chinese have begun to colonize more intensively the immense territories in the western half of their country. Manchuria and Inner Mongolia to the north, areas forbidden to most Chinese as long as the Manchus were in power, have also begun to feel the pressures of intense immigration. But all of China's territorial possessions, both in the North and in the West, are as yet relatively sparsely settled. More than 95 percent of the Chinese still live in Inner China, the part of the country east of the Tibetan Plateau and south of the Great Wall.

Inner China, the traditional homeland of the Chinese people, is divided naturally into two parts, the North and the South (see Fig. 2). North China is a treeless expanse of plain and plateau that extends south from the Great Wall over the area drained by the Yellow River and its tributaries. South China is the Yangtze River valley and the well-watered hills and valleys and rice-growing areas that lie to its south. These two regions, each of which is dominated by a great river, together form the geographical setting for Chinese civilization and history.

North China belongs climatically and geographically to the interior of the Asian continent. The entire western half of the region is a dry and dusty highland known as the Loess Plateau. Here, for 100,000 square miles, the hills and mountains are covered with a powdery yellow dust, called loess, that in places is as much as 300 feet thick. Loess is believed to have blown down from the deserts of Inner Asia into the western half of North China during the last Ice Age, when the north winds were unimaginably fiercer than anything known today. It erodes easily. The modern continental winds may be mild by comparison with those that blew in prehistoric times, but during the winter they are still powerful enough to raise great dust storms and fill the air with grit all the way to the Yellow

Sea. Sometimes the air-borne yellow powder is carried far enough east to sting eyes and faces in Korea and dust windows and gardens in Japan. To the east of the Loess Plateau lies the Yellow Plain. Its yellow soils, too, come from the Asian interior. This broad, flat flood plain of the Yellow River consists entirely of thick deposits of loess silt that have been built up over the ages. Where the Yellow River flows down from the mountains of the Loess Plateau, it is colored bright yellow by the soil that it and its tributaries have picked up in cutting through several hundred miles of loess deposits. At this point, the solids held in suspension sometimes make up almost half of the flow of the Yellow River by weight. As the river enters the flat Yellow Plain, it slows down abruptly and the silt begins to settle, building up the flood plain at a rate exceeded by no other major river system in the world. This river is with justice called "China's Sorrow." The Chinese have tried for millennia to keep the Yellow River within its banks by building elaborate systems of dikes. But as the silt in the water settles, the bed of the river rises higher and higher, and the dikes must also be built up higher to keep pace. Some dikes are forty or more feet above the surrounding land. Eventually the river must break through these restraining walls, and then it deposits thick layers of sediment over many miles of the surrounding countryside. In this way the yellow substance from the deserts of Inner Asia is spread over North China all the way to the sea.

The loess soils of the Loess Plateau and the Yellow Plain are fertile but relatively dry. In good years when rainfall is adequate, fine stands of wheat, millet, and other crops that require less water than rice can be and are grown. The traditional staples of the region are therefore noodles, breads, and other foods made from these grains. But water is too scarce or unpredictable to sustain the intensive irrigation that rice requires, and the bowls of this grain that are eaten in Peking must usually be shipped from South China.

The climate of South China is more oceanic. The colors are not brown and yellow, but green. Most of the region is protected from the northern continental winds by the Qinling Mountains, the range that forms the watershed between the Yellow and the Yangtze rivers, and the loess deposits of North China stop at this mountain barrier. The rivers and streams that flow from its southern slopes therefore do not pick up the characteristic yellow silt that is found in northern rivers. Here the prevailing winds are generally from the south—the so-called summer monsoons—and they bring with them moisture and warm air from the ocean. Summers in South China are hot and steamy; clothes and books mold and mildew. Winters are cooler and drier than summers, but in many areas they are still mild enough for crops to grow. South China is a region of rice fields and terraces, lakes, rivers, and canals; hilly or mountainous areas not under cultivation are often covered with trees and thick vegetation, which in the southwestern part of the country turn into the jungles of Southeast Asia.

The South has China's best farmland. Rainfall makes it a richer place than North China; population densities are higher, and the people are generally better nourished. In contrast with the North, with its harsh climatic extremes, the fresh and verdant lands of the South are almost ideal for the growing of rice. Around Canton, for example, two good rice crops are regularly grown each year. The region is also well suited to the cultivation of a variety of other warm-weather crops as well, including teas, cotton, tangerines and other fruits, and mulberry bushes for silk production.

THE Chinese language, like China itself, is geographically divided into the North and the South (see Fig. 5). The Northern varieties of the language, usually known in English as the "Mandarin dialects," are spread across the Yellow Plain and the Loess Plateau. This dialect area also creeps south to the Yangtze River and a long arm bends down to the extreme Southwest, extending across the provinces of Sichuan and Yunnan all the way to the Thai border. This southwestern branch is for the most part recently settled territory, as are Manchuria, Inner Mongolia, and the far Northwest, where Mandarin is the only kind of Chinese spoken. As a result of these accretions, the Mandarin area now covers more than three-fourths of the country. The Southern varieties of the language—the so-called "non-Mandarin dialects"—are confined to the wedge of land formed in the Southeast by the lower course of the Yangtze River and the South China Sea.

There is a qualitative difference between these two areas. The Mandarin area, on the one hand, is unusually uniform; virtually all of the dialects spoken there are mutually intelligible—or very nearly so. A native of Harbin, in the extreme northeastern corner of the Mandarin range, has little trouble conversing with someone from Chungking, a city in the extreme Southwest over 1,600 miles away. Mandarin has no more variety than French, say, or German. But the non-Mandarin area is extremely varied, and within it sharply divergent forms of speech are often separated by only a few miles. The Amoy dialect, for example, which is spoken on the southeastern coast opposite Taiwan, is completely unintelligible to anyone living much farther away than a hundred miles in any direction. The variety of the language in the South is so great that the dialects there can be classified into at least six groups, each of which is as varied as the entire Mandarin area.

This remarkable linguistic difference between a unified North and a fragmented South is a measure of how much life and society have been affected by geography. It is not surprising, of course, that the newly settled Mandarin territories are uniform; that is only to be expected. It usually takes time for regional differences to grow up—as we can see in recently populated areas of North America and Australia, where only the subtlest differences in speech can be detected across thousands of miles of land. What is unusual about Chinese is the difference in homogeneity between the North and the South of Inner China; both of these regions have long been inhabited by the Chinese people, and for much of that time the country has been culturally and even politically united. The correlation between the dichotomy in the language and the climatic and geographical division of the country is therefore all the more striking. The physical character of the land on which the Chinese live has apparently affected the ability to communicate.

One way the Chinese describe the contrast between the North and the South is with the catchword *Nán chuán běi mǎ*—in the South the boat, in the North the horse. In traditional times the horse was the best way to travel in North China. Mounted, one could generally move at will over the dry open terrain without encountering serious obstacles. Even the great Yellow River itself was in most places so shallow it could be forded. But in the South the horseman had to dismount. The lakes, rivers, and canals in the flat low-lying areas on the flood plains of the Yangtze and its tributaries could be crossed only by ferry. Still farther to the south, beyond the Yangtze Plain, the rugged hills and mountains with their high terraced rice fields and dense vegetation were difficult to cross even on foot, and on horseback virtually impossible. From the Yangtze on south, there were few roads of the kind that stretched across the North; in this southern half of China the highways were the rivers, streams, and canals that connected rice-growing area to market, town to town. The only efficient means of transportation in the South was by boat.

In the North there was much more freedom of movement. Water is an efficient medium of transport for bulk shipments of grain or freight, but it is less convenient for personal travel, because waterways and currents do not necessarily flow in the direction one wants to go. In the open spaces of the North, communication and transportation were quicker and easier than in the South, a region finely crosshatched with natural barriers.

The linguistic homogeneity of North China shows what a difference this has made. Mandarin has dialects, of course, especially in the hillier parts of the Loess Plateau. But there is nothing in the North to compare with the complex variety of the Southern dialects. The open terrain made possible linguistic cohesion.

South China, by contrast, has an abundance of the linguistic variety we expect to find where there are many barriers to communication and where people have stayed put for relatively long periods of time. Over much of the South the speech of each community—commonly a group of farming villages served by the same market—has tended to diverge from that of other, neighboring communities. The amount of divergence depends largely on the degree to which it is isolated from its neighbors. In general, the greater the barriers to travel and communication, the greater will be the differences in speech. Wuzhou and Taishan, for example, are both towns in the Far South that are served by Canton, the capital of Guangdong Province, as a commercial and cultural center. Wuzhou is a fairly new town that lies 120 miles directly upstream from Canton on the West River, a major shipping artery into the provincial capital. It was largely settled from Canton and still maintains close contacts with that city. Taishan, on the other hand, is only about 60 miles southwest of Canton, but several rivers must be crossed to get there. Thus in spite of the fact that Taishan is actually twice as close as Wuzhou to the provincial capital, it is much less accessible, and the dialect has diverged far more. A considerable number of linguistic changes separate Taishan from the cosmopolitan variety of Cantonese. An even sharper example of the effects of isolation can be drawn when the city of Swatow is brought into the picture. Although Swatow is located in Guangdong Province, it is separated from Canton by rows of rugged mountains. It was therefore settled from the north along the coastline and is still culturally and commercially independent of Canton. As a result, the dialect spoken there is totally unintelligible to a speaker of Cantonese.

Complicating this regional stratification, especially in the Far South, are the linguistic layers left by successive waves of immigrants. The modern city of Hong Kong with its hodgepodge of people from all over China is in any case exceptional; but commercial centers along the South China coast have long been places where different linguistic groups have lived side by side for extended periods of time. Also, to a slightly lesser degree, various groups have been able to coexist fairly close to each other in the geographically fragmented hill country farther inland. The physical isolation imposed by geography has helped to keep these groups from being assimilated.

A provocative question that remains to be answered is *how* linguistic unity was effected in North China. It is clear that physical geography was a necessary condition—the contrast with South China is enough to show that. But given this geographical fact, what further historical forces were then necessary to make this expanse of land cohere? Far broader plains and larger river valleys exist in this world. There have even been empires where comparable numbers of people have been brought together under one government. But nowhere before modern times has there ever been a linguistic unity like that of North China. Part of the answer, at least, must lie in the political and social institutions of traditional China. Linguistic uniformity is ample testimony to the efficiency and organizational strength of its central government. But were institutional factors alone enough?

The study of linguistic geography elsewhere in the world has shown us time and time again that homogeneity of the kind found in North China usually exists only in areas that have been settled fairly recently. One avenue that might be useful to explore, therefore, is the possibility that there has been extensive intraregional migration in the North. Could the populations of North China have moved around enough to homogenize the language? We know that there has been considerable local movement in both halves of China, but was the displacement of people in the North significantly greater than that in the South—and greater enough to reach a linguistically critical mass? There were, after all, reasons why peasant life might be more vulnerable in the North.

There was first of all greater economic stability in the South. Predictable rainfall meant that harvests could be depended upon from year to year, and that made farming a less risky occupation. The South was not free from natural disasters, but floods and droughts were seldom as frequent or as intense as those that struck the North. When the Yellow River abruptly shifted its course in 1194, a series of floods swept across the entire Northeast, devastating the economy and driving great numbers of peasants from their homes. The Grand Canal, an artificial waterway connecting the imperial capital in the North to the rice baskets of the Yangtze Valley, was of undeniable benefit for disaster relief, especially in areas immediately adjacent to the canal. But nothing could completely make up for the enormous disparity in economic stability between the South and the North.

Another consideration was personal safety. The North was more accessible to overland trade, but it was also more vulnerable to invading armies. The border skirmishes that China now has with Soviet troops give barely a hint of the almost unending wars that the Chinese once waged on their northern borders to hold the "barbarians" at bay. A weakened Chinese state brought invasion, and invasion brought death, destruction, economic chaos, and dislocation. But while this threat hung like a cloud over North China, the distant South lay well beyond the reach of most foreign armies. Not only was the South relatively safe because continental forces had to pass through the North first; the terrain of the South itself made the region almost impregnable. It was a stronghold for Chinese civilization. The northern invaders were cavalry, and horses were of little use in South China. How were horsemen to fight while crossing waterways and slogging through rice paddies? On his own ground, the mounted warrior was an efficient fighting machine, but when he came to South China he had to dismount like any other traveler—and on foot he faced Chinese infantries.

Even the invincible Mongols found the going hard in South China. In 1211 Chinggis Khan and his hordes swept down into North China, and in a series of lightning campaigns that lasted only four years they crushed resistance and seized control of all of China north of the Yellow River. But the Yangtze Valley, though protected by only a relatively weak Chinese state, escaped Mongol conquest for over half a century more. Long after Chinggis had died, his grandson Khubilai launched a series of flanking maneuvers that took his armies west and then south through the Tai kingdom of Nanzhao. Then, in 1268, after his encircling armies had already penetrated what is now Vietnam, Khubilai was able to mount his forces and attack the Song, moving down the river systems into central China. Finally, in 1279, sixty-eight years after they had first entered North China, the Mongols succeeded in destroying the Chinese government and in conquering South China. But even then, life was disrupted less than in North China, where the Mongols could move about quickly into any area.

Did the more frequent military incursions suffered by the North displace enough people to make significant changes in the language? Could floods and droughts have had a similar effect? If enough people were forced to leave their lands, if only for short distances, then North China could effectively have been returned to the state of newly settled territory in spite of the antiquity of its civilization. Could such a thing have happened? The study of the language alone cannot answer these questions;

without detailed demographic data linguistic information is more tantalizing than conclusive. It does, however, show us something about China
that needs to be explained. The linguistic unity of North China is an
extraordinary fact that may well require an extraordinary explanation.

3 THE SPREAD OF NORTHERN INFLUENCE

Many things have changed in China since the Communist Revolution, including some attitudes about the Chinese language. The writer Mao Dun, who had been one of the radical opponents of linguistic unification, became one of the most eloquent promoters of Putonghua, the Common Language. The man who in the 1930s had scorned any idea of subordinating Cantonese or other local forms of speech to a national standard—there was no such thing, he had scoffed, as a "modern Chinese common language"—later changed his public stand completely. In 1978 he wrote a pronouncement advocating that the Chinese people "firmly hold to the task of popularizing the Common Language." "The final goal of spreading the Common Language," Mao Dun concluded, "is to have all Han people speak it. At present we are still a long way from realizing that goal. We must devise methods to hasten toward it."

The standardization of Chinese is a matter of high priority in the People's Republic, and there is now almost no one who questions that goal. Discussion ended with the articulation of the official language policy in 1956. Two years later, in 1958, Premier Zhou Enlai emphasized in a speech on language reform how vital the government considered the implementation of that policy. "Spreading the use of the Common Language, which takes the Peking pronunciation as the standard, is an important political task," he said. Through the Hundred Flowers Movement, the Cultural Revolution, the reign of the Gang of Four and their subsequent downfall, the government has never altered this objective. The policy of standardization has moved slowly and deliberately ahead.

In North China, this policy has been of little or no consequence. Broad discrepancies from the Peking norm are tolerated as acceptable variations in the Common Language, and people who speak natively any dialect of Mandarin have simply continued to use the same speech patterns that they have always used. But in the non-Mandarin dialect areas of South China, where speech is substantially different from that of Peking, the effects of language standardization have been real and considerable. The lives of virtually everyone in the South have in varying degrees been touched by the policy.

Passive exposure to the standard language comes via film, radio, and television. In squares and marketplaces the ubiquitous loudspeaker fills the air with broadcasts from Radio Peking. Books, magazines, and newspapers are all written in the standard colloquial style, and dialect publications—such as the Cantonese newspapers commonly seen in Hong Kong, for example—have apparently became rare in the People's Republic. We have no word as to the fate of dialect literature, but none seems to appear in any officially sanctioned outlets. More active linguistic ability is required for such things as political rallies, meetings, and classes. Refugees in Hong Kong report that in such sessions both teachers and students often revert to their native dialect as soon as a topic becomes complicated or the debate heated. But the official medium is nevertheless the standard language, and a genuine effort is made to maintain that rule.

The school occupies a special place in this program of standardization: the government has concentrated its efforts on changing the speech habits of the very young. In 1956 it issued a State Council directive that all school instruction, from the first grade through university, be conducted in Putonghua. This step represented a radical departure from the past and one difficult to carry out, because most teachers in the South were at that time almost as unfamiliar with Peking speech as their students were. Workshops for teachers were opened, and within two years 721,000 were said to have been trained in Peking phonetics. There was probably considerable variation in the level of skill that these teachers acquired, and the thoroughness of subsequent training programs are perhaps open to question as well. But for the present generation of Chinese children, the cumulative results of these efforts are undeniable. For a child growing up in Canton or Shanghai, Putonghua *is* the language of education. Immersion might be less complete in rural areas, but in city schools today the primary medium of instruction from the end of the first year on is the standard language.

The first grade is where Southern children learn this new form of speech. On the first day of school they hear only the familiar sounds of their own language (or dialect, as the Chinese would insist). But gradually, over a period of months, the teacher begins to use more and more words and phrases of the standard language, and before the end of the first year most classroom subjects are discussed in Putonghua. This is not, in the strictest sense, foreign language instruction: we must remember that the Chinese do not think of the "dialects" as different languages, and the schools reflect this fact. Formal instruction is given only in reading and writing properly, and exposure to the spoken version of the standard language is for the most part treated as incidental to this process. The children simply "pick up" speaking skills based on the model of the teacher. Nevertheless, due to the tender age at which they begin this process, the children become effective users of Putonghua fairly quickly. Observers report that although they have pronounced local "accents," even pupils in the lower grades are able to converse fluently on almost any school subject.

This high level of fluency does not always last. As Mao Dun once lamented, most of these children gradually lose their ability to speak the Common Language after they leave school because the people all around them speak the local dialect. Certainly, the language of the streets in Shanghai, Fuzhou, or Canton has not become Putonghua; most Southerners still speak the same dialect or dialects that their parents and grandparents did. But it would be surprising indeed if any of today's schoolchildren did not retain at least some linguistic skills into later life. Experience with the standard language during these early years is critical.

In South China today Putonghua is the language of the government, and Southerners tend to use it for all activities associated with public life. For everything outside the public sphere the language is usually the local dialect. In the case of schoolchildren, the resulting formula is simple: in school use Putonghua, outside school use the home dialect. For adults the rules are more complicated; government penetrates their lives much more intricately, and the importance of the standard language to an individual depends upon a wide variety of factors—obviously a young telegrapher or a tour guide or a cadre member has more contact with the Common Language than an old farmer or street sweeper. But almost no one completely escapes public activity and the standard language. As the official language of China, Putonghua, the Common Language, reaches wherever the government does, and whatever contact a Southerner has with public life, there he finds in some measure the standard language.

Throughout the South an increasing number of ordinary people, adults as well as children, are becoming familiar with Putonghua and are even able to speak it. Recent visitors to South China have noted that it is now possible in almost any Southern city to shop, buy tickets, or ask directions using only the standard language. With it, it is even possible, they say, to strike up conversations with people in the streets. As any old China hand will attest, this is a far cry from prerevolutionary China, where any outsider who did not know the local dialect could quickly find himself hopelessly lost.

The rapid spread of Putonghua in South China does not mean that the dialects will soon die, however. A Southerner does not forget all the other varieties of Chinese he knows as soon as he learns the standard one. On the contrary, Putonghua complicates (or enriches) his life by adding another dimension to it. It becomes a useful tool, but at the same time it remains highly inappropriate and inconvenient in certain situations. There are many times and places where a Southerner must unavoidably speak his local dialect—that is, unless he wants to sever his ties completely with the social groups in which he grew up. The role of the dialect may be developing into something not unlike that of Swiss German, which has coexisted alongside standard High German in Switzerland for generations.

In the linguistically complex land that South China already is, Putonghua represents yet another layer of language. This Northern import cannot and will not immediately replace the many other varieties of Chinese that are already there. But even on levels farthest removed from public life its influence is already being felt. In Shanghai, which is a sophisticated Southern metropolis close to the leading edge of the Mandarin dialect area, some educated families have begun to use the standard language in their homes. For children growing up in such households, Putonghua is already a second home language. In Canton, a city far down in the Deep South and a stronghold of regional pride, the home is reportedly still the exclusive domain of Cantonese. But even there the vocabulary and locutions of new ways of life will eventually reach the most intimate levels of language.

The kind of linguistic changes that language standardization is bringing about are not completely new, however. The promotion of Putonghua is the product of modern nationalism, and its methods are those of twentieth-century technology (without modern transportation and communication the standard could never be spread so quickly). But in accelerated form, the spread of Putonghua is a continuation of much the same linguistic process that has been going on in China for a long time. One of the most consistent themes of Chinese history has been the flow of Northern influence into the South, and the language standardization policy of the People's Republic is in some ways only the most recent surge in the process.

IN Confucius's time, some 2,500 years ago, probably very little Chinese of any kind was spoken south of the Yangtze River. In those days, during the Classic age of China, the Chinese people lived in the North, and the southern part of the subcontinent belonged to other peoples and other cultures. These pre-Han inhabitants of South China appeared strange and wild to the Chinese, and for Confucius and his contemporaries the southeastern coast must have seemed as far away and exotic as California did to English settlers in Colonial America. The names of some of these Southern groups, such as the "Hundred Yuè" (or*gywät, as that ancient name might be reconstructed), are preserved in some of the early historical records. But the Chinese often referred to them collectively as the Mán, or "Southern Barbarians." Some idea of who these ancient Southerners were and what they were like can be found in the remote hills and forests of South China, where some of their descendants still live and preserve their languages and ways of life. But these scattered communities—which are now known as "non-Han minorities"—give barely a hint of what must have once been a veritable Babel of languages. Isolated from each other by geography, the early inhabitants of South China were probably as ethnically and linguistically diverse as the peoples of Southeast Asia or Central New Guinea.

From very early on, the North began to affect the South; but it took a considerable amount of time before the territories where these Southern groups lived could legitimately be called "Chinese." At first Sinification meant simply that the peoples of the South began to adopt a smattering of Chinese culture as the civilization developing in the Yellow River valley began to make its presence felt. The middle of the first millennium B.C.—again, Confucius's day—was an era of unparalleled energy and creativity in Chinese history, and the cultural pressures that were exerted upon neighboring peoples must have been strong in spite of distances and barriers to communication. The Yue groups living along the southeastern coast, for example, were already partially Sinified by the time that large numbers of Chinese settlers began to arrive in the middle of the third century B.C. Eventually, as time went on, more and more of these people adopted Chinese language and culture.

Direct migration from the North increased. As populations grew on the Northern plains, large numbers of pioneers moved into frontier regions of the South. Some of this migration resulted from government policy. In 221 B.C., the dynamic and aggressive "First Emperor" of the Qin dynasty ordered over five hundred thousand military colonists to fill newly conquered territories and to "live among the various Yue peoples." There were similar proclamations in later dynasties. But most migration was probably of the voluntary sort that responds naturally to the rhythms of population pressure; Chinese settlers moved into areas where farmlands would support them and spilled over into other areas when these were filled. For at least a thousand years and in some cases probably much longer, southeastern China was a complex mixture of Chinese and non-Chinese, the Sinified and the partly Sinified, all living in close proximity and in complex relationships with one another. During that time most parts of the South were nothing more than Chinese backwaters, places with a sprinkling of outposts of Chinese culture—perhaps a little like China's northwestern territories today. The South was, in other words, a Chinese frontier. It was different from the North, which was where Chinese civilization had begun.

In the literature of the early Tang period, there are frequent references to a North-South dialect division, and so it is certain that the Chinese were then aware of fundamental linguistic differences between the North and the South. But it is often difficult to know what the Southern "dialects" mentioned in these sources were. Oftentimes the references were undoubtedly to regional varieties of Chinese, spoken either by Northern immigrants or by Sinified groups, or both. But such "dialects" could also have been totally unrelated languages. The Chinese term we now translate as 'dialect'—*fāngyán*—literally means 'regional speech,' and in traditional times it was used rather indiscriminately to refer to anything different from the speech of the imperial capital. (In official glossaries compiled in late imperial times by the Translators' Bureau, even such foreign tongues as Korean, Japanese, Mongolian, Manchu, and Vietnamese were called *fāngyán*.) Without concrete linguistic facts we can know very little about these early "dialects," and pre-Tang and early Tang source materials contain precious little of that kind of information. Most of what can be known about the "North-South dialect division," at least until modern times, must therefore be surmised from what was happening to Chinese society at any particular time and supplemented by modern linguistic clues.

The South became an integral part of China in stages. The first region to become totally Sinified was the Lower Yangtze basin. Today this area focuses on the industrial and port city of Shanghai, but for the better part of its history, the Lower Yangtze had as its economic, cultural, and political centers the cities of Hangchow and Soochow (Hangzhou and Suzhou), situated in the fertile rice-growing delta south of the Yangtze. In A.D. 610 the great canal-building activities of the Sui emperor Yangdi succeeded in linking Hangchow to Chang'an, the imperial capital, which was located on the Loess Plateau in the Northwest. The completion of this system of waterways, known as the Grand Canal, brought about a period of extremely rapid population growth in the Lower Yangtze region and made it into the agricultural and economic center of the country. When the non-Chinese, Tungusic tribes known as the Jurchen conquered and then ruled North China during the twelfth and thirteenth centuries, the Southern Song made Hangchow their capital, and it became the repository of Chinese civilization, as well as a haven for Chinese immigrants from the Northeast.

The rest of the South took on a Chinese shape a little later than the Lower Yangtze. The rice-growing areas along the middle course of the Yangtze and in the Southeast finished filling up with people between the eighth and the eleventh centuries. The most important wave of migration during this period occurred around the turn of the tenth century, when, in the wake of the social upheavals that accompanied the collapse of the Tang government, large numbers of Northern Chinese refugees fled south. Among these immigrants were elite families who were protected by well-organized armies and followed by dispossessed peasants. Such groups formed the social and administrative core of the kingdoms that were subsequently established in the South, and these Sinitic kingdoms in turn provided the base for the complete assimilation of the South into Inner China when China was reunified by the Song a half century or so later. From the eleventh century on, the North and the South were no longer separated by the Sinitic versus the non-Sinitic; they had become part of the same Chinese world, moving together through similar cycles of cultural development.

The exception is Sichuan in the Southwest. Like the rest of the South, Sichuan began to be settled early, and it too was populated and Sinified in about the same time frame. But then in the thirteenth century the population of Sichuan and the entire Upper Yangtze region dropped precipitously. Just what caused this disaster is not totally clear, but it is suspected to have been been due at least in part to a series of plagues (bubonic?) that are reported to have swept over the region around the time of (and perhaps beginning slightly before) the Mongol invasions. The net result was that the population of Sichuan was reduced back to the level of a frontier. For several hundred years the region remained stagnant. But with the introduction of New World crops, the economy picked up and the population began to rise again, especially in the eastern part of the region around Chungking. In the two centuries between the beginning of the Qing period and the middle of the nineteenth century, the population of Sichuan climbed to its modern levels and the province became one of the most populous areas in all of China.

In spite of some superficial resemblances, the Sinification of South China was different from the march of the white man across the American West. In China, as in America, a technologically superior people pioneered and colonized an enormous territory, easily overwhelming scattered and disparate native cultures in the process. But there was a striking difference in the way that this was done. There is first of all the time scale. Whereas the American expansion across the continent took little more than a century, the Chinese movement southward, by even the most conservative reckoning, took well over a millennium—and in some respects is still going on in the remoter reaches of the South and Southwest. More important still is the difference in the fates that the native inhabitants suffered. The tragedy of the American Indian is not so much that he lost his lands and his culture, but that he more often than not lost his life as well. In the American West there was little assimilation or intermarriage, and many—perhaps most—native American groups have disappeared without so much as a genetic trace. In China, by contrast, the eradication of minority cultures was more benign, because the history of Chinese expansion was not so much one of displacement as of slow but continuous absorption.

Countless groups in South China gradually gave up their original ways of life and became Chinese. As time went on and contact with Chinese settlers increased, more and more native groups took up Chinese dress, customs, social values, and of course the Chinese language, which was crucial to the whole process of acculturation. Non-Chinese often gave up native names and even surnames in favor of Chinese ones, thus obscuring these potentially lasting differences between them and the immigrants from the North. For their part Chinese settlers tended to mix freely with native inhabitants. White settlers in the American West lived in isolated communities, but Han immigrants in South China tended to settle in native villages and mingle with the people who were already living there. Since pioneers into newly colonized areas were predominantly male, they frequently married local women, and the children were brought up as Han Chinese. Even military colonies were not always segregated, and we know that in most periods troops were dispersed among the native hamlets of an area. A sixteenth-century travel guide to the Southwest described the Chinese living there as indifferent to "mixing the races." Similar situations obtained in earlier periods as well. In short, immigrant and native blended together and became indistinct from one another in South China, with the language and culture of the dominant people— the Han Chinese immigrants from the North—eventually becoming the language and culture of all.

When a language spreads through transference—that is, when communities or large numbers of people who speak a different language learn a new one—the result can often be different from the spread of a language solely through immigration. An example of the latter sort is the English language in the New World. There is virtually nothing in the American language to tell us that Indian groups originally lived on the land where it is spoken. Aside from place names, some terms for local flora and fauna (e.g., *opossum, pecan, skunk*), and a scattering of colorful (and often jocular) native words such as *powwow, pemmican,* and *papoose,* little remains to speak of the linguistic richness that once existed on the American continent. Certainly there is nothing in the structure or the sounds of the American language that would give us a clue. The dialects of English spoken on the American continent descend directly from the language and dialects spoken in the British Isles, and scarcely a feature cannot be explained as deriving from there. (That is, if we leave aside such nettlesome questions as the amount of African influence on the formation of varieties of Black English; problems such as these of course have nothing to do with American Indian languages.) The spread of English in North America was one of complete displacement.

In the process of language transference, however, the language that is suppressed sometimes affects that of the intruder. A well-known case of this is Chilean Spanish. Because of the ferocity of the Indian tribes that inhabited the colony, the Spanish government was forced to send large numbers of soldiers to Chile to subdue them. These soldiers settled in the colony permanently and married native women, and the children of these mixed marriages became the core population of the new country. Unlike most of the rest of Latin America, Chile has lost its native Indian languages, and the people speak only Spanish. But the variety of Spanish that they speak differs from those spoken in the other countries of Latin America, because Chilean Spanish has features that once characterized the Indian languages spoken there. Linguists believe that the reason for this is that the children of the Spanish soldiers and Indian women learned much of their Spanish from their mothers, who, as non-native speakers, had mastered the language only imperfectly, retaining in their speech some of the characteristics of their native language. Another example of language transference is that of the Indo-European languages of India. Historians assume that the original Indo-European invaders came in small numbers and established themselves as a ruling caste. Many of the conquered peoples spoke Dravidian (and Munda) languages, and when they gave them up to speak Indo-European ones, they retained some of the features of Dravidian, such as its series of retroflex consonants. This imperfect transference is used to explain why, of all the Indo-European languages, only those spoken in India regularly have such consonants. (Even in the English that Indians speak, many consonants are pronounced as retroflexes, with the tip of the tongue raised high behind the alveolar ridge.) These same linguistic "substrata" are also believed to be the reason why an original Indo-European distinction between *l and *r is confused in the Indian languages; the Dravidian languages spoken in India at the time are thought to have had only one (or neither) of these two sounds.

In similar ways and for similar reasons, the varieties of Chinese spoken in South China still have some of the features of earlier, non-Sinitic languages. Of course, in the strictest sense, all of these varieties of Chinese descend from a language that was once spoken in the ancient Chinese homeland to the north. The linguistic influences from the North dominated almost completely, after all, and a detailed comparison of the Southern dialects is crucial to the reconstruction of earlier stages of Chinese. No people are prouder than Southerners—especially the Hakka—of the fact that ancestors of theirs once lived on the North China plain. And, as immigrants often do, Chinese in the South have tended to be more conservative in their language use than their compatriots who stayed in the homeland; features that were lost long ago in the speech of Peking, for example, are still very much part of the living dialects of South China. Yet, in spite of the fact that the South is now as staunchly Chinese as the North ever was, the Southern varieties of the language still bear faint traces of what the area was linguistically like before the Chinese came. When seen in the larger view, vestiges of pre-Han South China can still be seen in these dialects of Han Chinese.

The farther south one goes from the Yangtze, the more tones one hears in the Chinese dialects along the way. Some linguists believe this tendency is related to the fact that large number of tones are found in the surviving aboriginal languages of South China (and Southeast Asia).

In Chinese morphology a modifier normally precedes what it modifies. Thus the standard Peking word *gōngjī* 'rooster' is composed of *gōng* 'male' plus *jī* 'chicken,' in that order. But in the Southern dialects the order in such constructions is reversed, because sex markers are suffixed; in Cantonese, for example, *kaikong* 'rooster' is composed of *kai* 'chicken' plus *kong* 'male.' The elements have the same origins as those in the Peking word, but the way they have been put together is reversed. Other vocabulary items are constructed similarly. Alongside Peking *kèrén* '[literally] guest-person,' we find Cantonese *yanhak* 'person-guest.' Such morphological reversals in the Southern dialects have caught the attention of linguists because the order is the same as that of many of the aboriginal languages in South China, such as those of the Tai group, where modifiers regularly follow what they modify. Such constructions in the Southern dialects appear to be instances of a Tai substratum.

Some of the Southern dialects also have such peculiarities in their syntax. A few Cantonese adverbs, for instance, follow the verbs that they modify. (The Mandarin order is the adverb before the verb.)

sik to   ti
eat more some (= eat some more)

The various dialects often use totally unrelated grammatical forms—for the perfective suffix, for example.

meaning	Peking	Cantonese	Min (Fuzhou)	Hakka	Wu (Shanghai)
perfective	-le	-tso	0	-e	(reduplication)

These grammatical differences are believed to reflect differences in the substrata of the dialects.

In vocabulary, too, there is evidence for non-Han substrata. In the process of language transference, many humble words of everyday life are likely to be carried over into the newly acquired "higher" language (one thinks, for example, of the Yiddish words used conversationally by Israelis even after Hebrew was revived as the official state language). In all of the Chinese dialects there are many colloquial words that are never written down and for which, in fact, no written graphs exist. Such words are far more numerous in the Southern dialects than in the North and are thought to represent various linguistic layers, including the oldest, non-Sinitic substrata.

We must be careful, of course, not to exaggerate the importance of these substrata in the structure of the modern Chinese language. The Southern dialects are not "mixed languages," they are Chinese. The effects of the substrata on the formation of the Southern dialects have also been attenuated by many hundreds of years of later Chinese influence. More importantly, we must take care to avoid what Leonard Bloomfield once called "the mystic version of the substratum theory," in which later changes—in modern Cantonese, say—are attributed to some original "Tai substratum." That would make little more sense than to say that such changes are due to the "racial character" of the ancestors of the Cantonese. The peculiarities of a substratum come out in the first generation, when the speakers of one language attempt to master a second and do so imperfectly, retaining an "accent" when they speak the new language. The modern Cantonese people have no active memory of any ancestral Tai language; *new* linguistic changes in that direction would be farfetched indeed.

Nevertheless, we must not ignore the non-Sinitic substrata that exist in South China. They are unquestionably there, and a better understanding of them can teach us much about the historical processes that formed the Chinese language.

The structures of the Southern dialects are also complicated by later, various overlapping layers of Chinese. After Sinitic or Sinified populations became well established in the South, new waves of settlers and culture continued to arrive from the North. These deeply influenced local speech patterns.

The clearest such layers are the so-called "colloquial" and "literary" strains that are found in every dialect. The colloquial strain is invariably the older of the two levels, consisting of words that have been in the dialect ever since it was formed. The literary strain consists of words that were introduced into the dialect later. As the names imply, the "colloquial" level is made up mostly of informal, everyday words; the "literary" words are usually the more elevated terms of higher culture, which as a general rule came into the dialect through the local tradition of reading literary texts. But words from both levels are equally natural and common in everyday speech. The way they are mixed together is reminiscent of the relationship in English between native, Anglo-Saxon words and the Latinate vocabulary (mostly introduced into the language during the Renaissance). English *sweat* and Latin *perspiration* coexist in the language, as do *manly* and *masculine*. English *sweat* is more of an everyday word than Latin *perspiration*; but it would be hard to maintain that *manly* is more commonly used than *masculine*—and *feminine* wins out over *womanly* hands down.

Some colloquial words in the Chinese dialects have no literary equivalents. These usually cannot be represented with written characters (or if they can, the characters are used uniquely in that dialect). Here are a few examples of such words in the Cantonese dialect:

tsi:t^{7a}	'tickle'	te^3	'fretting, peevish'
ngao^1	'scratch'	te:ng^5	'throw'
mou^1	'squat'	lön^{6}tsön^6	'clumsy'
pot^{7a}	'spoon up'	li:m^{1}tsi:m^1	'nagging, fussy'
k'a:i^2	'naughty'	la^{4}tsa^3	'dirty'
nou^1	'angry'	pa^{1}poi^5	'boisterous'
le:k^{7a}	'smart'	hom^{6}pa^{6}lang^6	'all'
ling^5	'glittering'		

In other cases colloquial and literary words exist side by side in the dialect. The meaning of a colloquial word will often be somewhat different from that of its literary counterpart, and its use in actual speech is almost certainly not the same. But since the two ultimately come from the same ancient source, they will both be written with the same Chinese character. The result is a series of double readings for characters. Here are some Cantonese examples of colloquial and literary words written with the same graph:

Colloquial	Literary	
ts'e:ng[1]	ts'ing[1]	'blue, black'
ts'ong[4]	tsong[6]	'heavy'
p'o[1]	fo[3]	(measure word for 'tree')
tsa:ng[1]	ts'a[1]	'lack'
sei[5]	si[5]	'four'
li:t[7b]	ki:t[7b]	'knot'
ts'ön[o]	lön[3]	'egg'
yong[2]	nong[2]	'dark, thick (refers to tea)'

Northern influence in the South was especially great close to the border between the two areas, and the Southern dialects retreated very early from their natural geographical border along the watershed of the Yangtze to the banks of the river itself. Today Southern dialects continue to be pushed back, and Mandarin dialects are now well established in many places well across the Yangtze. Nanking, on its southern banks, is the representative dialect of the Southern Mandarin group. Danyang, a city located south of the Yangtze on the leading edge of the Mandarin area, has been described as having a dialect intermediate between Mandarin and Wu, the Southern dialect group of which Shanghainese is a member. The country dialects spoken just north of Danyang are still classified as Wu-type, but because Northern influences have already penetrated Danyang, the city upon which they are culturally dependent, these rural areas will probably soon begin to become "Mandarinized" themselves. One of the few non-Mandarin places still left north of the Yangtze is the area around Jingjiang, near the river's mouth; this area, however, used to be an island, until the northern channel grew so small as to leave it stranded on the northern side of the river in what is otherwise a Mandarin-speaking region.

Sometimes new waves from the North completely supplanted broad expanses of older varieties of Chinese. The most striking case where this has happened is in Sichuan (together with the immediately adjacent province of Guizhou and the northern part of Guangxi). This enormous area—Sichuan is the largest of China's twenty-two provinces—is entirely Mandarin-speaking in spite of the fact that it is geographically in the heart of the rice-growing South. Clearly, the large-scale migrations into Sichuan between the sixteenth and nineteenth centuries, well after the historical formation of Mandarin in the North, fundamentally changed the kind of Chinese that was spoken there. The fact that Sichuan is dialectally one of the most uniform places in all of Inner China is further evidence that the varieties of Chinese spoken there have been formed relatively recently.

Yunnan, to the southwest of Sichuan, did not become part of China until the thirteenth century, when the Mongols conquered the Tai groups living there and incorporated the area into the Chinese part of their empire. Yunnan was for this reason settled long after the rest of South China, and, as a result, the only varieties of Chinese spoken there are Mandarin.

4 THE STANDARD (PRONUNCIATION)

> Normalizing the Chinese language means fixing
> standards in phonology, vocabulary, grammar, and
> all aspects of the united national common language,
> so that our language can have a single standard in
> respect to both speech and writing.
> —1956 PRC pamphlet

The leaders of China have been clearest about what the pronunciation of standard Chinese should be. It is the part of the language that has been given the most attention.

The standard pronunciation is defined as the speech sounds of the Peking dialect. These are represented in written form by a Romanized alphabet that is taught in all the nation's schools. This system of Romanization is generally known as *Pīnyīn*. The name is short for *pīnyīn zìmǔ* 'phonetic alphabet,' but by itself it means simply 'spelling.' Pinyin has been the official spelling system of Mainland China since 1958. It is based primarily upon the earlier scheme of Latinization (called "Latinxua") that had been put together by the leftist Qu Qiubai in collaboration with Soviet experts. (The *x*'s, *q*'s, and *zh*'s that look so strange and unnatural to the English-speaking world thus reflect at least in part the graphic choices of Russian linguists.) But Pinyin also incorporates some of the insights and notational conventions of the National Language Romanization developed by Y. R. Chao and other Guoyu proponents.

Peking Mandarin has, according to government linguists, 405 basic monosyllables. Tones added to these basic monosyllables produce approximately 1,200 syllabic distinctions. (Since there are four tones, we might expect the number to be around 1,600. Many syllables, however, do not occur in all four tones.) This is a relatively small number of syllables compared to those of a Southern dialect such as Cantonese, which has undergone far fewer historical simplifications. The number is tiny in comparison with a language like English, which has many thousands of different possible syllables.

Each of these basic monosyllables is traditionally divided into an "initial" and a "final." The initial is the beginning consonant. The final is the rest of the syllable. The syllable *huang*, for example, has *h-* as its initial and *-uang* as its final. If a syllable has no initial consonant at all, and instead begins with a vowel, it is said to consist entirely of a final; *ang*, for example, is such a syllable.

This bipartite division of the syllable is the way sounds are analyzed in Chinese culture. So, even though Pinyin is a true alphabet, the Chinese schoolchild does not spell a Pinyin syllable by reading each letter by its letter name (as we would do: "Dee-oh-gee spells 'dog'"). The letters of the alphabet have no common Chinese names. Instead, the schoolchild indicates a pronunciation by giving its initial and final. This is done by chanting the two together in a uniform high pitch, with a conventional vowel sound (usually *e* [ə]) added to the initial so that it can be read syllabically. The two are then combined and the appropriate tone added to the resulting monosyllable. Here is how the formula works for *gǒu* 'dog,' *táng* 'sugar,' and *rén* 'person':

```
gǒu: gē-ōu, gǒu
táng: tē-āng, táng
rén: rī-ēn,  rén
```

This is the way the Chinese "spell." To them, the initial and the final, together with the tone, are the elements of which the syllable is composed. (This traditional analysis, with a little variation, has a long and venerable history; see Chapter 7.)

The Initials

There are twenty-one initial consonants in Peking Mandarin. These are given below in the usual Chinese order (the order, for example, in which Chinese children are taught the Pinyin symbols in school). The letters of the widely used Wade-Giles system of Romanization are added for comparison. The symbols in brackets represent the conventions of phonetic transcription used in this book.

Pinyin	[phonetic value]	Wade-Giles
b	[p]	p
p	[p']	p'
m	[m]	m
f	[f]	f
d	[t]	t
t	[t']	t'
n	[n]	n
l	[l]	l

Pinyin	[phonetic value]	Wade-Giles
g	[k]	k
k	[k']	k'
h	[x]	h
j	[chy]	ch
q	[ch'y]	ch'
x	[sy]	hs
z	[ts]	ts, tz
c	[ts']	ts', tz'
s	[s]	s, sz
zh	[chr]	ch
ch	[ch'r]	ch'
sh	[shr]	sh
r	[r]	j

Some Pinyin syllables begin with *y*- or *w*-, and these two glides could also be considered to be initials. But the Chinese usually treat *y*- and *w*- as graphic variants of the medial vowels -*i*- and -*u*-, and hence part of the final. The syllable *wai*, for example, is said to consist entirely of a final; the same final recurs in the syllable *kuai* (*k*- + -*uai*).

Unlike most European languages, Mandarin Chinese has no distinctively voiced consonants. What are written in Pinyin as *b*, *d*, and *g*, may sound voiced to a speaker of English, but they are actually pronounced [b, d, g] only when they occur in neutral-tone syllables (-*ba* of *wěiba* 'tail,' for example); otherwise, they are always voiceless [p, t, k]. What are written in Pinyin as *p*, *t*, and *k* (and *q*, *c*, and *ch*) are aspirated consonants. There is a discernible puff of air following the release of one of these aspirated consonants, and it is usually accompanied by audible friction in the back of the throat.

Three consonant types, the palatals (*j*, *g*, *x*), the dental sibilants (*z*, *c*, *s*), and the retroflexes (*zh*, *ch*, *sh*, *r*), are distinguished from each other by the position of the tongue. To pronounce the palatals, the tip of the tongue is dropped to a place behind the lower front teeth and the blade of the tongue brought up to contact the palate; for the dental sibilants, the tip of the tongue is held against the back of the alveolar ridge; for the retroflexes, the tip of the tongue is brought up and behind the alveolar ridge. This three-way distinction is rare among Chinese dialects, most of which have no retroflexes.

The mark of elegant Peking pronunciation is the retroflex. This particular pronunciation, which strongly recalls the *r* of the American Midwest, is very much admired. The great majority of Chinese living outside of the capital itself are unable to pronounce this sound correctly when they speak Putonghua, and most do not even try to imitate it. In Southern dialects, and in some of the North as well, the retroflexes *zh*, *ch*, and *sh* are not distinguished from the dental sounds *z*, *c*, and *s*. As a result, *chūn* 'spring' sounds like *cūn* 'village'; *shì* 'business' sounds like *sì* 'four'; *zhǎo* 'look for' sounds like *zǎo* 'early'; and so on. There are many homonyms for people who do not make this distinction natively, and there is no easy way for them to know which words should be pronounced as retroflexes. Teaching the distinction is like getting Cockneys to put their *h*'s in all the right places. The problem is always discussed in Chinese schools, but in most places it is regarded as insoluble. About the only people in the provinces who approximate the pronunciation with any consistency are professional speakers, such as announcers and tour guides, and a few educators. The retroflex distinction is officially considered part of the standard language, but in practice most speakers of Putonghua get along without it.

The finals

A final may be composed of as many as three elements: (1) a medial, (2) a main vowel, and (3) an ending. A "medial" is a short vowel sound or glide (*i-, u-, ü-*) that comes before the main vowel. The "main vowel" is the principal carrier of the syllable. An "ending" is a short vowel sound (*-i* or *-u*) or consonant (*-n, -ng,* or *-r*) that comes after the main vowel. The final *-uang* (as in the syllable *huang*), for example, contains the following elements: the medial *u-*, the main vowel *-a-*, and the ending *-ng*.

PUTONGHUA FINALS

medial	open ending	-i		-u		-n		-ng			-r
none	a, e, i, u, ü	ai	ei	ao	ou	an	en	ang	eng	ong	er
medial -i	ia	ie			iao	iou	ian	in	iang	ing	iong	
medial -u	ua	uo	uai	uei			uan	uen	uang	ueng		
medial -ü	üe						üan	ün				

There are about thirty-five finals in standard Chinese. Five of these consist of a single vowel: *-a, -e, -i, -u, -ü*. In Pinyin orthography there is also an *-o*, as in *bō* 'wave,' but this vowel is really a shorthand way of writing the final *-uo*, as in *guō* 'pot,' which has a medial *u-*. (When it stands alone, *o* can only be an exclamation: *ō* 'Oh!.')

The remaining thirty finals are combinations of medials, main vowels, and endings. Notice that in Pinyin the ending *-u* is written as either *o* or *u*. The *-i-* in the two finals *-in* and *-ing* is phonetically the main vowel, as is the *-ü-* in the final *-ün*.

The vowel *a* is pronounced [ɛ] in the final *-ian*. (This is why the final is written *-ien* in Wade-Giles Romanization.)

The vowel *e* is pronounced in several different ways. When it forms a final by itself, as in *è* 'to be hungry' or *gē* 'song,' pronunciation begins with the back of the tongue held high, then, as the vowel is articulated, the tongue relaxes and moves down toward a more central position. This vowel sound is not totally foreign to English—it is a little like the *u* in emphatic or mock Texan: "Git yore g*u*n!"

When *e* comes before *-n* or *-ng*, it is pronounced with the tongue more in the center of the mouth: [ə] (something like the *u* in Midwestern American *uh*). After a medial *i-* or *ü-*, *e* sounds like [ɛ]. Before the ending *-i*, *e* is pronounced [e].

The vowel symbol *i* has phonetically complicated values. After one of the dental initials *z-*, *c-*, or *s-*, it is a syllabic *z*—like the buzzing noise American children make when they imitate the sound of a bee: *zzz*! After a retroflex initial, *zh-*, *ch-*, *sh-*, or *r-*, it is a sustained (syllabic) retroflex. After all the other initials, *i* is pronounced [i]. In Wade-Giles Romanization these three vowel sounds are written three different ways: *-ŭ*, *-ih*, and *-i*.

	Pinyin	*Wade-Giles*
After z-, c-, s-:	-i [z]	-ŭ
After zh-, ch-, sh-, r-:	-i [r]	-ih
Elsewhere:	-i [i]	-i

Writing all three with the same Pinyin letter causes no confusion because they never occur after the same initial—a reader who knows Chinese sees the initial and adjusts the pronunciation of the vowel automatically.

When the vowel pronounced *ü* occurs after the palatal consonants *j-*, *q-*, or *x-*, the two dots over the vowel are omitted; *jün* is written *jun* (as in *jūn* 'army'); *qü* is written *qu* (*qù* 'to go'); *xüe* is written *xue* (*xué* 'to study'); and so on. The omission of this diacritic greatly simplifies the orthography and causes no misunderstanding because the vowel sound *u* itself never occurs after a palatal. However, *ü* contrasts with *u* after an *l-* or an *n-*, and here the two dots are not omitted: *lǜ* 'green' is different from *lù* 'road,' and *nǚ-* 'female' is different from *nǔ* 'to exert.' Such words as these are the only places the two dots are necessary in Pinyin orthography. When *ü* is the first sound of the syllable—that is, when the syllable has no initial—it is written as a digraph *yu*. Hence, the syllable *üe* is written *yue* (e.g., *yuè* 'moon'); *üan* is written *yuan* (*yuán* 'round'); *ün* becomes *yun* (*yūn* 'dizzy'); and *ü* becomes *yu* (*yǔ* 'rain').

The tones

Standard Chinese has four tones, which are usually identified by number: the 1st tone, the 2nd tone, the 3rd tone, and the 4th tone. (From a comparative point of view, the "fourth tone" should properly be called the "fifth tone," since the distinction that became the fourth tone in other dialects was historically lost in Mandarin. [See the discussion in Chapter 7, below.] However, pedagogical convenience has long since sanctified the use of the term "fourth tone" when referring to this tone in the standard language.)

The first tone is high and level. It is pitched near the top of the speaking range and is held on a steady, sustained note.

The second tone is high and rising. It begins near the middle of the normal conversational range of the voice but rises quickly to the top.

The third tone is low. When a word with this tone is pronounced in isolation, the voice starts off low, drops to the bottom, then rises to or above the middle of its range. When the word is not in isolation and is followed by another word, the voice stays down low. Either way, this tone goes down so low the voice often gets creaky.

The fourth tone is high and falling. It begins on a pitch at the very top of the vocal range and falls immediately to the bottom. It is very short in duration.

Every stressed syllable in the language is pronounced with the distinctive melody of one of these four tones. Here are a few examples of words that contrast with each other:

1st tone	2nd tone	3rd tone	4th tone
mā 'mother'	*má* 'hemp'	*mǎ* 'horse'	*mà* 'to scold'
dā 'to put up'	*dá* 'to answer'	*dǎ* 'to beat'	*dà* 'to be big'
tōng 'to open up'	*tóng* 'copper'	*tǒng* 'tub'	*tòng* 'to ache'
piāo 'to float'	*piáo* 'dipper'	*piǎo* 'to bleach'	*piào* 'ticket'

The tone marks used in Pinyin are iconic—that is, their shapes are meant to suggest the musical pitch of each tone. The mark for the first tone is a straight, horizontal line (¯). The second tone mark rises obliquely to the right (´). The third tone mark dips in the middle (ˇ). The fourth tone mark falls from left to right (`). Arrowheads placed on these marks show how graphic they are:

1st tone	2nd tone	3rd tone	4th tone
⟶	↗	⌣→	↘

The tone mark of a syllable is placed over the main vowel: *jī* 'chicken,' *jiā* 'home,' *jiān* 'pointed,' *jiāo* 'teach.' Some syllables, however, are by convention written with the main vowel omitted—e.g., *(j)iou* is written *jiu*; *(d)uei* is written *dui*; *(l)uen* is written *lun*. The rule in such cases is to put the tone mark over the last vowel: *jiǔ* 'wine,' *duì* 'be correct,' *lún* 'take turns.' But for the inexperienced writer it is often difficult to decide where the symbol should be placed.

The standard language has some examples of what is called *tone sandhi*—that is, the tones of some words change when they occur together with other words. The most famous kind of tone *sandhi* in Mandarin is the change of a third tone to a second when it is followed by another third tone.

hěn hǎo 'very good' ⟶ hén hǎo
mǎi mǎ 'buy a horse' ⟶ mái mǎ

The Peking orthography does not reflect such changes in tone, however; the syllable subject to tone *sandhi* is always written with its basic, lexical tone: *hěn hǎo*; *mǎi mǎ*.

In the Peking dialect, an unstressed syllable pronounced weak and short does not have a discernible, distinguishing tone. Instead, its pitch is determined by the intonation of the sentence and the pitches of the surrounding syllables. The question particle *ma*, for example, is a toneless syllable, as are many non-initial parts of compound words. Such syllables are left unmarked for tone:

Gāo ma? 'Is it high?'
Tā cōngming. 'He's smart.'
Xièxie! 'Thank you!'

Southern speakers of Putonghua have a great deal of trouble mastering this part of Peking pronunciation. Many Southern dialects have almost no toneless syllables, and as a result some Southerners tend to overenunciate the tones of the standard language.

Like all languages, Chinese has intonation, and this affects the phonetic realization of tones—but only within certain limits. A fourth tone at the end of a sentence with question intonation will fall less than one at the end of a sentence with declarative intonation; a first tone at the end of a statement will not be as high-pitched as one near the beginning. The interaction of the tones with intonation has been compared to that of ripples on the surface of large waves. Each small ripple remains the same in relation to the ripple before it and the one after it, regardless of whether it is in the trough of the large wave or on its crest.

A special type of intonation used in modern China is that of the radio and television broadcast. All Radio Peking announcers, both men and women, broadcast in a pitch range noticeably higher than that of their normal speaking voices. Each sentence begins high and shrill. Then pitch falls gradually, reaching a lower key by the end of the sentence. Pauses are exaggerated, and the normal rise of a nonconcluding clause becomes longer and more drawn out. The devices of this strident intonation may well be borrowed, in part, from traditional Chinese drama and opera; but their use in the media today seems intended to arouse in the audience an impression of struggle and determination. In Taiwan, by contrast, announcers usually do not affect such deliberate intonation and instead broadcast in a lower, more conversational speaking voice. This difference between the two Chinas is noticeable even to listeners who do not know Chinese.

北　京　语　音　表

Table of the Speech Sounds of Peking Dialect

声母＼韵母	a	o	e	-i	er	ai	ei	ao	ou	an	en	ang	eng	ong	i	ia	iao	ie	iou	ian	in	iang	ing	iong	u	ua	uo	uai	uei	uan	uen	uang	ueng	ü	üe	üan	ün
b	ba	bo				bai	bei	bao		ban	ben	bang	beng		bi		biao	bie		bian	bin		bing		bu												
p	pa	po				pai	pei	pao	pou	pan	pen	pang	peng		pi		piao	pie		pian	pin		ping		pu												
m	ma	mo				mai	mei	mao	mou	man	men	mang	meng		mi		miao	mie	miu	mian	min		ming		mu												
f	fa	fo					fei		fou	fan	fen	fang	feng												fu												
d	da		de			dai	dei	dao	dou	dan		dang	deng	dong	di		diao	die	diu	dian			ding		du		duo		dui	duan	dun						
t	ta		te			tai		tao	tou	tan		tang	teng	tong	ti		tiao	tie		tian			ting		tu		tuo		tui	tuan	tun						
n	na		ne			nai	nei	nao	nou	nan	nen	nang	neng	nong	ni		niao	nie	niu	nian	nin	niang	ning		nu		nuo			nuan				nü	nüe		
l	la		le			lai	lei	lao	lou	lan		lang	leng	long	li	lia	liao	lie	liu	lian	lin	liang	ling		lu		luo			luan	lun			lü	lüe		
z	za		ze	zi		zai	zei	zao	zou	zan	zen	zang	zeng	zong											zu		zuo		zui	zuan	zun						
c	ca		ce	ci		cai		cao	cou	can	cen	cang	ceng	cong											cu		cuo		cui	cuan	cun						
s	sa		se	si		sai		sao	sou	san	sen	sang	seng	song											su		suo		sui	suan	sun						
zh	zha		zhe	zhi		zhai	zhei	zhao	zhou	zhan	zhen	zhang	zheng	zhong											zhu	zhua	zhuo	zhuai	zhui	zhuan	zhun	zhuang					
ch	cha		che	chi		chai		chao	chou	chan	chen	chang	cheng	chong											chu	chua	chuo	chuai	chui	chuan	chun	chuang					
sh	sha		she	shi		shai	shei	shao	shou	shan	shen	shang	sheng												shu	shua	shuo	shuai	shui	shuan	shun	shuang					
r			re	ri				rao	rou	ran	ren	rang	reng	rong											ru	rua	ruo		rui	ruan	run						
j															ji	jia	jiao	jie	jiu	jian	jin	jiang	jing	jiong										ju	jue	juan	jun
q															qi	qia	qiao	qie	qiu	qian	qin	qiang	qing	qiong										qu	que	quan	qun
x															xi	xia	xiao	xie	xiu	xian	xin	xiang	xing	xiong										xu	xue	xuan	xun
g	ga		ge			gai	gei	gao	gou	gan	gen	gang	geng	gong											gu	gua	guo	guai	gui	guan	gun	guang					
k	ka		ke			kai	kei	kao	kou	kan	ken	kang	keng	kong											ku	kua	kuo	kuai	kui	kuan	kun	kuang					
h	ha		he			hai	hei	hao	hou	han	hen	hang	heng	hong											hu	hua	huo	huai	hui	huan	hun	huang					
	a	o	e		er	ai	ei	ao	ou	an	en	ang	eng		yi	ya	yao	ye	you	yan	yin	yang	ying	yong	wu	wa	wo	wai	wei	wan	wen	wang	weng	yu	yue	yuan	yun

THE STANDARD
(GRAMMAR)

The grammar taught in Chinese schools is the grammar of written style. The ability to write properly, together with a knowledge of the rules of pronunciation, are felt to be enough to enable any Chinese to speak Putonghua with facility. Little direct attention is paid to standards for speaking. Putonghua grammar is defined in terms of written Chinese, not spoken Chinese, and the model of usage is "the exemplary literature written in the modern colloquial."

But the basis of the standard, written as well as spoken, is in any case still Peking Mandarin.

CHINESE AND THE MYTH OF THE PRIMITIVE LANGUAGE

From very early on, Chinese gained a reputation among Westerners as a language poor in grammar. When the eighteenth-century linguist James Burnett (Lord Monboddo) learned that Chinese did not distinguish word classes by form, he concluded that it was an "exceedingly defective" language. A people possessing a language like this, he reasoned, could never make any progress in philosophy. In the first grand linguistic typologies—that is, those formulated in Europe in the early nineteenth century—Chinese was classed as a language "without structure." It was said to differ fundamentally from Turkish, which had suffixes, and Indo-European, which had inflection. Before too long, this tripartite distinction became the basis of classification for all the languages of the world, with the still-famous labels used and made popular by the German philologist and diplomat Wilhelm von Humboldt. There were, von Humboldt said, (1) "isolating" languages like Chinese, (2) "agglutinating" languages like Turkish, and (3) "inflecting" languages like Indo-European.

This schema focused solely on word morphology, the linguistic feature in which the Indo-European languages were richest. Other differences between languages were considered of secondary importance or ignored entirely. Nevertheless, as the nineteenth century wore on, ever more profound significance was attached to Humboldt's classification. Max Müller at Oxford connected the language types with social organization: isolating languages were family languages; agglutinating languages were nomadic languages; and inflecting languages were state languages. Soon, Darwinism crept into the picture, and many began to see an evolutionary order in the three types. August Schleicher, one of the greatest of the nineteenth-century philologists, conceived of languages as living organisms that had evolved like biological species. First, he said, all languages had begun with the "simplest structure, such as that still found in Chinese." After that, they went through a period of agglutination, then they became inflecting. But Chinese, according to Schleicher, still kept the most primitive and ancient form. The strongest opposition to Schleicher's views came from William Dwight Whitney, the Yale Sanskritist, who did not like the notion of languages as living things. He preferred to look upon them as human creations that reflected the progress of civilization. Whitney opposed Schleicher's concept of linguistic evolution and rejected his attempts to use language typology as a way of classifying the races of mankind. Whitney realized that a person is not bound by nature to speak only the language of his race, because, as he pointed out, a child of any national origin can learn any language to which he is exposed. But even Whitney, who in matters of race was relatively egalitarian, assumed as did Schleicher and almost all other Europeans that the languages of some cultures were primitively constructed. Whitney put it this way: "One may possess by descent a genius upon which even English, with all its force and beauty, imposes a laming constraint; while, on the other hand, and much more probably, there will be others whose meaner powers would be more in harmony with some lower form of speech, as Chinese or Malay." In his day Whitney's words were considered measured and scholarly.

Such assessments by Western experts were at least in part responsible for the low esteem Chinese intellectuals came to have for their own language. It became fashionable around the turn of the century to blame the Chinese language for a variety of social and political ills. In advocating the abolition of Chinese in favor of Esperanto, Qian Xuantong was perhaps extreme, but he was expressing a desire common among Chinese reformers. Many of them would have liked to do something about what they perceived as the inadequacies of their language. It would have been very difficult for them to reconstruct spoken Chinese. But there were a number of conscious attempts to sharpen the way it was written. Around the late 1910s writers began to use three separate graphs to distinguish 'he,' 'she,' and 'it.' All three of these characters were pronounced exactly the same way, *tā*, since there was (and is) only one third-person pronoun in Mandarin. But the use of separate graphs gave the illusion that

Chinese had the same kind of gender distinction that many Western languages did. Efforts were also made to expand the use of 'it.' In Mandarin, pronouns usually refer only to humans. For example, in response to the question, "Do you like the new person?" one says, Wǒ xǐhuān tā 'I like him (or her).' But if the question is, "Do you like the new machine?" one normally says, Wǒ xǐhuān 'I like,' without the pronoun 'it' obligatory in English. Now, however, some users of baihua began to ignore this structural fact and to write an 'it' in places where the pronoun would be found in an English translation. This particular stylistic innovation was in the end not very successful, though some unnatural uses of tā 'it' do still sometimes occur as a result of English influence. But the three-way graphic distinction between 'he,' 'she,' and 'it' continues in Chinese writing to this day. Similarly, efforts were made to distinguish the uses of the subordinative particle de. One graph was used when de meant possession ('of' or ''s'); another character was selected when de meant '-(t)ic, -al'; and a third character was used to transcribe de when it meant '-ly.' This innovation is another graphic device that has been retained in modern PRC usage.

Around the same time that these innovations were being made in China, the study of language in the West turned in a different direction. The rapid rise of descriptive linguistics in the second decade of the twentieth century brought a new set of standards, and the field work of anthropological linguists such as Franz Boas and Edward Sapir finally dispelled—at least for linguists—the idea that some languages are by nature more primitive than others. The diversity of language outside Europe, especially in the preliterate American Indian societies, convinced professionals to set aside most of the then-popular assumptions about the nature of language. From that time on, such things as national character, or the relative state of development of a particular language, were no longer serious questions. The task of the linguist came to be the description of each language on its own terms.

But the notion that Chinese is somehow inferior in expressive power is a persistent myth. It remains as a baleful legacy of a European-centered past. Y. R. Chao tells of a question he was asked concerning the absence in Chinese of an abstract 'it,' as in 'it rains': "Since ... scientific thought presupposes an objective consideration of neutral matter, would not, then, the lack of a grammatical 'it,' and the consequent lack of the ability to consider objective, neutral matter, be the real explanation of the failure on the part of the Chinese to develop a system of natural science before the advent of Occidental sciences?" The question comes from a former US ambassador to China, and it represents a suspicion harbored by many Westerners.

Dilettantes are not the only people who raise this issue. Joseph Needham, the well-known historian of science, is a respected Sinologist who believes that ancient China was lacking in the logical rigor necessary for the development of modern science. And, he says, one of the reasons for this lack is that "differences of linguistic structure between Chinese and the Indo-European languages had influence on the differences between Chinese and Western logic formation." This was written in 1956. Other Sinologists besides Needham have also pursued this line of thinking, and in the professional literature we can still occasionally find remarks implying that an indifference of the Chinese toward logical problems should somehow be connected to the structure of the Chinese language.

Quite recently—in 1981—a book has appeared with the provocative title, *The Linguistic Shaping of Thought: A Study in the Impact of Language on Thinking in China and the West*. Written by Alfred Bloom, an American professor of psychology, the book has been hailed by a reviewer as a convincing argument for the "precise ways the Chinese language does indeed influence thought." As his point of departure, Bloom makes the following linguistic observation: English and other Western languages make finer distinctions in conditional clauses than does Chinese. For example, the sentence *Rúguǒ nǐ kàndào wǒ mèimei, nǐ yídìng zhīdào tā huáiyùn le* is said to be translatable into English in three different ways:

(1) Reality: If you see my younger sister, you will certainly know that she is pregnant.
(2) Imaginative hypothetical: If you saw my younger sister, you would know she was pregnant (*I could imagine* your seeing her).
(3) Imaginative counterfactual: If you had seen my younger sister, you would have known that she was pregnant (you *did not* see her).

In the English conditional clauses (i.e., those introduced by *if*), three different situations are supposedly distinguished by the form of the verb (see—saw—had seen). But for the Chinese sentence the listener infers from context what kind of situation is meant. Bloom places great stress on this fact. Because the Chinese language does not have formal grammatical devices that distinguish between "counterfactual" situations and reality, Bloom says, the Chinese people do not readily enter into completely abstract modes of thought. Thus, he concludes, abstract theoretical models are alien to Chinese culture. To prove that what he says about Chinese resistance to abstraction is true, Bloom has used a series of questionnaires to poll a large number of educated Chinese in Taiwan and Hong Kong. For comparative purposes, similar questionnaires were distributed in the United States and France. The questionnaires presented situations that could not occur in reality. One question, for example, that elicited clearly different responses was this one: "If all circles were large and this small triangle [a small printed triangle is shown on the questionnaire] were a circle, would it be large?" Bloom's American and French respondents almost unanimously answered the question in the affirmative, while the Chinese were simply perplexed by it. The triangle was obviously a triangle and could never be a circle, so, according to Bloom, the Chinese were pragmatically unwilling to speculate about what it would be like if it were a circle. Bloom concludes that it is this completely empirical bias on the part of the Chinese that separates them from the abstracting Westerner, and it is the language they speak that, at least in part, gives them this bias. These are sweeping generalizations indeed.

What are we to make of this? Technical problems with such things as polling techniques and translation aside—and these are not inconsiderable—it is not all clear what Bloom has measured. The very complexity of a society makes it extremely difficult to isolate any one factor in the background of the respondents as responsible for a particular set of results. And what is it that makes the backgrounds of a group of Chinese respondents in any way comparable to those of a group of American respondents? (I suspect that if Bloom had shown his triangle to a group of working-class Americans, he would have been met with looks as puzzled as any he saw in China.) It might make more sense to compare Chinese responses to Korean responses. The Korean language has a series of fine distinctions in conditional clauses—including so-called counterfactuals—and the East Asian people who speak it differ far less from the Chinese in their cultural heritage than Americans or Frenchmen do. This way, we might conceivably come closer to isolating the effects of language. Yet here too—or in any such comparison—we would have begged the question of cause and effect. Language mirrors the society in which it is spoken. Chinese and Koreans talk about what they want to talk about, and they do not talk about what they do not think about. To ask which causes the other is the proverbial chicken-or-egg question. It is pointless even to speculate as to how the existence of some grammatical construction might promote certain modes of thought. Should we believe that the Koreans are better able to master modern mathematics just because their language has counterfactual constructions? Or conversely, that the Chinese are mathematically handicapped because their language does not happen to have such things? If new ideas or new things come into a society, then the language adjusts in various ways to accommodate them. That this is true is shown in the fact that, as Bloom points out, the Chinese have recently begun to use and talk about Western concepts now that they have been thoroughly exposed to Western science and culture.

But comparing Chinese to Korean would probably be beside Bloom's point anyway, since it would tell us nothing about the differences between East and West. The Koreans, after all, did not develop modern science any more than the Chinese did. And, in this connection, we might remember that the Indic languages, which are Indo-European, also have counterfactuals aplenty; why then did the Indians, who also had an advanced native civilization, not develop modern science either? This, like similar musings about Chinese civilization, is a simplistic question without a simple answer.

We do not know why modern science developed in Western Europe and in no other place. But Y. R. Chao, when asked to respond to this question by the American ambassador, gave (in part) the following answer: "Modern Western science is only a matter of the last three or four hundred years, which is a very small fraction of recorded history and even a more minute fraction of the history of human culture. Any set of fortuitous circumstances—fortuitous in the sense of being non-racial and non-linguistic—would have been enough to lead to such a relatively small difference in the starting time of the scientific phase of history. It would indeed be of the greatest interest if research should bring out what those fortuitous circumstances were. ... But a full explanation will probably not be given tomorrow or even next year."

If people brought up in China do not talk about the same things people brought up in Western culture do, that is one matter. But to attribute that difference to the lack of some formal grammatical device in the language is quite another. Chinese verbs may not be marked for subjunctive mood, but they are not marked for tense, either: In the sentence *Wǒ bù zhīdao, tā zuótiān qù, jīntiān qù, háishi míngtiān qù* 'I don't know if he went yesterday, is going today, or will go tomorrow,' the form of the verb *qù* 'go (*or* went *or* has gone *or* will go)' is the same whether the action takes place today, yesterday, or tomorrow. From this fact can we conclude then that the Chinese have a dim perception of the passage of time? Even between languages as closely related as English and German grammatical differences exist. The German sentence *Morgen, um zehn Uhr, wenn du kommst, bin ich schon damit fertig* means, in English, both 'Tomorrow at ten, *when* you come [as planned], I'll have it ready' and 'Tomorrow at ten, *if* you come, I'll have it ready.' Does this linguistic fact mean that the German people do not understand the implicational difference between a when-clause and an if-clause? English speakers instinctively sense a difference between these two things and may wonder how Germans could possibly get along without the distinction. But in fact the message contained in a German conditional clause (whether that is 'when' or 'if') will be made as clear as it needs to be by the context in which it is said. What has been said before; what the speaker and the listener implicitly know, both about the real world and about each other; where they are when the statement is made—all of these things are part of the context and contribute in one way or another to the meaning. The same is of course true for Chinese. All human communication takes place within a context, and any time we take an utterance out of its context—including the cultural one—we run the risk of misunderstanding it or losing part of its meaning.

In English there is no grammatical marker to compare with the Chinese particle *le*, which (among other things) indicates a change of condition or state. When a speaker of Chinese says *Wǒ lèi le* 'I'm tired,' with the particle *le*, he means that he was not tired before but now has become so. This change of state is not necessarily implied by the English *I'm tired*. But if, say, two friends have been out jogging and one turns to the other and says, "I'm tired," the conditions under which he says this make the change of state clear. In this case *I'm tired* is fully equivalent to *Wǒ lèi le*. The meaning of the particle *le* is provided by context.

Counterfactuals in Chinese can be roughly divided into two types: first, those which are explicitly so, and will be interpreted as such in virtually all conceivable situations; and, second, those for which a counterfactual interpretation depends closely upon context. Here are two common colloquial examples of the first type:

Yàoshi wǒ zhīdao, wǒ zǎo jiù   qù le.
if   I   know   I   early then go CA
'If I had known, I would have gone.'

Yàoshi wǒ zhīdao, wǒ bú jiù   zǎo qù le ma?
if   I   know   I   not then early go CA ?
'If I had known, wouldn't I have gone?'

Such sentences as these are completely counterfactual. It is not only that a factual interpretation of 'If I know ...' would be awkward. The time word *zǎo* 'early, some time ago now' and the particle *le*, which (with action verbs) usually indicates completed action, also serve to rule out some future reality. The rhetorical question reinforces the counterfactual effect.

Time words, particles, and verb suffixes (among other things) can be combined in various ways to make statements counter to fact. The auxiliary verb *huì* 'can, be likely to' usually means 'would have' when it is used in reference to situations contrary to past fact. In the following examples, the elements most important to a counterfactual interpretation are italicized:

> Yàoshi tā yònggōng yìdiǎr, *xiànzài* jiù bú huì   bù jígé *le*
> if   he is-studious a little now   then not likely not pass CA
> 'If he had studied harder, he would have passed.'

> Yàoshi tā yònggōng yìdiǎr, *xiànzài zěnme* huì   bù jígé?
> if   he is-studious a little now   how   likely not pass
> 'If he had studied harder, how could he have failed?'

> Rúguǒ nǐ   zuìjìn   kàndào-*guo* wǒ mèimei, nǐ   jiù *huì*   zhīdao
> if   you recently see   ES my sister   you then likely know
> tā huáiyùn le.
> she pregnant CS
> 'If you had seen my younger sister recently, you would know
> she is pregnant.'

In other words, there are a variety of ways to say something specifically counter to fact in Chinese—when it is necessary. In most cases, however, the context makes the interpretation clear. The sentence *Rúguǒ nǐ huì yòng kuàizi, nǐ jiù néng chī fěnsī* seems to be ambiguous when considered in isolation, because it has two different English translations:

> 'If you know how to use chopsticks, you can eat *fensi*.'*
> 'If you knew how to use chopsticks, you could eat *fensi*.'

[* *Fěnsī* are a kind of clear, Chinese vermicelli that cannot be eaten with a spoon and require considerable skill to eat with chopsticks.] But in what kinds of situations would something like this be said? Suppose a Chinese is sitting with a foreigner in a restaurant and says this after studying the menu. If the foreigner is a new acquaintance, or if they are eating together for the first time, then the meaning is unambiguously 'If you know. ...' But if, on the other hand, the two have eaten together in Chinese restaurants before, or if the Chinese has had some other opportunity to observe the foreigner's lack of skill with chopsticks, then the meaning can only be the counterfactual 'If you knew. ....' Chinese speakers can certainly cope with all the questions of factuals and counterfactuals that they confront in their everyday lives.

Of course, technical work in mathematical logic requires—in Chinese as in English—specialized usages and vocabularies for dealing with logical constructs. Such concepts should not be confused with those that exist in popular usage, however. The technical field of logic is different from natural language. As Y. R. Chao said, in a playful reference to a statement by Bertrand Russell, the only generalization to make about language and science is to make no generalization.

When people say that Chinese has no grammar, they usually mean that it is not inflected for case, number, person, tense, and so forth. But inflection is not the only kind of grammar. The parts of Chinese are put together in a fashion every bit as orderly as that of any other language. Sound units are combined to make morphemes; these form words; and words are carefully ordered to make meaningful utterances. That is to say, Chinese does have grammar. This grammar is very different from that of languages with what is traditionally called inflection. But, in its own way, it is just as complex and just as regularly defined.

WORDS

We English speakers analyze our language into what we call words. Words are the entries in our dictionaries; they are the things we teach our children in school; they are the parts of language that we talk about in our everyday lives. To us, the word is the elemental building block of language.

Yet, these very words we know so well are not always easy to define. Why is *fingerprint* one word but *finger mark* two? (Or *textbooks* one word and *text materials* two?) Sometimes the reasons we make separate words have very little to do with language. *Seaplane* and *seaside* look pleasant enough on the printed page, but *seaair* and *seaurchin* do not and so are not written together this way. Why are *common sense, black sheep, top hat, high school*, and *hot seat* considered expression or idioms and not words? It often happens that British and American sensibilities are at odds in such matters. In *Lolita*, a novel written in British style, Nabokov's hero Humbert Humbert muses on the nature of *forever* and says: "The words 'for ever' referred only to my own passion. ..." The enigmatic thing about this passage for American readers is that *forever* is treated as a plural concept; for anyone educated in the United States this expression is a single, indivisible word. The point of view in other countries is yet again different. A German discussing English might insist that *youth hostel* and *traffic accident* are single words, as indeed they are in his own language (*Jugendherberge* and *Verkehrsunfall*). It is fortunate indeed that most people need not be concerned over such nettlesome questions. Lexicographers, copyeditors, and printers make decisions, and the layperson, for his part, accepts what the dictionaries say. Just as in matters of spelling, the conventions of orthography provide clear-cut answers where otherwise there might be room for confusion. The words of the English language do not always have sharp borders. There are many gray areas.

What people think of as the units of language varies from culture to culture. The Japanese word closest to the meaning of 'word' (*kotoba*) can refer to any meaningful expression—a monosyllable, a phrase, a saying, a statement—or even the language as a whole. Closer to home, there is the opening verse of the Gospel of St. John: "In the beginning was the Word, and the Word was with God, and the Word was God." The verse sounds strange and mysterious because "Word" imperfectly translates the Greek term *logos*.

The Chinese have no everyday word for 'word.' There is as yet no place in the Chinese psyche for syntactic units of that size. Instead, they think of their language as composed of individual syllables, which they call *zì*. Many of these syllables also happen to be words; *rén* 'person,' *gāo* 'tall, high,' *chī* 'eat,' *liù* 'six,' *shuí* 'who.' But some are not. The suffixes *-tou* and *-zi* form parts of words (e.g., *shítou* 'stone' and *shīzi* 'lion') but they are certainly not themselves words, at least in the familiar way that we use the term. Still, *-tou* and *-zi* are considered *zi* by the Chinese.

The syntactic unit to which the Chinese syllable most nearly corresponds is the morpheme. This unit, though it is an abstract and technical concept in the English-speaking world, is more easily defined than the word. Simply stated, the morpheme is the smallest linguistic unit that has a meaning. It is the atom of meaning. The word *friendly* can be divided into two elements, *friend* and *-ly*. *Friend* is a word, but *-ly* is not. Both elements, however, are morphemes because they are the smallest meaningful units in the word. The form *-ly* is a suffix and may not stand alone, but since it has a consistent meaning ('characteristic of'), it qualifies as a morpheme as much as does *friend*. In the same way, the Chinese suffixes *-tou* and *-zi* are also morphemes—atoms of meaning. Just as some highly volatile elements of the physical world occur naturally only as parts of molecules, linguistic elements such as prefixes and suffixes occur only as parts of words.

A native speaker of Chinese instinctively divides an utterance up into as many units as it has syllables, or *zi*, and each of these units is almost always a morpheme. *Zhōngguó*, the word for 'China,' is composed of two morphemes, *zhōng* 'middle' and *-guó* 'country.' The construction parallels English *Finland* ('Land of the Finns'), except that the suffix *-guó* cannot be an independent word, the way *land* can be. (The Chinese word for 'country' is a compound: *guójiā*.) Yet, to the Chinese, the name of their country is an expression composed of two syntactic units and constructed similarly to English *South Africa* or *United States*. As a result, they feel free to ignore Western rules of word division and Romanize it as *Zhōng Guó*. Western writers often go along with these Chinese feelings by writing the name with a hyphen, *Zhōng-guó* or *Chung-guo*, even though they would never think of writing *Fin-land*, *Switzer-land*, or *Eng-land*. (*Togo-land* or *Togo Land* might be more acceptable.) In the textbooks of Chinese primary schools, dissyllabic words such as *kǎoshì* 'test,' *lǎoshī* 'teacher,' and *xuéxiào* 'school,' are usually written in Pinyin as *kǎo shì*, *lǎo shī*, and *xué xiào*. If a Chinese wants to ask what the word *jīguāng* 'laser' means, he is likely to say, *Jīguāng, zhèi liǎngge zì shì shénma yìsi?* '*Jī* (and) *guāng*, these two *zì*, what do they mean?' In very recent years young Chinese have also begun to use a term meaning 'word,' because PRC policymakers have decided that this modern concept should be introduced in the schools. But the word for 'word' that they chose, *cí*, was a technical linguistic term. It was not part of the average person's vocabulary any more than the term *morpheme* is in English-speaking countries. *Jī* and *guāng* are both meaningful; they are morphemes that literally mean 'stimulated' and 'light,' and the Chinese have good reason to feel that each is a unit in its own right.

A handful of Chinese morphemes are longer than one syllable. *Húdié* 'butterfly,' *pútao* 'grapes,' *méiguì* 'rose,' *Bōli* 'glass,' *héshang* 'Buddhist priest,' and a few other such words thought to be ancient loans cannot be divided into smaller meaningful units. There are also some common expressions like *chóuchú* 'to hesitate,' *gēda* 'pimple,' *luōsuo* 'to chatter,' *fǎngfú* 'apparently,' and *hútu* 'muddle.' *Mǎmǎhūhū* 'so-so' is written 'horse-horse-tiger-tiger' and *dōngxi* 'thing' is written 'east-west,' but these are folk etymologies; the origins of expressions such as these are obscure. There are, in addition, modern loanwords. *Kāfēi* 'coffee,' *āsīpǐlín* 'aspirin,' *shāfā* 'sofa,' *Bùěrshíwéikè* 'Bolshevik,' and the like are part of the language now. But even in cases such as these, where it is clear that expressions are of foreign origin, the Chinese tendency is to try to make meaning of some kind out of the constituent syllables. The phonetic shape of the borrowing *làngmàn* 'romantic' is intended to approximate the sounds of the English word, but the two syllables of which it is composed also have the literal meanings of 'unrestrained' and 'free.' The syllables of *yōumò* 'humor' mean 'secluded' and 'quiet'; *xiūkè* 'shock' means 'be inactive and overcome'; *jùlèbù* 'club' means 'all-enjoyment unit.' In the 1930s, when Coca-Cola first began marketing its product in China, the company sponsored a highly publicized contest to find a suitable Chinese name for its soft drink. The winning name, submitted by a man from Shanghai, was *kěkŏu-kělè*. This name not only reproduced the English sounds fairly accurately, but the individual syllables put together also had the elegantly-phrased meaning 'tasty and enjoyable.' For this linguistic tour de force the winner received a $50 cash prize. In more recent years Pepsi-Cola has begun to challenge Coke's success in Chinese-speaking countries by selling its product under a similarly constructed name, *Bǎishì-kělè*, which means 'everything's enjoyable.' The linguist Y. R. Chao himself coined the playful Chinese name of the martini, *mǎtīni* 'horse-kicks-you.' The miniskirt is a *mínǐqún*—a "fascinate-you-skirt." *Léidá* 'radar' is 'thunder-reach'; *tuōlājī* 'tractor' is 'haul-pull-machine'; *Xímíngnàěr* 'seminar' is 'review-understand-accept-like that.' In Chinese, a completely meaningless syllable is an anomaly.

The close correspondence of the syllable to the morpheme is the sense in which Chinese is a monosyllabic language. Every syllable is not what we would call a word—if that were taken as the criterion of monosyllabism, we would be hard-pressed to find any monosyllabic languages at all in the world. But because every syllable usually means something, the label "monosyllabic" can indeed by a useful way to describe Chinese.

Writing Chinese Words

The most difficult problem in Romanizing Chinese is deciding what its orthographic words should be. Should they be equated with its monosyllabic morphemes? This solution would accord with most speakers' intuition and the traditional writing system. (The Vietnamese have been Romanizing their monosyllabic language this way for centuries.) Or should Chinese words be written as longer syntactic units, something more in keeping with the way words are written in Western languages? Romanization demands a clear definition of the word. As a matter of practical orthography, a form must either be written solid or written with spaces. If written solid, it is a word; if written with spaces, it is not.

Though there are as yet no clearly articulated standards, most Chinese linguists and government agencies seem to prefer Western-looking words—the trend these days is to write solid. The official Pinyin name of the country is spelled *Zhōnghuá Rénmín Gònghéguó*, divided into essentially the same syntactic words as the English 'People('s) Republic (of) China.' Some words are written longer than their English equivalents, in ways approaching German orthographic convention: the 'Chinese Communist Party' is *Zhōngguó Gòngchǎndǎng*; 'blind alley' is *sǐhútòng* (literally, 'dead alley'), 'lucky days' is *hǎorìzi* (at least in most of the latest Pinyin dictionaries). But the arbiters of language in China are by no means all in agreement, and the words of one publication often appear as phrases in another. And, as might be expected, each syllable is still written as a separate word in many of the popular Romanizations. We see this kind of monosyllabic Pinyin, for example, on shop signs and product labels.

One index of the confused status of the word in China is the Romanization of journal titles. Some titles on the covers of journals are written monosyllabically; e.g., *Zhe Xue Yan Jiu* 'Philosophical Research,' *Xue Shu Yue Kan* 'Academic Monthly,' and *Li Shi Dang An* 'Historical Archives.' Others, such as *Lishi Yanjiu* 'Historical Research' and *Zhōngguó Yǔwén* 'Chinese Linguistics,' are more in keeping with Western orthographic practice. But the editors of many journals have apparently taken the principle "write solid" too much to heart: *Anhuiwenxue* 'Anhui Literature,' *Jiefangjunwenyi* 'Literature and Art of the Liberation Army,' *Beifangquyi* 'Northern Folk (Performing) Art.' And occasionally there are even polysyllabic titles that look more like Polynesian than Chinese: *Shenyangshifanxueyuanxuebao* 'The Journal of Shenyang Teachers College.'

In time, a consensus will probably be reached and the words in all Pinyin dictionaries standardized. But the problem of the orthographic word goes beyond the listable entries of a lexicon; for in Chinese, there is no clear dividing line between word formation and syntax. The negative *bù*, for example, is sometimes used as a prefix 'un-,' and other times as an independent word 'not'—e.g., *bùfǎ* 'illegal,' *bùtóngde* 'different (= unlike)'; *bù tōng* 'not make sense,' *bú qù* 'not go.' A noun or adjective is often the same in form as a clause: *kānménde* 'doorman' is identical to *kān mén de* '(the one) who watches the door.' Verbal expressions are particularly troublesome. Verbs such as *shīxìn* 'break a promise' are surely to be classified as single words. But elements can intercede between the two syllables to make them seem less and less like a unit: *shīguo-xìn le* 'broke a promise'; *Tā yǐjīng shīguo liǎng-cì xìn le* 'He's already broken his word twice.' Obviously usages like these cannot all be listed in a dictionary; deciding whether a morpheme is a separate word or not demands paying close attention to the context in which it is used. Writing Chinese words in Romanization can be an exercise in parsing.

Word Formation

Many of the elements in Chinese that we would call words are monosyllabic morphemes. These short words make up much of the basic vocabulary of the language. However, except for this monosyllabic core, the vast majority of words consist of two or more morphemes. These more complex forms can be roughly classified into three categories: (1) reduplicated words, (2) morpheme plus suffix, and (3) compounds.

(1) *Reduplicated words.* Reduplication is a way of making a new word by repeating a morpheme or word. In English the process exists, but just barely—*hush-hush* and *pooh-pooh* are made up this way, as are, with slight modification, *dillydally* and *mishmash*. But in general reduplicated words in English are associated with the nursery—*dada, mama, wa-wa,* and the like; the process is certainly not productive in the speech of adults.

In Chinese, however, reduplication has been a normal and extremely useful way of making words for as long as we have had records of the language. Reduplicated words are found in historical works ranging from the philosophical essays of Mencius to the regulated verse of Li Bai. In modern Chinese, the process has a variety of functions.

Action verbs can ordinarily be reduplicated in order to soften the degree of action: *děng* 'wait,' *děngdeng* 'wait a bit'; *cháng* 'taste,' *chángchang* 'take a little taste'; *xiūxi* 'rest,' *xiūxixiuxi* 'take a little rest.' Reduplication makes a description more vivid: *pàngde* 'fat,' *pàngpàngde* 'pudgy fat'; *hóngde* 'red,' *hónghóngde* 'bright red'; *gānjìng* 'clean,' *gāngānjìngjìng* 'squeaky clean'; *píngcháng* 'usual,' *píngpíngchángchángde* 'quite usual and ordinary.' In certain cases reduplication is a totalizer that adds the meaning of 'every': *chùchu* 'everywhere,' *tiāntian* 'every day,' *rénren* 'everybody,' *zhāngzhang (zhǐ)* 'every sheet (of paper).' Many familiar kinship terms are also constructed this way: *gēge* 'older brother,' *dìdi* 'younger brother,' *nǎinai* 'grandmother.'

(2) *Morpheme plus Suffix.* Chinese has just a few prefixes. The most useful of these is probably *dì-*, which is used to make ordinal numbers: *dì-yī* 'first,' *dì-èr* 'second,' *dì-sān* 'third,' etc. Except for a limited number of true prefixes like *dì-*, most elements that serve as prefixes have primary functions as something else. The adverb *bù* 'not,' for example, doubles as a prefix when adjectives are formed: *búxìngde* 'unfortunate,' *bùguīzé* 'irregular' (*guīzé* is a noun meaning 'rule').

Suffixes, on the other hand, are numerous. This is particularly true in modern colloquial usage. In the classical language there were only a small number of such word-forming elements, and their occurrence was very restricted. But in the modern varieties of the language—and most especially in the Mandarin dialects—suffixes play a major role in the formation of words.

The most common noun suffix is *-zi.* It is also the oldest recorded suffix. The original meaning of this morpheme was (and still is) 'child' or 'offspring,' but fairly early in the history of the language it is said to have also been used as a suffix for certain nouns referring to humans—e.g., *qīzi* 'wife' (in the modern pronunciation of the word). By the Tang period the suffix had begun to spread widely throughout the Chinese vocabulary, and today a great variety of nouns are formed with *-zi.* Here is a small sampling of its range: *érzi* 'son,' *háizi* 'child,' *chúzi* 'cook,' *ǎizi* 'a short person,' *pàngzi* 'a fat person,' *kuǎzi* 'a person who speaks with a regional accent'; *dùzi* 'stomach,' *bízi* 'nose,' *nǎozi* 'brain,' *shēnzi* 'body'; *yǐzi* 'chair,' *dāozi* 'knife,' *kuàizi* 'chopsticks,' *bàngzi* 'stick, club,' *fángzi* 'house,' *wūzi* 'room,' *tīzi* 'ladder,' *jīnzi* 'gold'; *júzi* 'tangerine,' *màizi* 'wheat,' *lìzi* 'chestnut,' *jiǎozi* 'Chinese dumplings'; *pàizi* 'rhythm,' *yángguǐzi* 'foreign (Western) devil,' *shùlínzi* 'woods.'

A much less productive noun suffix is *-tou.* Its most common use is in the formation of place words—e.g., *shàngtou* 'top,' *qiántou* 'front,' *lǐtou* 'inside,' *wàitou* 'outside' (this particular usage, which today seems typically Mandarin, can be found in Chinese writings as far back as the early centuries of the Common Era). Here are some of the other modern nouns in which the suffix occurs: *gútou* 'bone,' *shétou* 'tongue,' *shítou* 'rock,' *niàntou* 'thought, idea,' *mántou* 'steamed bun.'

The suffix *-r* is the only morpheme in the language that is less than a syllable long. It attaches to a variety of morphemes to form nouns (and in certain cases other kinds of words), often with a familiar and diminutive—or sometimes even a pejorative—flavor. As a typical example, alongside *māo* 'cat' we find *māor* 'kitty cat'; there is *huà* 'to paint' and *huàr* 'picture'; *mǎ* 'horse' and *(xiǎo) mǎr* 'little horsey'; *guān(yuán)* 'official' and *guānr* '(petty) bureaucrat.' Sometimes the meaning change is greater: *yǎn* is 'eye' but *yǎnr*, with the suffix, is 'hole'; *xìn* is 'letter' but *xìnr* is 'news'; *shǒu* is 'hand,' *shǒur* is 'ability.' The only truly common verb with the suffix is *wánr* 'to play'; but there is also the less frequently used *cuānr* 'to get mad.'

The pronunciation of the suffix *-r* is complicated and difficult to describe in any simple way. The tip of the tongue must be raised to articulate the retroflex of this suffix, but the vowels of many syllables are not compatible with this gesture. The vowel *i*, for example, is pronounced with the tip of the tongue down, making retroflexion impossible. In such cases the vowel must change. Sometimes *e* is added between vowel and ending (*jī* 'chicken,' *jiēr* 'chick'); sometimes an ending vowel is dropped (*kuài* 'lump,' *kuàr* 'lump'); sometimes the -*r* changes the quality of the vowel in less dramatic ways (as it does in the added retroflex articulation of *o* in *bāor* 'small parcel'). An -*n* ending is dropped completely (*wánr* 'to play' is actually pronounced *wár*), but an -*ng* ending remains in the form of nasalization of the previous vowel (the *a* in *qiāngr* 'accent' is actually the last segment of the syllable but it is articulated with both nasalization and retroflexion). All of the complicated changes in pronunciation caused by this suffix are ignored in Pinyin orthography, and in each case an -*r* is simply added onto the end of the original syllable.

The retroflex suffix is rarely heard outside the Mandarin-speaking area, but in the colloquial speech of the Peking capital it is extremely common and productive. Partly because it is such a localized thing, and partly because it is so difficult to imitate or use for most Chinese in the provinces, the PRC government has been reluctant to incorporate the suffix completely into the standard. The tendency is to substitute synonymous expressions where they exist—e.g., *jīntiān* for *jīnr* 'today,' *míngtiān* for *míngr* 'tomorrow,' *dòuzi* for *dòur* 'bean,' *chóngzi* for *chóngr* 'insect'—or to leave the suffix off entirely where possible: *diànyǐng* instead of *diànyǐngr* 'movie,' *hútòng* instead of *hútòngr* 'alley,' *huā* instead of *huār* 'flower.' Institutionalized in Putonghua are only a few unavoidable words such as *zhèr* 'here,' *nàr* 'there,' *nǎr* 'where,' *huàr* 'picture,' *wèir* 'flavor,' *wánr* 'to play,' and *hǎohāorde* 'carefully, thoroughly.' To what extent other words with this retroflex suffix belong in the language is unclear.

There are a host of other noun suffixes, mostly with specialized meanings. The suffix -*rén* (from *rén* 'person'), for example, means '-er': *gōngrén* 'worker,' *zhèngrén* 'witness,' *fūrén* 'lady,' etc.; -*shī* 'specialist, teacher' is found in *gōng-chéngshī* 'engineer,' *lǜshī* 'lawyer,' *jìshī* 'technician,' and *mùshī* 'pastor'; -*qì* 'air, essence' occurs in *yǒngqì* 'courage,' *píqi* 'temper,' *tiānqi* 'weather,' *yùnqi* 'luck.' Many such suffixes have been newly tailored to translate Western words and concepts. For example, the venerable morpheme *xué* 'learning' serves as a suffix with the meaning '-ology, -ics': *shùxué* 'mathematics (literally, number-ology)' *dòngwùxué* 'zoology (animal-ology)', *jīngjìxué* 'economics,' *jǐhéxué* 'geometry (how-many-ology).' [*Jǐhé* means 'how many,' but it is also an imitation of the sound geo-.] The morpheme *xìng* 'nature, character' is employed as the equivalent of English '-ity, -ness': *kěnéngxìng* 'possibility,' *zhòngyàoxìng* 'importance, significance,' *suānxìng* 'acidity (sour-ness).' The list of modern suffixes goes on and on.

A rather special suffix in Chinese is the so-called plural ending -*men*. With pronouns, this suffix really does indicate plurals—*wǒ* 'I,' *wǒmen* 'we'; *nǐ* 'you,' *nǐmen* 'you all'; *tā* 'he, she, it,' *tāmen* 'they.' But otherwise, -*men* is not a real plural. Rather, it is used only in certain situations to emphasize that some people being talked about form a group. For example, *nèixiē háizimen* means specifically 'those children (as a group).' (The noun *háizi* itself means both 'child' and 'children.')

The most commonly occurring suffixes are those that attach to verbs to indicate aspect. The perfective suffix -*le*, which is really a weakened form of the verb *liǎo* 'finish,' has a wide range of complexly interrelated meanings, the most common of which are to indicate the completion of an action or a change in the situation. Progressive -*zhe* shows that the action or condition of the verb is still going on. The suffix -*guo* attaches to a verb to indicate that its action took place some time in the indefinite past. The use of these and other verbal suffixes will be discussed below, in connection with Chinese syntax.

(3) *Compounds.* By far the most important way of making up words in Chinese is compounding. Classical Chinese has relatively few such constructions, because it is based upon a much older variety of the language with far greater phonetic resources. (One ancient dictionary listed almost 4,000 distinct syllables, which is more than three times the number of syllables found in modern Mandarin.) As over time the syllable was simplified, compounding was the principal way of coping with the homonyms that resulted. Making the word longer reduced confusion. Today, many thousands of compound words exist in colloquial Chinese.

A compound can be created out of a wide variety of syntactic constructions. It can consist of a subject and predicate. For example, the simple sentence *Dì zhèn* 'The earth shakes' is the source of the noun *dìzhèn* 'earthquake.' The sentence *Tóu téng* '(My) head hurts' becomes the noun *tóuténg* 'headache.' Many compounds consist of coordinate words or morphemes with opposite meanings. *Fùmǔ* 'parents' is literally 'father-mother'; *dàxiǎo* 'size' is 'big-small'; *zuǒyòu* 'thereabouts' is 'left-right'; *mǎimai* 'business' is 'buy-sell.' An even greater number of compounds are made up of coordinate elements with similar meanings. Examples are *bàogào* 'to report,' which is 'announce-inform'; *shēngyīn* 'sound' is 'sound-tone'; *qíguài* 'strange' is 'strange-strange'; *gāngcái* 'just now' is 'just-just.' One word or morpheme modifying another can be transformed into a single word: *dàrén* 'adult' is from *dà rén* 'big person'; *rèxīn* 'enthusiastic' literally means 'hot heart'; *xiāngxìn* 'believe in, have faith in' is 'mutually believe.' There are verbs plus an object: *chīfàn* 'eat' is literally 'eat-meal'; *fàngxīn* 'relax' is 'release-mind.' And there are verbs plus a complement: *gǎiliáng* 'improve' is literally 'change (into) good'; *dǎpò* 'smash' is 'hit-broken.' The possibilities are essentially unlimited. All the grammatical resources of the language are available for compounding.

Sentences

In inflecting languages case, tense, mood, and the like are indicated by changes in the shape of a word (e.g., *drink, drank, drunk*). But Chinese is not an inflecting language. The shape of a word remains the same regardless of its function or place in the sentence. The grammatical relationships between the parts of a Chinese sentence are shown largely by two things: (1) the use of grammatical function words such as particles; and (2) word order.

Topics

The primary syntactic division of a Chinese sentence is between the *topic* and the rest of the sentence (which is often called the *comment*). The topic is a word or phrase that sets the stage for the statement or question that follows. It is what the sentence is about. Some sentences do not have a topic, but if there is one, it is always said first. Sometimes an actual pause in speech sets the topic off from the rest of the sentence.

In the following examples, the topic is italicized:

> *Zhè xiāoxí* wǒ zhīdao le
> this news I know CS
> 'This news, I've heard (it) already.' (= 'I've heard this news already.')

> *Xīnde Běijīng Zhōubào* nǐ mǎile méi-yǒu?
> new-SP Peking weekly you buy-CA not-have (bought)
> 'The new Peking Review—have you bought (it)?'

> *Zhèige dìfāng* kěyǐ tiàowǔ
> this-ONE place may dance
> 'This place, (one) can dance (here).' (= 'One can dance here.')

> *Dàxué* xiànzài duōbàn shi nánnǚ-héxiào.
> University now most be malefemale-sameschool
> 'Universities, most are coeducational these days.'

> *Běijīng* cóng sānyuè dào wǔyuè shi chūntian.
> Peking from March to May be spring
> '(In) Peking, spring is from March to May.'

> *Nèi liǎngge rén,* yíge xìng Zhāng, yíge xìng Lǐ.
> that two person one name Zhang one name Li
> 'Those two people—one is named Zhang and one is named Li.'

A word or phrase may be made the topic of the sentence if it has come up earlier in the conversation, or if it is something that the speaker assumes the listener knows about. In other words, the topic tends to have a definite reference—somewhat like a word with a definite article in English. Notice that in the following example *huàr* is translated as 'the painting(s)' when it becomes the topic:

Wǒ màigei ta *huàr* le.
I   sell-give she painting CA
'I sold her some paintings.'

Huàr,   wǒ màigei ta le.
painting I   sell-give she CA
'I sold her the painting(s) (that we had talked about, that you had looked at, etc.).'

There are also a number of other reasons to make a word a topic. Some syntactic constructions require that the object of a verb be transposed to the topic position. For example, the adverb *dōu* 'all, both' can only refer back to something already mentioned, and so if a speaker wants it to refer to objects of the verb, then the objects must be moved to the front of the sentence. 'I like both apples and oranges' is phrased *Píngguǒ, júzi, wǒ dōu xǐhuān chī* 'Apples, oranges, I like both.' One very common use of topics is to compare things; an item put in a topic position is often being contrasted with something else:

Wǒ jiù mǎi bǐ. *Shū* wǒ bù mǎi
I   just buy pen book I   not buy
'I'm just buying a pen. (As for) books, I'm not buying (them).'

Yīfu xīnde hǎo; *péngyǒu* jiùde hǎo
clothes new-SP good friends   old-SP good
'Clothes, new (ones) are good; friends, old (ones) are good.'

Sentence topics are an unusual concept for speakers of English. In our language, there is usually no straightforward way to render a topic, and this is why the clumsy phrase 'as for ...' is often found in rough translations of Chinese. In the languages of East Asia, however—including not only Chinese but also Japanese, Korean, Manchu, Tai, and so on—the topic-comment construction is a basic part of grammar. It is a grammatical feature that Chinese has in common with all of its close neighbors.

Ellipsis

Another feature characteristic of the languages of East Asia is the widespread use of ellipsis. In a normal Chinese conversation, an element of a sentence that is known from context and that need not be specifically talked about may be left unsaid. A typical answer to a question like 'Where's Meizhen?' is *Hái méi lái* '(literally) Still not come.' Since both speaker and listener already understand from the question that the person is Meizhen, she need not be explicitly mentioned again, and so the sentence has no overt subject. In the same situation the English answer would have to be "She still hasn't come," with the pronoun *she* standing for Meizhen. The pronoun adds no new information; it is simply filling the subject slot required by English grammar. Chinese grammar is not so constrained. If a waiter brings several kinds of dessert to a table, one of the diners might say *Wǒ shi bīngqílín*, literally, 'I'm ice cream.' What is implicitly meant is of course '(What) I (ordered) was ice cream.' The affirmative answer to 'Did you hear what he said?' is *Tīngjiàn le* 'Heard.' In a conversation about families, one of those talking could say of someone *Tā yě shi yíge Měiguo zhàngfu* 'She is also (a case of being married to) an American husband.'

Ellipsis is one of the main reasons Chinese and the other languages of East Asia often seem vague to Westerners.

Nouns and measures

In Chinese, there is no grammatical number, gender, or agreement, such as is found in French: *les bonnes filles* 'the good girls.' But Chinese does have a kind of concord that is just as strictly defined. Each noun, depending on its nature or shape, has a specific measure word associated with it, and when the noun is counted or used with a demonstrative pronoun, the measure word intervenes. In the following phrases, the measure word is glossed in small capitals:

liǎng-běn   shū   'two books'
two-VOLUME book

 yì-tiáo   hé   'one (*or* a) river'
one-STRIP river

 nèi-tiáo   hé   'that river'
that-STRIP river

wǔ-bǎ   dāo   'five knives'
five-HANDLE knife

zhèi   sān-wǎn   fàn   'these three bowls of rice'
this three-BOWL rice

As the translation of the last example shows, English too has some measure words. Compare also: "five sheets of paper" (not "five papers"); "fifty head of cattle" (which, to a rancher at least, is not the same thing as "fifty cows"); "two pieces of toast"; and the like. Chinese, however, has far more such measure words and they are more widely used. A good Chinese dictionary should always give the appropriate measure under the entry for each noun, much as a French dictionary should always indicate the gender for each of its nouns.

The most generally used measure is *-ge*: *liǎng-ge rén* 'two people'; *sān-ge píng-guǒ* 'three apples'; *sì-ge xīngqī* 'four weeks.' It is sometimes possible to substitute *-ge* for more specialized measures: *zhèi-ge shān* 'this mountain' instead of *zhèi-zuò shān*. The use of *-ge* seems to be spreading, both within Mandarin and also from Mandarin to other dialects.

Modification

A modifier precedes what it modifies in Chinese. In English, by contrast, some modifiers precede, but other modifiers follow. We say both "my book" and "a book of mine"; "life's secrets" and "the secrets of life." Chinese has only the "my-book" kind of ordering.

A Chinese noun may be modified by another noun, an adjective, or a relative clause. In most cases the particle *de* comes between the modifier and the modified noun. This particle, which is used to link the modifier to the modified, is sometimes known as the *subordinative particle* (SP). Nouns that typically modify other nouns *without* the subordinative particle *de* are names of countries: *Zhōngguó huàr* 'Chinese paintings'; *Rìběn xuéxiào* 'Japanese schools'; *Fàguó cài* 'French dishes'; etc. Pronouns may also modify nouns without an interceding *de* in case a close personal relationship is expressed by the modification: *wǒ lǎoshī* 'my teacher'; *nǐ māma* 'your mommy'; *tā dìdi* 'his younger brother'; *wǒ péngyǒu* 'my friend'; and so on. But these are exceptions. When a noun modifies another noun, the rule is usually to mark the modification with the subordinative particle *de*. This is also true of pronouns when no personal relationship is involved. Here are a few examples: *Wǒ de shū* 'my book'; *nǐ de xìn* 'your letter'; *tāmen de xuǎnshǒu* 'their athletes'; *dìdi de gāngbǐ* 'brother's pen'; *jīntian de bào* 'today's paper'; *mòshuǐ de yánsè* 'the color of the ink'; *mùtou de zhuōzi* 'table (made) of wood'; *wūzi de mén* 'the door of the room'; *wúchǎnjiējí de zhèngdǎng* 'a party of the proletariat.'

A noun is often modified directly by a simple adjective; e.g., *hǎo rén* 'good person.' The use of *de* with such simple adjectives changes the meaning slightly, bringing prominence to the adjective and making it function more like a relative clause: *hǎo de rén* 'a person who is good.' Here are a few contrasts: *suān júzi* 'a sour orange' and *suān de júzi* 'an orange that is sour'; *kōng wūzi* 'an empty room' and *kōng de wūzi* 'a room that is empty'; *piányi zhǐ* 'cheap paper' and *piányi de zhǐ* 'paper that is cheap.' An adjective that is complex to begin with or is modified by an adverb requires the subordinative particle *de* in any case: *yǒumíng de lǎoshī* 'famous (literally, having-fame) teacher(s)'; *hǎokàn de háizi* 'good-looking children'; *hěn hǎo de rén* 'a very good person.'

Relative clauses are explicitly marked as modifiers by *de*:

wǒ mǎi *de* dōngxi
I buy SP thing
'the things that I bought'

mài le   *de* fángzi
sell CA SP house
'the house that was sold'

mài bào   *de* nèi- xiē   rén
sell paper SP that-SEVERAL person
'those people who sell newspapers'

zuótian   dào zhèr lái   *de* rén
yesterday to here come SP person
'the person who came here yesterday'

yǐjīng   zhànqǐlái *de* Zhōngguo rénmín
already stand up SP China   people
'the Chinese people, who have now stood up, ...'

The modified noun may sometimes be omitted, leaving a phrase or clause ending in *de*. This kind of ellipsis is roughly equivalent to our use of the pronoun "one" in English (e.g., "the one that ...").

Qián   shi wǒ *de*
money is I   SP
'The money is mine.'

Wǒ yào   shàngtou *de*
I   want top   SP
'I want the one that is on the top.'

Nǐ   mǎi *de* wǒ dōu xǐhuan.
you buy SP I   all like
'I like all the ones you bought.'

Zhèi-fēng xìn   shi yào jìdao   Rìběn qu *de*.
this- SEAL letter is want send-to Japan go SP
'This letter is the one that will be sent to Japan.'

Adverbs also precede the word they modify: *zài shuō* 'say again'; *hěn hǎo* 'very good'; *bù hěn hǎo* 'not very good'; *zhēn bù hěn hǎo* 'really not very good.'
Chinese has two kinds of adverbs: (1) fixed, and (2) movable. "Fixed" adverbs have a fixed position in the sentence. They precede the verb and follow the subject: *Wǒ xiān zǒu* 'I'll go first (= I first go).' Some common examples of fixed adverbs are: *tài* 'too,' *yě* 'also,' *cháng(chang)* 'often,' *cái* 'just,' *zài* 'again,' *duó(ma)* 'how?' *dōu* 'all, both,' *gèng* 'still more,' *zuì* 'most,' *yǐjīng* 'already,' *bù* 'not.' The majority of adverbs are fixed adverbs. Movable adverbs, which are far less numerous, are "movable" in that they can stand before the subject, as well as immediately before the verb:

Běnlái   tā yào qù.
originally he want go
'Originally he wanted to go.'

Tā *běnlái* yào qù.
he originally want go
'He originally wanted to go.'

Some of these movable adverbs function, in translation, as conjunctions:

Shū guì, *kěshi* bào bú guì.
book dear but paper not dear
Shū guì, bào *kěshi* bú guì.
book dear paper but not dear
'Books are expensive, but not newspapers.'

Besides *kěshi* 'but,' movable adverbs that serve as conjunctions include: *yàoshi* 'if,' *suīrán* 'although,' *yīnwèi* 'because,' *háishi* 'or,' *suǒyǐ* 'so,' etc. The use of these adverbs is the principal way to link clauses in Chinese.

Predicates

There are three kinds of predicates in Chinese: (1) verbal, (2) adjectival, and (3) nominal. One of the characteristic features of Chinese is that nominal predicates may have no verb.

A nominal predicate serves to link a noun or noun phrase to the subject. In English, as in most other Western languages, two nouns are equated by using a form of the verb "to be." In Chinese, however, two noun phrases can sometimes be linked by simply juxtaposing them with no intervening verb at all:

Tā èrshi suì.
she twenty year (of age)
'She (is) twenty years (old).'

Zhèi-běn shū shí-kuài qián.
this- VOLUME book ten-DOLLAR money
'This book (is) twenty dollars.'

Some speakers are even reported to say things like:

Zhāngsān hǎo rén.
Zhangsan good man
'Zhangsan (is) a good man.'

It is far more common in modern Chinese to equate the two phrases with the copula *shi*: *Zhāngsān shi hǎo rén* 'Zhangsan is a good man.' And when the sentence is negated, the use of *shi* is obligatory: *Zhāngsān bú shi hǎo rén* 'Zhangsan is not a good man.' (*Zhāngsān bù hǎo rén* is ungrammatical in the extreme.)

But the copular pattern linking nouns with a verb 'to be' is a relatively recent historical development. When the word *shì* appeared between two nouns in Classical Chinese, it was a demonstrative pronoun meaning 'this' or 'that.' Here is an example (transcribed in modern Mandarin pronunciations) taken from the *Analects* of Confucius: *Fù yŭ guì, shì rén zhī suŏ yù yě* 'Riches and honor, *these* [are] what men desire.' Philologists believe that through constructions such as these, *shì* became idiomatically identified as the linking element, and its use as a copula spread. In any event, the old verbless pattern for nominal predicates remains in common use to this day in modern Mandarin.

Adjectives

Predicate adjectives are verbs in Chinese. They can stand by themselves: *Xiǎoxīn!* 'Be careful!'; *Hǎo* '(That) is good, (I) am well'; *tián* '(it) is sweet'; *bái* '(it) is white'. The sense of "is" in the English translations is contained within the Chinese adjectives themselves. Hence *tián* means not just 'sweet' but '*is* sweet'; *bái* means not just 'white' but '*is* white.' Another name for the adjectives of Chinese is "stative verbs," because they are verbs that describe a quality or state.

Some adjectives are idiosyncratically used as adverbs. For example, *hǎo* 'good' is often used in the meaning of 'very, quite' to modify another adjective: *Jīntian hǎo lěng* 'Today is quite cold.' *Mǎn* 'full' means 'really' as an adverb: *Wǒ mǎn xiǎng qù kàn ta* 'I really want to visit her.' *Lǎo* 'old' becomes 'always': *Tā lǎo dào zhèr lái* 'He comes here all the time.' *Bái* 'white' can mean either 'free of charge' or 'uselessly': *Zuótian wǒ bái chī le* 'Yesterday I ate without having to pay for it'; *Tā bái qù le* 'He went in vain.' *Màn* 'slow' is used to mean 'not so soon' in idiomatic phrases, such as that said to departing guests: *Màn zǒu* 'You don't have to hurry.' Oftentimes the semantic connections are so loose, the adverbial usages might well be considered separate lexical items. Reduplicated adjectives, which have a vivid and intense flavor, can always be used as adverbs: *hǎohāorde yánjiū* 'study very diligently'; *mànmānrde kàn* 'look at slowly and carefully.'

But, in Chinese, the manner of an action is normally expressed by a predicate adjective instead of an adverb. This is done by changing the sentence with an action verb into a modifying clause (with *de*) and letting it stand before a predicate adjective that describes the appropriate manner:

> Tā chī de màn.
> he eat SP slow.
> 'He eats slowly.'

In other words, what in English is expressed adverbially, "He eats *slowly*," is in Chinese expressed as a predicate: 'His [manner of] eating *is slow*.' In this standard pattern for describing manner, the *de* in the modifying clause comes immediately after the verb. If the verb has an object, the object must be moved, either by transposing it to the topic position at the front of the sentence, or by giving out both verb and object, then repeating the verb with *de*:

> Tā de Yīngwén, shuō de hěn hǎo.
> she SP English   speak SP very good
> 'Her English, speak's (manner) is very good.'

Tā shuō Yīngwén, shuō de hěn hǎo.
she speak English   speak SP very good
'She speaks English, speak's (manner) is very good.'

'She speaks English very well' can be expressed in either of these two ways.

Verbs

Chinese verbs are varied and their behavior is complex. What they all have in common is that they can be negated by *bù* 'not,' and this is how they are usually defined as a class.

The one exception to this rule is the verb of existence *yǒu*, for which there is the special existential negative *méi*: *Yǒu píjiǔ ma? Méi yǒu.* 'Is there any beer?' 'No, there isn't'; *Zhèr méi yǒu rén* 'There is no one here.' The verb *yǒu* is also used to show possession, but this function follows from its primary sense of existence; without stretching the point too much, a sentence like *Wǒ yǒu qián* 'I have [some] money' can be thought of as meaning '[By *or* to] me there is money.' Among the languages of the world a basic verb of ownership seems to be rare—even English "to have" probably had an original meaning in Germanic more like 'to hold, grasp'—and among the languages of East Asia possession is generally expressed in terms of existence.

Normal sentence order in Chinese is subject-verb-object:

Tā huà   huàr.
she paint picture
'She paints pictures.'

Wǒ děi   guā   húzi.
I   must shave beard
'I must shave (my) beard.'

If a verb takes both an indirect object and a direct object, the order in standard Mandarin is first the indirect object, then the direct object:

Wǒ gěi nǐ   qián.
I   give you money
'I'll give you (some) money.'

Tāmen gěi   tā yíge xīngqī de jià.
they   give he one week   SP holiday
'They gave him a week's leave.'

In Southern dialects such as Cantonese and Shanghainese the direct object often comes in front of the indirect object, but when that order is used in Putonghua it is considered substandard.

Some transitive verbs in Chinese are closely associated with generalized objects and appear together with them in cases where the verb alone would be used in English. The Chinese say, for example, *chī fàn* '(literally) eat a meal' where English uses an intransitive "eat" (with the object "meal" only implied); *shuō huà* 'speak speech' means 'talk'; *chàng gēr* 'sing songs' means 'sing.' If the verb has a specific object, it replaces the generalized object:

> Wǒ yào   chī fàn.
> I   want eat meal (*or* rice)
> 'I want to eat.'

> Wǒ yào   chī miànbāo.
> I   want eat bread
> 'I want to eat (some) bread.'

But a specific object understood from context is normally omitted, leaving the verb with no object at all. In reply to the question, 'What happened to the bread?' the answer might be, *Wǒ chī le* 'I ate (it).' In such cases the grammar of English requires the object "it."

Sometimes the action of a verb is linked by a postverb to the object. For example, *zài* 'be at' is used as postverb in the sense of 'at, in, on': *Tā zhù-zai Déguo* 'she lives *in* Germany.' *Dào* 'arrive' is used postverbially to mean 'until': *Wǒmen zuò-dao bā-diǎn* 'We work *until* eight.'

Verbs may be followed by a directional complement that shows the direction of motion. These complements always end in *lái* 'come,' which indicates direction toward the speaker, or *qù* 'go,' which shows direction away from the speaker. For example, *bān* 'move' may take as its complement *jinqu*, which is composed of *jìn* 'enter' plus *qù* 'go'; the resulting verb form *bān-jinqu* means 'move in (there).' If this verb form takes an object, the object comes immediately before *qu* (or *lai*): *bān-jin wūzili qu* 'move into the room.'

Another kind of complement that typifies the behavior of the Chinese verb is the "resultative ending." When a resultative ending is added to a verb it indicates the result of the action. Here are a few examples of verbs with resultative endings: *tīng-dǒng* ('hear-understand') 'understand (what one hears)'; *chī-bǎo* ('eat-full') 'eat one's fill'; *xǐ-gānjing* 'wash clean'; *dǎ-sǐ* ('hit-die') 'beat to death.' If the result of the action has not been attained but is only potentially there, then the action is phrased as being either possible or impossible. Possible attainment is expressed by placing *-de-* (which comes from the verb *dé* 'get, obtain') between the verb and the resulative ending; impossible attainment is expressed by using the negative *-bu-* in that intermediate position:

> tīng-de-dǒng   'can understand (what one hears someone say)'
> tīng-bu-dǒng   'cannot understand'
>
> xǐ-de-gānjing   'can wash clean'
> xǐ-bu-gānjing   'cannot wash clean'

Chinese verbs are not distinguished for voice. The direction of action of a verb can be either away from the subject (active) or toward the subject (passive). The verb *suǒ*, for example, can mean either 'lock (something)' or 'be locked': *suǒ mén* 'lock the door'; *mén suŏ le* 'the door is locked.' There are a number of locutions that express an explicit passive, but their use in the colloquial language is very restricted. They are becoming more widespread, however, through the translation of passive constructions in various Western languages.

Modality is expressed in a number of ways. One important way, which resembles that of English, is with auxiliary verbs. In the following examples, the auxiliary verb is italicized:

Wŏ bu *gāi*   lái.
I   not should come
'I should not have come.'

Nèi- ge háizi *gāi*   dă.
that-ONE child should hit
'That child should be spanked.'

Nĭ *găn* dă tā ma?
you dare hit he?
'Do you dare hit him?'

Wŏ *děi*   zŏu le.
I   must go CS
'I must leave now.'

Nĭmen *kěyĭ* zŏu le.
you-all may go CS
'You may go now.'

Nĭ yàoshi dă ta, tā *huì* shēngqì.
you if   hit he he will be-angry
'If you hit him, he'll probably get mad.'

Tā bú *huì* shuō Yīngwén.
she not can speak English
'She does not know how to speak English.'

Wŏ de yănjīng téng, bù *néng* kàn shū.
I   SP eye   hurt not able read book
'My eyes hurt (so) I cannot read.'

Other kinds of modality are more exotic for English speakers. One of these is the potential construction with a resultative ending (which was discussed above):

Wŏ zŏu-bu-dòng   le.
I   walk-not-move CS
'I can't walk any farther.'

Tā méi yŏu yănjìngr kàn-bu-jiàn.
he not have glasses   look-not-see
'He can't see without his glasses.'

Tense is not a feature of Chinese grammar. An act or event is located in time by time words or context, not by the form of the verb. However, Chinese grammar does have a system for indicating *aspect*, which is a somewhat different way of looking at events. Instead of showing when something happened or existed, a Chinese predicate expresses such things as whether the act has been completed or not; whether the situation described by the verb represents a continuation of a previous state or, rather, represents a change. In other words, a Chinese predicate does not reflect so much *when* an act occurred, but *how* the act was performed.

Aspect is marked in Chinese mainly by a system of verbal suffixes and sentence particles. The most important and complex of these aspect markers is *le*, of which there are two different kinds: (1) a verbal suffix, and (2) a sentence particle.

Verbal-suffix *le* means 'completed action' (CA). Here are a few examples:

> Tā bìyè   *le*.
> she graduate CA
> 'She graduated.'

> Tā dào shūdiàn   qu *le*.
> she to   bookstore go CA
> 'She went to the bookstore.'

> Shuǐwèi   yǐjīng   dī   *le* liǎng-mǐ.
> water-level already drop CA TWO-METER
> 'The water level has fallen by two meters.'

> Nǐ xiān qù, wǒ xià   *le* bān jiù   qù.
> you first go I   get-off CA duty then go
> 'You go ahead. I'll go right after work.'

As the last example shows, a completed action need not have happened in the past though in practice that is usually the case; it can also be completed, in the future, relative to some other action or event.

Sentence-particle *le* indicates a change of status (CS)—i.e., that a situation has changed. A number of specialized uses are subsumed under this general meaning, some of which fit under the rubric CS better than others. Here are a few of the applications of this very complicated particle:

(1) General change of status:

> Tā hǎo *le*.
> she fine CS
> 'She is fine now.' (She must have been sick before.)

> Shuǐguǒ huài   *le*.
> fruit   be-bad CS
> 'The fruit has spoiled.' (It has gone bad.)

Tā bù máng *le*.
he not busy CS
'He is no longer busy.' (He was busy before.)

Zhè shi tā de *le*.
this is he SP CS
'This is his now.' (It was someone else's before.)

Wǒ yǒu qián *le*.
I   have money CS
'Now I have money.' (I did not have any before.)

Wǒ méi yǒu qián *le*.
I   not have money CS
'I don't have any money.' (I had some before.)

(2) Completed action (i.e., the same meaning as verbal-suffix *le* = CA):

Wǒ yǐjīng qǐng tāmen *le*.
I   already invite them CS
'I have already invited them.'

Tā gěi wǒ qián *le*.
she give I money CS
'She gave me money.'

(3) Imminent action (The action has been decided upon and will take place in the very near future; this meaning is often distinguished from completed action in the past by use with adverbs meaning 'soon' or the like.):

Tā kuài lái *le*.
she soon come CS
'She'll be here shortly.'

Wǒ děi zǒu *le*. Zài jiàn ba!
I   must go CS again see !
'I must be going. See you later!'

Háizi kuài hǎo *le*.
child soon fine CS
'The child is almost well.'

Wǒmen jiù yào chī fàn *le*.
we   then want eat meal CS
'We're just about to eat.'

(4) Excessiveness (used together with the adverb *tài* 'too (much)'):

Tā jiā lí zhèr tài yuǎn *le*.
he home from here too far CS
'His house is too far from here.'

Zhāng Tàitai tài kèqi *le.*
Zhang Mrs. too polite cs
'Mrs. Zhang is too polite.'

(5) Idiomatic (the changed-status meaning has eroded somewhat through frequent use):

Dui   *le.*
correct cs
'Right.' (a general expression of assent or agreement)

Búyào wàng *le*!
don't forget cs
'Don't forget!'

Both suffix *le* and particle *le* can appear in the same sentence when the verb is followed by an object. If the object is being counted—i.e., preceded by a number—the sentence particle gives the implication that the action will continue into the future:

Tā chī *le* fàn   *le.*
he eat CA meal cs
'He has eaten.'
Tā chī *le* liǎng-wǎn fàn *le.*
he eat CA two-BOWL rice cs
'He has eaten two bowls of rice already (and may eat more).'

Strictly speaking, suffix *le* and particle *le* should probably be considered two separate morphemes (and that is how they are usually analyzed by linguists). The two have completely different etymological sources; verbal-suffix *le* comes from a weakened pronunciation of the (post)verb *liǎo* 'to finish,' while sentence-particle *le* seems to be a weakened form of the complement *lái* 'come.' That they are homonyms in modern Mandarin is thus an historical accident. Yet, the fact remains that these two elements overlap in meaning and they *do* sound exactly alike. If a verb which comes at the end of a sentence is followed by a *le*, it is sometimes next to impossible to decide which *le* it is. Both are written with the same character. Undoubtedly for all of these reasons, native speakers of Chinese think of them as the same morpheme. In most textbooks of Chinese suffix and particle are introduced as variant uses of the same basic element.

There are several other aspect suffixes. The progressive suffix *-zhe* 'is …ing' indicates that an action or state is continuing. It is often used in conjunction with the progressive particle *ne.*

Mén xiànzài guān-*zhe* ne.
door now   close-ing PP
'The door is closed now.'

Bié   zhàn-*zhe*, zuòxia ba!
don't stand-ing sit-down!
'Don't keep standing; sit down.'

Zhuōzi-shang fàng-*zhe* hǎoxiē   dōngxi.
table-top   put-ing good-many thing
'There are a lot of things lying on the table.'

Tā ná-*zhe*   shū shuìjiào.
she hold-ing book sleep
'She went to sleep holding a book.'

Another aspect marker is the experiential suffix (ES) -*guo*, which means that something has happened at least once in the past. When used in a question, it means 'have you ever …?' When used in a statement with the existential negative *méi*, it often means 'I have never….'

Nǐ qù-*guo* Rìběn ma?
you go ES Japan?
'Have you ever been to Japan?'

Wǒ méi qù-*guo*.
I   not go ES
'I've never been (there).'

méi jiàn-*guo* de dà hàn
not see ES SP big drought
'an unprecedented drought'

Coverbs

Coverbs function like English prepositions. They include such words as *dào* 'to,' *zài* 'at, in, on,' *gěi* 'for,' *zuò* '(go) by,' *cóng* 'from,' *gēn* 'with,' and many more. But they are actually verbs. They can be negated by *bù* 'not': *bú dào Běijīng qù* 'not go to Peking.' They are all derived from action verbs, and many can still be used as main verbs in modern Mandarin. Thus, the phrase 'not go to Peking' might literally be thought of as 'not-arriving-Peking go'; *gēn wǒ qù* 'go with me' means (when we think of the source) 'following me, go.'

A coverb and its object precede the main verb and form a setting for the action.

[A small number of such verbs, including *zài* 'at, in, on' and *dào* 'to,' follow the main verb under certain conditions. But when they do, their syntactic usage and sometimes their meanings are different. Here, as in most textbook treatments of Chinese, we classify these occurrences as postverbs, not coverbs (see above).]

Let us look at a few of the most important coverbs to see how they work:

(1) *Zài* '*at, in, on*': As a main verb, *zài* means 'be at, in, on.' For example, *Tā zài Xiānggǎng* 'He is in Hong Kong.' Hence it works as an existential predicate with a meaning similar to *yǒu* 'be, have' (see above discussion). The main functional difference between *zài* and *yǒu* is one of word order; the thing that is

existing occupies the subject position in the case of *zài*, and the object position in the case of *yǒu*: *Qián zài zhèr* 'The money is here'; *Zhèr yǒu qián* 'There's (some) money here.' As these English translations show, the difference in word order affects the meaning; a noun in initial position tends to be definite and one that follows the verb tend to be indefinite. *Zài* is also unlike *yǒu* in that it can be negated by *bù* (*yǒu* is only negated by *méi*). In addition to its use as a main verb, *zài* can also function as a postverbal complement. Here are a few examples of *zài* being used as a coverb:

> Tā *zài* Xiānggǎng zuò shēngyi.
> he in Hong Kong do business
> 'He does business in Hong Kong.'
>
> Nǐ bú *zài* jiā   chī fàn ma?
> you not at home eat meal?
> 'Aren't you eating at home?'
>
> Tāmen *zài* fángzi-hòumian xiūlǐ   diànshìjī.
> they   at house behind   repair television
> 'They repair televisions behind their house.'

   (2) *Cóng* 'from' and *dào* 'to': *Cóng* signifies motion away from some point, and *dào* indicates motion toward some point. They are used together with *lái* 'come' or *qù* 'go' as the main verb. *Cóng* itself is no longer used as a main verb in the colloquial language, but in literary usage it means 'follow': *cóng sú* 'conform to custom.' *Dào* means 'arrive': *Huǒchē dào zhàn le* 'The train has arrived (at) the station'.

> Wǒ xiǎng *cóng* xuéxiào qu.
> I   think from school   go
> 'I'm thinking of going from school.'
>
> Tā *cóng* Měiguo *dào* Zhōngguo lái.
> he from America to   China   come
> 'He is coming to China from America.'

   (3) *Zuò* '(go) by': As a main verb *zuò* means to 'sit on'; as a coverb it indicates the means of conveyance—provided it is a vehicle on which one can sit down.

> Nǐ míngtian *zuò* shénma chē qu?
> you tomorrow by what   car go
> 'What sort of vehicle are you taking tomorrow?'
>
> Wǒmen dōu *zuò* gōnggòng-qìchē qu.
> we   all by public   car go
> 'We all go by bus.'

   (4) *Lí* 'from': *Lí* is used to indicate distance between places. It has a classical meaning of 'leave, separate from.'

Wáng Xiānsheng jiā   *lí*   zhèr hěn yuǎn.
Wang Mr.   home from here very far
'Mr. Wang's house is very far from here.'

(5) *Gěi 'for, for the benefit of'*: *Gěi* as a main verb means 'give.' It can also be
used as a postverb.

Guō Xiǎojiě yào   *gěi* wǒmen zuò Zhōngguo fàn.
Guo Miss   want for us   do China   meal
'Miss Guo wants to cook a Chinese meal for us.'

(6) *Tì 'for, in place of'*: As a main verb *tì* means 'substitute for.'

Nǐ   *tì*   wǒ mǎi piào ba!
you for I   buy ticket!
'Buy a ticket for me, will you?'

(7) *Yòng 'with, by means of, using'*:

Tā yòng kuàizi   chī fàn.
she with chopstick eat meal
'She eats with chopsticks.'

Zhèige shi *yòng* jīqi   zuò   de.
this   is with machine make SP
'This is (something) made by machine.'

(8) *Gēn 'with, in company of, and'*: As a main verb *gēn* means 'follow,' as in
gēn-zhe Dǎng zǒu 'follow the Party.'

Lǐ Xiānsheng *gēn* ta péngyǒu dào Niǔyuē   qu le.
Li Mr.   and he friend   to New York go CA
'Mr. Li and his friend went to New York.'

Tā *gēn*   wǒ huílai le.
she with I   return CA
'She came back with me.'

Bié   *gēn* tā xué.
don't with he study
'Don't learn from him.'

Gēn nǐ   méi yǒu guānxi.
with you not have connection
'It has no connection with you.'

(9) *Duì 'to, toward, facing'*: As a main verb *duì* has a large range of meanings,
including 'check (one thing against another)'; 'suit, agree with'; 'be correct';

'treat (someone some way)'; and so on. But the basic meaning from which the coverb is derived is 'to face.'

> Tā *duì* nǐ   shuō shénma?
> she to   you say   what
> 'What is she saying to you?'

> Wǒ *duì*-zhe tā zuò-zhe.
> I   face-ing he sit-ing
> 'I'm sitting facing him.'

(10) *Guānyú* 'about, regarding': *Guānyú* is a compound made up of the literary elements *guān* 'connect' and *yú* 'in, to, on, (etc.)'; as a main verb in Classical Chinese, *yú* means 'compare with.'

> *Guānyú* tā de shìqing bié   gēn wǒ shuō.
> about   she SP matter don't with I   talk
> 'Don't talk to me about her affairs.'

(11) *Bǐ* 'compared with, than': This coverb is used when comparing people or things. As a main verb it simply means 'compare.'

> Tā *bǐ*   wǒ gāo.
> she than I   tall
> 'She's taller than I am.'

> Tā shuō Yīngwén, *bǐ*   wǒ shuō de hǎo.
> he speak English   than I   speak SP good
> 'He speaks English better than I do.'

> Zuò fēijī bu *bǐ*   zuò huǒchē kuài.
> by plane not than by train   fast
> '(Going) by plane is not faster than (going) by train.'

(12) *Bǎ (taking)*': The so-called "*bǎ*-construction" is used to move the direct object of the main verb toward the front of the sentence. This is often done when the object has a definite reference and the main verb has some other kind of object or complement—the commonest is perhaps a directional complement ending in *lai* or *qu*. Beyond this rough generalization about the use of *ba*, it is very difficult to specify precisely when the construction should be used; it is one of the more complicated problems of Mandarin grammar. At the very least, however, it is clear that the main verb form must always be complex or at the least polysyllabic. *Bǎ* means 'take hold of, grasp (with the hand)' when used as a main verb, and so, in a sense, the *bǎ*-construction may be thought of as meaning 'taking (the object) do (something to it).' In Southern Mandarin, and in the Southern dialects in general, the *bǎ*-construction is not used; sometimes, in its place, a similar construction using *jiāng* '(bringing)' is used. Because of Southern influence, this *jiāng*-construction has made its way into the written forms of both Putonghua and Guoyu (used in Taiwan).

In the following examples, *bǎ* is glossed simply "BA":

Nǐmen míngtian   kěyǐ *bǎ* nǐmen de shū   dài-lai.
you-all tomorrow may BA you-all SP book take come
'You may bring your books tomorrow.'

Tā *bǎ* lùyīnjī   mài le.
he BA recorder sell CA
'He sold the recorder.'

Qǐng   nǐ   *bǎ* shū   fàng-zai zhèr.
request you BA book put-at   here
'Please put the book here.'

Nǐ   wèishénme bù   *bǎ* zhèige dà zhuōzi bān-chuqu?
you why   not BA this   big table   move out-go
'Why don't you move this big table out?'

Tā *bǎ* wǒ de dōngxi ná-zǒu le.
she BA I   SP thing   take-go CA
'She took my things away.'

(13) *Bèi* '*by*' *(marks the agent)*: Mandarin has several coverb constructions that can be used to express an explicit passive. The most common of these passive-marking coverbs is *bèi*. The *bèi*-construction, like all the other explicit passives in Mandarin, carries the connotation that something distinctly unpleasant has happened. Such is not the case when *bèi* is used to translate passive constructions from various Western languages, but this bit of translationese has just begun to permeate the spoken language. For most people, in most situations, a *bèi*-construction still represents something unfortunate.

Bèi is an unusual coverb because it does not always take an object. If it does not, it is simply marking an (adverse) passive; if it does, the object is the agent of the passive construction.

Tā *bèi* shā le.
he BEI kill CA
'He was killed.'

Měizhēn nèige shǒubiǎo *bèi* tā gēge   ná-zǒu le.
Meizhen that watch   by she brother take-go CA
'That watch of Meizhen's was taken away by her brother.'

Nèi-suǒ   fángzi zǎo yǐjīng   *bèi* biéren mǎi-qu le.
that-PLACE house early already by others buy-go CA
'That house has long since been bought by others.'

Sentence types

In Chinese, as in other languages, sentences can be classified as statements, questions, commands, and exclamations. To these four sentence types Chao adds a fifth, called "vocatives." Vocative expressions are never full sentences with a subject and predicate; they are words or phrases used to get the listener's attention. Chao gives these examples: *Mā!* 'Ma!'; *Gèwèi!* 'Ladies and gentlemen!'; *Lǎo Wáng a!* 'Wang!'; *Huǒji!* 'Waiter!'; *Xiū yángsǎn de!* '(You) who repair umbrellas!'; and a few more.

There are several ways to ask a question in Chinese. One way is simply to add question intonation to a statement: *Tā qù?* 'He's going?' This kind of question has about the same range of use as its equivalent in English. Another way to ask a question is with a question word—*shuí* 'who?' *shénme* 'what?' *zěnme* 'how?' *nǎr* 'where?' or the like. A Chinese question word occupies the same position in the sentence as the word it replaces; e.g., *Tā shi shuí?* '(literally) She is who?' This is different from the English pattern, in which the question word is moved to the front of the sentence: "Who is she?" Another difference between English and Chinese is that in Chinese question words also function as indefinite pronouns. *Nǐ yào shénme?* means 'What do you want?'; with a question particle added at the end, *Nǐ yào shénme ma?*, the sentence means 'Do you want something?'

One of the simplest and most frequently used ways to make a question is to add a question particle at the end of a statement: *Tā hěn máng* 'She is very busy'; *Tā hěn máng ma?* 'Is she very busy?' The most common question particle is *ma*. The particle *a* is used to soften a question, as in *Shuí a?* 'Who is it (please)?'; *Nǐ bu qù a?* 'You're not going?' This particle is phonetically interesting because it begins with the sound that ends the preceding syllable; after an *-n*, for example, it sounds like *na*: *Zhèige hěn nán na?* 'Is this very hard?' Also, it develops a *y*-sound after *-a*, *-e*, or the main vowel *-o*: *Wǒ ya?* 'Me?'; *Zhèige tài dà ya?* 'This is too big?' In spite of the difference in sound, *a* and *ya* are the same particle, just as "a" and "an" are the same article in English. The particle *ba* is used in some questions, as is *ne*, which, among other things, marks follow-up questions of the kind 'And what about ...?': *Wǒ xiǎng qù kàn diànyǐng, nǐ ne?* 'I think I'll go to a movie. How about you?' All of these question-particle questions have a slightly rising, question intonation.

The last main way to ask a question is to present the listener with a choice: *Nǐ chī fàn chī miàn?* 'Are you going to eat rice (or are you going to) eat noodles?' *Táishān gāo, háishi Huàshān gāo?* 'Is Taishan high(er), or is Huashan high(er)?' The choice-type question is very common. It can be used to ask what in English would be answered with yes or no—this is done by putting together the positive and negative forms of the verb:

> Nǐ máng bu máng?
> you busy not busy
> 'Are you busy?'

> Nǐ xǐhuān bu xǐhuān?
> you like   not like
> 'Do you like it?'

This pattern is perhaps a little more abrupt than the corresponding question-particle questions: *Nǐ xǐhuān ma?* 'Do you like it?' But the difference is slight. The

Chinese choice-type question is certainly not comparable to the more jarring English "Do you like it or not?"

Commands can be a verb form, or a predicate, alone: *Lái!* 'Come!'; *Guāi!* 'Be good!' (said to small children); *Kuài lái chī fàn!* 'Come quickly and eat!' But the second-person pronoun is used with the verb more often than in English: *Nǐ lái!* '(You) come!' A command may be made milder by adding the sentence particle *ba*, which gives it the effect of a request or suggestion: *Gěi wǒ ba!* 'Better give it to me'; *Wǒmen zǒu ba!* 'Let's be going.' A polite imperative is made with a verb such as *Qǐng* 'invite,' *láojià* 'trouble (you),' or *máfan* 'bother (you).' *Qǐng* is the verb form most often used in this pattern: *Qǐng nǐ màn yidiǎr shuō* 'Please say it a little slower.' Negative commands are made with *búyào* '(literally) not-want' or *bié* 'don't,' which originated as a contraction of *búyào*: *Nǐ búyào qù!* 'Don't go!'; *Nǐ bié qù!* 'Don't go.' *Bié* is considered a little more polite than *búyào*.

The most common kind of exclamatory sentence ends with the particle *a*, which is drawn out longer than usual: *Nà zhēn hǎo a!* 'That's really good!'; *Xiǎo Dì a! Nǐ hái méi shàng chuáng a?!* 'Little Brother! You still haven't gone to bed?!' These exclamations are pronounced with a lowered intonation at the end of the sentence.

Linking

The way words, phrases, and clauses are linked together epitomizes much of the grammatical difference between Chinese and English. In English, connections are ordinarily made explicit by conjunctions, relative pronouns, special verb forms, or the like. In Chinese, the basic linking device is simple juxtaposition.

Nouns in a coordinate relationship ('A and B') usually follow each other in succession without pause: *Tāmen mài shū bào* 'They sell books (and) newspapers': *Cáo Xiānsheng Wú Xiānsheng yě hǎo ma?* 'Are Mr. Cao (and) Mr. Wu also well?' The same is true of verbs: *Chén Xiāngméi hěn huì chàng gēr tiàowǔ* 'Chen Xiangmei can really sing (and) dance.' There are several Chinese words that can be translated as 'and' and which often function like conjunctions—e.g., *gēn, hé, tóng*: *Wǒ yào bǐ gēn zhǐ* 'I want a pen and some paper.' But the presence of these words is usually not necessary. They are special words, used when confusion might otherwise result, or for certain stylistic reasons. They are fundamentally not conjunctions, but coverbs, most often used like prepositions in the sense of 'with.'

Similar situations obtain for other conjunctional relationships. We have already seen how choice-type questions express the meaning 'or': *Nǐ chī fàn chī miàn?* 'Are you going to eat rice (or) eat noodles?' If the speaker desires to stress the choice aspect—and thus the meaning 'or'—he may add the adverb *háishi* '(literally) still is' between the choices. But the use of *háishi* is mainly a stylistic decision, for it is not required by Chinese grammar. In a choice between nouns, juxtaposition might be taken to mean 'and,' and so the meaning 'or' is usually made explicit by an adverb such as *huòshi* 'perhaps, maybe': *Gěi wǒ yi-zhī qiānbǐ, huòshi yi-zhī gāngbǐ* 'Give me a pencil or a pen.' But here too the adverb may be omitted if the meaning is clear: *Húluóbo wāndòu, dōu kěyǐ* 'Either carrots (or) peas are all right.' The meaning 'but' is often expressed by a slight pause: *Nǐ jiàn-guo de bú shi wǒ, shì wǒ gēge* 'It wasn't me, (but) my brother that you met.' A variety of adverbs such as *yàoshi* 'if' function as subordinating conjunctions, but they too are frequently omitted. *Yǒu rén zhǎo wǒ, nǐ shuō wǒ jiù huílai* '(If) somebody asks for me, say I'll be right back.' Where the subordinating conjunction 'that' might be used in English, Chinese verbs always take an unaltered sentence as object: *Wǒmen yíxiàng jiù zhīdao tā yào dào Xiānggǎng qu* 'We always knew (that) she wanted to go to Hong Kong'; *Tā shuō ta yào mǎi dōngxi* 'He says (that) he wants to go shopping.'

Chinese has no relative pronouns. Where 'that' would introduce a relative clause, Chinese marks the clause with the subordinative particle *de* at the end (see above discussion): *Nǐ kàn-guo dàjiāhuǒr zhí shuō de nèi-běn shū le ma?* 'Have you read the book (that) everybody's talking about?' This same construction with *de* serves where English would have the relative pronouns 'who,' 'where,' 'which,' etc.: *Gāng jìnlai de nèige rén shi lǎobǎn* 'The man (who) just came in is the owner'; *Wǒmen yào qù de nèige fànguǎnzi guān mén le* 'The restaurant (where) we wanted to go was closed.'

In English, a verb can function as a substantive if it is in the infinitive ("to do") or the gerund ("doing") form. In Chinese, the shape of a verb does not change when it is used as a noun: *Yóuyǒng hěn yǒuyìsi* 'Swim(ming) is a lot of fun'; *Wǒ hěn xǐhuān chī píngguǒ* 'I really like (to) eat apples.' Chinese verb phrases can thus come one after the other in a number of complex relationships. For example, the first may be the subject of the second: *Xué Éwén bù róngyi* 'Learn(ing) Russian is not easy.' The second may be the direct object of the first: *Wǒ yào qù* 'I want (to) go.' The second verb may serve as a complement to the direct object of the first verb: *Wǒ méi yǒu fàn chī* 'I don't have (any) food (to) eat.' The second verb may be a purpose clause: *Tā qù Rìběn niàn shū* 'She's going to Japan (to) study.' The predicate adjectives *hǎo* 'be good,' *róngyi* 'be easy,' and *nán* 'be hard' are often followed by an action verb to form a compound descriptive phrase with the meaning 'good (to do),' 'easy (to do),' or 'hard (to do)': *Píngguǒ hěn hǎo chī* 'Apples are very good (to) eat'; *Éwén bù róngyi xué* 'Russian is not easy (to) learn.' *Zài* 'be at, in' followed directly by an action verb shows that the action of that verb is continuous and still going on: *Tā zài chī fàn ne* 'He is eat(ing).' Series of verbs such as these, and a rich variety of other linking constructions, hold together without grammatical glue of the kind found in languages like English.

The modern dialects are usually classified into seven major groups. In the list of those groups below, the population estimates are based upon a total Han Chinese population of 950 million.

Dialect Group	Estimated Population	Where Spoken
NORTH		
1. Mandarin	679,250,000 (71.5%)	all of North and Southwest
SOUTH		
2. Wu	80,750,000 (8.5%)	coastal area around Shanghai, Zhejiang
3. Gan	22,800,000 (2.4%)	Jiangxi
4. Xiang	45,600,000 (4.8%)	Hunan
5. Hakka	35,150,000 (3.7%)	widely scattered from Sichuan to Taiwan
6. Yue	47,500,000 (5.0%)	Guangdong, Guangxi (and overseas communities)
7. Min	38,950,000 (4.1%)	Fujian, coastal areas of South

NORTH

Mandarin

The Northern varieties of Chinese are usually known as the Mandarin dialects. They are typified by the Peking dialect, which is the basis of the standard language and of "Mandarin" in a much narrower—and older—sense. These dialects are spoken by more than two-thirds of the Chinese people. With the total Chinese population having now passed the billion mark, this proportion means that there are around 700 million Mandarin speakers in the world—considerably more than the number of people who speak English as their first language. The area where these Mandarin dialects are spoken covers more than three-fourths of China. (See Fig 5.) It extends over all of North China and Sichuan, as well as the more recently Sinicized territories of the Northwest and Southwest.

This enormous dialect area is customarily divided by Chinese linguists into four subgroups: (1) Northern Mandarin, spoken in the Northeast and including the Peking dialect; (2) Northwestern Mandarin, which includes the dialects of the Loess Plateau and the territories to the west of it; (3) Southwestern Mandarin, spoken in Sichuan and adjacent regions; (4) Eastern, or Lower Yangtze Mandarin, represented by the dialects spoken around Nanking. The actual linguistic differences between these groups are relatively slight and are difficult to delineate in any systematic way.

Almost all of the Mandarin dialects are mutually intelligible. They are characterized by a number of common features, which, when taken together, distinguish them fairly clearly from the other dialect groups. Here are a few of those features:

Mandarin dialects do not have a series of voiced stops, with sounds such as English *b*, *d*, or *g*. (The Peking consonants that are written with these letters in Pinyin Romanization are phonetically unvoiced.) This feature separates Mandarin from Shanghainese and the other Wu dialects (as well as from some of the Xiang dialects of Hunan).

The tone system of the Peking dialect is typical of most Northern speech. The great majority of Mandarin dialects have just four tones (although a few places in the extreme north have just three tones, and a few other dialects near the Yangtze have five or six). There is a great deal of variation in how these tones are actually pronounced—for example, the third and fourth tones have pitch patterns in the Sichuan dialect that are almost exactly the reverse of those in the standard language. But the four tone *categories* are almost always the same.

Unlike Cantonese and other Southern dialects, Mandarin does not have -*p*, -*t*, -*k*, or -*m* as final consonants.

The pronoun system is one of the most distinctive features of Mandarin. The third person pronoun *tā* is found in virtually all Mandarin dialects; completely different forms are used for this pronoun in Southern dialects. Plurals are indicated in Mandarin by the suffix -*men* (e.g., *wǒ* 'I,' *wǒmen* 'we'; *tā* 'he, she,' *tāmen* 'they'). Many Mandarin dialects have the inclusive pronoun *zámen* 'we (you and I),' which is different from *wǒmen* 'we (he or they and I).'

The subordinative particle in Mandarin is -*de* or -*di* (e.g., *wǒde shū* 'my book'). This particle is as a rule not found in the dialect groups spoken south of the Yangtze River.

SOUTH

Wu

The Wu dialects are spoken in the Yangtze delta and the coastal region around Shanghai. This is an area in the most fertile and densely populated part of China. There are more than eighty million speakers of Wu, and they live in a space approximately the size of the state of Georgia (which has a population of about five and a half million).

The heart of this Wu-speaking area is Shanghai, China's largest city. Located on the flatlands of the rich Shanghai delta, this great metropolis of eleven million people serves as the economic and cultural focal point for the entire Yangtze basin. It is, above all, a city of industry and commerce. Its 8,000 factories produce everything from shoe polish and sweets to automobiles and steel, and altogether account for one-eighth of China's total industrial output. Its port, which is connected to the Yangtze estuary by the muddy Whangpoo River, accommodates a volume of cargo that ranks it among the twelve busiest in the world. The cultural impact of Shanghai on the rest of China is considerable. Of all the PRC's urban areas, it is by far the most cosmopolitan. Of course, Communist reform long ago destroyed the wicked opulence of what was once called "the Paris of Asia"—there are no more opium dens or prostitutes, posh foreign restaurants, hotels, or bars. Shanghai's old racetrack, for example, has become People's Park. Yet, in spite of more than thirty years of reeducation and reorientation, an atmosphere of smart sophistication still remains in Shanghai. Clothing is more colorful and, by Western standards, more stylish than elsewhere in the country. After the fall of the Gang of Four, Shanghai's women took up permanent waves and makeup again more quickly than did their counterparts in other cities. Nanking Road, which runs through the heart of what was formerly the British settlement, still has its reputation for better shopping, and bureaucrats from elsewhere seldom leave Shanghai without a visit to its stores. The appearance of downtown Shanghai, too, has changed little since 1949, and much of it still looks like the Paris of Asia. The foreign communities may have been disenfranchised, but the streets and buildings where they once lived are still there, occupied by others and used for different purposes. The look of this European architecture stands in sharp contrast to that of the monumental mixture of imperial and Stalinist style to be seen in Peking. Nothing else in China is quite like Shanghai.

By Chinese standards Shanghai is a new city. It began to be built up by foreign capital in the latter half of the nineteenth century; before that, it was an insignificant Southern town. Ancient records tell us that around 200 B.C. it was the site of a tiny fishing village, which was part of the kingdom of Wu. (The Wu dialects are named after this ancient "barbarian" state.) Soochow was the most important city in the area then; it was the capital of Wu. After Wu territory became Chinese, Soochow kept its position of prominence in the Yangtze delta, continuing as a cultural and literary center through all the succeeding Chinese dynasties. Shanghai, meanwhile, became the port for Soochow in about A.D. 500, and its fortunes remained tied to that other city until the mid-nineteenth century. Then, with the granting of the foreign concessions, its orientation changed, and it quickly came to eclipse Soochow in population and money. The needs of the foreign community, which was bent on the exploitation of all of China, made it a boom town, as skilled and semi-skilled labor poured in from the surrounding areas to take advantage of economic opportunity. Many of these migrants were also refugees, for the enclaves of Shanghai offered those willing to cut their roots with tradition a sanctuary against the very real physical dangers of living in a Chinese countryside that was rapidly becoming chaotic. By the end of the nineteenth century the population of Shanghai had swelled to over four million. Now it is three times that large.

The language of Shanghai reflects this turbulence. It comes in many varieties, depending on neighborhood and social group, and there is evidence of rapid generational change. Earlier missionary descriptions indicate that around the turn of the century it still had a sound system and vocabulary much like that of Soochow. But increased immigration of artisans and clerks from slightly farther down the coast began to give the metropolitan area a more Southern flavor, and today colloquial Shanghai speech is different from that of Soochow, with an apparent mixture of elements from various places in the Wu dialect area. In discussing the linguistic state of affairs, one Western writer notes this mixing and refers to "the so-called Shanghai dialect," saying that it is "not a pure dialect at all, but a metropolitan hodge-podge."

Nevertheless, in the Wu dialect area today, Shanghai is clearly the place to be from, and anyone from anywhere near the metropolitan area will identify himself as "Shanghainese." The upper-class dialect of Soochow, which was once the object of esteem and envy even in Shanghai itself, is now thought of as slightly old-fashioned or quaint. The majority speech of downtown Shanghai has become by far the most important of the Wu dialects.

The feature for which Shanghainese and the rest of the Wu dialects are best known is a three-way distinction in the initial consonants; for example, between p and p' and b. This is their defining characteristic. It sets them apart from Mandarin, which has only a two-way distinction: p versus p' (written b and p in Pinyin). Let us look at some words in the Shanghai dialect that illustrate this distinction and compare these words to their equivalents in standard Mandarin:

Shanghai initial	example	Peking pronunciation
p-	pu¹ 'wave'	po¹ (bō)
p'-	p'u¹ 'slope'	p'o¹ (pō)
b-	bu² 'old woman'	p'o² (pó)*
t-	tong¹ 'east'	tong¹ (dōng)
t'-	t'ong¹ 'be open'	t'ong¹ (tōng)
d-	dong² 'be alike'	t'ong² (tóng)*
k-	kuong¹ 'light'	kuang¹ (guāng)
k'-	k'uong¹ 'frame'	k'uang¹ (kuāng)
g-	guong² 'mad, wild'	k'uang² (kuáng)*

[* In these words the Mandarin correspondence is aspirated *p'-, t'-,* or *k'-*. But in other cases, depending on the tone, the correspondence is unaspirated *p-, t-,* or *k-*.]

We see that Shanghainese has a series of voiced consonants *b, d, g* (as well as other voiced sounds) that Mandarin does not have. The Wu dialects are very conservative in this respect, because the distinction that this voiced series represents historically has been lost in other parts of the country. In the Northern Plains, for example, it was lost some time during the Tang period.

The voiced consonants of Shanghainese are phonetically unusual. They are pronounced with a breathy quality, or murmur, that gives the auditory impression of aspiration. Therefore, like similar consonants found in the languages of India, they are known as "voiced aspirates." The breathiness is acoustically quite prominent; it pervades the entire syllable, beginning in the initial consonant and lasting throughout the syllable vowel. It is associated with a lowered register of the voice, and the syllables where it appears are all pitched in one of the lower tones. This breathy feature, which is so characteristic of the Wu dialects today, may well be an indication of how voiced sounds were pronounced at earlier stages of the Chinese language. In all of the ancient descriptions of voiced consonants, the Chinese invariably called them "muddy"; perhaps it was breathy voice of the kind heard in modern Shanghai that these early scholars were trying to describe.

Shanghainese has twenty-eight initial consonants and semivowels (see chart). Notice that, in addition to the voiced consonants not found in Mandarin, Shanghainese also has an initial velar nasal (*ng-*):

	Shanghai	Peking
'tooth'	nga²	yá
'mistake'	ngu²	wù
'I'	ngu²	wǒ

Shanghainese Consonants

	Labial	Denti-labial	Dental	Retro-flex	Alveo-lar	Palatal	Velar	Post-velar	Glottal
Voiceless stop	p		t				k		
Aspirated stop	p'		t'				k'		
Voiced stop	b		d				g		
Voiceless affricate			ts			chy			
Aspirated affricate			ts'			ch'y			
Voiced affricate						jy			
Voiceless fricative		f	s			sy			h
Voiced fricative		v	z			zy			ɦ
Nasal	m		n				ng		
Voiceless nasal									
Lateral			l						
Voiceless lateral									
Flap or trill									
Voiceless flap									
Semivowels	w					y			

There are an especially large number of vowels in Shanghainese: *i, e, ε, a, z, ə,* *ɜ̃, ɔ, u, o, ü, ö, er.* The vowel that is written here as *z* is pronounced with the blade of the tongue so close to the alveolar ridge it has a fricative quality. It is similar to the vowel of Mandarin *sì* 'four,' and it only occurs after the consonants *ts-, ts'-, s-,* and *z-.* The central vowel *ɜ̃* is very unusual; it is pronounced with the tongue bunched up in the center of the mouth, but how the articulation differs from that of schwa (ə) is uncertain. The acoustic impression is that it has rounding of some kind. The retroflex vowel *er,* which is pronounced like its Mandarin equivalent, is heard mostly in learned words; *er²* 'ear,' for example, is the form a Shanghainese doctor uses in the term for the ear-nose-throat department of a clinic. The usual, colloquial word for 'ear' is *ni²* (or *ni²tu*).

This large inventory of vowels is in part the result of historical changes. Many vowels, for example, come from original diphthongs. Others occur in syllables where a final nasal has been lost. In such cases Mandarin has been more conservative. Compare the following words:

	Shanghai	Peking
'come'	le²	lái
'good'	hɔ³	hǎo
'dog'	kɜ̃³	gǒu
'plate'	bö²	pán
'full'	mö²	mǎn
'rice'	vε²	fàn

A Shanghainese syllable can only end in a vowel, a glottal stop (*q*), or the nasal *-ng.* The final nasal is sometimes heard as a real velar consonant [ng], and sometimes just as nasalization on the preceding vowel—the word for 'square,' for example, can be pronounced as either [fɔng¹] or [fɔ⁵¹]. Let us compare some more Shanghainese words to their equivalents in Canton and Peking:

	Shanghai	*Canton*	*Peking*
'pay'	nəq	nap	nà
'happiness'	foq	fuk	fú
'arise'	faq	fat	fā
'square'	fɔng¹	fong¹	fāng
'powder'	fəng³	fen³	fěn

As can be seen from the first three examples, the glottal stop is all that remains of what was once a series of stop distinctions in final position (i.e., *-p*, *-t*, and *-k*). These final consonants have been preserved in Cantonese and completely lost in Peking dialect.

As can be seen from the last two examples, the Shanghai native does not distinguish between a final *-n* and a final *-ng*; for him, the words that end in these consonants in the Peking dialect all sound the same. Thus when a Mr. Chen from Peking happens to introduce himself in Shanghai, his host will probably not know whether his name in *Chén* or *Chéng*. This inability to tell the two sounds apart is an annoying problem for the Shanghainese trying to master the standard language; not only must he learn to pronounce an *-n* different from *-ng*, but he must also memorize which sound goes in which word.

Shanghainese has five tones. Wu dialects as a rule have seven or eight tones, but in Shanghai, tones 4, 5, and 6 have been lost as separate categories. The remaining five categories are pronounced as follows: Tone 1 starts high and falls; tone 2 is low in register (and associated with breathy voice); tone 3 starts medium high and may rise; tone 7 is high and ends abruptly with a glottal stop at the end of the syllable; tone 8 is in lower register (and associated with breathy voice) and ends with a glottal stop.

The Shanghai tone system is greatly complicated by what is often called tone *sandhi*. In Shanghainese—and in fact in all the Wu dialects—the tone of a word can change radically when it occurs in combination with another word in a compound. For example, *yǎ²* 'oil' and *diɔ²* 'strip' are both pronounced in isolation with a very low register. But when they combine in the colloquial compound *yǎ²diɔ²* 'a Chinese-style cruller (*yóutiáo*),' they lose their individual tones and the compound word as a whole is pronounced with a single tone envelope, which rises from low to high, then begins to fall again at the end of the compound. The rules describing this kind of tone *sandhi* are notoriously complex.

There are only a few important differences in grammar between the Wu dialects and Mandarin. However, the Wu speaker does have the Southern habit— also found in Cantonese—of putting the direct object before the indirect object. The order is the opposite of that of standard Mandarin, where the indirect object precedes. This aspect of the Wu dialects is so widely known in China it is associated with a Shanghai stereotype. The linguist Y. R. Chao illustrates the association with an anecdote: In a certain Chinese movie shown a number of years ago, one of the characters says (in Mandarin), "*Xièxie Nǎinai, gěi zhōu wǒmen chī!*" (Thank you, Grandma, for giving congee us to eat!), at which point the audience watching the movie murmurs, "That's Shanghai dialect!"

More subtle are differences in function words such as particles. The Wu forms are sometimes completely different, and they may not be used in a way that corresponds in a simple, straightforward way to anything found in Mandarin. For example, the Shanghai coverb $ləq^8$ '(be) at, in' has no cognate form in Mandarin even though it usually *means* much the same thing as *zài* '(be) at, in.' 'He is in Shanghai' would be expressed:

Shanghai		Peking		
ɦi²	ləq⁸	zɔng²hɛ³	Tā zài	Shànghăi.
he	is-at	Shanghai	he is-at	Shanghai

But where Mandarin *zài* is usually preceded by *zhèng* 'exactly' when it is used to express continuous action, Shanghai $ləq^8$ is reduplicated into $ləq^8ləq^8$ to express the same function. For example, 'He is eating':

Shanghai				Peking			
ɦi²	ləq⁸ləq⁸	ch'yəq⁷	vɛ².	Tā zhèngzài	chī	fàn.	
he		eat	meal	he		eat	meal

Much work still needs to be done to document these subtle contrasts between the various Chinese dialects.

To illustrate the speech patterns of Shanghainese, let us look at how some sentences are used in a longer context. In the following passage (excerpted from Michael Sherard's *Shanghai Phonology*) the Peking cognate—if there is one—and an English tag translation are given below each Shanghai word or morpheme. The abbreviation "SP" stands for "subordinative particle" (the usage corresponds to that of standard Mandarin *de*).

Zɔng²hɛ³	Syang¹ɦio²-də̃²
shànghăi	xiāngxià tóu
shanghai	country-SUFFIX

Me¹-vong²	ka³ jyi²	ngu² jyə̃²	təq⁷	ngu²-gəq⁸	bang²yə̃²—niəng²
mĕi fēng	jiàqī	wŏ jiù	—	wŏ—	péngyŏu rén
every-OCCASION	holiday I	then with I	-SP		friends people

vəq⁸-we³	tu¹-gəq⁸,	tsö³	tu¹	ɦia²-vəq⁸	ts'ɔ¹-ku³
wú huì	duō—	zuì	duō	—wú	chāo guò
not can	be-many -SP	most	many	still-not	exceed-over

sɛ¹-gəq⁸	niəng²—da²ka¹	daq⁸	chyaq⁷daq⁸ts'o¹	tɔ³	syang¹ɦio²
sān ge	rén dàjiā	tà	jiăotàchē	dào	xiāngxià
three-ONES	people everyone	step-on	bicycle	to	country

ch'yi³	bəq⁸	syang¹.
qù	—	—
go	play-around	

Yə²-gəq⁸ zəng²kuɔng¹ yaq⁷-hɔ³   ch'yi³ tang³ tiɔ³,
yǒu — chénguāng yuē hǎo   qù dǎ niǎo
exist-SP time   agree-done go hit bird

kəq⁷məq⁸ me¹ niəng² yəq¹-po³   ch'i³ch'yang¹. Chya³sz² yaq⁷-hɔ³   ch'yi³
— — měi rén yī bǎ   qìqiāng   jiǎshǐ yuē hǎo   qù
then   every person one-HANDLE air rifle   if   agree-done go

tiɔ³   ng²-gəq⁸ fie²fio², koq⁷ niəng² ta³   zz²ka¹-gəq⁸ tiɔ³ng²-ka¹sang¹.
diào yú — xiánhuà gè rén tài zìjiā —   diào yú jiā —
go-fish fish-SP story   each person bring oneself-SP fishing-tools

Sö¹zö²   yə²-gəq⁸ zəng²kuɔng¹ yəq⁷-tsaq⁷ tiɔ³ fia² tang³-vəq⁸-zaq⁸
suīrán yǒu — chénguāng yī-zhī   niǎo— dǎ wú zháo
although exist-SP time   one- HEAD bird even hit-not-receive

yəq⁷-diɔ² ng² fia² tiɔ³-vəq⁸-zaq⁸, dɛ²zz² tɔ³ syang¹fio²-də̄²
yī tiáo   yú — diào wú zháo dànshì dào xiāngxià tóu
one-STRIP fish even fish-not-receive but   to country-SUFFIX

bəq⁸syang¹ tsong³kuɛ¹ zz² k'ɛ¹k'ɛ¹syiəng¹syiəng¹-gəq⁸—yəng¹we²
— — zǒngguī shì kāikāixīnxīn   — yīnwéi
play-around anyhow is happy-   -SP because

syang¹fio²-də̄² ch'yəng¹zyəng² k'ong¹ch'yi³ fii²   hɔ³ — yə̄² jyi²
xiāngxià tóu qīngjìng   kōngqì   —   hǎo yóuqí
country-SUFFIX peaceful   air   and- also good especially

zz² syɔ³fiu² bɔng²piə¹-gəq⁸ zz²yəng¹ fio²-də̄²   gɛ²gɛ²
shì xiǎo hé pángbiān—   shùyīn   xià tóu   — —
is stream side-of -SP tree-shade down-SUFFIX loll-around

da²ka¹   ts'z¹ts'z¹   niə̄²pi³.
dàjiā   chuī chuī   niúpí
everyone blow-blow cowhide

[TRANSLATION]

THE SHANGHAI COUNTRYSIDE

Every holiday my friends and I—never very many of us, at most never more than three—would all ride our bikes out to the countryside to play around. Sometimes we would arrange to hunt birds, then everybody would have an air rifle. If we had decided to go fishing, then each one would bring his own fishing gear. Although there were times when we never shot one bird or hooked one fish, going to the country to play always made us happy— because the countryside was so peaceful, the air was fresh—especially when we would just loll around in the shade of a tree next to a stream and shoot the bull.

Gan

To the west and somewhat south of the Wu area are the Gan dialects. These little-known and little-studied varieties of Chinese are spoken mostly in Jiangxi, a province that stretches from the hills and mountain passes along the border of Guangdong northward to the great bow of the Yangtze River as it bends south to touch Boyang Lake. Some Gan dialects are also spoken in the eastern part of Hunan, next to Jiangxi, and perhaps in the southeastern corner of Hubei Province as well; very few details are known about the distribution of Gan dialects in these peripheral regions, however. The Gan dialect area is not clearly differentiated from the dialect areas adjacent to it. Through the center of Jiangxi flows the Gan River, the most prominent geographical feature of the region. It has given its name to the region and thus also to the dialect group.

For Chinese linguists the most noteworthy characteristic of the Gan dialects is that they have no voiced stops such as the *b*, *d*, *g* found in neighboring Wu areas. In this respect they are like Mandarin. But they differ from Mandarin in the way that the original voiced (and murmured or aspirated) consonants found at the Middle Chinese stage of the language were lost. In Mandarin the development of these consonants varied, depending on the tone, while in the Gan dialects they consistently became aspirated *p'*, *t'*, *k'*, and so on.

	Middle Chinese (7th century)	*Gan*	*Peking*	*Shanghai*
'level'	b-	p'iang²	p'ing² (píng)	bing²
'double'	b-	p'əi⁶	pei⁵ (bèi)	ba²
'white'	b-	p'ak	pai² (bái)	baq⁸
'lift'	d-	t'ia²	t'i² (tí)	di²
'brother'	d-	t'i⁶	ti⁵ (dì)	di²
'enemy'	d-	t'it	ti² (dí)	diq⁸

But in a larger, areal perspective the Gan dialects are important as a transition between North and South. The Gan River is one of the most accessible routes into China's Deep South, and so the dialects spoken along its banks have been tinged by Northern influence. Southern features become progressively fewer the closer to the Yangtze a dialect is spoken. Final *-p*, *-t*, and *-k*, for example, are said to be distinguished quite clearly in the southernmost parts of the Gan area. But in Nanchang, a large city near the mouth of the Gan, final *-p* has merged with *-t*. The younger generation of the city confuse *-k* and *-t* as well.

Xiang

The Xiang dialects are also a Southern group in transition—even more so than Gan. They are exposed to Mandarin from several directions. Hunan, the place where they are spoken, borders Mandarin-speaking territory on its north, west, and southwest. The densely populated center of the province is easily accessible from the Yangtze via the Xiang River and its tributaries. As a result of these inroads from the North, the Xiang dialects have become complex mixtures of older Southernisms and Mandarinized, newer features.

The Xiang dialects are divided into two types of speech, usually referred to as "New Xiang" and "Old Xiang." New Xiang is spoken in the northwestern part of Hunan, as well as in larger towns and cities all over the province. Old Xiang is the form of Chinese generally heard in mountain areas and farming communities. These two types of Xiang are reportedly very different. According to Chinese linguists:

> The general impression is that communication between New Xiang and Southwestern Mandarin is actually not difficult, while between New Xiang and Old Xiang there is a great barrier. For this reason some people prefer to classify New Xiang as Southwestern Mandarin.

In other words, the urban variety of Xiang—that is, "New Xiang"—has significantly diverged from its more conservative, rural counterpart; it has been so affected by Mandarin influence it appears to be very close to becoming Mandarin itself.

The index of a Xiang dialect is whether it has voiced consonants such as *b*, *d*, and *g* or not. Old Xiang dialects preserve these consonants in most cases, but—unlike the voiced consonants found in Wu dialects—they have no murmur or aspiration associated with them. In the New Xiang dialects, original voiced consonants have developed into unvoiced, unaspirated consonants (*p*, *t*, *k*, etc.).

	Middle Chinese (7th century)	Old Xiang (Shuangfeng)	New Xiang (Changsha)	Peking
'crawl'	b-	bo^2	pa^2	p'a^2 (pá)
'field'	d-	din^2	tien^2	t'ian^2 (tián)
'together'	g-	gang^6	kong^6	kong^5 (gòng)

In all varieties of Xiang, both New and Old, final *-p*, *-t*, and *-k* have been historically lost, just as they have been in Mandarin.

The grammar of these dialects is very close to that of Mandarin. In New Xiang, even pronouns are generally of Mandarin type.

Yue (Cantonese)

The Yue dialects are popularly known as the Cantonese dialects. They are spoken in Guangdong and Guangxi, in the area around the southernmost point in the curve of the South China coastline. The speech of Canton City, which is Cantonese in its narrower sense, is the best known and most generally esteemed of the Yue dialects.

These dialects are also spoken in North America. Unlike people from other parts of China, the people who speak Yue dialects—the "Cantonese"—have settled in fairly large numbers in the United States and Canada. An estimated 86 percent of Chinese-Americans trace their ancestry to Guangdong Province, and usually to Taishan, a tiny, rural district about sixty miles southwest of Canton. Taishan was only one of the ninety-eight districts of Guangdong (which was only one of some twenty Chinese provinces), but it had the advantage of being accessible from the sea when American sailing vessels came to recruit cheap labor in the middle of the nineteenth century. Immigration from the South has given the American Chinatown a distinctive and lasting regional flavor.

The Yue-speaking people are relatively distinct from Northern Chinese. Named after an ancient "barbarian" state located in the Deep South, the Yue are true Southerners. The word "Southern," in fact, is sometimes used as an exclusive synonym for "Yue." (In the world of Chinese restaurants, for example, South Chinese cooking almost always means Cantonese cooking, and anything north of Guangdong is considered Northern.) If there is a well-defined subgroup of the Han Chinese today, it is the Yue. They may not be as numerous as speakers of Wu, but they have a far better developed sense of group identity. The person from Shanghai knows that his speech is somehow very similar to that of Soochow or Hangchow, but he has usually never heard of a Wu dialect area and certainly does not think of a Wu culture distinct against the greater background of China. The Yue speaker, by contrast, will always identify himself as "Cantonese." He looks to Canton as the center of his local culture. He recognizes Canton dialect as standard.

The Yue refer to themselves as "people of the Tang." They call their country "Tang Mountain," their cuisine "Tang food," and their clothing "Tang clothes." The American Chinatown is known even in Mandarin as the "Tang People's Neighborhood" (*Tángrénjiē*). The Yue have a strong tradition of reciting the classics that dates back to the Tang, and the phonological categories of their dialects derive almost entirely from those of the literary standard of that period. Apparently, the mixture of native and immigrant in Guangdong must have reached a critical mass of acculturation during the Tang dynasty.

Among the Yue people the dialect of Canton has enjoyed prestige for centuries, at least since the Ming dynasty, by which time the Pearl River delta had become the most important economic and cultural center in the Deep South. From that time on, Cantonese had no local rivals. A vernacular literature grew up, including the enormously popular *Yuèōu*, which were ballads sung to the accompaniment of the Chinese lute, the *pípá*. A kind of epic poetry, chanted to the clacking beat of two pieces of wood called *mùyú* thrived in late imperial times. *Nányīn*, or "Southern melody," usually sung by a blind girl, was also popular—it survives best today in some of the airs of Cantonese opera. In addition, there was some writing of fiction and other kinds of vernacular literature. These styles of colloquial writing were relatively crude and unambitious, and they were never used for formal compositions; yet they were important enough to make Cantonese the only modern Chinese dialect (besides Mandarin) with widely recognized, nontraditional graphs for colloquial words and expressions. A few of these Cantonese characters are known to people all over China. Today such dialect writing is largely suppressed in the PRC, but it continues in Hong Kong and overseas Chinese communities, where Cantonese newspapers and other colloquial publications are sold on almost every newsstand. Cantonese is being challenged these days by Putonghua and the language policies of the Peking government. But, as yet, its speakers retain their own separate traditions.

Cantonese is thus more than a widely spoken dialect. It is a genuine regional standard. In Guangdong Province, even people whose home language is not Yue, including some national minorities whose home language is not even Han Chinese, use it and respect it as a model for speech. No other Southern dialect, including Shanghainese, has this kind of stature.

Cantonese is said to be a conservative dialect, and to a certain extent this reputation is deserved. In its sound system it preserves with great fidelity the final consonants and tonal categories of the Tang dynasty literary standard. This means that a Tang poem read in Cantonese keeps more of its original patterns of rhyme than when read in Mandarin—or in any other dialect. Perhaps, as has sometimes been suggested, immigrants far from home were more careful about language and tradition. But, on the other hand, perhaps it was more important that the immigrants moved into a geographical area where such distinctions were likely to be preserved. The aboriginal Tai people of Guangdong with whom the

Chinese mixed spoke languages with relatively large numbers of tones and final consonants. Cantonese is today the southernmost of the Chinese dialects—it is the closest both geographically and typologically to Southeast Asia.

At the beginning of a syllable, where it has lost many distinctions, Cantonese has been less conservative. It resembles the surviving Tai languages of southern Guangdong and Guangxi in having a simple system of initial consonants. In addition, standard Cantonese has no medial vowels at all anymore—such as the -i- or -u- of Mandarin *piē* 'skim off' or *tuǒ* 'appropriate, proper.'

Cantonese has nineteen initial consonants (see table). There is only one series of sibilants in this system: *ts, ts', and s*. These consonants are usually articulated with the front part of the blade of the tongue against the alveolar ridge. Some speakers, in some cases, pronounce them with the tip of the tongue, but never in contrast with the other kind of sibilant articulation. This means that no Cantonese speaker distinguishes two separate series of consonants—the way English speakers do, for instance, in making the difference between *seep* and *sheep*, or *seat* and *sheet*. For a Chinese dialect, the system is simple. Mandarin, by contrast, has three different series of consonants—the palatals, the dentals, and the retroflexes—corresponding to the one series of sibilants in Cantonese.

	Canton	*Peking*
		(palatals)
'liquor'	tsau^3	jiǔ
'fetch'	tsip^{7b}	jiē
		(dentals)
'again'	tsoi^5	zài
'word'	tsi^6	zì
		(retroflexes)
'paper'	tsi^3	zhǐ
'middle'	tsung^1	zhōng

Cantonese speakers learning the standard language seldom master these Mandarin consonants.

Another striking historical change that has taken place in Cantonese is the weakening of **k'*- to become *h*- in most words. (This same change also occurred in the Chinese loanwords of Vietnamese, a coincidence for which there is as yet no compelling explanation.) In some Cantonese words the consonant **k'*- has even changed into *f*-. In all of these cases it is Mandarin that has been conservative.

	Canton	*Peking*
'look'	hon^5	kàn
'polite'	ha:k^{7b}hei^5	kèqi
'bitter'	fu^3	kǔ
'quick'	fai^5	kuài

CANTONESE CONSONANTS

	Labial	Denti- labial	Dental	Retro- flex	Alveo- lar	Palatal	Velar	Post- velar	Glottal
Voiceless stop	p		t				k,	kw	
Aspirated stop	p'		t'				k',	k'w	
Voiced stop			ts						
Voiceless affricate			ts'						
Aspirated affricate									
Voiced affricate									
Voiceless fricative		f	s						h
Voiced fricative									
Nasal	m		n				ng		
Voiceless nasal									
Lateral			l						
Voiceless lateral									
Flap or trill									
Voiceless flap									
Semivowels	w					y			

In Taishan, the Yue dialect spoken most widely in American Chinatowns, this tendency toward the weakening of stop closures has progressed even farther, and there *t'-*, also, has changed into *h-*.

There is more nasality in Cantonese than in Mandarin. Cantonese has, first of all, the nasal consonant *ng-*, an initial sound that has completely disappeared in most of the North. Some Cantonese speakers even put this nasal on the front of words where it does not originally belong. Then there is the initial *m-*; Cantonese has preserved this nasal consonant in words where Mandarin has historically lost it.

	Canton	Peking
'tooth'	nga²	yá
'I'	ngo⁴	wǒ
'bank'	ngan²hong²	yínháng
'tail'	mei⁴	wěi
'ask'	man⁶	wèn
'literature'	man²hok⁸	wénxué

Cantonese also has completely nasal syllables, in which *m* and *ng* function as vowels. The most common word for 'not' is pronounced *m*² (in usage this corresponds to Mandarin *bù*). Syllabic nasal *ng* is the form of the word for 'five', *ng*⁴, and of two common surnames, *Ng*² and *Ng*⁴ (*Wú* and *Wǔ* in Mandarin).

Cantonese has seven vowels: *i, e, a, u, o, ü, ö*. It has none of the retroflexed or buzzing vowels typical of Northern dialects. At one time, a Mandarinlike, *z*-type pronunciation of the vowel in the syllables *tsi, ts'i,* and *si* was the admired cachet of many old families in Canton City, but that style of pronunciation no longer seems to have much prestige.

What is unusual about the Cantonese vowels—at least for a Chinese dialect—is that they can be distinctively long (again, this is remarkably like pronunciation in the Tai languages of South China). Moreover, a difference in length can change the quality of the vowel. When *a*, for instance, is pronounced long, as it is in the word *ka:m*³ 'to feel,' it sounds like [α]—similar to the vowel in English *calm*. But when short, it is phonetically closer to [ə]. This is why the word *kam*³ 'brocade' with a short vowel sounds to an American ear like *gum*. (Think of the spelling "subgum" for the word *sap*⁸*kam*³ 'mixed, assorted' on the Englished version of a Cantonese menu!) A short *i* is pronounced much lower than a long *i*. The short vowel in *sik*⁸ 'eat,' for example, is even lower than the *i* in American *sick*, sounding more like the *é* in French *été* 'summer.'

A Cantonese syllable can end with the main vowel, an offglide *-u* or *-i* (which sounds like [ü] when it follows the main vowel *ö*), or with one of six final consonants: *-m*, *-n*, *-ng*, *-p*, *-t*, *-k*.

These six final consonants of Cantonese are exactly those of the Tang dynasty literary standard. Mandarin, which has been notably less conservative at the end of the syllable, only has two ending consonants, *-n* and *-ng*. Here are some comparisons that illustrate what has happened:

	Canton -m	*Peking -n*
'feel'	ka:m³	gǎn
'drink'	yam³	yǐn
'snack, lunch'	tim³sam¹	diǎnxīn
	Canton -n	*Peking -n*
'a minute'	fan¹	fēn
'person'	yan²	rén
'see'	kin⁵	jiàn
	Canton -ng	*Peking -ng*
Chang (a surname)	tsöng¹	zhāng
'surname'	sing⁵	xìng
'Mr.'	sin¹sa:ng¹	xiānsheng
	Canton -p	*Peking*
'pagoda'	tʻa:p⁷ᵇ	tǎ
'enter'	yap⁸	rù
'ten'	sap⁸	shí
	Canton -t	*Peking*
'cough'	kat⁷ᵃ	ké(sòu)
'brush'	pat⁷ᵃ	bǐ
'moon, month'	yüt⁷ᵇ	yuè
	Canton -k	*Peking*
'hundred'	pa:k⁷ᵇ	bǎi
'color'	sik⁷ᵃ	(yán)sè
'National Language'	kwok⁷ᵇyü⁴	guóyǔ

Cantonese is particularly rich in tones. There are nine basic tones, three of which belong to the so-called "entering tone" category and thus end abruptly with a *-p*, *-t*, or *-k* stop at the end of the syllable. The nine tones are usually numbered and described as follows: Tone 1 is high falling, and tone 2 is low falling; tone 3 is high rising, and tone 4 is low rising; tone 5 is mid-level, and tone 6 is low level. Tone 7a, the first entering tone, is high level and usually very short; tone 7b, the second entering tone, is mid-level and almost always pronounced long. (The distinction between tone 7a and tone 7b, which is found only in Cantonese and the other Yue dialects, arose historically because of phonetic differences in vowel length.) Tone 8, the last entering tone, is low level in pitch.

Here is a schematic representation of these tones, with a vertical line given as a reference of pitch height:

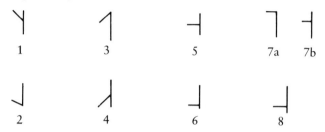

1   3   5   7a   7b

2   4   6   8

Besides these nine basic tones there are two additional and special tones known as "changed tones." One of these two extra tones has a high-level pitch, as in the word *yin⁰* 'tobacco.' The other tone, which is far more common, has a long, high rising pitch, as in *t'oi** 'table.' These two changed tones are transcribed with the degree symbol and the asterisk instead of numbers. They are different from the basic tones. The reason they are different is that a word with a changed tone is usually derived from an older word with one of the basic tones. For example, *yin⁰* 'tobacco' is derived from *yin'* 'smoke'; *t'oi** 'table' is derived from *t'oi²* 'terrace, stage.' Moreover, while a basic tone is not associated with a particular meaning any more than a consonant or a vowel is, a changed tone has a morphological meaning something like: 'that familiar thing one often speaks of.' Thus a word with a changed tone is a colloquial, everyday expression. It is never used in a literary combination or context.

Here are some examples:

Word with basic tone	*Corresponding word with high-level "changed tone"*
mui⁶ 'younger sister'	mui⁰ 'girl'
yat⁷ᵃ-ko⁵ yan² 'one person'	yat⁷ᵃ-ko⁵ yan⁰ 'alone'

Word with basic tone	*Corresponding word with long rising "changed tone"*
nöi⁴- 'female'	nöi* 'daughter'
t'ong² 'sugar'	t'ong* 'candy'
ts'a:k⁷ᵇ 'thief'	ts'a:k* 'stealer'
mat⁸ 'honey'	mat* 'bee'
wong² 'yellow'	wong* 'yolk'
-söng⁵ 'appearance'	söng* 'photo'
ma⁴t'ai² 'horse's hoof'	ma⁴t'ai* 'water chestnut'

The "changed tones" are frequently used to naturalize Western loanwords. (Cantonese is one of the few Chinese dialects that has a significant number of such loans.) A stressed syllable in English is usually approximated by the high-level tone, and a final, unstressed syllable is often pronounced with the high rising tone.

po^0 'ball'	kit^{8}t'a^0 'guitar'	si^{6}pan^0 na* 'spanner, wrench'
pam^0 'pump'	fa^{0}san* 'fashion'	sek^0 si^6 fung^0 'saxophone'
mai^0 'mile'	to^{0}si* 'toast'	tsü^{0}ku^{0}lik^0 'chocolate'
sin^0 'cent'	fei^{0}lam* 'film'	fa^{0}si^{6}ling^2 'Vaseline'
ta:i^0 'tire'	so^{0}fa* 'sofa'	
	ku^{0}li^0 'coolie'	

Tones are also used as a kind of rudimentary inflection. Tonal differences distinguish degree deictics ('this much,' 'that much') from manner deictics ('this way,' 'that way'). A change in the tone of a verb changes the aspect of the action:

lai^2 'come'   →   lai* 'have come'
ma:i^4 'buy'   →   ma:i* 'have bought'

In the Taishan dialect pronouns are pluralized by changing the tone.

Most of the vocabulary of Cantonese is the same as that of the other Chinese dialects. This is particularly true of elevated or formal speech—in general, the more learned a Cantonese expression the more likely it is to have an exact equivalent in Mandarin. The greatest dialectal differences are found in grammatical function words and in very colloquial expressions.

Cantonese vocabulary is noted for a certain kind of conservatism. Some of its everyday words, especially monosyllables, correspond in Mandarin to very archaic lexical items used only in literary expressions; such words include vocabulary as basic as min^6 'face,' keng^3 'neck,' hang^2 'to go, walk,' sik^8 'to eat,' and wa^6 'to say.'

In the syntax is where we find the greatest uniformity among Chinese dialects. But here, too, there are differences. For example, in Cantonese direct objects precede indirect objects, and certain adverbs follow the verb. The opposite order obtains in Mandarin. Here are sentences illustrating these and other contrasts in syntax:

Canton	Peking
K'öi^4 pei^3 sa:m^1-pun^3 sü^1 ngo^4.	Tā gěi wǒ sān-běn shū.
he give three-VOLUME book me	he give me three-VOLUME book
'He gave me three books.'	
Ngo^4 höi^5 ka:i^1 ma:i^4 ye^4 sin^1.	Wǒ xiān shàngjiē mǎi dōngxi.
I go market buy things first	I first go-market buy things
'I'm going to market to buy some things first.'	
K'öi^4 kou^1-kwo^5 ngo^4.	Tā bǐ wǒ gāo
he tall pass me	he compare me tall
'He's taller than I am.'	

Kiu⁵k'öi⁴ loi².   Bǎ tā   jiào lái.
call him come   take him call come
'Ask him to come.'

Ngo⁴ höi⁵ Pak⁷ᵃking¹.   Wǒ shàng Běijīng qù.
I   go Peking   I   up-to Peking go
'I'm going to Peking.'

m² t'ai³-tak⁷ᵃ-kin⁵   kàn- bú- jiàn
not lookcan see   look not see
'cannot see'

Nei⁴ sik⁸ fa:n⁶ m² sik⁸?   Nǐ chī bù chī fàn?
you eat rice not eat   you eat not eat rice
'Do you eat rice?'

Some differences between Cantonese and Mandarin grammar are very subtle. Almost any Mandarin grammatical pattern can be used in Cantonese and be understood, but such locutions are often not idiomatic. Typically, a sensitive and forthright native speaker will say of such Mandarinisms: "You *could* say it that way—that sentence pattern exists in Cantonese—but actually that's not the way we say it, we say it *this* way: ..." A colloquial Cantonese discourse always has a number of patterns that would sound peculiar in Mandarin.

The following story is told in a very colloquial style:

Pak⁷ᵃfong¹   t'ong²   Yat⁸t'au²
běifēng   tóng   rìtóu
north-wind together   sun

Pak⁷ᵃfong¹ t'ong²ma:i²   yat⁸t'au², yau⁴ yat⁷ᵃ-tsi⁵ hai²sü⁵
běifēng   tóng —   rìtóu   yǒu yī cì   — chù
north-wind together-with sun   exist one-TIME in-process-of

tsang¹lön⁶ k'öi⁴   löng⁴-ko⁵ tsi¹tsong¹ pin¹   yat⁷ᵃ-ko⁵ pun³si⁶
zhēnglùn —   liǎng ge zhīzhōng —   yī ge běnshì
dispute   he/they two-ONES among   which one -ONE power

ta:i⁶. Sik⁷ᵃtsik⁸ ko³-tsan⁶   si*, yau⁴ yat⁷ᵃ-ko⁵ yan², tsök⁷ᵇ-tsü⁶
dà   shìzhí —   zhèn shí yǒu yī ge rén   zháo zhù
great just-then that-PERIOD time exist one -ONE person wear -ing

yat⁷ᵃ-kin⁶   nün⁴nün⁴-ke⁵   ts'öng²p'ou* hai² ko⁵ sü⁵ king¹-kwo⁵.
yī jiàn   nuǎnnuǎn —   chángpáo   — — chù jīng-guò
one GARMENT warm-warm SP long-robe be-at there   pass by

K'öi⁴   löng⁴-ko⁵ tsau⁶ ts'ing²yün³   lap⁸ yök⁷ᵇ,   yü²kwo³
—   liǎng ge jiù qíngyuàn   lì   yuē   rúguǒ
he/they two-ONES then be-willing-to set-up agreement if

pin^1-ko^5 yau^4 pun^{3}si^6, nang^2 sin^1 sai^3-tak^{7a} ko^3-ko^5 yan^2
— ge   yǒu běnshì néng xiān shǐ-dé   — ge   rén
which-ONE exist power can first cause-get that-ONE person

ts'öi^2-tso^3 k'öi^4 ko^3-kin^6 p'ou*, tsau^6 sün^5 pin^1-ko^5-ke^5
chú —   — jiàn   páo   jiù   suàn   — ge —
take-off -ed he/his that-GARMENT robe   then be-regarded which-ONE SP   .

pun^{3}si^6 ta:i^6.
běnshì dà
power great

Pak^{7a}fong^1 kam^3 tsau^6 yong^6-tsön^6 k'öi^4-ke^5
běifēng —   jiù yòng-jìn — —
north-wind thereupon then use-exhaust he   SP

lik^8 lai^2 ts'ui^1 la^5. Sui^2 tsi^1 k'öi^4 yüt^8 fa:t^{7b} ts'ui^1-tak^{7a}
lì   lái chuī la shúi zhī   — yuè fā chuī dé
strength come blow!   who know he   the-more blow get

ka:u^{1}kwa:n^1, ko^3 -ko^5 yan^2 yüt^{8}fa:t^{7b} la:m^{3}sat^8 k'öi^4 kin^6 p'ou*
jiāo guān   — -ge rén   yuè fā lǎn shí   — jiàn   páo
intense   that -ONE person the-more pull tight he/his GARMENT robe

wai^2 -tsü^6 k'öi^4-ke^5 san^1 po^5,   tsöt^{7a}tsi^1 kin^5-tak^{7a} tou^1 hai^6
wéi zhù— — shēn —   zú zhī jiàn dé dōu —
wrap-ing he -SP body PAUSE finally see get all is

m^6 tsai^5-tak^{7a}-kwo^5-ke^5 lo^5, pak^{7a}fong^1 tsau^6 m^6 tsai^5
— zhì dé guò — le běifēng   jiù — zhì
not doable   ! north-wind then not do

la^5. Ko^3 tsan^6 si*   ko^3 -ko^5 yat^{8}t'au^2 tsau^6 sai^3 -ts'öt^{7a}
la — -zhèn shí — -ge rìtóu jiù shǐ   chū
-ed! that -PERIOD time that -ONE sun   then cause come-out

hou^3 nün^4 ke^5 yit^{8}hei^5. Ko^3 -ko^5 ha:ng^2 lou^6 -ke^5 yan^2,
hǎo nuǎn — rèqì   — -ge xíng lù — rén
really warm SP heat   that -ONE go road SP person

tsik^{7a}hak^{7a} tsau^6 tsöng^1 k'öi^4 ko^3 -kin^6 p'ou*
jíkè   jiù jiāng — — -jiàn   páo
immediately then taking he   that-GARMENT robe

thüt^{7b}-lak^{7a}-tso^3. Kam^3-yöng^3 ne^1,   ko^3 -ko^5 pak^{7a}fong^1 tsau^6
tuō — —   yàng ne   — -ge běifēng jiù
take-off -ed this way PAUSE that-ONE north-wind then

kam⁵tsü⁶ tsiu⁵ying⁶, wa⁶ ko³-ko⁵   yat⁸t'au² hai⁶
— zhù zhào rèn huà — -ge   rìtóu   —
force   admit   say that -ONE sun   is

lek⁷ᵃ-kwo⁵   k'öi⁴ tsi⁶kei¹ lo⁵.
— guò   —   zìjǐ   le
capable-pass he   himself!

[TRANSLATION]

THE NORTH WIND AND THE SUN

Once upon a time the North Wind and the Sun were arguing over which one's power was greater. Just then a man wearing a very warm coat happened to pass by. [Seeing him,] the two of them decided to make an agreement: whichever one had the power to make the man take off that coat of his first, then the power of that one would be regarded as greater. Thereupon the North Wind blew with all his strength. Who would have thought that the harder he blew the tighter the man pulled his coat around his body! Finally, seeing that it was all of no use, the North Wind gave up. Then, the Sun sent out some really warm heat, and the man walking down the road immediately took off his coat. In this way, the North Wind was forced to admit that the Sun was greater than he was.

Min

The Min-speaking part of China is Fujian Province and the northeastern tip of Guangdong. The best-known dialects in the area are those of Fuzhou, Amoy, and Swatow.

Speakers of Min are also found outside of this dialect area. Because they are seafarers and fishermen, many Min have settled along the coastal areas of Guangdong, especially around the Leizhou Peninsula and the periphery of Hainan Island. Other Min are found even farther south, in the various countries of Southeast Asia. Taiwan, too, is Min-speaking. Lying about one hundred miles off the Fujian coast, the island was populated mainly by immigrants from Southern Fujian who sailed across the Formosa Strait during the late Ming period. The dialect called "Taiwanese" is very close to that of Amoy, and the people who speak it still outnumber all other groups on the island, including the Mainlanders who fled to Taiwan following the Nationalist defeat at the hands of the Communists in 1950.

Fujian is relatively isolated from the interior of China. The entire province is mountainous, with few navigable rivers, and the small number of overland links it has with the rest of the country are poor. Access is easier by sea. Fujian was the last part of southeastern Inner China to be settled by Chinese, and most of the early immigrants had to travel down the coast to reach it.

This geographical isolation has kept the Min dialects somewhat out of the Chinese linguistic mainstream. Certain historical changes have not taken place in Min, leaving these dialects with some very archaic features not to be seen in other varieties of Chinese. The consonant *f*, for example, which first appeared in the Northern dialects during the Tang period, never did develop in the Min dialects. An even more conservative feature is the preservation of dental stops (*t* and *t'*) in words where even Middle Chinese, the literary language of the seventh century, already had palatal stops (*ty-*, *t'y-*, *dy-*). In modern Mandarin these consonants have undergone further changes and become retroflexed affricates, *zh* and *ch*.

	Middle Chinese (7th century)	Min (Amoy)	Peking	Canton
'divide'	p-	pun¹	fēn	fan¹
'point, tip'	p'-	p'ang¹	fēng	fung¹
'tie up'	b-	pok⁸	fù	fok⁸
'know'	ty-	ti¹	zhī	tsi¹
'penetrate'	t'y-	t'iat⁷	chè	ts'it⁷ᵇ
'hold'	ty-	ti²	chí	tsi²

The Min dialects are the most heterogeneous in China. Though they all share certain broad classificatory features—such as the historical developments described above—they are also, at the same time, highly differentiated. According to one Chinese linguist there are at least nine mutually unintelligible groups of these dialects in Fujian. To this number must be added the groups of Min dialects spoken in northeastern Guangdong. It is common practice among Chinese linguists to divide Min as a whole into a Northern group, as typified by Fuzhou dialect, and a Southern group, usually represented by Amoy dialect. However, recent evidence suggests that a more basic division exists between the inland dialects in the western part of Fujian and the coastal dialects—including Fuzhou and Amoy—which are spoken along the relatively accessible eastern seaboard. This more recent evidence makes Fujian appear to be an even more complex place than it had originally been thought to be.

Somewhat arbitrarily, let us look more closely at the Southern Min dialect of Amoy, which is essentially the same dialect as Taiwanese.

Amoy has sixteen (or nineteen) initial consonants and semivowels (see chart). The nasal consonants *m-*, *n-*, and *ng-* only occur before nasalized vowels (e.g., *ã*); elsewhere—that is, before oral vowels—they have historically lost their nasaliza-

AMOY CONSONANTS

	Labial	Denti-labial	Dental	Retro-flex	Alveo-lar	Palatal	Velar	Post-velar	Glottal
Voiceless stop	p		t				k		
Aspirated stop	pʻ		tʻ				kʻ		
Voiced stop	b						g		
Voiceless affricate			ts						
Aspirated affricate			tsʻ						
Voiced affricate			dz						
Voiceless fricative			s						h
Voiced fricative									
Nasal	(m)		(n)				(ng)		
Voiceless nasal									
Lateral			l						
Voiceless lateral									
Flap or trill									
Voiceless flap									
Semivowels	w					y			

tion and become *b-*, *l-*, and *g-*: e.g., mi > bi; nu > lu; ngi > gi. This historical change is one of the salient differences between Southern Min and Northern Min, since the latter group of dialects have kept the original nasals; for example, Amoy (Southern Min) bɔ³ 'mother' corresponds to Fuzhou (Northern Min) muɔ³.

There are six vowels in Amoy: *a, ɔ, o, e, i, u*. Sometimes vowels are nasalized; e.g., *ã, ɔ̃, ẽ, ũ*.

A syllable can have a medial vowel, *-i-* or *-u-*. It can end with the main vowel or with an offglide or final consonant: *-m, -n, -ng, -p, -t,* or *-k*.

There are seven tones in Amoy. (But they are customarily numbered to eight; tone category 4 has historically merged with tone 3 to produce the present seven.) The phonetic values of these tones change in very complex ways in context—Min tone *sandhi* is of a complexity rivaling that of Wu.

One of the most provocative aspects of the Amoy dialects is the sharp contrast between the literary and colloquial pronunciations of characters. Although all Chinese dialects have differences between reading and spoken vocabularies, nowhere are these differences so great as in Southern Min. Just why this is so has yet to be explained satisfactorily. Here are a few examples:

	Amoy literary	Amoy colloquial
'yellow'	hɔng²	ng²
'round'	wan²	hng²
'shoes'	hai²	ue²
'below'	ha⁶	e⁶
'boil'	hut⁸	pʻu⁸
'prostrate'	hɔk⁷	pʻak⁸
'tile'	wa³	hia⁶
'rain'	u³	hɔ⁶, hu⁶

Hakka

Scattered over most of South China are communities of Hakka. Villages of these unusual people can be found in the countryside from Sichuan to Taiwan and are especially common in the hillier parts of Guangdong, Guangxi, and Southern Fujian. The area around Meixian ('Plum County'), in the mountainous northeastern corner of Guangdong, and the adjoining counties of Jiangxi and Fujian is considered their homeland. In this remote part of South China, the Hakka outnumber all other groups. Everywhere else, they remain a distinct and recognizable minority.

The name "Hakka" is a word of Cantonese origin that literally means 'guest' or 'stranger.' The Hakka were called this when they began migrating into Yue-speaking territory, and the exotic name seems to have stuck quite simply because, until fairly recently, many Cantonese and Min mistakenly thought that the Hakka were not Chinese at all, but rather some kind of strange non-Han "barbarians" like the Tai or the Miao. In many parts of South China, these "guests" are still treated as outsiders and intruders even though everyone now concedes that they are Han Chinese.

The Hakka identify themselves as Northern Chinese, and this contention has some basis in fact. Local genealogies and other historical records indicate that many of the ancestors of the Hakka were people originally from the Northern Plains who in a series of waves migrated deeper and

HAKKA CONSONANTS

	Labial	Denti-labial	Dental	Retro-flex	Alveo-lar	Palatal	Velar	Post-velar	Glottal
Voiceless stop	p		t				k		
Aspirated stop	p'		t'				k'		
Voiced stop			ts						
Voiceless affricate			ts'						
Aspirated affricate									
Voiced affricate									
Voiceless fricative		f	s						h
Voiced fricative		v							
Nasal	m		n			(ny)	ng		
Voiceless nasal									
Lateral			l						
Voiceless lateral									
Flap or trill									
Voiceless flap									
Semivowels						y			

deeper into the South. What remains to be explored, however, are the contributions made by local populations to the formation of the Hakka people, and how these differed from those that made up the Yue or the Min. For no matter what the ethnic origin of the Hakka, the group is *linguistically* Southern Chinese. The Hakka dialects are historically allied to the other Southern dialects around them. They have some unmistakably Northern features, but they are actually not much more like Mandarin than Cantonese is. The Hakka dialects were formed in the South—almost surely in northeastern Guangdong—and the present widespread distribution of their speakers is the result of large-scale migrations that took place out of Meixian during the Qing dynasty.

Middle Chinese voiced consonants became aspirated consonants in Hakka. This historical development is often considered to be the most important characteristic of the dialect group. Since the Gan dialects of Jiangxi—just to the north of the Hakka-speaking area—underwent the same change, many linguists used to group Gan and Hakka together as Gan-Hakka. But since there are no other good reasons for this grouping, it has now generally been abandoned. Gan and Hakka are nowadays usually classified separately.

	Middle Chinese (7th century)	Hakka	Peking
'level'	b-	p'in²	p'ing² (píng)
'white'	b-	p'ak⁸	pai² (bái)
'lift'	d-	t'i²	t'i² (tí)
'younger brother'	d-	t'i⁵	ti⁵ (dì)
'flag'	g-	k'i²	ch'yi² (qí)
'together'	g-	k'iung⁵	kung⁵ (gòng)

The dialect spoken around Meixian is considered to be standard Hakka.

It has seventeen initial consonants (see chart). The nasal *ny-*, which is articulated with the blade of the tongue against the palate, occurs only before the vowel *i*; e.g., *nyit⁷* 'sun,' *nyiet⁸* 'moon.' It does not contrast with the velar nasal *ng-*, which never occurs before *i*, and so the two can be regarded as the same phoneme even though they are pronounced very differently. The initial *v-* developed historically from **w-*, and some linguists still treat it as a semivowel.

There are six vowels in Hakka: *i, ə, e, a, o, u*. After the initial consonants *ts-*, *ts'-*, and *s-*, the vowel *ə* is pronounced like the buzzing minimal vowel heard in Mandarin *sì* 'four,' for example. But, unlike this similar-sounding Mandarin vowel, the Hakka vowel contrasts with *i*; e.g., *sə¹* 'to think,' *si¹* 'west.' As in other Southern dialects, *m* and *ng* sometimes function as vowels.

A syllable can have a medial vowel -*i*- or -*u*-. It may have an offglide -*i* or -*u* or a final consonant -*p*, -*t*, or -*k*.

There are six tones in Meixian Hakka. (But they are numbered to 8 since earlier tone categories 4 and 6 have merged with categories 3 and 5.) This tone system has a number of peculiarities that are not found among the tones of other dialect groups. For example, in Mandarin and most other dialects, very few syllables beginning with a nasal consonant or *l*- have tone 1; but in the colloquial Hakka vocabulary such syllables are common.

	Hakka	Peking
'take'	na¹	ná
'hair'	mau¹	máo
'fish scale'	lin¹	lín
'mother'	me¹	mǔ
'horse'	ma¹	mǎ
'carp'	li¹	lǐ

Peculiarities like this suggest that the historical development of the Hakka tone system was unusual and possibly unique.

Hakka has more Northern words than Yue and Min dialects do, but overall its vocabulary is characteristically Southern. Its syntactic structure, too, is generally of the Southern type.

The following folk tale illustrates many of the structural features of the Meixian Hakka dialect. The story is built around a Hakka explanation for the origin of a peculiar birdcall.

> Ko¹tsə³ ts'ok⁸ ts'ok⁸, Oi¹tsə³ p'ak⁸sok⁸
> gē zǐ záo záo — zǐ bái —
> brother chisel bore mother waste-thoughts

A¹sun⁵ t'ung² A¹nyi⁵ he⁵ liong³ hiung¹t'i⁵.
Āshùn tóng Āyì xì liǎng xiōngdì
Asun with Anyi be two brothers

A¹sun⁵ he⁵ ts'ien²oi¹   kiung¹-ke⁵, A¹nyi⁵ he⁵ heu⁵oi¹   kiung¹-ke⁵.
Āshùn xì qián —   —   — Āyì xì hòu—   —   —
Asun be before-mother bear SP Anyi be stepmother bear   SP

Heu⁵oi¹   tso⁵nyin² m² kung¹t'au⁵, ts'i¹ka¹-ke⁵ ts'in¹sen¹   tsə³
hòu —   zuòrén — gōngdào zì jiā — qīnshēng zǐ
stepmother behavior not just   oneself SP one's own son

ts'iu⁵ k'on⁵tso⁵ pau³pi⁵, A¹nyi⁵ oi⁵ mak⁷-ke⁵ ts'iu⁵
jiù kànzuò bǎobèi Āyì ài —   — jiù
then regard-as treasure Anyi want something then

mak⁷ke⁵, tui⁵ A¹sun⁵ sim¹kon¹ ts'iu⁵ m² he⁵ an³yong⁵.
— — duì Āshùn xīngān jiù — xì — yàng
something toward Asun feelings then not be this-way

A¹sun⁵ sət⁸ m² pau³, tsok⁷ m² sau¹, han² sə²song² ta³ ki².
Āshùn shí — bǎo zháo — — hái shícháng dǎ —
Asun eat not full wear not warm also often hit him

Heu⁵oi¹ tsung³ siong³ hoi⁵si³ A¹sun⁵.
hòu — zǒng xiǎng hàisì Āshùn
stepmother always think murder Asun

Yu¹ it⁷-pai³, heu⁵oi¹ na¹ liong³-tsak³ vong²t'eu⁵, it⁷-tsak³
yǒu yī — hòu — ná liǎng zhī huángdòu yī zhī
exist one-TIME stepmother take two SEED soybeans one SEED

sang¹-ke⁵, it⁷-tsak³ suk⁸-ke⁵, suk⁸-ke⁵ pun¹ A¹sun⁵, sang¹-ke⁵
shēng — yī zhī shú — shú — fēn Āshùn shēng —
raw SP one SEED cooked SP cooked SP give Asun raw SP

pun¹ A¹nyi⁵, vong³ ki² liong³-ke⁵ nyin² to⁵ t'ai⁵ su⁵
fēn Āyì — — liǎng — rén dào dà shù
give Anyi tell he/them two ONE person to big tree

lung¹ tu³-li³ k'i⁵, vong²t'eu⁵ yung⁵ nai² t'un²-kin³ k'i⁵,
lóng dǔ lǐ qù huángdòu yòng ní — jǐn qù
hole belly inside go soybean use mud cover tight go

k'on⁵ man³nyin²-ke⁵ sien¹ pau⁵nga², ts'iu⁵ man³nyin² sien¹
kàn — rén — xiān bào yá jiù — rén xiān
see who SP first sprout then who first

tson³ vuk⁷-ha¹. Hang² to⁵ pan⁵-lu⁵, A¹nyi⁵ k'on⁵-to³ kia¹ ko¹ke⁵ t'eu⁵tsə³
zhuǎn wū xià xíng dào bàn lù Āyì kàn dǎo— gē — dòuzǐ
return home walk to half road Anyi see fall his brother SP bean

ko⁵ t'ai⁵, ts'iu⁵ t'ung² kia¹ ko¹ kau⁵.
guò dà jiù tóng — gē —
pass big then with his brother trade

Ko⁵-e² ho³ kiu³, A¹sun⁵-ke⁵ t'eu⁵tsə³ sien¹ pau⁵nga², ki²
guò — hǎo jiǔ Āshùn — dòuzǐ xiān bào yá —
pass -ed really long Asun SP bean first sprout he

ts'iu⁵ tsau⁵ kia¹ me¹-ke⁵ fa⁵ sien¹ tson³ vuk⁷-ha¹ k'i⁵-e².
jiù zhào — mǔ — huà xiān zhuǎn wū xià qù —
then reflect his mother SP speech first return home go -ed

Kia¹ me¹   k'on⁵-to³ ts'i¹ka¹- ke⁵ ts'in¹sen¹   tsə³ mo² tson³-loi²,
— mŭ   kàn dǎozì jiā — qīnshēng zǐ — zhuǎn lái
his mother see   fall oneself SP one's own son not return come

ts'iu⁵ miang⁵ nga¹ m² mai⁵-e², kiak³kiak² tseu³ k'i⁵ k'on⁵.
jiù mìng — — — — — — zǒu qù kàn
then life   even not want -ed quickly   run go see

Mang² ti¹   tsə⁵ A¹sun⁵ ts'ut⁷-loi²   heu⁵, san¹sən²   t'u³t'i⁵
— zhī   zì · Āshùn chū lái hòu shān   shén tŭdì
where know from Asun emerge come after mountain god earth

sə³-e² fap⁷, su⁵ lung¹ set⁷-pet³-e².
shĭ — fǎ   shù lóng sāi — —
use -ed magic tree hole fill-in away -ed

Heu⁵oi¹   ts'iu⁵ vong³ A¹sun⁵ na¹ it⁷-pa³   ts'ok⁸tsə³
hòu —   jiù — Āshùn ná yī bǎ   záozǐ
stepmother then tell Asun take one HANDLE chisel

k'i⁵ ts'ok⁸-k'ai¹ su⁵ lung¹ loi², mang² ti¹   ts'ok⁸-k'ai¹- loi²
qù záo kāi shù lóng lái — zhī záo kāi lái
go bore open tree hole come where know bore open come

mak⁷-ke⁵ ya¹ mo².
— — yě —
something also not-exist

Tsung³ yu¹ it⁷-tsak⁷ tiau¹-tsə³ pi¹-ts'ut⁷-loi², kiau⁵-ten³,
zǒng yǒu yī zhī niǎo zǐ fēi chū lái jiào —
assemble exist one HEAD bird   fly emerge come call -ing

"Ko¹tsə³ ts'ok¹ ts'ok¹, Oi'tsə¹ p'ak⁸sok⁸!"
gē zǐ   záo záo — zǐ bái —
brother chisel bore mother waste-thoughts

pi¹-to⁵ pan⁵t'ien¹ k'i⁵-e².
fēi dào bàntiān qù —
fly to half day go -ed

T'ang¹kong³ mi¹-nyian²-ke⁵ ha⁵ki², ki² ya⁵-ya⁵
tīngjiǎng   měi nián — xiàjì — yè yè
hear say   each year SP summer he night night

a¹ tiau⁵-ten³ su⁵va¹-hong⁵, kiau⁵-ten³, "Ko¹tsə³ ts'ok⁸
— diào — shùchà shàng jiào — gē zǐ záo
even drop-ing tree-crotch top call -ing brother chisel

ts'ok⁸, Oi'tsə³ p'ak⁸sok⁸!"   oi⁵   kiau⁵-tau⁵ tsoi⁵
záo — zǐ bái —   ài   jiào dào zǔi
bore mother waste-thoughts want call   until mouth

kok⁷t'eu² ts'ut⁷hiat³ tsang⁵ m² kiau⁵.
jiǎo tóu chūxuě —   — jiào
corner bleed   finally not call

[TRANSLATION]

"BROTHER BORED WITH A CHISEL, MOTHER WORRIED IN VAIN"

Asun and Anyi were two brothers. Asun was the son of the first wife, and Anyi was the son of the stepmother.

The stepmother's behavior was not just. Her own son she considered a treasure, and whatever Anyi wanted he got. But her feelings toward Asun were not like this. Asun did not have enough to eat, his clothing was not warm, and he was often beaten. The stepmother was thinking of murdering Asun.

One day, the stepmother took two soybeans, one raw and one cooked. The cooked one she gave to Asun, and the raw one she gave to Anyi. She told the two of them to go inside the hollow of a great tree and to cover up the soybeans with mud. The one whose bean sprouted first was to return home. When they had gone about halfway, Anyi noticed that his brother's bean was bigger and traded with him.

After a long time, Asun's bean sprouted first, and, following his mother's orders, he returned home. When his mother saw that her own son had not returned home, [she was in such despair] she didn't even want to live. Quickly she ran off to look. How could she have known that after Asun had come out, the mountain god had used magic and filled up the hollow in the tree! The stepmother then told Asun to take a chisel and bore open the hollow in the tree. How could she have known that when it was bored open there would be nothing in it! There was only a bird, which flew out crying, "Brother bored with a chisel, Mother worried in vain!" and flew about for half the day.

They say that each year in the summer, night after night, he sits in the fork of the tree crying, "Brother bored with a chisel, Mother worried in vain!" He cries until the corners of his mouth bleed, before finally not crying any more.

The Source

Our history of the sounds of Chinese begins in A.D. 601, when the celebrated rhyming and pronouncing dictionary *Qièyùn* was completed. One of the formative works of Chinese civilization, this medieval book is also the foundation for what we know about China's linguistic past.

In his preface, the compiler Lù Fǎyán describes how *Qieyun* was created:

> Once about fifteen or twenty years ago Liu Zhen and others—in all eight persons—came to visit me and stayed the night. When it grew late and we had been drinking wine for most of the evening, we began discussing the sounds and the rhymes.
>
> Modern pronunciations are naturally varied; moreover, those who have written on the sounds and the rhymes have not always been in agreement. In Wu and Chu the pronunciation is too light and shallow; in Yan and Zhao, too heavy and turbid. In Qin and Long the departing tone is pronounced like the entering tone; in Liang and Yi it is the even tone that is similar to the departing tone. Furthermore, some authors make single rhymes out of a number of different rhyme categories; some argue that other rhymes have the same final sounds. If one wishes to widen the circle of readers, then it is all right to allow clear and muddy pronunciations to be interchanged; but if one has discriminating tastes, then there must be a distinction between light and heavy. Lü Jing's *Yun ji* [and other works of its kind] all have idiosyncrasies; the rhymes they use from the lower Yangtze region are different from those taken from the area north of the Yellow River.
>
> So we discussed the rights and wrongs of the North and the South and the comprehensible and incomprehensible of the ancients and moderns. We wanted to select the precise and discard the extraneous, and there was much of this that was decided by Xiao and Yan. Then Compiler Wei said to me, "Up to now we have been talking and arguing and all the questionable points have been resolved. Why don't we write down what we have said? If the several of us decide on something, then it is settled once and for all."

So under the candlelight I took up my brush and jotted down an outline. We consulted each other extensively and argued vigorously. We came close to getting the essence.

At this point I went off into various other studies while pursuing my career as a minor official, and for more than ten years I did not have leisure to put the collection of rhymes into order.

Now I have retired from government service and am giving private instruction in composition to several students. Whenever dealing with writing where elegant style is important, one must be very clear about the tones and the rhymes. But since I am living in seclusion in the country with my relationships and contacts cut off, there is no place to ask when there are things that I have doubts about. As for those among my acquaintances who have died, the roads of life and death have parted and in vain do I harbor a regret that I am not able to consult with them again; as for those who are living, there is now a social barrier between those noble people and the base person that I have become, and this has insured the disruption of friendship. Consequently, I have taken the sounds and the rhymes of the various specialists and the dictionaries of the ancients and moderns, and by arranging what those before me have recorded, I have made up the five volumes of *Qieyun*. The splits and analyses are exceedingly fine and the distinctions abundant and profuse.

Why should I be concerned with recognition? I would not wish to be like that ancient man whose presentation of jade was repeatedly and unjustly rejected by the king; nor do I think my work can match that of the ancient master who offered gold to anyone who succeeded in improving a single word of his perfect text. The ancients were amazed at Sima Qian's boasting when he said he would store his work on a famous mountain for future generations; now I sigh in sympathy with the stammering Yang Xiong who was fearful that his book would only be fit for covering sauce jars. The present work is not my wanton invention—I am merely transmitting the ideas that all the worthies have left us. Would I dare hope to become well known in the world without having gone out of my gate, simply because I present and circulate this book?

Written in the year *xinyou*, the first year of *Renshou* of the Great Sui (A.D. 601).

This relatively short preface is followed by the body of the dictionary itself, a five-volume work that contains a total of about 12,000 character entries.

Qieyun was intended above all as a guide to the recitation of literary texts. This was not the first such work that had ever been written in China; after all, reading the classics correctly had long been perceived as one of the most important of society's needs—Lu Fayan in fact mentions the names of six other rhyming and pronouncing dictionaries that were in circulation at the time. But *Qieyun* is the oldest guide to Chinese pronunciation that has been preserved. The others have long since been lost.

Lu Fayan arranged the dictionary as a book of rhymes. First he sorted all the characters by tone and made them into separate volumes. Since the first, or "even," tone had an especially large number of characters, it occupied two volumes by itself. The other three tone categories of the Chinese of that day took up one volume each. This made five volumes altogether. Then, within each of these volumes, Lu grouped the characters together by rhyme. The resulting rhyme groups, 193 in all, form the framework of the dictionary.

But what made *Qieyun* useful as an aid to pronunciation was the fact that it contained within this framework a system for "spelling" the readings of characters. This "spelling" system, called *fǎnqiè* in Chinese, is one in which the reading of a character is indicated by using two other, presumably known, characters. The first or upper character represents the initial consonant, and the second or lower character represents the rest of the syllable—the "final" and its tone. Using this system, the modern Mandarin syllable *kuāng*, for example, could be spelled with two characters pronounced, respectively, *kè* and *huāng*, i.e., k(è) + (h)uāng = kuāng. Such *fanqie* spellers may seem a rather crude and cumbersome expedient, but they were the most powerful tool for describing actual pronunciations available in China at the time. Until the early centuries A.D. the only way a pronunciation had been indicated was with a homophone. If no homophone or near-homophone existed, the reading simply could not be recorded. In this kind of situation, the invention of the *fanqie* system was something of a major linguistic breakthrough. Lu Fayan and his contemporaries were not the innovators—the system had already been in use for several hundred years by their time. But the examples of *fanqie* that they gave us in *Qieyun* are the oldest that have been preserved intact.

Lu Fayan used *fanqie* to detail a general literary standard. These *fanqie* and the literary standard that they represented were carefully constructed to reflect the tastes and sensibilities of upper-class Chinese from all areas of the country. They did not represent an actual dialect spoken by Lu Fayan or by any other single person. The nine gentlemen at the wine

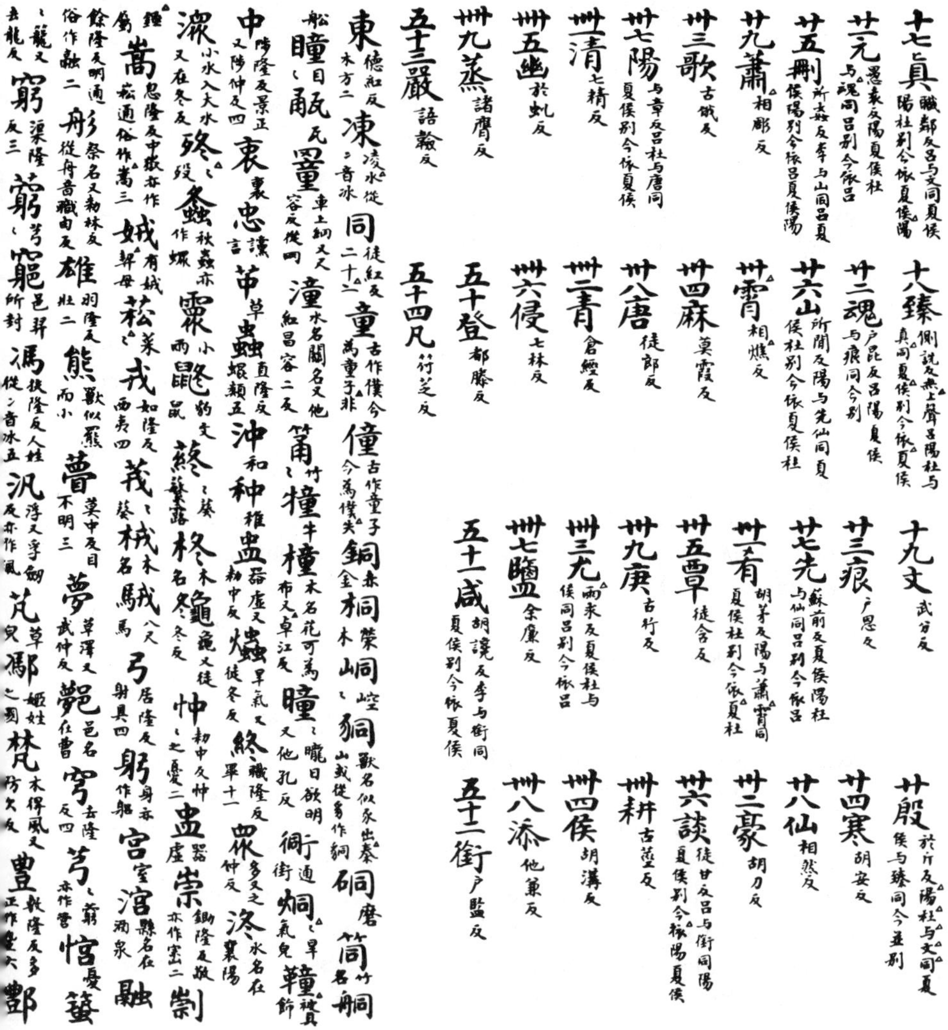

Figure 7. A page from the *Qièyùn* Rhyming Dictionary.

This page shows the beginning of the first rhyme in the first volume of the dictionary. The first character in the rhyme is 東 'East.' Under its entry can be found the *fǎnqiè* reading 德紅, which has been deciphered as follows: $t(\partial k) + (gh)ung^1 = tung^1$, the Middle Chinese pronunciation of 東 'East.'

party chose readings from among the "rights and wrongs of the North and the South" and various writings ancient and modern, and what Lu finally wrote down that night was something very eclectic. It was a dialect compromise designed to satisfy everyone, and that is perhaps one reason why *Qieyun* was in the end so successful.

Lu Fayan probably never suspected how important his *fanqie* spellers would become. Literary matters were his main concern, as is evident throughout the preface that he wrote for the dictionary. To be sure, he complains about the strange accents heard in certain areas of the country, but only because they affected the proper reading of classical texts. "Pronunciations are naturally varied," he wrote; and he probably had never given a thought to changing these natural, regional variations in speech. The formal recitation of literature was what mattered. Lu Fayan lived in an aristocratic age. He and the guests at his wine party were Chinese gentlemen, and their world extended no farther than the "gates and gardens" of a few rich and powerful families. Lu Fayan was writing for a relatively small, elite group of men with "discriminating tastes" who were interested in the fine points of literary elegance.

Yet, more than any other work, *Qieyun* and the *fanqie* spellers that it contained helped standardize pronunciations of Chinese characters in every land reached by Chinese civilization. This dictionary was the model for everything that came after it. Copied, recopied, revised and expanded several times over, *Qieyun* spread, in various forms and under several names, to all parts of China and the rest of East Asia. At the time that education was becoming more widespread in this part of the world, generation after generation of schoolboys all over China, Japan, Korea, and Vietnam learned to read Chinese with a system of pronunciation based on the readings given in *Qieyun*. As a pronouncing dictionary it never had any rivals; the system that it detailed was almost universally accepted as standard throughout the medieval Chinese period.

The Tradition

The *fanqie* formula—using two known characters to identify the pronunciation of a third, unknown one—continued to be the way the Chinese "spelled" words, from before the time of *Qieyun* down to the present century. Even today, in the Nationalist version of the encyclopedic *Cíhǎi*, the readings of the characters are indicated by *fanqie*. In the intervening years there had been a significant increase in the understanding of phonology in China, but no easier or more straightforward way to indicate pronunciation was ever devised. In this respect lexicography remained at a standstill. The limitations imposed by the nature of the writing system could not be overcome. Had the Chinese begun to use an alphabetic notation, even in a supplementary way, *fanqie* could quickly have been replaced by letter spelling. (And this could theoretically have easily been done since Buddhist scholars of the Tang period were familiar with Indic alphabets.) But as long as the Chinese continued to write exclusively with the traditional character system, the *fanqie* would remain about the most efficient way to indicate pronunciations.

Problems with the *fanqie* began to become apparent almost from the very beginning. When Lu Fayan compiled *Qieyun* the Empire had just been reunified by the Sui. Less than two decades later the dynasty had collapsed and the reins of government taken up by the Tang. The Tang rulers kept the capital in the North, in Changan, and enthusiastically accepted *Qieyun* as their literary standard. But the very strength of this new central government meant that the spoken basis of the standard became ever more firmly entrenched in the North. It was not long before actual pronunciations must have differed considerably from the categories of *Qieyun*, which had incorporated elements from other areas of the country, some of them in the South. After some time had elapsed, people must have begun to puzzle over a few of the *fanqie*. As more time passed, the more the language naturally changed, and the more serious the problems became. Clearly, there needed to be some supplementary instructions on what pronunciations were indicated by the *fanqie*.

It was at this time in Tang Dynasty China that there grew up a native phonological science whose sole purpose was to clarify the literary standard, and thus the *Qieyun* system. This Chinese science was called *děngyùn-xué*, which meant 'the study of graded rhymes.' Indian linguistic theory, which had been brought into China along with Buddhism, provided the stimulus, and many of the categories and concepts used in the Chinese study of sounds are borrowed from Indian tradition. Even the *fanqie* themselves are believed to have developed at least in part under the influence of Indian linguistic science. But, just as the Buddhist sutras themselves were translated into Chinese before becoming sacred canon, so too was linguistic learning translated and transformed to fit the East Asian mold. One clear example is the alphabetic principle itself. A Sanskrit word for alphabet is *matrika*, whose stem, *matr̥*, means 'mother.' This association of 'mother' with sound unit (which seems to have come originally out of Hindu mythology) was

韻	日	來	喻	匣	曉	影	禪	審	牀	穿	照	斜	心	從	清	精
冬東		籠	○	洪	烘	翁						○	檧	叢	蔥	葼
東	○	○	○	○	○	○	○	○	崇	○	○					
鍾東	戎	隆	○	容	肓	邕	鱅	舂	重	充	終					
鍾		○	融	○	○	○						松	嵩	從	樅	蹤
董		曨	○	澒	嗊	蓊						○	敕	○	○	總
	○	○	○	○	○	○	○	○	○	○						
腫	冗	隴	○	○	洶	擁	歱	○	○	蠢	腫					
腫		○	勇	○	○	○						○	悚	○	怂	縱
送		弄	○	鬨	烘	甕						○	送	瘶	認	糭
送		○	○	○	○	○	○	○	剓	○	○					
用送	鞣	曨	○	○	趜	雍	○	○	重	銃	眾					
用送		○	用	○	○	○						誦	○	從	趣	縱
沃屋		祿	○	縠	殸	屋						○	速	族	瘯	鏃
屋		○	○	○	○	○	○	縮	○	珿	縬					
燭屋	肉	六	○	○	蓄	郁	熟	叔	○	俶	粥					
燭屋		○	育	○	○	囿						續	肅	歠	鼀	足

Figure 8. One of the Rhyme Tables from *Qièyùn zhǐzhǎng tú*.

Qièyùn zhǐzhǎng tú was the Song Dynasty set of rhyme tables Karlgren used for his reconstruction of Middle Chinese. In the particular table shown above, the character 東 'East' appears at the intersection of the fifth initial with the first final of the even tone. The circles in the grid indicate syllable types that are expected but do not in fact occur.

taken over intact by the Chinese. The term *zìmǔ*—literally, 'mother of words'—which today means any alphabetic letter, referred in Tang times specifically to an initial consonant. Chinese phonologists gave names to these 'mothers of words' by choosing representative characters, which themselves had those initial sounds. These 'mothers of words' (which were also called 'mothers of sounds') were actually rather close to being alphabetic symbols and are the easiest part of the phonological tradition to interpret. The problem came with the rest of the syllable. If Chinese phonologists had followed through with the Sanskrit-style analysis, which they had begun in the initial consonants, they would have segmented the rest of the syllable into vowel units and, in many cases, a final

奉	敷	非	明	並	滂	幫	娘	澄	徹	知	泥	定	透	端	疑	羣	溪	見	二
			蒙	蓬	○	○					農	同	通	東	嵸	○	空	公	平
			○	○	○	○	○	○	○	○					○	○	○	○	
馮	豐	風	瞢	○	○	○	濃	蟲	忡	中					顒	窮	穹	弓	
			○	○	○	○					○	○	○	○	○	○	○	○	
			蠓	菶	○	埲					穠	動	桶	董	○	○	孔	○	上
			○	○	○	○	○	○	○	○					○	○	○	○	
奉	捧	覂	鶒	○	○	○	重	寵	冢						○	渠	恐	拱	
			○	○	○	○					○	○	○	○	○	○	○	○	
			幪	○	○	○					齈	洞	痛	凍	○	○	控	貢	去
			○	○	○	○	○	○	○	○					○	○	○	○	
鳳	賵	諷	夢	○	○	○	挶	仲	踵	中					○	共	焢	供	
			○	○	○	○					○	○	○	○	○	○	○	○	
			木	瀑	扑	卜					○	獨	禿	縠	擢	○	哭	穀	入
			○	○	○	○	○	○	○	○					○	○	○	○	
伏	蝮	福	目	僕	○	轐	朒	逐	畜	竹					玉	驧	麯	菊	
			○	○	○	○					○	○	○	○	○	○	○	○	

consonant (i.e., *-m, -n, -ng, -p, -t, -k*). But they did not. Instead, they treated everything after the initial consonant as a single sound unit and called it a *yùnmŭ*, literally, a 'mother of rhyme' (we call this the *final*). In other words, Chinese phonologists did not analyze the syllable into units smaller than those already indicated by the upper and the lower *fanqie* characters. They simply classified and organized the raw information of the *fanqie* spellers. This contribution to an understanding of the *Qieyun* system, important though it may be, falls far short of the sophisticated analyses of Indian tradition.

The essence of Chinese phonological learning is embodied in what are called "rhyme tables." A rhyme table is a large chart that is marked off by intersecting horizontal and vertical lines into a grid. The characters of *Qieyun* are placed in the squares of the grid. The vertical columns represent the initials, and the horizontal rows the tones and, subdivided under the tones, the finals. That is, all the characters in a single column of the rhyme table shared the same initial consonant, and all the characters in a single row across the page had the same final. All of these many rows and columns were further arranged in a systematic fashion on the page so that sounds which shared similar features were grouped together. Since the number of initial consonants was small and manageable, they could all be put into a single table. But the number of finals, which represented all the many possible combinations of vowels and ending consonants that could occur in a Chinese syllable, was very large indeed, and there was no way that they could all be included on a single sheet of paper. Therefore, in order to display the entire *Qieyun* system, Chinese phonologists made up *sets* of rhyme tables, each table being a group of finals that seemed to share the same kind of acoustic or articulatory quality. These complex sets of tables were circulated throughout China as explications of the *Qieyun* dictionary. For many centuries they were used all over East Asia as the keys to the standard literary pronunciations.

For us today, these rhyme tables are exotic and esoteric in the extreme. The organization of knowledge that they represent cannot be translated in any one-to-one, straightforward fashion into the terminology and categories of twentieth-century linguistics. Of course we freely interpret, for example, the arcane labels 'clear' and 'muddy' as meaning 'voiceless' and 'voiced,' because our modern linguists have deduced those particular articulatory qualities for the initial consonants so designated. But surely such picturesque words as 'clear' and 'muddy' evoked other acoustic associations for the medieval Chinese scholar. (One is reminded of voice teachers in our own classical tradition who instruct their students to sing "pear-shaped notes.") Especially problematic are the designations for the finals because there are so many possibilities. Did two finals contrast because they had different medials or because they had different nuclear vowels? Or was the difference some combination of the two? Among modern scholars there have been many debates over various interpretations, and some of the Chinese phonological classifications remain mysterious to this day.

The heyday of the *dengyun-xue* tradition was the Song. The most important surviving rhyme tables date from that period, even though a few of the earliest examples may represent redactions of prototypes from the mid-Tang. Even the *Qieyun* itself became available to post-Song generations principally through the expanded Song edition of 1008 known as *Guǎngyùn*. After the Song, Chinese scholarship turned from the compilation of rhyme tables to other matters. The body of works comprising the tradition was now closed.

Sounds of the Past

Anyone who studies a language from the past wants to know what it sounded like. In the case of earlier stages of English, this is often a simple matter. To know something about Middle English, say, we need only scan a line or two of *The Canterbury Tales*.

> Whan that Aprill with his shoures soote
> The droghte of March hath perced to the roote ...

A reader of this famous opening couplet sees at once that the word 'sweet' could rhyme with the word 'root' in the fourteenth century. He does not need a rhyming dictionary; the old spellings *soote* and *roote* alone are enough. All he need do is learn a few simple orthographic rules—such as, "long *o* [o:] was spelled *oo* in Middle English"—and the words of Chaucer begin to ring in his head.

By comparison, the classical poems of China are mute. The modern reader does not hear a Tang verse the way it sounded when it was written. Instead, he customarily reads the characters with Mandarin (or perhaps Fukienese, Cantonese, or Shanghainese) pronunciations, and in so doing treats the poem as if it had been written in a modern Chinese dialect. This removes it more than a thousand years from the time of the poet. It would be no more of a distortion if we were to pronounce the last words of Chaucer's opening line *showers sweet* instead of *shoures soote*. When read in this way, the Tang poems become, in effect, modern works in an archaic syntax. The sounds of classical Chinese verse were not recorded in the sense that those of *The Canterbury Tales* were, and, as a result, they can never be known with quite the same degree of certainty.

The *Qieyun fanqie* and their reworkings in the Song rhyme tables attest sounds only in the abstract. They show in great detail what the phonological system of Tang poetry was—that is, what contrasted with what and what rhymed with what. But they do not reveal how Lu Fayan or, after him, the poets of the Tang actually pronounced their standard language. They tell us that character A had the same initial as character B, character B the same initial as character C, and so on, and from this information a series of equations can be made that takes the form A = B = C. But these values are nothing more than mathematical abstractions, and the entire *fanqie* system itself an enormous matrix of equations relating these abstractions to each other. In other words, *Qieyun* gives a great deal of *structural* information about the literary standard of the seventh century, but it does not tell us anything *concrete* about it.

In order to recover Lu Fayan's language in anything like its original form, the sound values must be inferred from evidence other than that given in *Qieyun*. This task was first accomplished in the early part of this century by a young student from Sweden.

The work of Bernhard Karlgren

Bernhard Karlgren (1889–1978) came to Sinology by chance. Nothing in the early years of this remarkable man would indicate any particular interest in China. The passions of his youth were the folk tales and dialects of his native Sweden, and it was in this field that he distinguished himself in the academic world while still a boy in his teens. When he entered the university at Uppsala, his experience in linguistics and dialectology brought him under the tutelage of a well-known professor of Slavic dialectology, who guided his gifted student into the study of Russian. Karlgren took a degree in that field in 1909 and left almost immediately for St. Petersburg to continue his studies. But, as it happened, within a few months a grant to study dialects in China became available. Karlgren had no background at all in Chinese studies, but his Slavicist teacher at Uppsala gave him a strong recommendation anyway because of his outstanding linguistic training and personal qualities. Karlgren won the grant and in February 1910, set sail for the Far East. At the time he knew no Chinese.

This would not appear to be a very auspicious beginning for what Karlgren had to accomplish. On the face of it, it seems naive, almost foolhardy, to have sent a young European to do research in the Chinese countryside. Rural China was a dangerous and hostile place in those days, not only for Westerners but for the Chinese as well. The Empire was tottering on the verge of collapse, and civil order was tenuous at best. Within a few months revolution would spread across the country. Such political uncertainty compounded manyfold the cultural problems already facing the Westerner in rural China, and it was under these most adverse of conditions that Karlgren had to carry out his research.

Yet, here is how another linguist would later describe that most extraordinary period in Karlgren's life:

> It is overwhelming, nay beyond comprehension, what the young Bernhard Karlgren achieved during his first stay in China. In a few months he acquired a knowledge of spoken Chinese sufficient for him to go out into the field, and a knowledge of written Chinese sufficient for him to establish and apply a questionnaire containing 3,100 Chinese characters. He travelled during long periods from

town to town, and from village to village, alone with his servant and his horse, clad and behaving like a Chinese, usually accepted everywhere, and by virtue of his quick mind and his upright personality, able to escape unhurt from many a dangerous situation.

Karlgren stayed in China for two years. When the money in his grant ran out, he made a living by teaching French and English (the latter he had never been taught but had picked up on the boat coming over from Europe!). During that time he collected enough materials to make phonological descriptions of twenty-two different Chinese dialects—nineteen from the Mandarin-speaking area and one each from Shanghai, Fuzhou, and Canton—plus the Japanese and Vietnamese pronunciations of the characters in his questionnaire. To these materials he then added data from nine other dialects described in various published sources. Though his transcriptions would later be amended somewhat and greatly supplemented by the Chinese and Western linguists who would follow him, Karlgren's materials were in 1912 by far the greatest body of dialect data that had ever been assembled in China.

Karlgren packed up the results of his researches and returned to Europe. After a few months' study in London, he went to Paris, which was then the center of Chinese studies in Europe. There he got to know Paul Pelliot (1865–1945) and Henri Maspero (1883–1945), two men who would soon come to dominate the French school of Sinology. These two scholars must have had an enormously stimulating effect on Karlgren, because they had both long been concerned with the perplexing problem of how Chinese sounds from earlier historical periods could be recovered. But it was Karlgren of course who had the modern dialect materials, which would prove to be the key, and he had already determined what had to be done with them. He spent two years in Paris building a solid foundation in Sinological studies and Chinese phonological tradition, and, after a couple of short visits with scholars in Germany, he returned to Sweden.

In May 1915, Bernhard Karlgren was awarded the Ph.D. degree. His dissertation, which would be published as the first part of *Études sur la phonologie chinoise*, won an important scholarly prize, and Karlgren himself was appointed to a position at the University of Uppsala. He was twenty-five years old.

Études sur la phonologie chinoise, a work Karlgren published in full between the years 1915 to 1926, gave concrete sound values to the categories represented by the *fanqie* spellers. It was a reconstruction of the literary language of the seventh century. Karlgren called this reconstruction "Ancient Chinese," and today it is usually known as "Middle Chinese." The literary scholars of traditional China had known the *Qieyun* system in intimate detail and had worked out precisely how many initial and final categories there were. But they had not been able to reconstruct the sounds of Middle Chinese because they did not have a methodology with which to do it. Such a methodology only became available with the development of the comparative method in European linguistics during the nineteenth century, and the Chinese as yet had no knowledge of this new Western science. The first person to apply the comparative method in any thoroughgoing way to Chinese was therefore a Westerner, Bernhard Karlgren, and *Études* was the work in which he presented the results.

The key to the application of the comparative method in Europe lay in the existence of what were called "genetic relationships" between languages. Scholars had found that if languages resembled each other in certain systematic ways, it was because they were later, changed forms of what had once been the same language. The Romance languages, for example, were related because they had all descended from the language of ancient Rome. The Romans had spread their language over the greater part of Western Europe, and, with the passage of time, it had changed in various ways into "Spanish," "French," "Italian," and so on. Because these modern Romance languages had come from one and the same ancestral language, the ways in which they now differed from each other were the cumulative results of the changes that each had undergone. Once this central fact was understood, the history of each language, as well as the original form of the ancestral language itself, could all be reconstructed through a careful comparison of the systematic differences between the modern forms.

Karlgren used the comparative method to reconstruct Middle Chinese. The literary pronunciations in the various modern dialects were now very different from each other, but that was because over a thousand years had passed. In fact, they had all descended from the same source. Each provided concrete forms that, through the use of the comparative method, could be used in reconstructing the original language.

But Karlgren also realized that the comparative method had a very unusual role to play in China. In a language family like Romance, the method could be and was applied quite independently of Latin. The sounds of Italian, say, were compared to the sounds of Spanish, French, and so on, quite deliberately without regard to what the distinctions had been in Latin. This way, the reconstructions had their own independent validity. The variety of proto-Romance that was thus reconstructed could be used to illuminate some dark etymologies of Latin, or to reveal how popular pronunciations and usages had differed from those of the standard. But proto-Romance and Latin were fundamentally separate things. Latin was the language written down by the lettered aristocracy; proto-Romance was a reconstruction of the speech of the average Roman citizenry, the people who had actually spread Romance over Europe. There would always be something uncertain about a language that was completely reconstructed the way proto-Romance was; but such an independent thing was valuable because of the hints that it would otherwise not be able to give about the language of the plebeian Roman—the soldier, the trader, the settler, the housewife, the craftsman, the illiterate. As for the more patrician sounds of Latin, the modern Romance languages were not needed to find out about them; they had already been recorded in a rich and extensive alphabetic literature. For Chinese, however, this kind of independent reconstruction was a luxury. For unlike the sounds of Latin, the sounds of early Chinese literature were still unknown, and the comparative method was the only way to find out what they had been. Karlgren therefore reconstructed not some unattested and consequently abstract proto-language, but rather the pronunciations of the actual literary standard as they had been laid out by Lu Fayan in A.D. 601. Karlgren's was not a pure application of the comparative method. He adapted his materials to a unique situation and put together what in effect was a hybrid—a combination of the reconstructed and the attested, a blend of Western techniques and Chinese philological tradition.

To reconstruct Middle Chinese, Karlgren began by listing the initial and final categories set up by the Song phonologists. These he then compared with the modern dialect pronunciations. The arrangements of the *Qieyun fanqie* (or the *Guangyun fanqie*) given in the rhyme tables thus became the framework that he fleshed out with his dialect materials. The whole process was of course enormously complex, but to illustrate the method, here are a few simple examples of how Karlgren arrived at the phonetic values for three of the initial categories:

Characters with Initial 1:	*Peking*	*Shanghai*	*Fuzhou*	*Canton*	*Sino- Japanese (Go'on)*
多	t-	t-	t-	t-	t-
當	t-	t-	t-	t-	t-
帶	t-	t-	t-	t-	t-

Characters
With
Initial 2:

扡	t'-	t'-	t'-	t'-	t-
湯	t'-	t'-	t'-	t'-	t-
泰	t'-	t'-	t'-	t'-	t-

Characters
With
Initial 3:

駝	t'-	d-	t-	t'-	d-
唐	t'-	d-	t-	t'-	d-
大	t-	d-	t-	t-	d-

From these examples it is amply clear that Initial 1 must have been *t-, and that Initial 2 must have been *t'-. The modern Chinese dialects have all preserved these values. The only difficulty is in reconstructing the pronunciation of Initial 3. But since both Shanghainese and the Go'on pronunciations of Japanese consistently have a *d*- in these readings, Karlgren felt confident that the original consonants must have been similarly voiced. (Karlgren also believed that these consonants were aspirated, for reasons that we will not go into here.)

Karlgren reconstructed thirty-six initial consonants for Middle Chinese, including "zero" (0) in case there was no actual consonant and the syllable began with a vowel. These initial consonants are given in the table here. The symbols in brackets represent phonetic transcriptions

MIDDLE CHINESE CONSONANTS

	Labial	Denti-labial	Dental	Retro-flex	Alveo-lar	Palatal	Velar	Post-velar	Glottal
Voiceless stop	p		t			t̂[ty]	k		•[q]
Aspirated stop	p'		t'			t̂'[t'y]	k'		
Voiced stop	b'[b]		d'[d]			d̂'[dy]	g'[g]		0
Voiceless affricate			ts	ts[chr]		tś[chy]			
Aspirated affricate			ts'	ts'[ch'r]		tś'[ch'y]			
Voiced affricate			dz'[dz]	dz'[jr]		dź'[jy]			
Voiceless fricative			s	s[shr]		ś[sy]	χ[x]		
Voiced fricative			z			ź[zy]	γ[gh]		
Nasal	m		n			ń[ny],	ng		
Voiceless nasal						ńź[nzy]			
Lateral			l						
Voiceless lateral									
Flap or trill									
Voiceless flap									
Semivowels									

used in this book. These consonants were for the most part reasonable reconstructions. Not only was the philological and dialect evidence fairly clear, but the resulting system of the thirty-five or six distinctions had a reassuring look of reality about it. Surely Lu Fayan had read his characters with pronunciations not very different from these!

The reconstructed vowels, on the other hand, were a different matter. There were fifteen of them:

This was an exceedingly intricate system. It had six different kinds of *a*'s, for example. Could Chinese spoken in the seventh century really have been so complex? As Karlgren himself clearly realized, it was very unlikely that any single language or dialect could ever have had so many fine distinctions in pronunciations. He offered the following explanation: "The rhymes of *Qieyun* were set up by a linguist (or several linguists?) who was extremely well-trained, and he recorded all of the very delicate nuances of sound." In other words, Karlgren believed that Lu Fayan was a consummate phonetician who had fine-tuned his ear to hear the slightest differences in pronunciation, even those nondistinctive ones of which the speaker himself was normally unaware. In Karlgren's view, therefore, Lu had recorded every phonetic detail. But there was also at least another reason for this great complexity in the finals and the rhymes. *Qieyun*, as Lu Fayan had stated in his preface, was compiled from many sources. It represented a composite of the speech of many different areas, and the sum of all the distinctions was naturally greater than those of any one of the living dialects. Therefore, no matter how the *Qieyun* system might be interpreted, the result was bound to be complex. Still, this overabundance of vowels was the least satisfying part of Karlgren's reconstructions.

In the years and decades following the publication of *Études* there were naturally many criticisms and improvements on this monumental work, not a few by Karlgren himself. Some were the result of more and better information. Research was bound to lead to advances in the primitive state of dialectology and descriptive linguistics in China, and much better philological sources, too, were soon discovered. Karlgren had carried out all his research, for example, without once having seen *Qieyun* itself, relying completely on the Song redaction, *Guangyun*. In his day only fragments of *Qieyun* were known to exist. More recently, however, a Tang copy of *Qieyun* (which had apparently been pilfered somehow from the Palace Library) was found at a used bookstore, and this particular copy is a complete one. The newly discovered text has understandably led to improvements in our knowledge of Lu Fayan's language.

But other suggested changes in Karlgren's reconstructions were the result of different minds at work, and of different intellectual currents in linguistics. Karlgren was a proud man, and as the years passed he became increasingly intolerant of criticism. He was particularly disdainful of the American Structuralists, and of their tampering with his carefully constructed edifice. He believed that they had become obsessed with the "phonemic principle" and had reduced linguistics to an intellectual sport. "This craze is inconvenient and harmful," he declared in 1954, and was convinced that it would soon pass out of fashion. About that he was of course correct; for within a few short years of this prediction Noam Chomsky's Transformational Grammar had appeared on the American linguistic scene and largely swept away the classical Structuralist School. But what Karlgren could never have expected was that this new movement would not bring a return to the sober, data-oriented philology of his youth, but rather a far more extreme preoccupation with theoretical "breakthroughs" and formalisms. The era of the Sixties and early Seventies was a time when the best and brightest young minds of a generation indignantly scoffed at collecting data, unless it was for the express purpose of illuminating the general theory of human language. It is surely more than coincidence that these excesses of the linguistic community coincided roughly with the period of political radicalism on campuses around the world; at the same time that young American linguists were excoriating their elders for not being concerned with the right issues, Red Guards were rampaging in Karlgren's beloved China. This was not a movement with which Karlgren could sympathize and he discreetly let it pass without comment. He spoke out only once in the Sixties; the occasion was to oppose some revisions in his reconstructions suggested by Edwin Pulleyblank, an English-trained Sinologist whose highly individualistic brand of linguistics was still within the Structuralist framework. Among many suggestions, Pulleyblank had proposed reducing Karlgren's unwieldy number of vowels by reanalyzing a number of them as diphthongs. Karlgren found all of Pulleyblank's revisions unacceptable and labeled the diphthongs "eccentricities." After this one outburst, Karlgren refrained from critical comment on the work of his colleagues. He increasingly withdrew from the scholarly discussions of the field, and the debates surrounding his many works, which had now become classics, continued without him.

Middle Chinese (or Ancient Chinese), Karlgren's reconstructed language of the *Qieyun* dictionary, is the hub of our understanding of the history of Chinese. It is the oldest attested sound system. Still older stages of the language are adumbrated in ancient Chinese literature, of course—after all, Chinese writing was well over two thousand years old when Lu Fayan picked up his brush at the wine party that night. But where older works give only tantalizing hints, the *Qieyun* dictionary gives an explicit statement of the system of oppositions. The *fanqie*, cumbersome though they may be, make all the difference in the world. Without them the history of Chinese before modern times would be dark indeed.

Then, too, there is the relationship of Middle Chinese to the modern dialects. All of the major groups of dialects are related to each other through this system, and their individual historical developments are customarily described in terms of its categories. In the colloquial pronunciations of each and every part of the country—and especially in the Min dialect area—there are elements that predate the *Qieyun* system. But so far these traces of a more remote past remain more talked about than identified and correlated. From our time perspective it is almost impossible to separate out all these tiny strands from the greater *Qieyun* fabric. For the foreseeable future, at least, the dialects will continue to be described as the descendants of Middle Chinese.

As AN illustration of how Tang verse is thought to have sounded, the following poem is transcribed in a somewhat simplified version of Karlgren's reconstructions:

Ch'yun¹-miɑng⁵ Springtime-gaze	春望
Kuək p'ɑ⁵, shrɛn¹ ghɑ¹ dzəi³. nation broken mountains rivers be	國破山河在
Zyɛng¹ ch'yun¹, ts'ɑu³ muk syim¹. city springtime weeds trees deep	城春草木深
Kom³ zyi¹; xuɑ¹ tsiɛn⁵ lui⁵. grieve times flowers splash tears	感時花濺淚
Ghən⁵ byɛt; teu⁵ kiäng¹ sim¹. heartsick parting birds alarm heart	恨別鳥驚心

Piong¹-xuα³ liɛn¹   sαm¹-ngywät.   烽火連三月
beacon fires connect three-month

Ka¹-syiu¹   dei³ miän⁵-kyim¹.   家書抵萬金
home letters trade myriad gold

Bak-dou¹ sαu¹   käng⁵-tuan³,   白頭搔更短
white head scratch more short

Ghuən¹-yok piət-syiəng¹ chrim¹.   渾欲不勝簪
almost   not sustain hairpin

[TRANSLATION]

LOOKING AT SPRING

Our nation may be defeated, but our mountains and rivers are still there. In the city it may be spring, but the weeds and trees are thick. We are moved by the times; the flowers splash our tears. We are grieved by separation; the birds startle our hearts. Beacon fires have burned for three months in a row. For a letter from home I would pay ten thousand in gold. My white hair I've scratched till it is even shorter, so that it will almost not even hold a hairpin. —Written in 757, in Chang-an, by Du Fu when he was captive of the rebels.

OLD CHINESE

The language reflected in the earliest Chinese literature is called "Old Chinese." There are two main philological sources: (1) The rhymes in *The Book of Odes (Shī jīng)*, and (2) the phonetic hints provided by the structure of many Chinese characters. With information gleaned from these two types of materials, linguists have attempted to reconstruct Chinese spoken around the time of Confucius (550 B.C.) and earlier.

The Structure of Chinese Characters

An understanding of Old Chinese is based in large part upon the graphic relationships between Chinese characters. Although these symbols are not alphabetic, they do give certain clues to the pronunciation of Chinese because of the way that they are structured.

Writing is believed to have developed independently in China, but the pattern of development was the same as in the Middle East. In both cases the shapes of written symbols evolved out of simple drawings. In China such drawings can be found on fragments of ancient pottery that have been dated to around 2,000 B.C.; the designs were probably traditional and already ancient at that time. Similar pictures were also incised on many of the earliest bronzes. Some of the drawings were quite realistic, and it is often easy to see that they were intended to portray some animal, bird, or other natural object. But their meanings—if indeed they had meanings in a linguistic sense—are less clear, since the symbols appear to have been little more than decorations. They were not messages or texts to be read as language and so cannot be considered actual examples of writing. Rather, these pictures were the prototypes of Chinese characters.

The earliest authentic specimens of Chinese writing have been found on shells and bones dating from the second millennium B.C. These late Shang period artifacts are usually called "oracle bone inscriptions" because they were used mainly for divination. A question was inscribed on the plastron of a turtle or the scapula of a cow, then a prayer was offered and heat applied to the back. The cracks that formed in the shell or the bone were interpreted as divine messages. These oracle bones not only were used to foretell the future, however; they also served as records of certain kinds of events, which were then carefully stored in royal archives. In modern times around 100,000 shells and bones with inscriptions on them have been excavated. Altogether, these inscriptions contain a total of about 3,000 different characters, of which perhaps 800 have been conclusively deciphered.

The shell-and-bone characters represented writing in the true sense of the word. They were not pictures. Many of their shapes had evolved out of earlier pictographic designs, but the symbols themselves were no longer pictorial in nature. Indeed, Shang scribes seem to have deliberately distorted the shapes to produce a stylized effect. Perhaps the symbols seemed more mystical to the early Chinese when they did not look like familiar objects; in any event, the symbols had been transformed into abstractions without obvious reference points in the real world. Each of these abstract symbols was used to represent a word or morpheme in the Chinese language, not objects or ideas.

The early Chinese created an effective writing system out of stylized drawings by means of a crucial discovery. This discovery was the orthographic principle of the rebus. In twentieth-century Western society, rebus writing is relegated to the Sunday comic page or to riddles for children. In these rebus games a picture of an eye represents the pronoun 'I,' a lumberjack's saw stands for the verb 'saw,' a drawing of a duck's bill suggests the name 'Bill,' and so on until an entire English sentence emerges. But in early Chinese society, as well as in early Middle Eastern societies, the rebus was no game. Before the invention of the alphabet, the rebus was the most efficient way that people knew of to represent most words.

It was easy enough to write a single horizontal line to represent 'one,' or two lines to represent 'two'; but how could a scribe record the number 'ten thousand'? The solution that the Chinese hit upon was to use the stylized drawing of an insect much like a scorpion, because their word for this insect sounded like their word for 'ten thousand' (now pronounced *wàn* in Peking dialect). Thus, in an account book a picture of a scorpion indicated in rebuslike fashion the number that was meant. The word for 'that' (*qí*) sounded very similar to the word for 'winnowing basket' (*jī*) so that a schematic drawing of a basket could suffice for both; the graph for 'to come' (*lái*) was derived from the drawing of the near-homonym, '(a stalk of) wheat.' This kind of rebus association is the principle that underlies the structure of the majority of Chinese characters. For a comparable writing system, where the rebus principle is just beginning to be exploited, see the section on Naxi writing in Chapter 11.

One more orthographic technique was devised as a refinement on the rebus, however. This technique consisted of adding what is often called a "radical" to the borrowed character to give a hint as to the meaning. Since widespread use of 'borrowed characters' produced whole series of words transcribed with the same graph, there was potential for confusion; under these circumstances the addition of a second element was necessary to show which of the various homonyms or near-homonyms was being transcribed. In other words, the rebus-type association hinted at the pronunciation, and the radical gave an additional clue by hinting at the meaning. By forming compound graphs in this way, the Chinese were able to represent unambiguously any word in their language.

Here are some examples of how the system worked (the pronunciations given are those of modern Peking):

Rebus clue (phonetic)	Word	Graph	Meaning determinant (radical)
皮	pí 'skin, hide'	皮	
	pī 'split open'	披	扌 'hand'
	pí 'exhausted'	疲	疒 'disease'
	bì 'argue'	詖	言 'speech'
	pò 'break'	破	石 'stone'
	bǒ 'walk lame'	跛	足 'foot'
	bō 'wave'	波	氵 'water'
	bèi 'coverlet'	被	衣 'clothing'
	pō 'slope, bank'	坡	土 'earth'

弟	dì 'younger brother'	弟		
	tì 'glance at'	睇	目	'eye'
	tì 'shave'	剃	刂	'knife'
	tì 'weep, tears'	涕	氵	'water'
	tī 'wooden stairs'	梯	木	'wood'
	dì 'order, sequel'	第	竹	'bamboo'
干	gān 'shield'	干		
	gān 'liver'	肝	月	'flesh'
	gàn 'dusk'	旰	日	'sun'
	kān 'carve'	刊	刂	'knife'
	hàn 'drought'	旱	日	'sun'
	hàn 'sweat'	汗	氵	'water'

About 90 percent of all characters were made up this way. (Only a tiny fraction were ever directly derived from pictures.) The Chinese writing system is therefore structured almost entirely according to the phonetic principle of the rebus, and this fact can be used to investigate the pronunciation of earlier Chinese.

The Sounds of Old Chinese

What did Old Chinese sound like? Here there is much that remains in the realm of speculation. The facts surrounding Old Chinese are completely different from those of Middle Chinese, where the modern dialects reveal in detail what pronunciations were like. For Old Chinese, there is no comparable basis for reconstruction; its sounds can only be surmised by projecting the reconstructions for Middle Chinese back a thousand years in time. There is no key like *Qieyun* for Old Chinese. Nothing exists to tell us how many distinctions there were. We know only that if two words rhymed in *The Book of Odes* or are written with characters that share the same phonetic element, they must have once sounded similar. But the question is, how similar? What phonological features did they share and which ones made them different? Such questions cannot be answered with certainty, and so many of the most basic features of the language remain in doubt. For example, we do not know how many tones Old Chinese had. In the case of its better-known descendant Middle Chinese, we know with certainty that there were exactly four tone categories; we know because Lu Fayan explicitly listed them and gave the tone for every word in his dictionary. But since there is no comparable information for Old Chinese, we do not even know whether the language had any tones at all. Some linguists, in fact, now maintain that it did not; if they are right, the tones of Chinese developed only much later, as a kind of phonological compensation, when certain consonant distinctions at the end of the syllable were lost. The majority of Sinologists probably do not ascribe to this view, but few indeed can agree on how many tones Old Chinese did have. The issue is controversial and not likely to be resolved in the foreseeable future.

What we can be sure of is that Old Chinese was very different from Middle Chinese (and of course from the modern dialects). We know this to be true because in *The Book of Odes* many words rhyme that no longer did so later, at the Middle Chinese stage of the language. In the same way, characters in the same phonetic series were often read with quite different pronunciations by the time of Middle Chinese. For example, the character used to write *kam*[1] 'inspect,' with a consonant *k*, served as the phonetic for *lam*[1] 'indigo (blue)' and *lam*[3] 'see,' which had initial *l*'s. Similarly, *tsuət* 'soldier,' with a final *-t*, was the phonetic for *tswi*[5] 'drunk,' which had no final consonant at all; since the two words also rhymed with each other in *The Book of Odes*, their final sounds were undoubtedly close in Old Chinese.

From these kinds of facts linguists reason that simplifications must have taken place in the Chinese consonant system. They believe that unlike any variety of the language known today, Old Chinese had complex consonant clusters, such as **kl-*, **dr-*, and the like. It had a variety of ending consonants, such as perhaps **-s*, **-r*, and **-g*. There were almost surely prefixes, such as **s-* and **h-*, and probably suffixes as well. On the other hand, Old Chinese seems to have had far fewer vowels than Middle Chinese; some say as few as four. Vowel distinctions apparently proliferated before the time of Middle Chinese to offset the loss of so many consonant distinctions.

Today scholars offer a variety of alternative reconstructions for Old Chinese, and opinions differ as to which ones might be correct. For practical reasons the most widely used are still those of Bernhard Karlgren (whose name for Old Chinese was "Archaic Chinese"). As in the study of Middle Chinese, Karlgren was a pioneer in this area of Sinology as well. He was the first to produce a complete set of reconstructions for Old Chinese, and his are still the most accessible; an index to them is available in dictionary form in the 1940 volume *Grammata Serica*, as well as its 1957 revision, *Grammata Serica Recensa*. Other well-known reconstructions of Old Chinese include those of Dong Tonghe, Wang Li, Zhou Fagao, Edwin Pulleyblank, and Fang-kuei Li (Li Fanggui). Fang-kuei Li's reconstructions, in particular, have won praise in recent years for their internal consistency, as well as for their daring and innovative solutions to certain problems. However, Li has not yet published a dictionary of his reconstructions for Old Chinese, and so the reconstructions given by Karlgren in *Grammata Serica Recensa* remain more accessible to non-specialists.

FROM MIDDLE CHINESE TO PEKING MANDARIN

Each modern dialect developed differently. The principal changes that have shaped the standard dialect since Middle Chinese are as follows:

Tones

Two main changes have taken place in the tones. (1) The first, or "even" tone of Middle Chinese has become two separate tones in Mandarin. (2) The "entering tone" category has been completely lost.

(1) *Tone split.* Middle Chinese had four tone categories, called the "even tone" (*píngshēng*), the "rising tone" (*shǎngshēng*), the "departing tone" (*qùshēng*), and the "entering tone" (*rùshēng*). These are the "four tones" of Chinese tradition. (For the sake of convenience, linguists customarily assign the numbers 1, 3, and 5, respectively, to the first three of these tones, reserving the even numbers for the tones that later "split off" from these basic categories in most of the dialects. The last, or "entering," tone needs no number, because syllables in this category can be readily identified by their *-p*, *-t*, or *-k* ending consonants.)

At some point in time—at least by the late Tang—the Middle Chinese even tone "split"; that is, it became the Mandarin *first* tone in some words, and the Mandarin *second* tone in other words.

	Middle Chinese	*Peking*
'east'	tung¹	tung¹ (dōng)
'pass through'	t'ung¹	t'ung¹ (tōng)
'boy'	dung¹	t'ung² (tóng)
'agriculture'	nuong¹	nung² (nóng)

As can be seen from these examples, the split was caused by the phonetic quality of the initial consonant. A syllable with a *voiceless* initial consonant developed tone 1 in modern Mandarin, while a syllable with a *voiced* initial consonant developed tone 2.

(2) *The entering tone.* The Chinese have always regarded syllables that ended in *-p*, *-t*, or *-k* as being in a separate tone category, which they call the "entering tone." This treatment is not frivolous or illogical, though it may seem that way to most Westerners. In Middle Chinese, the syllables with these final stops, and *only*

the syllables with these final stops, never had an even, a rising, or a departing tone. In other words, they were not subject to the three-way pitch distinction that applied to all other syllable types. If the entering tone were not actually a tone of some kind, we would expect the syllables in that category to be evenly distributed among the three "real" tones the way other syllable types are. Whatever pitch shape syllables ending in -p, -t, or -k may have had, it was functionally distinct from the other three tones.

Peking Mandarin does not have an entering tone, because the final -p, -t, and -k stops of Middle Chinese have been lost in that dialect. The syllables that had originally been in that category acquired one of the other tones when the consonants were lost.

	Middle Chinese	Peking
'virtue'	tək	tə² (dé)
'six'	lyuk	liu⁵ (liù)
'kill'	shrat	shra¹ (shā)
'snow'	sywät	sywe³ (xuě)
'answer'	tap	ta² (dá)
'stand'	lyəp	li⁵ (lì)

Initials

The Middle Chinese initial system changed into that of Peking Mandarin through four important processes. (1) Under certain conditions the labials p-, p'-, and b- developed into f-; and, under the same conditions, initial m- was lost. (2) Voiced consonants became devoiced. (3) Certain consonants became pronounced with the tongue retroflexed, or retracted. (4) Velar consonants (k-, etc.) and dental affricates (ts-, etc.) became fronted and pronounced as the palatal consonants chy-, ch'y-, and sy-.

(1) Development of f. Middle Chinese did not have an f-. Instead, this Mandarin consonant developed out of certain occurrences of Middle Chinese p-, p'-, and b-. At the same time and under the same conditions, some Middle Chinese m-'s changed first into v-, then were lost entirely. This entire process, called "dentilabialization" by specialists, was the first of the major changes in the Middle Chinese consonant system.

CHANGE

	Middle Chinese	Peking
'is not'	pywei¹	fēi
'calf (of leg)'	bywei¹	féi
'literature'	myuən¹	wén

No Change

	Middle Chinese	Peking
'sad'	puai¹	bēi
Pei [a surname]	buai¹	péi
'gate'	muən¹	mén

(2) *Devoicing.* Middle Chinese had voiced consonants, but Mandarin has lost the feature of voicing on these consonants.

	Middle Chinese	Peking
'head'	dəu¹	t'ou² (tóu)
'bean'	dəuˢ	touˢ (dòu)
'accompany'	buai¹	p'ei² (péi)
'double'	buaiˢ	peiˢ (bèi)

As can be seen from these examples, the Mandarin consonant is aspirated in case the word had a first, or "even," tone in Middle Chinese; otherwise, the consonant is unaspirated.

(3) *Retraction.* Nine of the consonants of Middle Chinese are ordinarily reconstructed as palatals—that is, as consonants articulated with the blade of the tongue against the palate. They include the following: *ty-, t'y-, dy-, chy-, ch'y-, jy-, sy-, zy-,* and *ny-* (or *nzy-* if Karlgren's reconstruction is followed). Sometime before the fourteenth century these consonants became retracted, or retroflexed, and pronounced with the tip of the tongue against the palate. When this happened, the series merged with the consonants that had already been retroflexed in Middle Chinese: *chr-, ch'r, jr-,* and *shr-*. Today all of these consonants are pronounced as retroflexes in the Peking dialect (and are written *zh-, ch-, sh-,* and *r-* in Pinyin).

	Middle Chinese	Peking
'middle'	tyiung¹	chrung¹ (zhōng)
'numerous'	chyiungˢ	chrungˢ (zhòng)
'strong'	chriangˢ	chruangˢ (zhuàng)

(4) *Fronting.* The last major change was fronting. It took place in two stages. In the first part of the process, the velar consonants *k-, k'-, g-,* and *x-* became pronounced in the front of the mouth as palatal consonants *chy-, ch'y-,* and *sy-* (written *j-, q-,* and *x-* in Pinyin) whenever they were followed by an *i* or by the low front vowel *a*. In the latter case, a medial *-i-* developed between the initial and the *a*.

	Middle Chinese	Peking
'capital (city)'	kyəng¹	chyəng¹ (jīng)
'home'	ka¹	chyia¹ (jiā)

Shortly after the velars changed, the dental consonants *ts-, ts'-, dz-, s-,* and *z-* also changed. They became the same palatal consonants *chy-, ch'y-,* and *sy-* whenever they were followed by an *i*.

	Middle Chinese	*Peking*
'ford'	tsien[1]	chyin[1] (jīn)
'west'	siei[1]	syi[1] (xī)

This complex process of fronting did not begin to take place until after the fourteenth century. Many older Western spellings reflect the way Chinese place names were pronounced before the change: "Peking," for example, is the English name for what is now pronounced *Běijīng*; "Tientsin" is pronounced *Tiānjīn*; "Sian" is pronounced *Xī'ān*. Many Mandarin dialects outside of Peking have still not undergone the change. Also, the conservative stage pronunciations of Peking opera preserve artificially some of the earlier distinctions.

Finals

Middle Chinese had a very rich vocalism, and many vowel distinctions were lost before the formation of the Mandarin dialects.

The most important changes between Middle Chinese and modern Mandarin took place in the ending consonants. These changes radically affected the structure of the language.

(1) *The ending -m.* Sometime after the fourteenth century the ending *-m* merged with *-n*.

	Middle Chinese	*Peking*
'man, male'	nam[1]	nán
'difficult'	nan[1]	nán

(2) *The ending -p, -t, -k.* The Middle Chinese ending consonants *-p*, *-t*, and *-k* merged by the fourteenth century into a glottal stop. The glottal stop later disappeared completely, leaving no trace of the original consonants. This loss affected both the vowels and the tones.

	Middle Chinese	*Peking*
'white'	bɑk	bái
'abundant'	pak	bó
'north'	pǝk	běi
'answer'	tap	dá
'pull'	lap	lā
'end, tip'	muat	mò

8 CHINESE WRITING
  TODAY

> The Chinese script is so wonderfully well adapted to
> the linguistic condition of China that it is indispensa-
> ble; the day the Chinese discard it they will surrender
> the very foundation of their culture.
> —Bernhard Karlgren (1929)

Will the Chinese one day write with an alphabet? Many people in this century have thought so. In an open letter written around 1919, Hu Shih, for one, expressed the belief that phonetic writing was inevitable. To him, the coming of the alphabet appeared so likely he was concerned that the old characters might be phased out with too much haste. Other intellectuals of the time, especially leftists like Lu Xun, were convinced that alphabetization was necessary for China's survival; they looked forward hopefully to the day when Chinese would be completely Romanized.

The prospects for alphabetic writing soared with the victory of the Communists in 1949. The revolutionary ideal was then—and ostensibly remains today—the promotion of literacy through the abolition of characters and the substitution of some kind of alphabetic writing. Accordingly, on the eve of the Revolution, one supporter of the Latinization Movement ecstatically predicted that at long last China was about to be "liberated from the shackles of monosyllabic Chinese characters."

As soon as the new government consolidated power, script reform emerged as an important issue and discussions began. There were two concurrent approaches. The first approach was to design a new phonetic writing system; out of these plans eventually came the Pinyin system of spelling. The second approach to script reform was the simplification of characters, a measure originally represented as a supplementary expedient. Some of the more ardent advocates of Romanization objected to character simplification because they thought it would only divert attention from the main goal, which was the alphabet. But the argument that prevailed was that character simplification would not hinder but rather enhance phonetic writing. A reform of the characters would, it was explained, serve as a transition stage that would prepare people for the eventual changeover to an alphabetic system. Plans for both phonetic writing and character simplification thus began simultaneously.

In early 1950 it could be thought that the new Communist government was sincerely dedicated to a true revolution in letters. China seemed poised on the verge of what Turkey had experienced under the authoritarian reformer Kemal Ataturk. Yet, in retrospect, it is clear that even then most of the leaders of China were not committed to total change.

The turnaround in policy seems to have come in July of that year, when Mao Zedong gave instructions to begin the reform of the writing system with character simplification. After this point in time, the alphabet faded in importance. The Communists continued to pledge themselves to alphabetic writing, and in public pronouncements they reaffirmed that as the ultimate objective. Mao Zedong himself supported the plan. But while a phonetic writing system was held up as a distant ideal, character simplification became the practical task at hand. Within one year character lists had been drawn up, and by the next year—1951—a two-volume dictionary of simplified characters had been compiled. In 1952 an official Committee on Language Reform was established and given character simplification as its most urgent mission. It began work immediately and by 1954 research and planning in this area were complete. In 1956 the first official list of simplified characters was published.

Plans for the alphabet, meanwhile, moved at a much slower pace. Phonetic writing was not the priority of the Committee on Language Reform, and because of the long-range nature of the objective, there tended to be more theoretical discussion than pragmatic planning. One of the major stumbling blocks was nationalism, and for the first few years the Latin alphabet came under repeated attacks as something too "foreign." Mao Zedong had in his 1950 directive suggested that phonetic writing should be based upon the shapes of Chinese characters, and this idea appealed to nationalistic sentiments. Other factions were in favor of using the Cyrillic alphabet. After long and arduous debates alternative schemes were rejected; Romanization was approved; and in 1958 the Pinyin system of spelling was finally adopted. But by this time the issue was of minor importance. The Roman alphabet was not intended to be the primary writing system of China, and support for the traditional characters had grown ever stronger and more public. Guo Moruo, once one of the strongest supporters of the Latinization Movement, gave a speech in 1955 praising the role the characters had played in China's cultural heritage. In this speech Guo touched briefly on the official goal of alphabetic writing, but only to make it clear that the goal lay at a very great distance in the future. For a long time to come, he said, the Chinese people would have to continue to depend upon their own traditional writing system for culture and education and communication. Other high-ranking officials expressed similar views. Complaints that the revolutionary ideal had been betrayed were too weak and too late. The Chinese would not discard their script after all.

In a definitive report given on 10 January, 1958, Zhou Enlai made known what the government's policy toward writing was to be. It was the most revealing pronouncement on language that has ever come out of modern China. Zhou began his speech by announcing that top priority in government planning would be given to character simplification. As for the role of the newly developed alphabetic script, Zhou said: "At the outset, we should make clear that the purpose of Pinyin Romanization is to indicate the pronunciation of Chinese characters and to spread the use of the standard vernacular; it is not to substitute a phonetic writing system for the Chinese characters." Zhou did not defend the characters; he did not need to. He simply stated that they would continue to be used. Then, near the end of his speech, he had this to say:

> There is yet another question that troubles everyone; the question is, what is to become of the Chinese characters in the future? Historically, Chinese characters can never be eradicated; we are all agreed on this point. As for what will happen to Chinese characters in the future: Will they never again change? Should they change? Will the forms of the characters themselves change? Will they be replaced by phonetic writing? These are questions for which we shall be in no hurry to draw conclusions.

With these words Zhou shelved indefinitely all public debate on the future of Chinese characters. The issue was not one of the immediate tasks of writing reform, he said.

This 1958 report formalized the shift in emphasis of the reform program from alphabetic writing to character simplification. In his discussion Zhou Enlai gave this measure an air of legitimacy by describing the simplification of characters as a revolutionary action that had been opposed by "rightists." Just the opposite was true. No one had publicly criticized simplified characters because they were too radical; the main opposition had come from certain idealists on the Left who believed that priority should be given to phonetic writing. Character simplification was actually a reformist measure that fell short of the revolutionary ideal, and in effect it represented a victory for the more conservative factions.

Simplified Characters

The conscious distinction between simplified characters and complex characters is modern. In earlier centuries the important distinction for the writing of characters was between "vulgar characters" (súzì) and "correct characters" (zhèngzì). The correct characters were the prescribed standard forms. If a graph was not one of these standard characters, it would be thought of as vulgar, no matter whether it was simple or complex in terms of its number of strokes. The terms "simplified characters" (jiǎntǐzì) and "complex characters" (fántǐzì) themselves, so much a part of the modern Chinese vocabulary, are neologisms coined near the end of the nineteenth century.

The basic guide to simplified characters used in the PRC is the second, 1964 edition of Jiǎnhuàzì zōngbiǎo (A Comprehensive List of Simplified Characters). This edition superseded the much shorter list of 1956. Altogether, in its several tables, the 1964 list contains some 2,238 simplified characters, about a third of the seven to eight thousand total characters required to write modern Chinese.

In the year following publication, over five million copies of this definitive list were printed and distributed around the country. Through this act the Committee on Language Reform intended not only to propagandize the characters on the list, but also to bring simplification under some measure of control. New ways to write characters had proliferated with the suspension of old standards, and the committee had become concerned that unofficial variation was getting out of hand. In his 1958 report Zhou Enlai had fretted over this matter:

> In society now there is some confusion in the use of simplified characters. Some people on their own arbitrarily create simplified characters, and no one but they themselves may be able to read them, which is bad. The random creation of simplified characters has to be properly controlled. How one writes characters in making notes or in personal correspondence does not concern anyone else; however, when we write announcements or notices for everyone else to read, we should observe a uniform standard. In printed and typewritten documents, particularly, the random use of simplified characters must stop.

The publication of the 1964 list was meant to clarify what the limits were.

These limits again became obscure, however, with the beginning of the Cultural Revolution in 1966. Character simplification had been represented all along as a kind of Marxist, proletarian process; as a consequence, coining and using new characters became a popular way to show that one's writing was being done in right spirit. Wall slogans, signs, and mimeographed literature of all kinds began to be embellished with abbreviations never seen before. Within a short time the Committee on Language Reform has turned to the task of collecting characters "simplified by the masses" and in 1973 published a small dictionary called *Hànzì zhèngzì xiǎo zìhuì* that included many of these new forms. An expanded list was then under preparation, and a formal publication was targeted for some time around 1975. However, these plans were suspended after the death of Mao and the fall of the Gang of Four. The publication that emerged in 1977 was a reissue of the 1964 list with a "draft" list of new characters added as an appendix. In subsequent publications the draft appendix was withdrawn, and copies of the official list printed in the early 1980s are essentially reproductions of the 1964 list.

THE simplified characters used officially in the PRC come from a variety of sources but are seldom new creations. The majority, in fact, are printed adaptations of forms that have been used for centuries in shorthand or script. Hence, the work of the Committee on Language Reform was more one of selection than invention. Here are a few common examples:

	Complex form	Shorthand simplified form
tóu 'head'	頭	头
dāng 'just at'	當	当
chóu 'grievance'	讐	仇
gè ONE [a measure]	個	个
jiù 'old'	舊	旧
wàn 'ten thousand'	萬	万
lǐ 'ceremony'	禮	礼

The "running hand" or script styles of Chinese calligraphy provided the inspiration for many simplifications, either of whole characters or of recurring components.

	Complex form	Calligraphic simplified form
wéi 'become'	爲	为
shū 'book'	書	书
chē 'car'	車	车
mǎ 'horse'	馬	马
jiàn 'see'	見	见
mén 'door'	門	门

Some archaic variants of characters that had fewer strokes than their modern equivalents were made standard.

	Complex form	Archaic simplified form
zhòng 'multitude'	衆	众
shā 'kill'	殺	杀
wǎng 'net'	網	网
cóng 'follow'	從	从

Even simplified characters unfamiliar to the majority of literate Chinese often had a solid philological basis. A considerable amount of historical research went into the compilation of the simplified character lists. Librettos for popular dramas, old prints of colloquial novels, shop account books, medical prescriptions, and other kinds of texts and manuscripts were known to contain a wealth of little-used or forgotten abbreviations, and the committee was given a mandate to collect these and examine them for suitability. A systematic study of "vulgar characters" had already been done under the Nationalists during the 1930s, and researchers of the 1950s built upon this extensive earlier work. The result was that some rather specialized relics were revitalized and brought into the mainstream. Examples of obscure forms treated in this way include the characters now used to write *yin* and *yang*.

	Complex form	Simplified form
yīn 'yin [the feminine principle in nature]'	陰	阴
yáng 'yang [the masculine principle in nature]'	陽	阳

Here the complex right halves of the original characters were replaced, in the case of *yin* by the graph for 'moon' (月) to suggest the dark, the lesser, the feminine; and in the case of *yang* by 'sun' (日) to suggest the bright, the greater, the masculine. These two abbreviations were not in common use at the time of the Communist Revolution, but they were both found in the texts of colloquial novels dating from the fourteenth century.

The simplified characters that are genuinely new have usually been constructed by extending shorthand conventions. The easiest and most direct way to simplify was just to leave off parts of the original character. Here are a few examples:

	Complex form	Simplified form
xí 'practice'	習	习
fēi 'fly'	飛	飞
chǎng 'factory'	廠	厂

In other cases, a stroke or simple combination of strokes stands for a complex element, somewhat after the fashion of running-hand calligraphy.

	Complex form	Simplified form
bì 'currency'	幣	币
Dèng [a surname]	鄧	邓
shù 'tree'	樹	树

The most common simplification technique was to substitute for a complex element a simple character with a pronunciation that suggested the sound. This method was in essence a restructuring of the basic relationships that obtained between the characters. (Cf. "The Structure of Chinese Characters" in Chapter 7, above.)

	Complex form	Simplified form	Character used as phonetic loan
yì 'art, skill'	藝	艺	乙 (yǐ)
rèn 'recognize'	認	认	人 (rén)
tài 'form'	態	态	太 (tài)

Reducing the number of strokes needed to write a character was not the only kind of simplification. Yet another aspect of the language reform program was the elimination of graphic distinctions. According to traditional writing conventions, each of a very large number of homonymic syllables in modern Chinese had to be written with its own separate and individual graph. Now, syllables that are pronounced the same are sometimes written with the same character, especially if by doing so a complex character can be done away with. The morphemes lǐ 'inside' and lǐ '(Chinese) mile,' for example, are in today's orthography both represented by the single character 里. This particular character was once used only to write the lǐ which means 'mile'; but since the character for 'inside' (裏) was relatively complicated, the use of the simpler character was extended. Here are a few other cases where graphic distinctions have been leveled: The character 千 is used to write both qiān 'swing' (鞦) and qiān 'thousand' (千); the character 姜 is used for jiāng 'ginger' (薑) as well as for the surname Jiāng (姜); 谷 represents both gǔ 'millet' (穀) and gǔ 'valley' (谷); 系 is the character for xì 'related' (係), xì 'to tie' (繫), and xì 'system' (系). As can be seen from these examples, some of the traditional graphic distinctions were linguistically real. Gǔ 'millet' and gǔ 'valley' are quite different words even though they are pronounced the same, and writing them with the same graph negates one linguistic advantage the character system affords. But other graphic distinctions had questionable validity, and here the reform measures produced some desirable results. Though graphically distinct from earliest times, *xì* 'related,' *xì* 'to tie,' and *xì* 'system' are almost certainly etymologically related, and encouraging people to think of them as the same morpheme does away with much orthographic confusion.

Results of the Reforms

Character simplification is usually represented as progress in China's drive toward modernization. Yet, fundamental questions about this kind of script reform remain. How has the use of simplified characters contributed to literacy in China? More people can presumably read and write now, but that is not necessarily because the writing system is easier to learn. The experience of Taiwan where the literacy rate approaches that of Japan and other developed countries, and where simplified characters are scrupulously avoided in print, shows that the old system can be taught and taught well. To a very large degree, it has simply been assumed that the wider use of simplified characters has simplified the learning process. Very little evidence has been properly documented.

The number of symbols that must be learned in China today is approximately the same as before the reform. The characters have not been— nor can they easily be—significantly restricted in number the way they have been in Japan, where obscure words are represented by a phonetic notation. Moreover, simplified characters have not completely replaced the corresponding complex characters. For certain purposes the full forms of the characters are still preferred; in a series of footnotes, the official list of simplified characters makes explicit provisions for some of the older characters in cases where there is believed to be the possibility of confusion of meaning. Moreover, the tendency to use complex characters has increased in this more conservative, post-Gang of Four era. Historical and classical documents, such as the dynastic histories, are now printed in the traditional way without simplified characters. Deluxe editions of Mao Zedong's poetry are always written in classical style. Even in more ordinary printed materials a number of the old, complex characters may sometimes be seen.

For highly educated Chinese the language reform program does not represent a very significant change; one must still master both simplified characters and complex characters in order to be completely literate. The principal difference is the order in which the forms must be learned. In the old days the "correct" characters were studied first, in formal classes, and shorthand styles and abbreviations were learned either *sub rosa* or during the study of more advanced calligraphic styles. Now, lessons begin with the simpler forms, and many of the regular characters that they replaced are not seen until much later. Texts written in complex characters may sometimes be annoyingly slower going because of the reading habits formed earlier in life; but for the intellectual elite they are certainly readable.

For the less educated, however, the situation is different. Those people who spend the minimum number of years in school never see anything but simplified characters. To what extent have reform measures made their precious hours of formal training more effective? Has the amount of time spent memorizing characters been lowered appreciably? How much has the reduction in the number of strokes that make up the characters made them easier to recognize and remember? These are questions that have never been explored in any systematic way. The information that has come out of China has been almost completely anecdotal. Here are some examples of what Zhou Enlai said in his 1958 pronouncement on language reform to justify character simplification:

> When one old primary-school teacher in Henan introduced the simplified characters to his students, he told them that from now on they would write the first character in *fēng shōu* 'good harvest' in its simplified form—three horizontal strokes and one vertical stroke. The children were very happy, they clapped their hands and cheered. A worker in Tientsin said that he had been trying to learn the three characters for *jìn* 'all, entirely,' *biān* 'side, boundary,' and *bàn* 'to do, handle, attend to' for a long time but he could never remember them; when he could simplify them to [the new forms], he could remember them immediately.... When Comrade Li Fenglian sent a book of simplified characters to her brother, he was very happy and replied, "These new characters are much easier to learn," and he scolded his sister for not having sent the book to him sooner.

The only real studies conducted before the reforms went into effect seem to have been statistical ones showing the average number of strokes saved by simplified characters in running texts.

Fewer strokes make writing faster but not always easier to learn. The elements that recur in Chinese characters can be useful to the memory. The character for *yán* 'speech' consists of seven squarish strokes: 言. As a full character it is considered simple enough and so there it has not been touched by the reform. But when this same graphic element is used as a radical, as it is in a host of common characters, it has been simplified to two flowing calligraphic lines: 讠. This change effects a tremendous savings in stroke count in a running text, but now there are two elements meaning 'speech' instead of one that must be learned. The same is true of *shí* 'food,' which is represented by 食 and 饣; of *jīn* 'metal,' written 金 and 钅; and of a number of other graphs. A stroke saving that seems particularly counterproductive is the simplification of common characters but not graphically related ones that occur less frequently. A typical example is the character for the everyday word *ràng* 'let, allow," which has been simplified from 讓 to 让. Here the phonetic element 襄, with seventeen strokes, has been abbreviated to something with only three strokes. But the same element appears in its full form in 瓤 *ráng* 'pulp,' 壤 *rǎng* 'soil,' 嚷 *rǎng* 'make up uproar,' 囊 *náng* 'bag,' 齉 *nàng* 'snuffle,' and a number of other characters. These complex characters do not occur frequently enough to affect the number of strokes in a text significantly, but by the same token they are that much harder to remember. If the phonetic element still appeared in its full form in 'let, allow,' the frequency of that common character would reinforce the memorization of the more obscure characters.

Equally deserving of attention are the mechanics of reading, which are different from the process of learning how to write characters. Some studies on the perception of Chinese characters have been conducted in Japan, but the results may or may not obtain for Chinese subjects. One finding that would seem to apply more or less universally is the discovery that eye movements for horizontal writing are smoother than those for vertical writing. The decision of the PRC to print texts in horizontal lines instead of the traditional vertical lines would therefore seem to be one that facilitates the reading process.

A simplification in the shapes of words does not necessarily increase legibility. Studies on the Roman alphabet indicate that just the opposite may be the case. Although differences in type style seem to have little effect on legibility, texts written in lower-case letters are read far more easily than texts printed all in capitals. This greater legibility is thought to be due to the variety ascending and descending lower-case letters give to word shapes as compared to the block outlines of capitals. For reading, it is not simplicity or complexity that is important, but rather relative confusability. Lowercase *c* and *e*, for example, are Roman letters that are easy to confuse. Are 辦 *bàn* 'do, handle' and 爲 *wéi* 'do, act' more easily confused now that they are written 办 and 为? What about 旧 *jiù* 'be old' and 归 *guī* 'return'—or is the context always foolproof? There is much that we do not know about how Chinese read.

CHINESE characters have recently been the object of script reform in most of the countries of East Asia. The Vietnamese stopped writing with them altogether in the early part of the twentieth century, choosing instead to Romanize using the missionary-inspired *quoc-ngu* system. Chinese writing has also disappeared in North Korea, where the Korean alphabet has been in exclusive use since the end of World War II. In South Korea, the characters have fared somewhat better, and the old, "correct" forms are still being used there, mixed in with the native alphabet in newspapers, technical works, and specialized writings of various kinds. But their existence in South Korea is precarious. Energetic, nativist opponents continue to press for their abolition, and Ministry of Education policy changes with every shift of the political winds. As a result, education in Chinese characters is disorganized and spotty at best. In Japan, including the Ryukyus, reforms were instituted during the Allied occupation. The principal reform came in 1946, when the Japanese Cabinet and Ministry of Education promulgated a list of 1,850 characters restricting the number of characters in government and general public use. The document was entitled *Tōyō kanji hyō* (Table of Chinese characters to be used for the time being) in anticipation of more thoroughgoing reforms, but it was not superseded until 1981, when an expanded list of 1,945 characters was issued. This latter list is called the *Jōyō kanji hyō* (Table of Chinese characters for common use), showing that it was drawn up in a spirit quite unlike that of the earlier, "temporary" list. The *Jōyō kanji* also differ from the *Tōyō kanji* in that they are intended to serve as guidelines, not as absolute restrictions. Thus, it would seem that the future of Chinese characters has become more secure in Japan. Still, even in that conservative country important changes have taken place. A great many of the characters that appear on the *Tōyō kanji* and *Jōyō kanji* lists are simplified characters. Although these simplifications are almost invariably "vulgar" abbreviations that have been used in China and Japan for centuries, they rarely take the same form as the simplified characters that were adopted a few years later in China. The only countries where the general public still uses the traditional, "correct" Chinese characters on a daily basis are the peripheral Chinese communities of Taiwan and Hong Kong.

In China itself, the future of Chinese characters seems settled for now. Further changes do not seem to be in the offing. Given the conservative nature of the present regime, it is unlikely that the government will institute many more simplifications. Nor can one reasonably expect a restoration of the complex characters, especially since the Nationalist government in Taiwan actively promotes itself as the champion of these traditional forms. A small but vocal minority continues to advocate the wider use of Pinyin, and these reformers have recently joined forces with young computer specialists who believe that Romanization would smooth the development of modern technology. The arguments of this latter group are new and compelling and may yet make an impression on pragmatic leaders frustrated with trying to mechanize the cumbersome traditional writing system. Such an eventuality does not appear very likely, however, because the overwhelming majority of the Chinese people at all levels seem content with the present system. Yet, there are those both in China and in the West as well who believe that it is only a matter of time before the characters must give way to a simpler system of writing. If they are right, that day would bring easier access to literacy for China's citizens, as well as increased internationalization of China's culture. But, at the same time, these advantages would be at a cultural cost far higher than the present generation of Chinese would ever be willing to pay.

PART II THE MINORITY LANGUAGES OF CHINA

9 THE CHINESE AND THEIR NEIGHBORS

"The people of China are all one nationality."
—Sun Yat-sen (1924)

"Our country is a land of many nationalities."
—PRC publication, dated 1981

The borders that China claims today derive from events that took place two hundred years ago. Between 1755 and 1792, imperial armies waged a series of successful wars and campaigns against native groups on almost all of the Empire's frontiers. The results were dramatic. By the end of the Qianlong period in 1795, the Qing imperial government controlled Chinese Turkestan, Mongolia, Tibet, and all of South China from Yunnan to Taiwan. Never before had any Chinese domain been so large. It was a high-water mark that established permanently, as far as the Chinese are concerned, the traditional boundaries of their country.

CHINA still has the ethnic and territorial composition of the Empire. The People's Republic controls virtually all of the possessions of the Qing dynasty, and these territories extend far beyond lands occupied by Han Chinese. In the frontier regions inherited from the Empire can be found a wide variety of ethnic and linguistic groups who have not been assimilated into the Chinese nation. Outside of China's heartland and yet within her international boundaries live Tibetans, Mongols, Kazakhs, Uighurs, Tais, Koreans, Manchus, and many other groups and races who are different from each other and from the Han. In a world neatly divided into nations and states, these people are Chinese—and yet they are not Chinese. They live in China and are citizens of the People's Republic, but they are not the heirs of Chinese civilization, literature, history, or tradition. In the modern Chinese state, the non-Han people left over from the Qing Empire have become the national minorities.

The government of the People's Republic presently recognizes fifty-six distinct ethnic, religious, and linguistic groups among its citizenry, and only one of these is the Han, that group of people traditionally known as the "Chinese." The other fifty-five are minorities. Of course, the Han are overwhelmingly greater in number than all of the minorities combined.

Theirs is also the national language, history, and culture of China. But the sixty-seven million non-Han citizens of China are far from a negligible constituency, even in a country of over a billion people. The Chinese government puts each of its fifty-six different nationalities on a theoretically equal footing and considers its minorities to be just as much *Zhōng-guórén*, or "People of the Middle Country," as the Han are. This means that the word "Chinese" has now been redefined along the lines of citizenship, and its use as an ethnic term is actively discouraged. The ethnic majority is officially referred to as the "Han."

Instead of Chinese culture—which is now supposed to be used only in connection with the customs and trappings of the modern Chinese Communist state—there is "Han culture." Instead of the Chinese language, there is the "Han language" (*Hànyǔ*), a word that had always been used in the same meaning but with a slightly literary flavor. And so on. But how far these new definitions have penetrated into actual usage can be questioned; even in official sources inconsistencies can be found, and in dealing with foreigners, of course, the word "Chinese" must almost always be used in its older, more familiar meaning. But the efforts of the government to apply the name "Chinese" to all its citizens show the importance it places upon the minorities.

The minorities also enjoy theoretical autonomy. The areas in which they live have been designated by the government to be autonomous regions, counties, and districts, thus making China, at least on paper, a multinational, federal state on the pattern of the Soviet Union.

There are good reasons for the attention the minorities receive. The territories that they occupy comprise over half of the country's total land area. These territories also form the strategically important frontier regions that lie along the borders that China shares with the Soviet Union, India, and Vietnam. For the most part, the lands are thinly settled, sometimes only by nomads, and so offer hope for relief from population pressures in China's heartland. The minority areas also contain most of China's mineral and forest resources, as well as over 80 percent of the herds of livestock from which the country derives its meat and wool. Properly exploited, these lands could considerably enrich the material well-being of all of China's citizens, Han and non-Han alike.

But the minorities are important not only for the lands that they occupy. Their condition is essential for the image that the People's Republic wishes to project to the world. Minorities happily and enthusiastically integrated into the life and functioning of the Chinese state are the best kind of advertisement for a successful and benevolent government.

But discontent, or worse, open rebellion—such as the Tibetan revolt of 1959—can be an embarrassment of serious proportions. When an estimated seventy thousand Uighurs, simultaneously pressured by the government to institute social reforms and attracted by a higher standard of living, fled across the lightly guarded Xinjiang border in the early 1960s to join their brethren living in the Soviet Union, the result was a major propaganda victory for the Soviets at Chinese expense. On the other hand, there was great rejoicing in Peking in 1974 when members of a minority militia participated in the capture of a Soviet helicopter; the event was highly publicized, and the Chinese press made much of the alleged determination of those people to defend their homeland against aggression. The minorities have political power, both real and potential, that must be constantly reckoned with in China today.

The authorities have therefore been cautious in how they implement policy. Special concessions are granted to minorities; rules that apply to the Han majority are often suspended. Until quite recently, for example, minorities were exempt from the draconian laws on birth control, and even today local cadres in places like Xinjiang are probably wary of pushing strict adherence to the rules for fear of precipitating political unrest. Divorce laws, especially in the case of Muslims, and sumptuary laws regulating funerals do not affect most minorities. Minorities also enjoy certain rights and privileges not granted to Han Chinese. They often have preferential treatment, for example, in the case of university and professional school admissions along guidelines not completely unlike those of the affirmative action policies implemented in American educational institutions, and analogies could be drawn on several levels. Such policies seem justifiable and perhaps laudable in certain cases, because non-Han people do not usually speak the standard language natively, and, since they often live in very underdeveloped areas, the primary and secondary educational facilities available to them may sometimes be far inferior to those in Han areas. But some minority privileges, such as the higher stipends granted to non-Han students, are difficult to explain in these terms.

Minorities are officially encouraged to preserve their own languages and cultures, and a great number of pronouncements have been released reaffirming their rights to do so. The 1954 Constitution has several articles to this effect. In designated minority areas, the government recognizes local languages as official media of communication, and they are used by the state in its dealings with the populace in those areas. Even Han Chinese working there are required to learn the local language (though it is unclear what level of fluency is deemed sufficient or how strictly the requirement is observed—some say it is often ignored). The medium of education in elementary school is the minority language for the first three years, and it is taught as a subject through middle school. In minority areas, such things as newspapers, books, and magazines are often published in the local languages, and in Peking the Nationalities Publishing House (Mínzú Chūbǎnshè) regularly issues books in the five major minority languages: Tibetan, Mongolian, Uighur, Zhuang, and Korean. Similarly, local radio stations broadcast in minority languages as well as in Chinese, and the Central Broadcasting System in Peking puts together programming in the major minority languages.

Language usages also reflect politics. We have already mentioned that the word "Chinese" is used in a way that implies equality among the various groups. The standard language is no longer called the "National Language" (Guoyu), as it was in Republican days (and still is on Taiwan), but rather the "Common Language" (Putonghua). The Chinese names of some groups have been changed from words with pejorative connotations to more positive, or at least neutral, terms. The old name "Lolo," which referred to a large Tibeto-Burman group in South China, was once used condescendingly by the Chinese and has therefore since been replaced by the name "Yi" in Communist usage. The Jingpo, another Tibeto-Burman people, are no longer—at least in public— known as the "Wild Men" (Yěrén). The word 'Fān' was formerly used by the Chinese almost innocently in the sense of 'aborigines' to refer to ethnic groups in South China, and Mao Zedong himself once used it in 1938 in a speech advocating equal rights for the various minority peoples. But that term has now been so systematically purged from the language that it is not to be found (at least in that meaning) even in large dictionaries, and all references to Mao's 1938 speech have excised the offending word and replaced it with a more elaborate locution, "Yao, Yi, and Yu." "Tribe" (bùluò), a somewhat demeaning word frequently used by Chiang Kai-shek, has disappeared from general use. Potentially dangerous words such as "assimilation" (tónghuà) have been changed to euphemisms such as "amalgamation" (rónghé) when applied to minorities, and the dictionary entries for the older terms are predictably prescriptive; the definition of the expression tónghuà zhèngcè, for example, is now given as "the policy of national assimilation (as pursued by reactionary rulers)," implying that such policies do not exist in socialist states. Graphic pejoratives, the most common way the Chinese used to write the names of peoples they considered inferior, have been purged from the writing system. The "beast-radical," for example, which was once attached as a meaning determinative to the characters for such names as "Yao," has been replaced by radicals that are less offensive.

The People's Republic prides itself on the independence and the evenhanded treatment it gives its minorities. And, with certain shameful exceptions, such as the persecutions that took place during the Great Leap Forward and the Cultural Revolution, it is true that the Communist government has been reasonably cognizant of the sensibilities of its non-Han peoples. But there are limits to the amount of local autonomy that it can allow. Modernization obviously demands the sacrifice of some local color—such as the belief of the Wa that crops will not grow unless fertilized with a freshly severed Han Chinese head. Nor can some extreme forms of social stratification, such as the complex slave-owning society of the Yi, be completely left alone. Many of the religious practices of the Tibetans have fallen victim to the same kind of reasoning. But then too, the state orthodoxy demands interference in a variety of other matters as well: Heretical teachings are as much anathema to Communist dogma as they are to that of other state religions. Minorities are indeed free to hear broadcasts and read books and speak in their own languages. But what about the content? Old themes and old stories have been replaced by translations of the same subject matter the Han read, hear, and say. The "folk songs" that are sung by troupes of minority performers may often be in the minority's own language, but the themes of the lyrics are now "revolutionary."

Even with the best of intentions, the Chinese cannot help but alter the languages and cultures of all these peoples. Even improvements in the quality of life, especially better transportation, communication, and education, all serve to strengthen the links to Peking and inevitably to weaken the fibers of local life. There may be official toleration toward those who do not learn the standard language, but those who succeed in the society are not those who remain stubbornly nationalistic at the expense of learning the standard language, Putonghua. The only way to get advanced skills and training is to master Chinese—Han Chinese—and reports of minority groups "learning it enthusiastically" are surely not all exaggerated. The sheer weight of 950 million people and the vitality of Chinese civilization are bound to be felt even in the remotest corner of the country.

This does not mean, of course, that all the citizens of China will one day register themselves as Han nationals. Tibet is unlikely to be absorbed into China in spite of the maps cartographers draw, and the Mongols can always verify their separate identity through the existence of the Mongolian People's Republic next door. Those groups with strong ethnic identities will probably continue to have them. The question is how much the minorities will have to sacrifice in order to participate in the greater Chinese system.

THE CLASSIFICATION OF THE MINORITIES

The Chinese do not have a strong tradition of ethnography. In imperial days the authorities considered it necessary to know only enough about the non-Han peoples to keep them under control, and the attitude of the court toward its subjects can most generously be described as benign neglect. When the last imperial government was overthrown, the new Chinese leaders began to take more interest in the identity of the peoples under their control. They gave the country the sobriquet "The Republic of Five Nationalities" and made their national flag with five stripes, one for the Han and the other four for the Mongols, Manchus, Tibetans, and Tatars. (The PRC flag today continues the tradition with five stars instead of five stripes.) But extraordinarily little was actually known about the minorities at the time, as this rather simplistic classification into what were thought to be four representative groups shows. Large areas of China were then ethnographically unmapped and unexplored, and the Nationalist government was never in a position to do much about it.

Major ethnographic research began in China when the Communists consolidated control of the country in 1950. Among the Soviet advisors to the Chinese were many excellent, well-trained ethnographers, and under Soviet guidance the new government immediately launched an investigation of minority languages. There were three announced aspects to the program: (1) the development of writing systems for languages that had never been written down and the introduction of systems of Romanization for languages that were being written with other kinds of writing systems; (2) scientific research into the spoken languages; and (3) the training of language cadres. The project continued for a while, and at the end of the first ten years, forty-two languages were said to have been studied and about a dozen writing systems worked out.

In 1956 the scope of investigation was broadened beyond language with the beginning of long-term social history projects for the various minority groups. There were eight different areas to be investigated: Sichuan, Yunnan, the Northwest, Guizhou-Hunan, the "Tibetan Region," Guangxi-Guangdong, Inner Mongolia, and the Northeast, each of which would have a separate team of investigators. Around two hundred people were involved in the projects, including experts from a variety of fields, such as anthropology, history, literature, music, and art. Though it had other objectives as well, the primary purpose of the investigation was simply to list and classify the various minority groups.

Up until the time that the projects began, no one had agreed on just how many minorities there were in China. In 1950 one authority had guessed that there might be over a hundred groups, but other estimates varied widely. When voters in the elections of 1954 were asked to report their nationality, hundreds of names were submitted. The situation continued to be chaotic until the late fifties, at which time the names and numbers began to stabilize, presumably because of the official findings of the projects. Since then, the list of minorities has slowly gotten longer as new names have been added; forty-five minority groups were reported in 1956, forty-six in 1957, fifty-one in 1959, and fifty-three in 1963. As of 1981, there were fifty-five names on the official list, the tiny group of Vietnamese living in China (they are known as the Gin) and the Jino of Yunnan Province in Southwest China having most recently been granted minority status.

The government projects of the 1950s thus produced results, and, because of them, more is known about the peoples of China than was ever the case in the past. But there is still much more to be learned. The projects were only a first step, and yet little was done beyond them over the next two decades. The enthusiasm for ethnography that Soviet colleagues attempted to plant in Chinese soil in the fifties appeared at first to take firm root, but the xenophobic excesses of Chinese politics in the Sixties soon brought a halt to most serious scholarship. The information that had been flowing out of China slowed to a trickle and then effectively stopped. Until recently a formal listing of names and numbers and places seemed to have satisfied most of the Chinese curiosity about the peoples with whom they share their country.

The official list of the minorities is still the foundation for systematic study. It therefore takes on an importance far beyond simple classification. It has become the basis of much of our knowledge of the ethnic composition of China. The list itself is no mean accomplishment, of course. The censuses and surveys that went into its compilation were carried out on a geographical scale unknown in China before that time, and it represents the marshalling and distillation of a great deal of information. Yet in order to know how it should be interpreted, some important questions still need answers. Perhaps most fundamentally,

THE OFFICIALLY RECOGNIZED NATIONALITIES OF CHINA

Name of Group	Population	Language Family	Location
Achang	20,441	Tibeto-Burman	South: Yunnan
Bai	1,131,124	—	South: Yunnan
Bao'an	9,027	Mongolian	North: Gansu
Benglong	12,295	Mon-Khmer	South: Yunnan
Blang	58,476	Mon-Khmer	South: Yunnan
Bouyei (*see* Buyi)			
Bulang (*see* Blang)			
Buyi	2,120,469	Tai	South: Guizhou
Dagur	94,014	Mongolian	North: Manchuria
Dai	839,797	Tai	South: Yunnan
Daur (*see* Dagur)			
Dong (*see* Kam)			
Dongxiang (*see* Santa)			
Drung	4,682	Tibeto-Burman	South: Yunnan
Dulong (*see* Drung)			
Elunchun (*see* Oroqen)			
Evenki	19,343	Tungus	North: Manchuria
Gaoshan (*see* Kaoshan)			
Gelao	53,802	—	South: Guizhou
Gin	11,995	—	South: Guangxi
Han (Chinese)	950,000,000	Sinitic	countrywide
Hani	1,058,836	Tibeto-Burman	South: Yunnan
Hezhen	1,476	Tungus	North: Manchuria
Hoche (*see* Hezhen)			
Hui	7,219,352	Sinitic	countrywide
Jing (*see* Gin)			
Jingpo	93,008	Tibeto-Burman	South: Yunnan
Jino	11,974	Tibeto-Burman	South: Yunnan
Kam	1,425,100	Tai	South: Guizhou
Kaoshan	1,549	Austronesian	Taiwan
Kazakh	907,582	Turkic	North: Xinjiang
Kirghiz	113,999	Turkic	North: Xinjiang
Korean	1,763,870	—	North: Manchuria
Lahu	304,174	Tibeto-Burman	South: Yunnan
Lhopa	2,065	Tibeto-Burman	Tibet
Li	817,562	Tai	South: Hainan
Lisu	480,960	Tibeto-Burman	South: Yunnan
Loba (*see* Lhopa)			
Lolo (*see* Yi)			
Manchu	4,299,159	Tungus	North
Maonan	38,135	Tai	South: Guangxi
Miao	5,030,897	Miao-Yao	South
Monba (*see* Monpa)			
Mongolian (proper)	3,411,657	Mongolian	North

Name of Group	Population	Language Family	Location
Monguor	159,426	Mongolian	North: Qinghai
Monpa	6,248	Tibeto-Burman	Tibet
Moso (*see* Naxi)			
Mulam	90,426	Tai	South: Guangxi
Mulao (*see* Mulam)			
Nakhi (*see* Naxi)			
Naxi	245,154	Tibeto-Burman	South: Yunnan
Nu	23,166	Tibeto-Burman	South: Yunnan
Orochon (*see* Oroqen)			
Oroqen	4,132	Tungus	North: Manchuria
Primi	24,237	Tibeto-Burman	South: Yunnan
Pumi (*see* Primi)			
Qiang	102,768	Tibeto-Burman	South: Sichuan
Russian	2,935	Indo-European	North: Xinjiang
Salar	69,102	Turkic	North: Qinghai
Santa	279,397	Mongolian	North: Gansu
She	368,832	Miao-Yao	South: Fujian
Shui (*see* Sui)			
Sibo (*see* Xibo)			
Sui	286,487	Tai	South: Guizhou
Tajik	26,503	Indo-European	North: Xinjiang
Tatar	4,127	Turkic	North: Xinjiang
Tibetan	3,870,068	Tibeto-Burman	Tibet
Tu (*see* Monguor)			
Tujia	2,832,743	—	South: Hunan
Uighur	5,957,112	Turkic	North: Xinjiang
Uygur (*see* Uighur)			
Uzbek	12,453	Turkic	North: Xinjiang
Va (*see* Wa)			
Vietnamese (*see* Gin)			
Wa	298,591	Mon-Khmer	South: Yunnan
Xibo	83,629	Tungus	North
Yao	1,402,676	Miao-Yao	South
Yellow Uighur	10,569	Turkic	North: Gansu
Yi	5,453,448	Tibeto-Burman	South
Yugur (*see* Yellow Uighur)			
Zang (*see* Tibetan)			
Zhuang	13,378,162	Tai	South: Guangxi
Other national minorities (still to be identified)	879,201		

NOTE: Population figures are for 1982. All of the groups on the list have distinctive language(s) except the Hui, who are distinguished from the Han Chinese by their Muslim religion and customs only.

we need to know more of what constitutes a nationality in the People's Republic of China. How does a name get on the official list? From time to time, the names of other minority groups appear in Chinese publications—why are they not on the list?

The best information on the subject of nationality can still be found in a series of articles co-authored in 1956 by Fei Xiaotong and Lin Yuehua, two of the leaders of the social history projects. Fei and Lin's articles are not an explicit statement of how later decisions must have actually been made, but they are the best indication we have for what the authorities consider a nationality to be. In their discussion of how a minority was to be defined, Fei and Lin attempted to follow the general criteria laid down by Stalin: common language, common territory, economic ties, and psychological factors. In the end, however, the authors were unable to give hard and fast guidelines for how these criteria were to be applied. They went to great lengths to stress the difficulties involved in deciding which factors would be decisive in any particular case. But they did give some specific examples of actual decisions that were made, and these are perhaps the most helpful part of the work. In any event what Fei and Lin were clearest about was that the existence of a minority was not automatically established simply because a particular group considered itself to be one. Such decisions had to be made by the competent authorities and only after all the relevant facts of each case had been duly considered.

Fei and Lin's articles illustrate just how difficult and, finally, how arbitrary many of the decisions in such a taxonomy must be. In determining whether a group is a separate nationality, linguistic factors provide the best metric. But even speech is by no means an infallible indicator of what groupings should be made. How is one to decide when dialect differences become great enough to constitute different languages? (Recall the situation with Han Chinese itself!) One of Fei and Lin's examples was the case of the Miao. The Miao are scattered throughout South China, and the dialect differences among the various groupings are great enough to make communication difficult, and sometimes impossible. They could therefore be said to speak several different languages and, as a result, to form separate minority groups. But it is well known that the various groups of Miao all once spoke the same language, and that the differences are due to the fact that they have been separated from each other for a long time. Consequently, the Miao have been properly classified as a single nationality. And yet such a historical relationship is surely not sufficient grounds for classifying other groups together, or else, for example, all the speakers of the many Tibeto-Burman languages could be classified as but a single minority group.

There is also the problem of the relative degree of assimilation into another group—particularly the Han. Throughout Chinese history the Han have been gradually absorbing the people with whom they have come into contact, and that process is still going on. (Cf. Chapter 3.) This absorption is not a quantum change, but rather an almost imperceptible one that takes place over many generations. Many people living next to or in Han areas are probably only dimly, if at all, aware that they are different from their neighbors. If they have their own language, more often than not they also have fluency in the local variety of Han speech as well. Moreover, how are they supposed to know that their own language is not a kind of Han dialect itself? The Tujia, a Tibeto-Burman people living among Han groups in the northwestern part of Hunan Province, were not "discovered" until 1956 in spite of the fact that they numbered well over half a million. The official explanation given for their long anonymity was that they had hidden their identity out of fear of suppression by the Nationalists. But surely an equally plausible explanation is that neither they nor their Han neighbors had ever thought of them as being "non-Han." Other groups are reported to have applied for minority status only to be told that they were in fact Han, and that the reason they were different from other Han groups was that their speech and customs had diverged over the years; a comparative linguistic study was said to have revealed that their language was actually a dialect of Chinese.

The same is true of the individuals that make up a nationality. Intermarriage and living in close contact tend to blur the boundaries between groups so that many people are difficult to assign to one or the other. How are the so-called hyphenated groups, such as the "Tibetan-Han," to be classified? By the official count, the Tai group living in southern China known as the Zhuang has more members than any other ethnic group in China except the Han. But most of its more than thirteen million assigned members are said to consider themselves Han. Of 152 clans examined in one district of Guangxi Province, not one claimed to be non-Han. Many are reported to be so anxious to be Chinese they have falsified genealogical records in order to find a suitable Han ancestor. How all the false claims were separated from the real ones we are not told. In any case, if the Zhuang are so well assimilated, one wonders why the borderline cases were not permitted to go ahead and register as Han if they so desired. As the count stands, the Zhuang appear to be more important than the Tibetans, who are less than a third as numerous, but who are an incomparably more distinct nationality.

In the end, many decisions have to be made at least in part on the basis of personal judgment, and that surely must have been true in the case of the classifications made by Chinese authorities. Some decisions seem to have been politically motivated. The surveys turned up several million Manchus, in spite of the fact that Manchu is virtually an extinct language. Even "Henry" Pu-yi, the last male head of the Manchu royal house, was said to have known only a few greetings in Manchu. By finding so many hidden Manchus, the government was able to show how much the minority had been suppressed by the old Nationalist regime, which had been particularly proud of the fact that the Manchus were so well assimilated. The Hui, that powerful group of Chinese Muslims, are given nationality status in spite of the fact that they share a common language with the Han and live in the same areas. A few are thought to have ancestors among the soldiers of the Arab army that was sent by the caliph to help the Tang emperor during the An Lushan rebellion. But by far the majority have only Han ancestry. The Hui are a conspicuous and very devout religious group, but still a religious group nonetheless. They are neither somatically nor linguistically different from the Han. The fact that they are the only religious group recognized as a national minority by Peking is certainly not unrelated to the trouble that all Chinese governments in the past have had controlling them: Hui holy wars against the Han were still being reported in the 1950s.

The term "Hui" has also been used as a convenient label for groups of Muslims who have otherwise not been properly identified. On the southernmost tip of Hainan, the large egg-shaped island lying atilt off the South China coast, there is a village called Sanya where a small community of several thousand Muslims live. These Sanya villagers are officially classified as Hui. But, as we know from the reports of Hans Stübel, the German ethnographer who accidentally discovered them in the 1930s, these Muslims speak a language completely different from any other so far known to exist in China. Who the Sanya are and where they came from remains a mystery. According to their own traditions, their ancestors migrated south out of Central Asia. But Stübel's fragmentary reports indicate that the Sanya Muslims are more likely descended from seamen of the ancient Champa Empire of Southeast Asia. In any case they share little more than religion with all of the other people called Hui in China. It is unfortunate that the Sanya have been assigned to this larger "nationality," since the association is likely to discourage research directed specifically at this tiny group of Muslims.

Quite recently—with the advent of the Eighties—interest in minority languages has suddenly revived in China. The center of activity is the Department of Minority Languages in the Central Institute of National Minorities. For a period of more than ten years—from 1966 to 1978—none of the work of that department was allowed into print; now, in a different political atmosphere, the Institute has begun publishing as never before. Data and information from projects held in abeyance since the Fifties, as well as accounts of fresh research, have recently started to appear. Most linguistic papers and articles are published in *Mínzú Yǔwén* (Nationality Language and Literature), but there are also other outlets. The Institute even publishes some language monographs. Many of these works are of good quality. Less innovative or analytic than descriptive, they usually contain accurate phonetic transcriptions of a small but representative vocabulary, an analysis of the sound system, and a brief sketch of the grammar.

One of the most promising developments at the Institute seems to be a departure from the inflexible categories of the Minorities List. For example, there have recently been reports on the Be language of Hainan Island. The existence of the Be people had been known since foreign missionaries began sending out word of them in the late nineteenth century, but little has been written about them in the People's Republic, at least in part because they are not on the official list of minorities. An article on their language in *Minzu Yuwen* may mean a new kind of sophistication in research and reporting techniques. If so, then the answers to some old questions may not be far away. Who, for example, are the mysterious "boat people"—the Hoklo, the Tanka, the Xumin, and perhaps others— that one catches mention of from time to time? Presumably they still ply the waters in and around the South China coast, but little concrete is known about them. A number of years ago, some of these groups applied for minority status but were subsequently turned down, apparently in part because they were speakers of dialects of Han Chinese (Cantonese and Min). Do any of them also still speak other languages that have not been described? Some investigators suspect that they do. Other languages reported on only from Southeast Asia are said to be spoken in China as well, but as yet there has been no verification of this claim.

LINGUISTIC AREAS IN CHINA

The peoples of North China and the peoples of South China are very different from each other. To the Chinese, they are all "national minorities," just as in the past they were all "barbarians." But that only means that they are not Han Chinese. Were it not for the mediation of the great Chinese civilization that lies between them, there would be scarcely a thing that they would have in common. Their languages and their ways of life, as well as their respective places in China and Chinese history, are half a continent apart.

The peoples of the North live on the rolling plains of Manchuria and in the grasslands and the deserts of Mongolia and Xinjiang. They are the descendants of the horse-riding nomads of Inner Asia, the feared invaders who from time to time swept down into and sometimes conquered China itself. They were, among others, the Huns, the Türks, and the Mongols, the people against whom the Chinese found it necessary to build a Great Wall. Though some of them, such as the Uighurs, long ago settled into such civilized pursuits as dry-crop farming, most of these peoples were traditionally hunters and herders, or sometimes traders, who only under the influence of the Chinese began taking up the more sedentary ways of civilization. Throughout Chinese history, they ebbed and flowed across the northern plains and deserts, striking a delicate balance with the relative strength of the Chinese state.

The peoples of the South, by contrast, were the "aborigines"—the Mán—who were settled in South China long before the Han Chinese came into the area. Unlike the North, where the Chinese were never able for very long to expand far beyond their original homeland in the Northern Plains, the South was an area the Han could and did colonize and absorb all the way to the South China Sea. Although the natives of the South were not always docile, they were seldom able to mount serious military resistance against the Han newcomers, and so were either absorbed like their lands into the Han ranks or were driven into ever remoter regions of the country. Today an ethnographic map of South China shows clearly what has happened: The Han dominate the river valleys and rich farming lands, and the non-Han remnants live in the higher, remote mountains in isolated clusters, which increase in density toward the south and west, away from the direction of the original Han encroachments from the North. (See Fig. 4.) Although they are now technologically far below the level of the Han, recent archeological evidence indicates that these people were once dominated by an advanced Tai civilization that controlled most of what is now South China. It may eventually turn out that it was they who long ago taught the Chinese the arts of ceramics and bronze-casting and even rice culture. The issues surrounding the origins of East Asian civilization are still highly controversial. At any rate, unlike the peoples on the northern frontiers of China, many of the peoples of South China were familiar with the techniques of intensive agriculture long before they came into contact with the Chinese.

The minorities of China are part of two different linguistic areas. The languages of the North are almost all "Altaic languages." In structure they are much like Korean and Japanese, two languages on the easternmost fringe of the area which are often classified as Altaic as well. The languages of the South are an extension of the Southeast Asian linguistic area, with its rich profusion of tones and tendency toward monosyllabism.

All of the languages in a linguistic area are not necessarily members of the same family, or "genetically related." Many of course are, and this is especially true of the linguistic area in North China. But some are not. The diverse languages of South China, for example, do not all go back to a common ancestor (or, if they do, the connections are too far back in antiquity to be recovered). The languages in a linguistic area resemble each other for reasons other than genetic. Just as other aspects of culture—such as folk tales and legends, artistic themes, styles of clothing and cooking, and so forth—will often be shared by the various peoples living in a given area, in the same way, the languages spoken there will also usually have much in common. Not only do people in intimate contact borrow words and concepts from each other, but they tend to imitate each other's pronunciations and grammatical structures as well. As a result, languages found in the same general geographical region may be similar even when they are not genetically related. This is what is meant by a *linguistic area*.

The so-called "uvular *r*," found in both standard French and standard German, is a pronunciation feature of a large linguistic area in Northern Europe. This pronunciation began as an innovation in Parisian French, then spread through Huguenot influence and other ways across language boundaries into Belgium, Switzerland, Northern Germany, and Denmark. The result is that Northern Germans, for example, have a French pronunciation of *r*, while Southern Germans, who were not affected by the change, retain the older "apical *r*" pronunciation typical of Italian to the south. In India, the languages of the three different families, Indo-Aryan, Dravidian, and Munda, are unrelated to each other, but they all have the "domal" or "retroflex" (*r-like*) consonants peculiar to that linguistic area. The languages spoken in the Balkans, one of the best-known linguistic areas, are not very closely related to each other, but they are all remarkably alike in structure. For example, four of them, Romanian, Bulgarian, Madedonian, and Albanian, have postposed definite articles:

	Romanian	Albanian
'wolf'	lup	ujk
'the wolf'	lupul	ujku

This postposed definite article is a feature of the Balkan linguistic area. It does not occur in languages closely related to these languages but which happen not to be spoken in the Balkans: Italian does not have this kind of structure even though it is closely related to Romanian; and neither does Serbo-Croatian, though it is closely related to Bulgarian.

In this way, the languages of South China form a linguistic area. They have similar sounds and structures whether they are related or not.

Yet a third linguistic area is formed by Tibet and adjacent parts of West China. The dominant language spoken there is without question related to Burmese, and many believe it is related to Chinese as well. But the typology of Tibetan, its characteristic structure, shows that it has developed in a relatively isolated space over the last few millennia. Tibet's culture, too, is uniquely its own. Until roads and airfields were recently built linking it to China, Tibet was one of the most remote inhabited places on earth. Since this area has not been an organic part of China, it will not be discussed in this book.

The island of Taiwan on the other side of China is different from all of these areas. The native "Kaoshan" languages spoken there are Austronesian and are reported to be more varied than all the rest of that family put together. However, these languages would also take us too far afield from East Asia. They will not be considered here.

10 THE MINORITIES OF NORTH CHINA

Almost all of the languages in North China are Altaic. The only exceptions are Tajik, an Indo-European language spoken by an Iranian group living on the western fringe of Xinjiang, and Han Chinese itself, now spreading more and more into territory formerly occupied by only Altaic languages.

"Altaic" is the term used to refer to a large group of Asian languages believed by most investigators to be genetically related. Included in Altaic are three well-defined families of fairly closely related languages: Turkic, Mongolian, and Tungus. Korean and Japanese, which are very similar in structure to the Altaic languages, are sometimes classified together with them as a single language family. However, Japanese and Korean will not be included in the discussion here.

The Altaic languages are spoken over one of the largest continuous land masses on earth. They are found all across North Asia and into Southwest Asia, from Turkey to the northern coast of northeastern Siberia. The mountains in southwestern Mongolia for which this family is named, the Altai, roughly bisect the arc formed by the southern edge of their range. Most of this range is the part of the Eurasian continent that until modern times lay beyond the civilizations of Europe, the Middle East, India, and China. It is the part of the world often called "Inner Asia." Because of its harsh climate and geography, most of Inner Asia is not suited to intensive agriculture, and the Altaic people who live there are by tradition nomads who even today often make their living by herding. They did not develop great civilizations. They were excellent horsemen, however, who waged frequent and successful wars against each other as well as against other peoples. In Inner Asia, Altaic tribes interacted and influenced each other almost continuously for thousands of years.

Because of the cultural differences, Inner Asia has always stood in contrast with the areas on its periphery. The nomadic people who lived in Inner Asia were "barbarians," and the sedentary people around them represented civilization. The barbarians were impressed by the material culture and technology of others, but they had little to attract the interest of the civilized peoples in return. For this reason, the Altaic languages are rich in loans from Slavic, Semitic, Iranian, Indic, and Chinese. The languages of civilization, on the other hand, have taken little from Altaic, except the names of some objects associated with the barbarians, such as *yogurt, koumiss* 'liquor made from fermented mare's milk,' and *yurt* 'a nomadic dwelling.'

Altaic Structure

The Altaic languages are very much alike in structure. Their common features, when taken together, distinguish them from the other languages and language families of North Asia. What follows are some of the most salient of those features.

Phonology. Vowel length is often distinctive in the Altaic languages. For example, in standard Mongolian the vowel of the word *del* 'mane' is not the same as the vowel of the word *de:l* 'coat, robe,' which is pronounced much longer (and as a result is often written as a double vowel: *deel*); *tos* 'fat, butter, grease' and *to:s* (or *toos*) 'dust' are also not homonyms.

Although differences in stress and pitch are common in many other languages, they are seldom used to distinguish words in any of the Altaic languages. In English, for example, the noun *récord*, with a stress on the first syllable, contrasts with the verb *recórd*, which has a stress on the second syllable. In standard Japanese the word *káki* 'oyster' is pronounced with a higher musical pitch on the first syllable and thus contrasts with the word *kakí* 'fence,' which is given a higher musical pitch on the second syllable. In most of the Altaic languages, however, changes in stress or pitch do not change the meaning of the word.

One of the peculiarities of the Altaic languages is that the consonants *l* and *r* seldom occur at the beginning of a word. This is especially true of *r*. In Mongolian, for instance, there is not a single word that begins with an *r*. If a foreign word with an initial *r* is borrowed into Mongolian, an extra vowel must be put in front of the *r* so that it will not begin the word; in this way the word 'radio' became *araadi*, and the French word *rayon* 'district' was borrowed as *oryoon*.

Altaic languages also do not have consonant clusters at the beginning or end of a word. In this respect, they resemble modern Chinese but are quite different from the Indo-European languages, which are rich in consonant clusters. English is typical of the Indo-European languages in having many words that begin with *spr-*, *fl-*, and so on, and clusters such as *-lps* at the end of words are equally common. Other Indo-

European languages, such as Russian, have even more complicated sequences.

The best-known and most characteristic feature of Altaic phonology is the phenomenon known as "vowel harmony." Vowel harmony means that the vowels in any given word must "harmonize" or "agree" with each other. In the most typical kind of vowel harmony, the vowels harmonize if all are pronounced either with the tongue held in the front of the mouth or with the tongue held in the back of the mouth. They do not harmonize if one of them is a front vowel and another is a back vowel. In Turkish, a language with a very rigid system of vowel harmony, *köpek* 'dog' has two front vowels and is therefore a real, natural word. The word *kulak* 'ear,' with back vowels, is too. But forms like *ˣköpak* or *ˣkulek* would have a mixture of front and back vowels and therefore could not be native Turkish words. In other words, the speakers of a language with this kind of vowel harmony move the tongue either to the front of the mouth or to the back of the mouth when they begin to pronounce a word and keep it in that position through the end of the word. This restriction on which vowels can occur is most striking when suffixes are added to a word, for then the vowel of the suffix changes according to the vocalism of the stem. Thus, in Tatar, one of the Turkic languages, the plural of *at* 'horse' is *at-lar* 'horses,' but the plural of *et* 'dog' is *et-ler* 'dogs' because the vowel of the plural suffix *-lar/-ler* must be front if the vowel of the noun is front, and back if the vowel of the noun is back.

This kind of phonological process often seems very exotic to speakers of English, or Chinese, or other languages that are structurally different from Altaic. In fact vowel harmony is relatively common among the languages of the world, but most of the other languages and language families spoken around northern Asia do not have it.

(2) Morphology. Words and phrases are generally formed by adding suffixes. As a result, words can often be very long in these languages. Here is a typical build-up of word length through the addition of suffixes in Mongolian:

bari- 'to seize'
bari-lda- 'to seize each other' (= 'to wrestle')
bari-ld-aa 'the wrestling'
bari-ld-aa-tsi 'wrestler'
bari-ld-aa-tsi-d 'wrestlers'
bari-ld-aa-tsi-d-ta 'to the wrestlers'

As is illustrated by the last word in the above sequence, *barildaatsid-ta* 'to the wrestlers,' the Altaic languages have no such things as prepositions, and the equivalents of prepositional phrases are created through suffixation. Prefixes are also rare in these languages, and vowel changes of the kind found in the English *drink-drank-drunk* are virtually unknown.

This type of formative process in which words are created through suffixation is known as "agglutination" (from the Latin verb *agglutinare* 'to glue to'), and languages that use agglutination almost to the exclusion of other derivational processes are said to be "agglutinative." The Altaic languages are therefore called "agglutinative languages."

The words in an Altaic language fall into two very distinct classes—nouns and verbs. In English, there are many noun and verb look-alikes such as *a rate* and *to rate*, *a man* and *to man*, *a mark* and *to mark*, and so on, but in Altaic languages nouns and verbs are clearly distinguished from each other by their forms. The verbs end with verb endings that can never be suffixed to nouns. "Adjectives" function as verbs in these languages (except in Turkic) and generally take the same inflectional endings. This is different from European languages such as English or French, where adjectives often look like nouns. For example, in the English sentences *It was heavy* and *It was a horse*, both the adjective *heavy* and the noun *a horse* follow a form of the verb *to be* and therefore behave similarly. In an Altaic language, on the other hand, an adjective like 'heavy' would take inflectional endings and behave like a verb.

Relative pronouns and conjunctions are rare in these languages. Nor do we find in Altaic such things as gender (masculine, feminine) or agreement, as in French *les bonnes filles* 'the good girls' where each word must have the -*s* to mark the plural.

(3) Syntax. In Altaic languages the verb always comes at the end of the sentence or clause after all the other information has been given. Here are two examples taken from Mongolian:

manae xüü surguuli-da or-no
our   son school-into enter-s
'Our son will enter school.'

sine barilga   bari-ba
new building build-ed
'[He] built a new building.'

Dependent clauses and other types of complements normally precede the word or phrase that they modify; constructions are of the type 'the sitting person' rather than the type 'the person who is sitting.' (In English modifying clauses can either follow or precede the noun that they modify, but the tendency is toward complements that follow.) The following examples are from Mongolian:

ger-te   oro-son xun
yurt-into enter-ed person
'a person who entered the yurt'

minii atsar-san nom
my   bring-ed book
'a book I brought'

Structural differences in Altaic. Compared to an extremely varied language family like Indo-European, Altaic is structurally relatively uniform. This does not mean, however, that there are no differences to be found among the Altaic languages. Much of our discussion of the individual languages of North China will in fact be concerned with precisely those features that make each one different. They all have their own particular historical, geographical, and social settings. For example, the Mongolian languages that were left by the Mongol conquests isolated deep inside China, surrounded by typologically different languages, have diverged considerably from the Altaic pattern. But even within the Altaic continuum, there is a kind of linguistic gradient, in which the typological features gradually change across the land mass of Asia. Most of these Altaic details need not concern us because they have little directly to do with the linguistic situation in China. But a few examples deserve mention.

Most of the Altaic languages have no verb for *to have*; possession is generally expressed by a verb of existence, and instead of 'I have' one says 'to-me there-is.' In the eastern part of the Altaic range, in languages like Manchu, there is also a negative verb of existence that is used similarly to the literary Chinese negative verb of existence *wú*. Again, in the extreme east, especially in Manchuria, the languages tend to have fewer "cases" than languages somewhat farther to the west; Manchu, a Tungus language, has fewer cases than the closely related Tungus languages spoken in Central Siberia. Some languages in the east tend toward an "open syllable" phonological structure, in which words typically end in vowels; Manchu and Dagur, a Mongolian language spoken in Manchuria, are like this. There are marked differences in vowel harmony among the Altaic languages. The Turkic languages in the west have the most regular and rigid systems, and the front–back differences are consistently maintained. Mongolian, in the geographical center of Altaic, still has much of the same kind of harmony as Turkic, but some historical changes have created irregularities in the patterns. In the Tungus languages vowel harmony is of a different sort, generally high–low rather than front–back; and in some Tungus languages the vowel harmony relationships have almost completely broken down.

Altaic as a Language Family

The Altaic languages have long been thought to be genetically related. At first, this hypothesis was based almost solely upon the fact that there are so many close structural resemblances between them. But over the years the arguments have been improved, and today the Altaic hypothesis has become much more convincing. Not only are the languages similar at all levels of structure, but there are also many common elements, of apparently great antiquity, linking their vocabularies.

The hypothesis remains controversial, however. It is not as secure as, say, that of Indo-European, Semitic, Austronesian, or Tibeto-Burman. For these other groups of languages, the rules governing the correspondences between the members of the family have all been codified, so that, given a word in one of the languages, it is possible to predict the forms of the corresponding words in the other members of the family. But in the case of Altaic, the rules of correspondence have not been demonstrated to everyone's satisfaction. Within each of the three *branches* of Altaic—that is, within Turkic, or Mongolian, or Tungus—such rules unquestionably exist; the members of each of these subfamilies are all obviously related. The problem comes when one subfamily is compared to another subfamily. The rules relating each of the three branches of Altaic to the other two are not very clear, and for this reason many experts remain cautious. They are troubled, moreover, by the fact that there has been so much intimate interaction among these groups for so very long. A worry to many is the role of Mongolian. Mongolian is the center of Altaic linguistically as well as geographically. From the earliest historical appearance of the Mongols until now, groups of Mongols have lived between the Turkic peoples in the west and the Tungus peoples in the east, a geographical position that made it easy to transmit language or any other aspect of culture from one side to the other. Mongolian shares many more features with Turkic and, to a lesser extent, with Tungus than these two outer language families share with each other. Skeptics warn that convergence of the languages through the diffusion of structural features as well as vocabulary could have produced a mere illusion of genetic affinity. They would accordingly ascribe the common elements in the languages to very early borrowings, passed back and forth perhaps several times from one group to the other.

Linguists, then, are divided in their opinions as to what "Altaic" really means. Some consider it to be a true family of languages in the same sense that Indo-European is. They are confident that in time the details of the correspondences can, for the most part, all be worked out. Others remain unconvinced. They are not swayed by the evidence offered so far and prefer to believe that "Altaic" is no more than a group of structurally similar languages that have influenced each other over a time period spanning millennia.

Who is right? Although this is a question that cannot yet be answered with certainty, the arguments in favor of genetic affinity seem to be stronger. It is difficult to imagine that the many common elements in these languages could all have been caused by chance or by structural convergence. They are too numerous to be accidental, and there are limits to the amount and kinds of convergence that diffusion can cause. We will see later, in fact, some extreme cases of structural convergence between certain isolated Mongolian languages and neighboring non-Altaic languages. Yet, these Mongolian languages remain unmistakably Mongolian in many parts of their structure. We will assume, without further justification, that Altaic is an actual language family; however, we remain cautious because its innermost connections have still to be clarified. For details on the controversy and some technical references, see the chapter on "The Altaic Theory" in Nicholas Poppe's *Introduction to Altaic Linguistics* (1965).

TURKIC

Turkic is the western branch of Altaic. Although some of the Turkic languages are found as far north and east as the River Lena in northeastern Siberia, the great majority of them are spoken on the western side of Inner Asia and in the territory that stretches beyond it to the southwest into Iran and Turkey.

It is easy to confuse "Turkic" with "Turkish." Turkic is a large family of languages of which Turkish is only one member. Turkish is the best-known and most important of these languages, of course: it is spoken by some forty million people, far more than all the rest of the Turkic population combined; it is also the official language of the only independent

Turkic-speaking nation in the world. Nor can any other Turkic language compare with present-day Turkish for literary or cultural significance. However, Turkish should not be used to stand for all the Turkic languages, just as the citizens of modern Turkey should not be thought of as representative of all the Turkic peoples. Turkey is too Western. It is a Turkic colonization of territory formerly inhabited by Indo-Europeans, and both language and people show a strong mixture of these non-Turkic elements. Letting Turkish stand for Turkic can be almost as misleading as letting American English stand for Germanic.

The Turkic homeland is close to China. The original Turkic people—the Türks—were traditionally associated with the land known as Turkestan, a region now partitioned between Russia, China, and Afghanistan. "Chinese Turkestan"—the eastern, or Chinese, part of the region—is an older name for Xinjiang. The northern part of Chinese Turkestan, around the Ili River, became the focal point of the Türk empire around the time that this Turkic people began their westward expansion in the sixth century. Before that, the Türks lived only in western and central Mongolia. Their oldest literary monuments—the oldest of any Altaic-speaking people—were found written on steles erected in the valley of the Orkhon River, a tributary of the Selenga, in north central Mongolia. These Orkhon inscriptions date from the eighth century, about a century or so after the apogee of the Türk empire. Their location is important, because it is in the cradle of almost all of the nomadic empires and is the heart of the Altaic region. Because it was their ancestral homeland, this eastern part of their empire remained politically more important to the Türks even after the western part became militarily and economically far stronger. The Eastern Türks are said to have "preserved the national spirit," while the Western Türks became the link between civilizations East and West.

The Western Türks made conquests in the west and southwest, then began to infiltrate and settle the agricultural lands in that same direction. As they did so, they absorbed the local Iranian populations. (The Tajik, some of whom are still found in western Xinjiang, represent the unassimilated elements of that process.) Both the languages and the ethnic compositions of the Turkic peoples who now live in these areas show that they have lived and intermarried with the bordering, non-Altaic peoples for a long time. In general, the farther south and west one goes within the regions inhabited by Turkic peoples, the more the faces show Indo-Iranian features and the less they look Mongolian. The languages that these people speak are still very much Turkic, but their vocabularies have a great many borrowings from Persian. Some of them, including Turkish, also show a certain amount of Persian influence in their phonology, morphology, and syntax. Turkish has developed the consonants *j* (pronounced [zh]) and *h* because of this sustained Iranian contact, much as English developed the phoneme *zh* (the *z* in *azure* or the *g* in *rouge*) under the influence of French. Dialects of the Uzbek language, some speakers of which live in the extreme western reaches of Xinjiang, are said to have been so "Iranized" that they have only six vowels instead of the characteristic eight of most Turkic languages. Vowel harmony is also said to have been eroded.

This expansion of the Türk empire in the sixth and seventh centuries was the major phase in the spread of Turkic peoples across Asia. More were displaced by the Mongols under Chinggis Khan in the twelfth century, and still more by the Russians after that.

All of these widely scattered Turkic languages are quite clearly and recognizably alike. If one knows any one of them well, it is possible to analyze words and simple sentences of almost any other of these languages without very much difficulty.

The major exception to this generalization is Chuvash, a Turkic language spoken by about 1.7 million people in the middle course of the Volga River in the USSR. Chuvash is so different from all the rest of the Turkic languages we must assume that the original Proto-Turkic language split into two branches, East Turkic and West Turkic, a very long time ago, well before the beginning of the Türk empire. The only surviving descendant of West Turkic today is Chuvash. (We know, however, that the present-day Bulgarians also originally spoke a West Turkic language but eventually gave it up and began to speak Slavic instead.) The original speakers of West Turkic probably migrated across the Ural Mountains into Europe, while their kinsmen, the speakers of the East Turkic branch of the family, must have stayed together nearer home, beginning to disperse only much later, in the sixth and seventh centuries.

Chuvash, spoken in an area far to the west of China, is important to East Asia for the light some linguists believe it sheds on the nature of Altaic as a whole. Since it split off from the other Turkic languages so early, a comparative study enables the reconstruction of a much earlier variety of Turkic than would otherwise be possible. This reconstructed variety of Turkic, called Proto-Turkic, in turn gives a much earlier, more reliable base for the reconstruction of the Proto-Altaic language. The most famous fact about Chuvash is that it is a so-called "*r*-language." This is a shorthand way of saying that Chuvash has an *r* or an *l* in words where all the other surviving Turkic languages have a corresponding *z* or *sh*. Since *r* and *l* also appear in supposedly cognate words found in Mongolian and Tungus, the Chuvash situation is thought to confirm the belief that the Turkic consonants *z* and *sh* developed from what were originally *r*'s or *l*'s of some kind. Chuvash is thus said to have separated from Turkic before the changes took place. Here are some examples of these correspondences, along with the words in Mongolian and Manchu that are said to be related to them:

z-words in East Turkic	r-words in Chuvash	Mongolian	Manchu
iz 'trace'	yər 'trace'	ir 'blade'	iri 'edge'
uz-un 'long'	vər-əm 'long'	ur-tu 'long'	—

sh-words in East Turkic	l-words in Chuvash	Mongolian	Manchu
ta:sh 'stone'	chul 'stone'	chilaghun	—
yash-ur 'cover, hide'	—	dal-i 'cover up'	dal- cover, hide'

All of the modern Turkic languages other than Chuvash developed from East Turkic. There are around thirty of these modern East Turkic languages today, and seven of them are spoken in China.

Turkic Languages in China

The People's Republic of China recognizes seven Turkic minorities: Kazakh, Kirghiz, Tatar, Uzbek, Uighur, Yellow Uighur (officially called "Yugur" in China), Salar. Of these seven, the first four are principally nationalities of the Soviet Union whose range extends slightly over the Chinese border. Tatar, for example, is the fifth largest language of the USSR, while there are only some four thousand speakers of Tatar living in China.

Tatar. The Tatar were first known in Western Europe around 1300 as the "Tartars." This perverse spelling of their name resulted from a folk etymology. Since the fierce invading armies of the Tatar caused great panic in medieval Europe, they were thought to have come from *Tartarus*, a Latin and Greek word for 'hell.' Like "Huns" and "Turks," the word "Tartars" became a general terms used to describe savages or any other wild and violent people.

The Chinese, too, have in the past used the name "Tatar" loosely. In Sun Yat-sen's day all Turkic people were called Tatar. Sun Yat-sen and other Chinese were particularly aware of these "Tatar" because they looked so different; in spite of their high cheekbones and other Central Asian features, the Tatar (the Turkic peoples) seemed "white" or "Caucasian," especially to the Chinese eye. Thus when Chiang Kai-shek tried to smooth the way for assimilation by saying that the minorities were all of the "same racial stock" as the Han, and that China's ethnic diversity was not due to "race or blood but to religion and geographical environment," he was deliberately ignoring the "Tatar."

TATAR CONSONANTS

	Labial	Denti-labial	Dental	Retro-flex	Alveo-lar	Palatal	Velar	Post-velar	Glottal
Voiceless stop	p		t				k		q
Aspirated stop									
Voiced stop	b		d				g		
Voiceless affricate					ch				
Aspirated affricate									
Voiced affricate					j				
Voiceless fricative		f	s		sh		x		
Voiced fricative			z				gh		
Nasal	m		n				ng		
Voiceless nasal									
Lateral			l						
Voiceless lateral									
Flap or trill			r						
Voiceless flap									
Semivowels	w					y			

The 4,000 Chinese Tatar live in Xinjiang, as do almost all of the Turkic peoples of China. They are found in the immediate area of the Soviet border in the northern part of the region. They are horsemen and herdsmen.

The Tatar language is typified by certain historical changes that took place in its sound system. The voiced velar consonants, *gh* and *g*, that were originally in the final position in some words, were either completely lost or changed into *w*. For example, *sari* 'yellow' < **sarigh*; *taw* 'mountain' < **tagh*. There have been several changes in the values of the vowels in Tatar; mid-vowels have been raised to high vowels, and high vowels have been lowered.

Tatar has a typically Turkic, front–back kind of vowel harmony. There are nine vowels: *i, e, ä, ü, ö* (the front vowels) and *i, a, o, u* (the back vowels). Words are automatically stressed on the final syllable; for example, *urmán* 'forest,' *urman-chí* 'forest hut,' *urman-líq* 'forested area,' *urman-chilíq* 'forestry.' Tatar has a number of morphological peculiarities not found in most Turkic languages, such as the formation of verbal nouns with the suffix *-w: qaraw* 'seeing' < *qara-* 'to see.'

Kazakh. The Kazakh are a pastoral people. About 900,000 of them live in China, principally along the Soviet and Mongolian border areas in Xinjiang, though there is also a large patch of Kazakh territory in northern Qinghai Province.

As in Tatar, a language very closely allied to Kazakh, final velar consonants have historically been lost or changed to *w*: *yayaw* 'on foot' < **yayagh; uru:* 'clan, tribe' < **urugh; taw* 'mountain' < *tagh. The vowel shifts that happened in Tatar did not happen in Kazakh, but otherwise it has a similar nine-vowel system: *i, e, ä, ü, ö* (the front vowels) and *i, a, o, u* (the back vowels). It also has much the same consonant system as Tatar.

Kirghiz. The 114,000 Kirghiz who live in China are found mostly in the western corner of Xinjiang on the southern slopes of the Tianshan Range. The nearby Soviet border, which they once ignored and drove their flocks and Bactrian camels across at will, has now become difficult to cross. The Kirghiz winter over in communes now and, like the Kazakh, lead a semi-nomadic life only during the summer months.

The Kirghiz language has one of the strictest and most regular systems of vowel harmony found in all of Altaic. There are eight vowels in the system: four front vowels, *i, e, ü, ö*, and four corresponding back vowels, *i, a, u, o*. These vowels harmonize not only in terms of front versus back, but also in terms of rounded versus unrounded. In other words, let us say that the first vowel in a word is both front and rounded, either *ü* or *ö*; then, in such a word, every vowel that follows must also be *ü* or *ö* since these two are the only front rounded vowels in the language. Similarly, there are only two vowels that are back and unrounded; two that are front and rounded; and two that are front and unrounded. Accordingly, no matter how long a word may be, it can never contain more than two different vowels. This is an extremely rigid kind of system.

Except for this unusually regular vowel harmony, Kirghiz is a language much like Kazakh.

Uzbek. The Uzbek language has over ten million speakers, more than any other Turkic language except Turkish. It ranks third among all the languages of the Soviet Union.

The Uzbek people are not nomads. About 84 percent of them live in the irrigated lands of Uzbekistan, where they have been farming for centuries. In the southern part of this Soviet republic, they farm alongside Tajik, the Iranian people who were living in the area when the Uzbek settled there. Both the Uzbek and the Tajik spill over the still-disputed Chinese border into Xinjiang, where approximately 12,000 Uzbek and 27,000 Tajik are found on the eastern side of some of the highest peaks in the Pamir Range.

The Uzbek speak a language that has been strongly influenced over the years by their Iranian neighbors the Tajik. The Uzbek language once had a vowel system of eight or nine vowels, probably much like that of Tatar or Kazakh. But the distinctions between *u* and *ü*, *o* and *ö*, and *ï* and *i* have since been lost, so that there are now only six vowels, *i, e, a, o, ɔ, u*. The resulting vowel system is virtually identical to that of Tajik. Since the vocalic oppositions that were lost played an essential role in the workings of vowel harmony, there is little left in the language of the original system, and the remaining vowels are generally free to occur in all combinations. In this sense, too, Uzbek has come to resemble the non-Altaic language Tajik. Such fundamental changes could not fail to leave traces, however; in places where vowel differences were leveled, additional distinctions arose in the consonants.

There has also been some morphological convergence between the two languages. For example, some of the formative suffixes of Uzbek have been borrowed into Tajik.

The Uighurs and Their Kin

The Uighurs and their close relatives, the Yellow Uighurs and the Salar, are found almost exclusively within Chinese borders. They are both in name and in fact indigenous peoples of China.

Yellow Uighur. The Yellow Uighurs, who live far away from the Uighurs of Xinjiang, are given separate minority status. Nevertheless, they are also Uighurs. They have called themselves the "Yellow Uighur" (*Sarïgh Yughur*) at least since A.D. 840, when they first moved into their present-day home in Gansu following the destruction of the Uighur empire by the Kirghiz. Since that time they have lived separated from the other Uighurs, long enough for the languages to have become mutually unintelligible. By spending those centuries completely within the borders of China, the Yellow Uighurs escaped the conversion to Islam that the Uighurs living in Chinese Turkestan (Xinjiang) experienced, and were able to preserve their Buddhist faith, as well as the Uighur literary language and script. Through exposure to the Mongols, however, some of the Yellow Uighurs gave up their Turkic language and began to speak a variety of Mongolian. Most of the Yellow Uighurs, whether they speak Turkic or Mongolian, now know Chinese as well.

Salar. The Salar, like the Yellow Uighur, are also classified as a separate national minority by the Chinese government. But from a linguistic point of view, this is a mistake, since the Salar language is actually another dialect of Uighur. The main difference between the Salar and the Uighurs of Xinjiang is geographical: The Salar live far removed from the Uighur region in a small Turkic pocket in the eastern corner of Qinghai Province, where, according to their own traditions, they have been since the Ming period. Also, unlike the Yellow Uighurs, they are Muslims.

Uighur Proper. There are about six million Uighurs living in Xinjiang, which makes them the most numerous minority in North China. This number far exceeds the 173,000 found across the border in Soviet territory, most of whom migrated out of China in the late nineteenth century. The Uighurs are a Chinese people. They have played a long and unique role in Chinese history, and they are equally important in the People's Republic today.

The national minority known as the Uighurs are the sedentary Turkic population of Xinjiang. They are the principal ethnic group in the area, which as a result is named after them, the "Xinjiang Uighur Autonomous Region." The economy of the Uighurs is based upon the farming of fruits, cotton, wheat, and rice through extensive irrigation from the oases and streams scattered around this arid region. This way of life more than anything else separates them from the pastoral peoples of Xinjiang: the Kazakh, the Tatar, and the Kirghiz, who otherwise share much of the Islamic and Turkic culture of the Uighurs. Anthropologically, the Uighurs are probably closest to the Uzbek.

The Uighurs are often, and perhaps more properly, called the "New Uighur." Until early in this century, "Uighur" was not what they had called themselves; for in fact, they had no name at all. Those living on the Soviet side of the border had called themselves Taranchi, which meant nothing more than 'farmers'; and those Turkic people farming on the Chinese side of the border had taken the name of whatever oasis area they happened to live in. In 1921, at a meeting of the East Turkic people in Tashkent, delegates from both the Soviet and Chinese areas decided to take the name "Uighur," after the ancient Turkic kingdom that had flourished in Chinese Turkestan in the ninth century. Until that time, the only people who had continued to call themselves "Uighur" were the Yellow Uighurs of Gansu Province.

The "New Uighurs" are descended from the "Old Uighurs," who had continued to live in Chinese Turkestan (Xinjiang) even after their kingdom had been overrun several times and had broken up into a number of small, independent states. But in the ancestry of the "New Uighurs" there is also a mixture of many other peoples who have lived in the area. The Turkic people of Xinjiang are the racial and cultural product of a region that historically lay at the crossroads of East and West.

Xinjiang is actually two areas, separated from each other by the Tianshan Mountains, which extend from east to west. To the north lies a barren and sandy plain known as Dzungaria (Junggar). This plain in turn is bounded in the north by the Altai Mountains, which form part of the Chinese border with the Mongolian People's Republic. To the east and west, however, it is open, allowing a slight air flow to reach it and bring a little moisture to the area. To the south of the Tianshan Range lies the Tarim Basin, a deep depression encircled by mountains that block drainage to the outside. The center of the Tarim Basin is filled with nothing but sand dunes. It is even drier than Dzungaria. But in the summer, snows melt from the slopes of the mountains and form streams that bring water to the edge of the basin floor. From west to east around the north of the basin, the Tarim River and its tributaries flow in a great arc that terminates in the saline Lop Nur Lake, not far from where the Chinese now conduct their atomic tests. In such a place farming would be impossible without irrigation, but with it, the fertile soils grow a rich variety of crops.

For thousands of years people have farmed in this narrow band around the Tarim Basin, using methods much like those that served other early civilizations, such as those in the Mesopotamian and Egyptian river valleys. And from Roman times on, these settlements served as the link for trade between China and the West, the famous "Silk Road." It was a good place for a civilization to develop.

The Uighurs—the "Old Uighurs"—were a Turkic tribe in northern Mongolia virtually indistinguishable from the Türks. In 745, not long after the death of the last Türk *kaghan*, their traditional ruler, the Uighur tribe wrested power from the Türks and took over control of the empire. Some say that the passing of the Türk empire into Uighur hands was no more than a "change of administration," for the empire and its composition remained intact; the Uighurs had lived in northern Mongolia under Türk rule before 745, and the Türk became a tribe in the Uighur empire after that. In any event, for our purposes the important fact is that the Uighurs spoke the same language as the Türks. We know that that was true because an eighth-century Uighur inscription found at Shine-usu in Mongolia was written in a variety of Turkic almost exactly the same as that of the Orkhon inscriptions of the Türks, which had been written a few decades earlier.

When their empire in Mongolia was subsequently destroyed in 840 by the Kirghiz, another Turkic tribe from even farther north, the Uighurs were not absorbed into a new empire and lost to history the way many Altaic tribes before them had been. Instead, they fled south and established two kingdoms that thrived for many years. One of these two kingdoms was that of the Yellow Uighurs, who settled in the neck of Gansu in Chinese territory between the Great Wall and the Qilian Mountains, where their descendants still live today. The other, and far more important group, fled to Chinese Turkestan and created a civilization unmatched by any other non-Muslim Turkic people.

The Uighurs had already begun to develop a culture unique to Inner Asia even before they had left Mongolia. For one thing, unlike any nomadic power up until that time, they adopted a sophisticated formal religion, Manicheanism. For another, they had become a northern power consistently friendly to the Chinese, siding with the Tang during the An Lushan Rebellion (755–757) and remaining loyal after that. But it was only after the Uighurs settled into Chinese Turkestan that they developed the cosmopolitan culture for which they are known. The area had long been multiracial and multilingual when the Uighurs arrived—no doubt the oldest ethnic and linguistic layers were Indo-European, for this had been the home of the Sogdians, the Sakians, and the Tocharians, whose written records have played an important part in Indo-European studies. On top of these layers were a number of other elements, principally Turkic and perhaps also Semitic, that had preceded the Uighurs. The Uighurs absorbed and were influenced by all these elements, but they kept much that they had brought with them, including their language, and made the area Turkic for good.

In Chinese Turkestan the Uighurs gave up being nomads and settled into a more prosperous life. Their kingdom lasted for over four hundred years, from 847 to about 1270, long enough for them to make an indelible mark on North China. The degree of civilization they attained impressed even the Song Chinese. Among their cultural achievements, the Uighurs are especially known for two: the remarkable mural paintings found in their ancient capital city of Khocho, on the northeastern side of the Tarim Basin in what is called the Turfan Basin; and the so-called Uighur script—"so-called," because the Uighurs did not invent it. By the time the Uighurs arrived in Chinese Turkestan, it had already been in use for centuries; apparently, some other, unknown Turkic people must have been the originators, and they in turn had merely adapted it from the cursive script of the Sogdians, the Iranian forebears of the Tajik. But the

Uighur Consonants

	Labial	Denti-labial	Dental	Retro-flex	Alveo-lar	Palatal	Velar	Post-velar	Glottal
Voiceless stop	p		t				k		q
Aspirated stop									
Voiced stop	b		d				g		
Voiceless affricate					ch				
Aspirated affricate									
Voiced affricate					j				
Voiceless fricative		f	s		sh		x		h
Voiced fricative		v	z		zh		gh		
Nasal	m		n				ng		
Voiceless nasal									
Lateral			l						
Voiceless lateral									
Flap or trill			r						
Voiceless flap									
Semivowels	w					y			

Uighurs are associated with the script, first of all, because they created a literature with it—Uighur works on Manichean, Nestorian, and Buddhist teachings, as well as some astrological works and poetry are still preserved—and secondly, because they were instrumental in transmitting the script to others, the most important of whom were the Mongols.

THE modern Uighur language is divided into two dialect groups: Uighur proper and the "isolated" dialects, which include Salar. Uighur proper consists of the northern dialects and the southern dialects, a geographical division more convenient than meaningful. There is actually very little dialect diversity in Uighur proper, since it is spoken in the principal oasis areas, which have always been tied together closely by the main lines of commercial traffic.

Uighur has eight vowels: *i, e, ä, ö, ü, a, o, u*. A characteristic of this system is that there are two *e*-type vowels (*e* and *ä*), but only one *i*-type vowel. In the vowel harmony system, the two *e*-type vowels pattern the same way. The lone *i*-type vowel resulted when the distinction between the vowels *i* and *ï* was lost. The whole system is said to be unstable, and the pronunciations of the vowels to vary considerably. The phoneme /i/, for example, is often heard as [ï] as well as [i]; thus 'girl' can be pronounced as either *kiz* or *qïz*. For this reason, early Western investigators of the Uighur language described it as having as many as twenty-one vowels. The language has long vowels, as in the words *a:t* 'name' and *qa:r* 'snow.' In addition to the usual Turkic stress on the final syllable of a word, it also has a secondary accent on the first syllable.

Historically, the final consonants -*gh* and -*g*, which are still pronounced as such by the Yellow Uighurs (thus 'yellow' is *sarɨgh* in that language), have become unvoiced stops in Uighur proper: *sarɨq* 'yellow.' In addition, earlier -*d*- has become -*y*-: The word *adɨgh* 'bear,' found in the Orkhon inscriptions, is now pronounced *eyiq* in Uighur.

Uighur has been significantly affected by long contact with non-Turkic languages. The Uighur vocabulary has many loans from a variety of languages that have been spoken over the years in Chinese Turkestan, especially Iranian, Arabic, and Chinese. More interesting is the fact that the Uighur vowels, like those of the neighboring Uzbek language, are believed to have undergone structural changes during those centuries of contact. Iranian and Chinese influences are suspected of being responsible for the partial loss of vowel harmony in Uighur (but one wonders if the presence just next door of Uzbek, the Turkic language in which such changes have been the most pronounced, should not be given a share of the responsibility). In any case, it is only the front–back type of harmony that has partially broken down in Uighur, and the direct cause of that was the loss of the distinction between the vowels *i* and *ɨ*. Otherwise, the system still works. Also, the rounded–unrounded opposition is still very much intact, as is seen, for example, in the behavior of the adjectival suffix -*lük*/-*luq*: *süt* 'milk,' *süt-lük* 'milky'; *ot* 'fire,' *ot-luq* 'fiery.'

One unusual part of the Uighur vowel system—at least among the Turkic languages—is the presence of a process that in a sense works just backwards from the usual Turkic vowel harmony. To illustrate, let us return briefly to the Kirghiz system. In Kirghiz, the choice of the first vowel of the word determines the qualities of the vowels that follow; that is, if we choose a front unrounded vowel, such as *i*, then all the rest of the vowels in the word have to be front and unrounded as well (either *i* or *e*). Uighur, on the other hand, has developed a very different (regressive) kind of system called *umlaut* (after the name of a similar kind of process found in German). For example, the Uighur word for 'head' is *bash*, with a back vowel. But when we add to that word the personal possessive suffix -*im* 'my,' with a front vowel, we get the form *besh-im* 'my head,' with the original back vowel *a* of the stem now changed into the front vowel *e*. In other words, the vowel of the suffix has determined the quality of the vowel of the stem, rather than the other way around.

The morphology of Uighur is much like that of other Turkic languages. For example, one interesting process is the intensification of the meaning of an adjective by doubling the first syllable and putting a *p* in between: *qara* 'black,' *qap-qara* 'jet black'; *yoghan* 'fat,' *yop-yoghan* 'quite fat'; *tuz* 'salty,' *tup-tuz* 'very salty.' The one major non-Turkic development in Uighur morphology is the accretion of a respectable number of suffixes borrowed from Iranian and Arabic.

The syntax is also typically Turkic. For example, in Turkic languages an equational sentence usually requires a copula at the end. Here is a Uighur example using the copula *du(r)* 'is':

Ata-sɨ	Shahɨ Märdan	du.
father-your		is

'Your father is Shahi Mardan.'

But sometimes an equation is made by simply juxtaposing the two nouns. This kind of construction is particularly common in Uighur, especially in set phrases or proverbs such as the following:

Yaxshi: xo:tun   bihish.
good   wife   paradise
'A good wife is paradise.'

Uighur Writing. The old Uighur script was an alphabet with twenty basic symbols. These twenty were far from enough to represent all the phonemes in the Uighur language, and many differences in pronunciation were left for context to determine. Only one symbol, for example, was used for the four vowels *o, ö, u,* and *ü*; only one was used for both the consonants *g* and *k*; and, although *p* rarely occurred in initial position, the fact that the same symbol was used for both it and *b* could be very problematic medially. In many ways, the runelike script the Türks and the Uighurs had used in the Orkhon Valley in Mongolia had been a more efficient system, even though this script too had had only twenty basic letters. Nevertheless, in spite of its imperfections, the Uighur alphabet was easy to learn and use, and it was more than adequate for most purposes, as is shown by the readiness with which the Mongols and, after them, the Manchus took it up. In this way, the Uighurs brought literacy to much of Inner Asia.

The script itself was Semitic in origin. Like Arabic and Hebrew, the symbols are read from right to left across the page. The Sogdian alphabet, of which it was a variant, was very close to the Syrian and Aramaic alphabets.

These Middle Eastern writing systems flowed easily into the areas on China's nothern frontiers. By adopting a Semitic writing system, the Uighurs were only following a pattern of the Altaic peoples that had been established before, and that would continue after them. The runic alphabet that they and the Türks had used earlier had been an adaptation of the Aramaic script; and a few centuries later, with the introduction of Islam, almost all of the Turkic peoples would come to write their languages with Arabic letters.

One may well ask how it was that Semitic writing systems, from so far away, were so singularly successful among the Altaic peoples. The concept of representing words visually was known to these nomads well before they had even seen a single Semitic letter, and they had surely long been envious of the literacy of Chinese civilization. Part of the reason, at least for later developments, can be attributed to the power of Islam, and

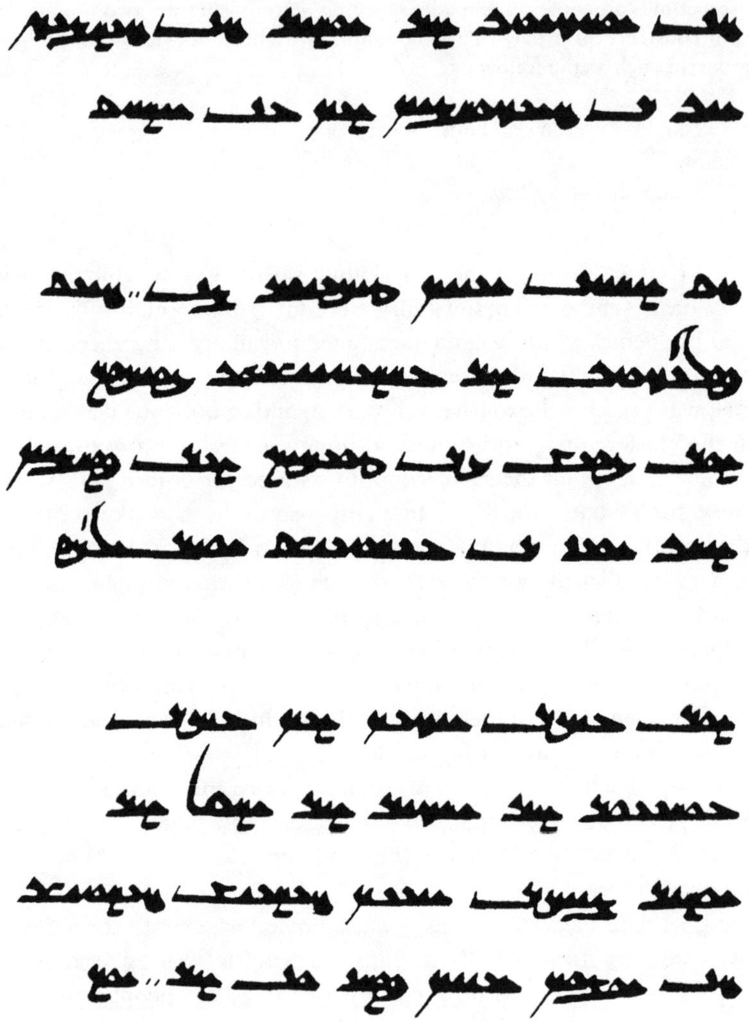

Figure 9. A Uighur Blockprint. (from Gabain 1950)
The lines of the text are horizontal and read from right to left,
as would be expected of a writing system from the Middle East.

that is certainly why most of the Uighurs finally gave up their alphabet in
favor of the Arabic script in the thirteenth century. But a more basic
problem was the nature of the Chinese writing system, the only other
kind of writing these peoples had had contact with. For of all the writing
systems that were ever used in Asia, the Chinese character system is surely the one most ill-suited for representing any language other than the

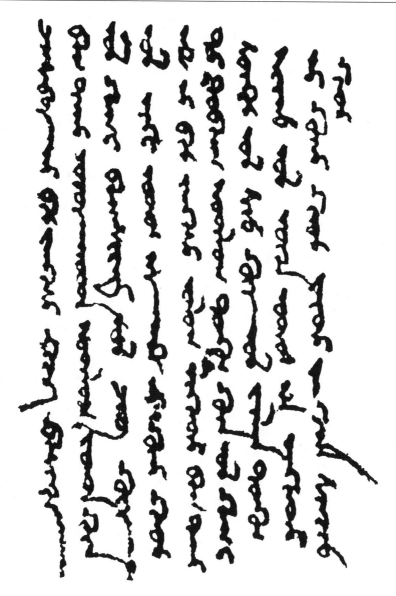

Figure 10. A Uighur Manuscript. (from Gabain 1950)

In this text, typical of late Uighur writing, the lines have become vertical
and follow one another from left to right across the page. The change,
apparently induced by the way the Chinese write, amounted to no more than
turning the page ninety degrees counter-clockwise. It was this vertical
Uighur script that the Mongols adopted.

one for which it had been originally designed. To use it, one simply had to learn Chinese and then write in that language. The enormous difficulties involved in adapting Chinese characters successfully to a polysyllabic, inflecting language like those of the Altaic family seem to have been beyond the determination of all the northern peoples but the Japanese, and theirs is probably the most unwieldy writing system still in use anywhere in the world today. Only two Altaic groups, the Khitan—the Altaic people who founded the Liao dynasty (907–1125)—and the Jurchen—the Tungusic founders of the Jin dynasty (1115–1234)—are known to have persistently tried to make a Chinese-style writing system for their own languages, and these two cumbersome systems quickly disappeared from use not long after they had been invented. The alphabetic scripts of the Middle East, on the other hand, in spite of their well-known deficiencies, could be used far more easily to accommodate these northern languages. Writing, then, became the most important gift of the Middle East to China's northern peoples, and the Uighurs played a key role in its diffusion.

With their conversion to Islam in the thirteenth century, the Uighurs gave up their "Uighur script" in favor of the sacred writing of the new religion. From that time until quite recently, they wrote their language with Arabic letters. In 1921 those Uighurs living in Russian Turkestan were forced by pressure of the Soviet government to switch to the Cyrillic alphabet. The Uighurs of China have continued to write with the Arabic script, except for a brief period in 1975 when the Peking government experimented with using a Pinyin-based Romanization. Objectively speaking, a decision to replace the Arabic script would be a practical development, for the Cyrillic and Roman alphabets are far better linguistic tools than the Arabic for the representation of a Turkic language. Although the structure of the Semitic languages usually obviates the need to write vowels, the Uighur language needs separate symbols to transcribe its eight vowels, and the three diacritic marks available in the Arabic script accommodates that need very poorly.

MONGOLIAN

Mongolian is a very closely related family of languages. Many of these languages differ so little from each other they could be thought of as dialects of the same language.

The main body of Mongolian speakers is concentrated in and around the Mongolian People's Republic and the parts of North China known as Inner Mongolia. Away from this center, however, groups of Mongols are found as far west as Afghanistan and the Volga River, as far east as Manchuria, and as far south as Yunnan in Southwestern China. These isolated pockets of Mongols are mostly the remnants of military garrisons left behind when the Mongol empire collapsed, but some remote settlements are the result of later migrations as well.

The Mongolian family of languages can be divided into Mongolian proper, with its closely allied languages and dialects, and the so-called "archaic" varieties of Mongolian. The archaic varieties of Mongolian are those that have been separated from Mongolian proper for the longest time—presumably since the Mongol empire expanded in the thirteenth century. They are the only varieties of Mongolian that can unquestionably be called different languages. They are said to be "archaic" because they have preserved many features that have been historically lost in Mongolian proper. (However, as we shall see, under the influence of neighboring languages they have undergone some rather radical changes of their own.) These archaic languages are in turn classified into three groups: Moghol; Dagur; and the dialects of the Gansu-Qinghai region of China. Altogether, then, there are four groups of Mongolian languages:

1. Mongolian proper: Besides the standard Khalkha dialect and related forms of Mongolian spoken throughout most of Mongolia, this group includes Buriat and Oirat, both of which are also spoken in North China. The Chinese government classifies this entire group as a single language.
2. Moghol: Moghol is a single language spoken in a remote corner of northeastern Afghanistan.
3. Dagur: Dagur is also a single language. The speakers of Dagur live in small settlements scattered around western Manchuria and northern Xinjiang.
4. The Gansu-Qinghai group: This group is divided into the Santa (or Dongxiang), Bao'an, Monguor, and the variety of Mongolian spoken by Yellow Uighurs (see sections on Uighur, above).

The languages in these latter three groups, the "archaic" varieties of Mongolian, are spoken by Mongols who have lived for many centuries completely surrounded by alien cultures. As a result, there have been two conflicting tendencies in these linguistic communities. On the one hand, like immigrants and other groups who become separated from the homeland, they have generally been more conservative about their speech than their compatriots who remained at home. They still make many distinctions that have been lost in Mongolian proper. Some sound changes have not occurred. In certain respects these languages resemble stages of Mongolian known in Mongolia itself only from earlier written records— thus philologists think of them as "archaic." But on the other hand, through widespread bilingualism and other forms of intimate social contact, these expatriate Mongols have adjusted their linguistic behavior in sometimes basic ways to conform to the other culture, occasionally resulting in bizarre typological blends.

Moghol is not spoken in China, but it is typical. Like the other archaic forms of Mongolian, Moghol derives from the speech of soldiers sent to man one of the distant Mongol garrisons, in this case the Khanate of Persia. And again like the other languages, Moghol is only spoken today by a very small community. Although there are several hundred thousand Mongols believed to be still living in the mountains of northeastern Afghanistan, most of these nomads have forgotten their Mongolian language and speak only an Iranian language, either Tajik or Afghan (Pashto). As for the rest—that is, those Mongols believed still able to speak Moghol—they are completely bilingual in Tajik or Afghan as well. Outside pressures have also accelerated the demise of this language; for out of fear of repression from the Afghan government, most Mongols usually try to pass themselves off as Tajik.

The few remaining speakers of Moghol have preserved almost intact most of the features of what is known as Western Middle Mongolian, a literary language recorded by Islamic authors from the thirteenth century to the fifteenth century. But at the same time, these people have developed some surprisingly un-Mongolian kinds of syntactic constructions; relative clauses, for example, are made Iranian-style, with a relative pronoun (borrowed directly from Iranian) and a verb in the finite form, which in other Mongolian languages only appears at the end of the sentence.

Mongolian Languages in China

Five Mongolian Languages are recognized by the People's Republic of China: Mongolian (proper), Dagur, Santa, Bao'an, and Monguor.

Little mention is made in official sources of the several thousand Yellow Uighurs known to speak a variety of Mongolian. Presumably this small group is classified together with their more numerous kinsmen, the Turkic-speaking Yellow Uighurs.

Yet another group of Mongols who have not received official recognition are the Yunnan Mongols, a small community of peasants who live about a hundred miles north of the Vietnam border in Hexi County, Yunnan Province. They were apparently a Mongol outpost during the

Yuan dynasty. Very little is known about the Yunnan Mongols except that they are supposed to be rice farmers and fishermen. In the late Fifties there were reported to be about 3,500 of them left, but most of them had at that time already given up their language and adapted themselves to the speech of neighboring groups, principally the Tibeto-Burman people formerly known as the Lolo, and now known as the Yi.

Dagur. The Dagur were Mongol soldiers originally stationed on the eastern flank of Mongolia, in the area around the Amur River (Heilongjiang) in northeastern Manchuria. In the seventeenth century the Russians had completed their eastward expansion across Siberia and had begun to develop the areas along the Pacific coast. Settlers discovered the Dagur living there, and the Russian Orthodox church sent missionaries to them in 1682. The Manchu government in China learned of this and, fearing the rapidly growing Russian influence in the area, resettled the Dagur to keep them from falling under Russian sway. They were placed in settlements scattered across northwestern Manchuria and what is now northeastern Inner Mongolia. Some were also sent across Mongolia to a corner of Northern Xinjiang. Today the largest community of Dagur is found in the Dagur Autonomous District in the Nen River valley near Qiqihar in Heilongjiang Province. Together with the Dagur found in other recognized communities, they number around 94,000. Most Dagur make their living as farmers or herders, or sometimes as hunters. They are said to be still strongly shamanistic. The Dagur have no script of their own but are often able to read Chinese or, at least in the recent past, Manchu.

There was once a great deal of confusion about the Dagur language. The first reports of it indicated that it was either a Tungus language or a strange mixture of Tungus and Mongolian; the reasons underlying these mistakes may be that investigators heard certain important differences in pronunciation between it and Mongolian proper. There is now no question, however, about the provenance of Dagur or its status.

As was mentioned above, Dagur is another of the Mongolian languages philologists refer to as archaic. Many words that are otherwise found only in old Mongolian literature can still be heard in colloquial Dagur. It is also true that a number of historical changes key to the classification of Mongolian languages have not taken place in Dagur. For example, in *The Secret History of the Mongols*, written around 1240, the word 'red' is recorded with an initial *h: hulaan*. In Mongolian proper, including the standard Khalkha dialect of the Mongolian People's Republic, the *h* has disappeared without a trace (and thus 'red' is *ulaan*); but in Dagur the consonant is still pronounced: *hulaan* 'red.' Hence this language is

DAGUR CONSONANTS

	Labial	Denti-labial	Dental	Retro-flex	Alveo-lar	Palatal	Velar	Post-velar	Glottal
Voiceless stop	p		t				k		
Aspirated stop									
Voiced stop	b		d				g		
Voiceless affricate					ch				
Aspirated affricate									
Voiced affricate					j				
Voiceless fricative			s		sh		x		
Voiced fricative									
Nasal	m		n, ñ						
Voiceless nasal									
Lateral			l						
Voiceless lateral									
Flap or trill			r						
Voiceless flap									
Semivowels	w						y		

often said to be at the "stage of Middle Mongolian," the last period of Mongolian proper in which the consonant was recorded. However, as conservative as it has been in certain respects, the Dagur language has not stood still. For one thing, the earlier Mongolian stock of seven vowels has been reduced to five vowels in Dagur: *i, e, a, o, u*. For another, all syllable-final consonants except *l* have become a uniform *r* in Dagur; for example, earlier **ulus* is now *olor*. Through this latter change Dagur has very nearly become an "open syllable" language like Japanese, since only this *r*, or an *l*, or (again like Japanese) the "syllabic nasal" *-ñ* can close a syllable. Moreover, according to one important linguistic analysis that has been made of this language, there is also a minimal vowel schwa after *r*'s and *l*'s; if this description is correct, Dagur comes to look even more like Japanese.

There are no accent distinctions since the stress falls automatically on a given syllable. Dagur sentences are constructed the same way as in other Mongolian languages. Particles marking case relationships are suffixed to nouns, and inflectional endings are suffixed to verb stems—most of these processes parallel similar ones in Korean and Japanese. Dagur also has several "emphasis particles" that can be added onto words and phrases; for example, the particle *-le* 'only, even' adds emphasis, and the particle *-(i)ni* 'as for' reduces emphasis on the word to which it attaches. These emphasis particles are reminiscent of the Japanese and Korean focus particles (*-mo* and *-wa* in Japanese, and *-to* and *-(n)in* in Korean).

The Mongolian Languages of the Gansu-Qinghai Area

In the Gansu-Qinghai area of China, scattered along the ethnographic border between the Tibetan and Chinese populations, clusters of

Mongol villages still thrive. These clusters are often cut off from each other and surrounded by Tibetans and Chinese. Some of the communities in this area speak Mongolian proper; these are relative latecomers. But there are three groups, the Monguor, the Bao'an, and the Santa, who speak "archaic" Mongolian languages, and they are believed to be the descendants of the Mongols who manned the Great Khan's garrison in the area.

Santa. The Santa live south of the Yellow River, about fifty miles southwest of Lanzhou, high in the mountains east of the Chinese town of Linxia. Because of this geographical location, which is east of the principal Chinese settlements, they have been given the appellation Dōngxiāng, or 'eastern villages' by the Chinese. The PRC government has followed this Chinese custom and officially named the group "Dongxiang," even though the people call themselves "Santa." There are approximately 280,000 Santa living in several towns and villages. Most of them make their living by farming. Like the Hui, who have settled all around them, the Santa are Muslims.

The Santa language resembles its relative Dagur in many respects. It has preserved the initial *h*'s of Middle Mongolian: *hulan* 'red.' (But long vowels have become short, as the originally long *a* in the second syllable of this word has done.) And, like Dagur, Santa has progressed noticeably toward an "open syllable" kind of structure—but by a slightly different process. Many consonants that once closed syllables, including *r*, have been lost in Santa. For example, Middle Mongolian *bulag* 'spring' has become *bula*; *marghasi* 'tomorrow' has become *magashi*. The consonants *-l* and *-m* have changed to *-n*. The result of these changes is that *n* is now the only consonant that closes syllables. In Santa the front vowels *ö* and *ü* have changed in pronunciation and are now not distinguished from *o* and *u*. Vowel harmony has been lost in the language. In Santa syntax, the genitive and the accusative are marked with the same particle.

More than likely, many of the changes that have taken place in Santa can be attributed to the centuries of contact that the speakers of this language have had with northern Chinese groups. The tendency toward an open syllable is typical of the Mandarin dialects, as is the change of final *-m* to *-n*. One particularly striking adaption to Chinese is the hybrid construction made in Santa using the Chinese copula *shi* 'is.' This copula is put into the sentence in Chinese syntactic order, between the nouns being equated; but the old Mongolian copula is also kept, appearing in its usual position at the end of the sentence. The result is a strange double-copula construction that is neither Chinese nor quite Mongolian. Here are two examples (the Chinese copula is given in small capitals):

Ene kɨwan SHI kienni we.
this youth is   whose is
'Whose boy is this?'

Bi kieliesen kun   SHI ene we.
I spoke   person is this is
'The person I was talking about is this one.'

Around 30 percent of the Santa vocabulary is reported to be borrowed from Chinese.

Bao'an. Almost directly west of the Santa area, at a distance of about thirty to forty miles, lives an even smaller group of Mongols, the Bao'an. "Bao'an" is the Chinese name for these people, and they are officially called that by the Chinese government. The Bao'an are also referred to as the "Bonan" or the "Paongan" in the linguistic literature. There are around 9,000 Bao'an living in the border area between Gansu and Qinghai provinces. There are also Hui, Han Chinese, Salar (a Turkic people), and Tibetans living in the immediate vicinity, and the Bao'an show the effects of this mixed environment. Those living on the Gansu side of the border are Muslims, like the Hui and the Salar; those living on the Qinghai side have become Lamaist Buddhists like the Tibetans.

Bao'an, though it is apparently a separate language, has many of the features of its nearby relatives, Santa and Monguor. For example, the genitive and the accusative are expressed by the same particle. Initial *h*'s are also still pronounced. Bao'an is also like Santa, however, in that it has no distinctive vowel length.

Monguor. The last of the Gansu-Qinghai Mongols, the Monguor, live across the Qinghai border, perhaps a hundred miles northwest of the Bao'an and Santa areas, in the delta formed by the confluence of the Datong and Xining rivers. Today there are some 160,000 Monguor, whose principal settlements are found near the town of Huzhu. The Monguor farm and keep livestock, mostly sheep and swine. Since the Monguor were well established in this area when the Han Chinese began migrating in, they are also called the Tǔ(rén), 'local people, aborigines,' even in official publications. This is an inconsistent lapse on the part of the Chinese government, which has made a point of avoiding condescending terms toward its minorities. The group should be known by their correct name, Monguor, which is their pronunciation of the word "Mongol" (-*l* and -*r* are indistinct at the end of the word in their language).

Though today the population in this part of Qinghai has become more heavily Hui and Han, the Monguor lived for centuries in the midst of Tibetans left from the old Tangut, or Xixia, kingdom. This experience has had a lasting effect. The social and economic system of the Monguor interlocked and often merged with that of the nearby Tibetans. Both groups participated in festivals and weddings. There were many intermarriages. The Monguor all converted to Lamaist Buddhism, and many of the men became monks. What education there was came from Lamaism and its rich Tibetan literature, and the Mongols took for their own many of the Tibetan legends, songs, and fairy tales. The Tibetan language was quite naturally considered by both groups to be more elegant than Mongolian.

The Monguor language is sometimes said to be the most divergent Mongolian language of all. It has apparently undergone none of the various changes that earmark the development of Mongolian proper. We see in the Monguor word *hulaan* 'red,' for example, that both initial *h* and long vowels have been preserved. The innovations that have taken place in Monguor are generally not to be found in any of the other Mongolian languages. (An important exception, however, is the breakdown of its vowel harmony system, something which has also happened in Dagur, in particular.) The effects of Tibetan can be seen everywhere in Monguor structure. The most noteworthy and perhaps the most surprising of these innovations is the development of the complex initial consonant clusters that can be found in Monguor; it seems to be the only Altaic language that has such clusters in native words. The first step in this development was the large-scale borrowing from the local Tibetan dialect of words that had a variety of initial consonant clusters. These words were pronounced with the clusters intact. For instance, the Lamaist term for 'sacrificial offering' was *xtorma*, and the Monguor borrowed it as such. Through a subsequent sound change, it became *storma*, the modern Monguor form of the word. The Monguor did not significantly change the pronunciations of such words in order to fit the structure of their own language, as, for example, the Japanese do when they borrow English words. (Thus in Japanese, vowels are inserted between the consonants in words such as *kurisumasu* 'Christmas.') To understand how the Monguor were able to do this, we must remember that many of them probably had native or near-native fluency in Tibetan for many centuries. They simply pronounced the words "properly," the way New York Hispanics often do when they put English words into their Spanish conversations. After these borrowings took place, the existence of so many foreign sounds in the Monguor vocabulary caused the pronunciations of many native words to change. Vowels separating consonants were elided, making clusters in native words. For example, the older, Middle Mongolian form *hudaru-* 'to destroy' changed first to **xtaru-*, making it look like a Tibetan word; this form in turn changed to modern Monguor *stari-*. The final detail, and the most interesting part of this linguistic story, is that the vowels separating consonants dropped only when the result would be a cluster identical to one of those already found in words the Monguors had taken from the Tibetans. The *u* in the first syllable of *hulaan* 'red,' for example, stayed put for just this reason.

Mongolian Proper

Mongolia—geographical Mongolia—is much larger than the Mongolian People's Republic. In the north it extends up to the Sayan and Yablonoi mountain ranges in the Soviet Union. In the south it is approximately demarcated by the Great Wall. All of this territory is inhabited by Mongols. The part of Mongolia that is now the Mongolian People's Republic is only the part that was known as "Outer Mongolia," that is, the Mongol territory "outside" of China. "Inner Mongolia," representing about half of what was once the Mongols' country, was administratively incorporated into China in the seventeenth century, about a hundred years before "Outer Mongolia" was finally subdued by Qing armies. The Mongols living still farther to the north than Outer Mongolia were conquered by Russians in the seventeenth century and made subjects of the tsar.

The Mongols will probably never be politically united again, any more than the German-speaking people of East and West Germany, Switzerland, and Austria will be. But, like the Germans, the Mongols are united by language. Dialects may vary from place to place in Mongolia, but rarely enough to cause a complete breakdown in communication. A visitor from Ulan Bator, say, would probably have fewer difficulties in Inner Mongolia than a Bavarian would in Low German-speaking areas. The common practice of dividing the Mongolian spoken in Mongolia into three different languages—Khalkha, Oirat, and Buriat—therefore seems to be more a matter of convenience than linguistic reality. The dialect groups formed along the lines of these old tribal alliances are by no means completely mutually unintelligible. If the Austrians and the Swiss can be said to speak German, there is no reason why the Oirat and Buriat cannot be said to speak Mongolian. We will follow the practice of the Chinese government here and classify them all as "Mongolian proper."

The number of speakers of Mongolian proper who live in China is around 3,500,000. They are spread out in the arc of the border that begins at the top of Eastern Manchuria and swings around through all of Inner Mongolia to the border of Xinjiang. On the leading edge of this arc newly arrived Chinese settlers overlap the Mongols and, in an increasing number of places, outnumber them; the Han are a clear majority in most of Inner Mongolia now. Patches of Mongols are also scattered around Xinjiang and Qinghai.

The Mongols of Inner Mongolia are economically divided into "agricultural" Mongols and "herding" Mongols. Many of the agricultural Mongols have been collectivized and make their living in ways similar to the Han living in the same areas. They plant barley, millet, buckwheat, sesame, beans, and other crops adapted to terrain and climate. For livestock, they usually keep swine and fowl instead of the more traditional sheep of their herding brothers. Houses are generally made of sod. The herding Mongols are still semi-nomadic. They follow their flocks in summer, living in the traditional felt tents called yurts (*ger* in Mongolian; "yurt" is a borrowing into Western languages from Turkic). In addition to the "agricultural" Mongols and the "herding" Mongols, a large number of Mongols are being drawn from both groups to work in the salt, iron, and coal mines of Inner Mongolia.

All of these Chinese Mongols, but especially the "agricultural" Mongols, have taken much from the Chinese—so much so, that when the Mongols in Outer Mongolia declared their independence in 1911, they did little to exhort their Inner Mongolian kinsmen to join them because they were suspicious of them as being too "Chinese." Yet, the Inner Mongolians have more in common with the Outer Mongolians than they do with the Dagur, the Monguor, and the other remnants of the Mongol garrisons in China. Much that was formative in the lives of the Mongols happened in the seventeenth century, after these garrisons had become isolated, but while all the Mongols of geographical Mongolia were still in contact. For this was the time of the rapid spread of Lamaist Buddhism among the Mongols, and almost all of those living in Inner and Outer Mongolia embraced the new faith. The monastery became the source of all education and literature, and all literate speakers of Mongolian (proper) read and wrote in Classical Mongolian well into the twentieth century, using the Middle Eastern alphabet they had borrowed from the Uighurs. This period had a lasting and unifying effect on the life and language of the Mongols. Even today, the alphabet is known in all parts of Mongolia, and in Inner Mongolia it is still the official script. In contrast with this kind of literacy, the Dagur, the Monguor, and the others who became isolated from the homeland in the thirteenth century have no knowledge at all of Mongol writing and literature and are unable to write their own language.

Most of the Mongols of Inner Mongolia speak varieties of the language differing little from the Khalkha standard, although some speakers of Oirat dialects are also found here and there in many regions as a result of the refugee movements that took place during the internecine warfare between them and the victorious Khalkha. One branch of the Oirat, the Kalmyk, went to Russia in 1630 and participated in the Russian conquest of the Caucasus. After the conquest, they stayed on and moved permanently into the Volga region. Later, in 1771, some of them returned and settled in modern-day Xinjiang. The Kalmyk are an extreme example, but they serve to show just how widely the Oirat became scattered.

The Khalkha dialect has a vowel system representative of the rest of Mongolian proper. It is a very Altaic system, far more so than Moghol or Monguor, which have been more influenced by non-Altaic languages. Its seven vowels—*i, e, ü, ö, a, u, o*—are much the same as the vowels of Middle Mongolian, the language of Chinggis Khan's time. They are arranged in a system of vowel harmony based on the opposition of front and back: *e, ü, ö* are the front vowels, and *a, u, o* are the back vowels. Except in loanwords, front vowels only appear with front vowels, and back vowels only appear with back vowels. For example, the particle used to mark what is called the "ablative" case is pronounced as either *-aas* or *-ees*, depending on the vowels of the noun to which it attaches:

> gar-aas 'from the hand'
> tüsimel-ees 'from the official'

One significant difference between this Mongolian vowel system and that of most of the Turkic languages is that in Mongolian the vowel *i* is a "neutral" vowel; that is, it does not harmonize with the other vowels. It can be in the same word with any vowel, regardless whether the vowel is front or back. Here is how the accusative particle *-iig*, which contains this neutral vowel, behaves.

> emeel-iig '[I saw, e.g.] the saddle'
> axa-iig '[I saw, e.g.] the elder brother'

It seems at first curious that a vowel so obviously pronounced in the front of the mouth would be "neutral" in a system in which "front" is the critical feature. But the fact is that at one time this vowel was not neutral, because there was then the

MONGOLIAN CONSONANTS

	Labial	Denti-labial	Dental	Retro-flex	Alveo-lar	Palatal	Velar	Post-velar	Glottal
Voiceless stop	(p)		t				(k)		
Aspirated stop									
Voiced stop	b		d				g		
Voiceless affricate			ts		ch				
Aspirated affricate									
Voiced affricate			dz		j				
Voiceless fricative		(f)	s		sh		x		
Voiced fricative									
Nasal	m		n				ng		
Voiceless nasal									
Lateral			l						
Voiceless lateral									
Flap or trill			r						
Voiceless flap									
Semivowels	(w)					y			

vowel $*i$, which was the back version of i. It was only after this vowel $*i$ that contrasted with i was lost that i became "neutral."

One peculiarity of modern Mongolian is that, unlike the Mongolian of an earlier time, its vowels are slurred or pronounced indistinctly when they are in an unstressed position. This is similar to what English speakers do. For example, the stressed vowel of the English word *fámily* is pronounced [ɛ]; but when the same vowel is not stressed, as in the word *familial*, its full quality is not articulated and it becomes a schwa [ə], much like the vowel sound of *uh*. In much the same way, Mongolians pronounce the second vowel in the word *ene* 'this' rather close to a schwa, because the syllable in which it appears is unstressed.

The consonants in parentheses in the table are alien to Mongolian and occur only in foreign words. Thus the Mongolian word *samping* 'abacus,' which contains a *p*, is a borrowing from Chinese *suànpan* 'abacus,' and the word *kapitaal* 'capital,' which contains both a *p* and a *k*, is a borrowing from Russian. Since many of the languages of the world have a distinction between *p* and *b* and between *k* and *g*, we might suspect that Mongolian at one time did, too. Our suspicions about *k* are confirmed when we compare Mongolian with Dagur, a closely related language that does have such a consonant. The word for 'blue' in Dagur is *kuke*, and the same word in Mongolian is *xüxe* (the phoneme *x* is a velar fricative, like German *ach* or the Putonghua consonant written with *h* in Pinyin). Mongolian did have *k*'s, but they all weakened and changed to *x*. Something similar happend to an original Mongolian $*p$, except that it happened much earlier. The word 'red,' for instance, originally began with a *p*: $*pulaghan$. The *p* weakened by Chinggis Khan's time to an *h*, which the conservative language Dagur still has: *hulaan*. Mongolian has progressed a step beyond this and completely lost the consonant: now the word for 'red' is pronounced *ulaan*, as can be seen in the name of the Mongolian capital, Ulan Bator (*ulaan baatar*), which means 'red hero.'

Something very characteristically Altaic about the Mongolian consonant system is that *r* and *l* do not appear at the beginning of a word. The consonant *r-* never does, and the tiny number of exceptions with *l-* are all loanwords; for example, the word *lüü* 'basket' has been borrowed from Chinese *lóng* 'basket.' Why these consonants should be so constrained in where they can occur we do not know; but the fact remains that they are similarly restricted in almost all of the Altaic languages.

In Mongolian speech, words are often abbreviated or run together into adjacent words. We have already mentioned that vowels are not always fully articulated; sometimes in rapid speech they are elided altogether, creating a jumble of consonants alien to more careful speech.

A Mongol puts his words together and constructs sentences in ways that would be familiar to a Korean or Japanese. The grammars are remarkably similar. A Mongolian sentence or clause consists of a loosely ordered series of nouns and noun phrases that terminate in the verb, which is the core around which the sentence is built. The order of the noun phrases is determined by relative emphasis; the importance of the nouns increases as the sentence builds toward the verb. The relationship of each noun to the rest of the sentence is indicated by suffixing to it various caselike particles. There are eight of these cases in Mongolian. Here are examples:

	case	form	
1.	absolute	dalae	'sea'
2.	genitive	dalae-ng	'of the sea'
3.	dative-locative	dalae-do	'to the sea'
4.	ablative	dalae-gaas	'from the sea'
5.	accusative	dalae-g	'[I subdued] the sea'
6.	instrumental	dalae-gaar	'by sea'
7.	comitative	dalae-tae	'with the sea'
8.	directive	dalae-ruu	'toward the sea'

One significant and often mentioned difference between this Mongolian case system and the similar systems of Japanese and Korean is that in Mongolian there is no particle to mark the subject, and so subjects are in the "absolute"; that is, the noun stem itself, bare of suffixed particles, is used as the subject. A direct object is also in the absolute if it is "indefinite," although it takes the accusative case marker -*(ii)g* if it is "definite":

zurag   zuraba
picture painted
'painted *a* picture' (INDEFINITE)

zurag-iig   zuraba
picture-ACC painted
'painted *the* picture' (DEFINITE)

Verb forms, too, are created with suffixes attached to a stem, and Mongolian is equipped with a variety of verb endings that function analogously to those of

Korean and Japanese. Mongolian, however, like other Altaic languages, is different from Korean and Japanese in that a simple imperative, such as *Yaba!* 'Go!' consists of nothing but the stem of the verb *yaba-* 'to go.' In contrast with this, the stems of verbs in Korean and Japanese never appear without a suffixed ending. In Korean and Japanese, there is a fundamental difference between verbs and the much freer, isolatable class of nouns.

Complements and clauses are also constructed and used in ways common to typologically similar languages like Japanese and Korean. Here is one example:

> Xarangxui shönö önggör-chi, xar   üül-te   tengger,
> dark(ness) night end-ing   black cloud-y sky
> xayaan-aas-aa gegeere-be.
> edge-from-its brighten-ed
> 'Dark night ended, and the sky covered with black clouds
> brightened on the horizon.'

Mongolian writing. The earliest historical glimpse of Mongolian comes from the inscription on a stele erected in honor of Chinggis Khan's nephew Yisüngge around 1225, shortly before the death of the great Khan. There are no written records older than that. What is known of "Ancient Mongolian," the language spoken by the Mongols before the time of Chinggis Khan, comes from a small number of words imperfectly preserved in Chinese documents, and a few ancient borrowings into languages with which the Mongols came into early contact. The features of Ancient Mongolian, so far as they are known, are almost entirely the product of reconstruction by linguists and philologists. The actual history of Mongolia does not begin until the early thirteenth century, the time of the oldest extant writings in the language.

The Mongols learned to write sometime in the twelfth century from the Uighurs, the Turkic people living to their west in Chinese Turkestan. These were the most highly civilized people that the Mongols had come into contact with before the conquest of China, and the commercial skills the Uighurs had sharpened from centuries of living on the main East–West trade routes were in great demand in Chinggis Khan's rapidly expanding government. The Uighurs became the core of his civil administration, and their alphabet became the medium of communication in the Mongol empire.

One of the earliest and most important uses that was made of the Uighur script was the recording, in Mongolian, of the code of laws that Chinggis Khan established for the Mongol nation. Unfortunately, no original version of this code has been preserved, but one can well imagine that many of the orthographic conventions governing the use of the Mongol writing system must have been fixed by that time. Since Chinggis

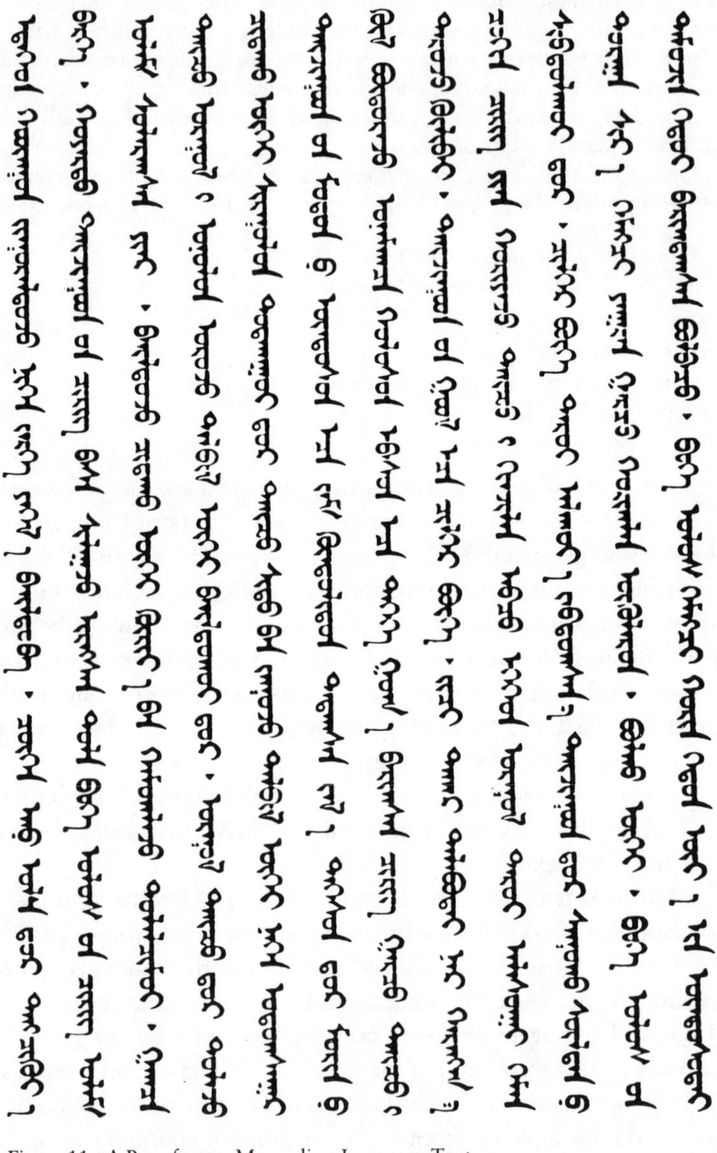

Figure 11. A Page from a Mongolian-Language Text.
The text, a history of the Mongol dynasty in China, was printed
in Peking, ca. 1920.

intended his legal code to be a higher authority than the Khan himself, he must have demanded a precise and consistent standardization. Many of the conventions and spellings found in the Yisüngge inscription of 1225 are still in use today among all the Mongols who employ the old alphabet, and this gives "Written Mongolian" a decidedly archaic quality. The words *maxa* 'meat, fish' and *uula* 'mountain,' for example, are still spelled *miqan* and *aghula*, just as Chinggis Khan might have pronounced them. This may seem to be excessive orthographic conservatism, but let us remember that the English-speaking world makes use of spellings such as *knight* and *taught*, which are only slightly less archaic.

Mongol writing has a pleasant but unusual appearance. The curves, loops and comblike serrations projecting off a thick baseline look Middle Eastern, as one might expect; but the lines run vertically down the page, Chinese-style. To produce this curious effect, the scribes of the Khan modified the Uighur script by rotating the page ninety degrees counterclockwise, resulting in vertical lines that progress successively from left to right. The Mongols—or their Uighur scribes—were not the only people in East Asia to make this modification, and some extant examples of Syriac and Uighur writing from Chinese Turkestan are also read from top to bottom. Apparently, the Chinese model of vertical writing had an influence even upon people using totally different writing systems and writing implements.

The Mongol script has twenty-four basic symbols, most of which, like the Uighur letters, have three different forms according to their position in the word: initial, medial, or final. The symbols are usually distinct in the initial position, but several of them look exactly the same in medial or final position. For example, the final forms of the letters for *a, e,* and *n* are all the same. Of course, if one knows the structure of the language this does not present a very serious problem, since the shapes of Mongolian words are largely predictable. Hence the symbol for *a, e,* or *n* cannot represent *n* if the letter immediately before it is a consonant, because no Mongolian word end in *-ln, -gn,* or the like. The rules of vowel harmony usually tell whether the symbol represents *a* or *e*. These particular letters do not present much of a problem to native Mongolians, but there are certain other letters that can be troublesome even for them. The Mongols do not distinguish in writing at all between the phonemes *o* and *u, ö* and *ü, t* and *d, k* and *g,* or *y* and *j*. This creates many homographs; for example, *unuqu* 'to ride horseback' and *onoqu* 'to understand'; *ger* 'house, yurt' and *ker* 'how'; *urtu* 'long' and *ordu* 'palace.' Pairs of words such as these can be told apart only by the context of the passage in which they

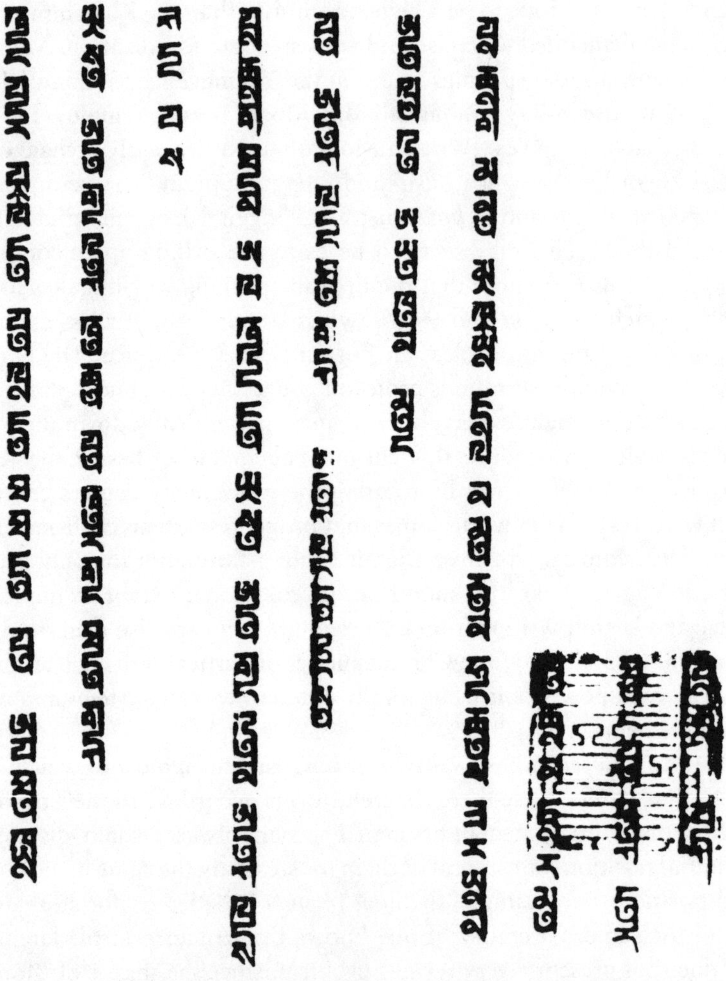

Figure 12. A hP'ags-pa Manuscript, dated 1305. (from Tucci 1949)

As this manuscript shows, the lines of hP'ags-pa writing are vertical and follow one another from left to right across the page. Tibetan, upon which the letters of the hP'ags-pa alphabet were patterned, was (and still is) written horizontally, from left to right.

appear. The problem is much like that of the English spelling *read*, which can be pronounced either as a homophone of the word *reed* or as a homophone of the word *red*. This confusion in written Mongolian is compounded by the fact that some letters, such as *gh* and *q*, are distinguished by dots placed next to the left of the letter, and in ancient manuscripts these dots are often omitted, just as in Arabic the superscripts indicating vowel qualities are usually left off. None of these deficiencies of Written Mongolian were ever corrected, and they are still found in the writing system today. It remained for the Manchus, who would later take over this script from the Mongols, to find ways to eliminate these inconveniences.

Meanwhile, within a few decades of Chinggis Khan's death, a different and briefer episode in the history of Mongolian writing began. Khubilai Khan, Chinggis's grandson and fourth successor, had a more grandiose concept of writing than his grandfather. Khubilai, as is well known from Marco Polo's accounts of him, cultivated an internationalism in the great Mongol empire under his rule. To this end he conceived of a kind of orthographic Esperanto, in which all the peoples of the realm would be served by one and the same script. He commanded his personal lama— for by this time Lamaism had become popular among the Mongol leaders—to construct a unified script. The lama, known to the world as hP'ags-pa (the Tibetan word for 'esteemed'), was of course Tibetan, and the script with which he was most familiar was the modified Indic alphabet used in his own country. Accordingly, hP'ags-pa devised an alphabet of forty-two squarish letters in imitation of the Tibetan model. Khubilai promulgated the new writing system in 1269, and it subsequently became known variously as the "hP'ags-pa script" after its inventor, or the "square script," because of its appearance.

The hP'ags-pa script was not a very imaginative invention. It was a slavish imitation of Tibetan and difficult to write. Nevertheless, the new alphabet was phonetically more precise than the Uighur writing system, and with it the distinctions in a number of languages could be represented. Mongolian and Chinese, and to a lesser extent Turkic and Persian as well, began to be written with the new alphabet. Khubilai encouraged the use of this script and gave rewards to those who learned it, and throughout his lifetime and the Mongol reign in China it was used for official decrees and inscriptions and on paper and coined money. In the end, however, the hP'ags-pa script was abandoned. Not long after the collapse of the Yuan dynasty in 1368, it fell into disuse, and everyone, including the Mongols, went back to their old scripts.

The reasons for abandoning a phonetically more accurate writing system may have been partially sentiment and attachment to the traditions of the great Chinggis Khan. It may also be true, as many claim, that the hP'ags-pa letters were clumsy and ugly; they are undeniably complicated and bulky and require far more effort to write than the relatively streamlined script of the Uighurs. But one suspects that the real reason was just habit. Khubilai had wanted to persuade people to use the new alphabet, but he never tried to purge the old writing systems. While the hP'ags-pa script appeared in all officially sanctioned places, the old Uighur script more than likely continued to be used as the medium for more private purposes, and in the end it was destined for a longer life.

Mongolian has also been recorded using other writing systems. Some of what is known about earlier stages of the language comes from Arabic and Persian glossaries of the thirteenth and fourteenth centuries. Still more information comes from Chinese sources. *The Secret History of the Mongols*, a semi-legendary account of Chinggis Khan and his ancestors, was probably first composed around 1240 using the Uighur script, but no original copy of this work has survived. Instead, what remains of the Mongols' greatest literary monument is a transliteration and translation of the work made in the fourteenth century using Chinese characters. The Ming government also produced various Chinese–Mongolian glossaries around the same time.

Tungus

Tungus is the eastern branch of Altaic. The best-known member of this family is Manchu, the now almost extinct language that was once spoken by the Altaic conquerors who ruled China from the seventeenth to the twentieth century. All the other Tungus languages are relatively little known and little studied.

The Tungus peoples—again, with the exception of the Manchus—are mostly small nomadic bands of hunters and reindeer breeders. Others live in fishing communities along the Pacific coast. The Tungus are not numerous. The largest of their groups are at most a few tens of thousands strong, and some number only in the hundreds.

There are two distinct groups of Tungus, the Northern Tungus and the Southern Tungus. A few of the Northern Tungus are found in Manchuria, but most of them live in the remote reaches of Eastern Siberia, isolated from the "higher" civilizations that surround Inner Asia. These tiny groups of nomads are spread thinly over an enormous territory. The entire eastern half of Siberia, from the Pacific Ocean in the east to the middle course of the Ob River in the west, is home to them. In the north they live on the very banks of the Arctic Ocean. When tsarist soldiers exploring Siberia reached the Yenesei River in 1607, they found the Northern Tungus people called the Evenki living there. This meeting with the expanding Russian empire, at such a recent historical date, marks the first

recorded modern contact any Northern Tungus had with a technologically advanced and literate culture; many of the other Northern Tungus
were not "discovered" by the outside world until as late as the nineteenth
century. How and why an almost negligible number of people became
diffused over such an enormous expanse of North Asia is not known.
Presumably there was some technological or social innovation that led to
a relatively rapid expansion of a much more compact group. But what
this innovation was, or when it was, can only be guessed; there are no
historical accounts of the migrations of the Northern Tungus. Neither
they nor the Siberian peoples that they displaced left any records. We
know only, from linguistic evidence, that the Northern Tungus began
from a common origin with the Southern Tungus that was probably
located on the eastern side of the Altaic area in the vicinity of what is now
Manchuria and Eastern Mongolia.

The Southern Tungus, represented most notably by the Manchus, live
nearer to what was probably the original homeland of the Tungus. They
are found dispersed throughout Manchuria and the adjacent coastal
areas of the Soviet Union, along the lower course of the Amur River and
on the island of Sakhalin, just off the northern tip of Japan. As late as the
seventeenth century, tribes of Southern Tungus also lived deep in the
northeastern part of the Korean peninsula. Because the Southern Tungus
have remained close to the zone of contact with Mongols, Koreans, and
Chinese, their languages have generally changed more than the relatively
conservative languages of the Northern group. Manchu not only has a
very large number of loanwords, but it also has a structure significantly
affected by its contact with Chinese. Its relationship to Evenki, the pro-
totypical Northern Tungus language, can be likened to the position that
English occupies within the Germanic family, since English structure and
vocabulary have also been altered through intense exposure to another
culture, namely that of the Norman French.

Tungus Languages in China

There is still considerable disagreement among experts as to how
many Tungus languages there are. Over the years many new names have
been suggested, but most of these probably represent dialect variants of
languages already reported upon.

Problems with classification notwithstanding, the People's Republic of
China has decided to recognize five Tungus groups among its minorities:
Evenki (also called Solon), Oroqen, Hezhen, Xibo, and Manchu.

Evenki. About 20,000 of these Northern Tungus nomads still live and hunt in the northernmost corner of the border region between Manchuria (Heilongjiang Province) and Inner Mongolia. The names given to this minority are confusing. The word *evenki* means nothing more than 'people' or 'human beings'; and 'Solon,' the name by which the Evenki living in China are usually known in the West, means only, 'those (people) from the upper course of the river.' As is common among the Tungus, the Evenki have never had a strong consciousness of their national identity, and so they themselves have no name for their group.

Until quite recently, the Evenki were the essential Tungus hunters, migrating from one campsite to the next with seasonal changes in hunting conditions. They camped in conical tents or yurts, which in summer were made of birchbark and in winter were made of pelts. Moves from one place to the next were accomplished using all-purpose domestic reindeer both as draft animals and as mounts. Of late, however, many Evenki have been forced to settle into more permanent dwellings and sometimes into communes. They still hunt and raise livestock, including the traditional horses and reindeer, but now some Evenki have also turned to farming.

The Evenki language has vowel harmony, the characteristic feature of Altaic. But the system, which is representative of the general Tungus type, has undergone some important historical changes. It no longer works like Turkic or Mongolian harmony (if it ever did). The way the vowels are arrayed makes a system in which the harmonizing feature can best be described as a matter of the relative height of the vowel. It is not as regular or as simple as the front–back opposition assumed to be the original Altaic kind of harmony. In addition, some of the vowel distinctions that once existed in Evenki have been lost, so that in the present-day system there are three "neutral" vowels. (For a discussion of what "neutral" vowels are, see the section on Mongolian, above.)

Evenki has a much more complicated morphology than Manchu. Its case system is said to be the richest of all the Tungus languages. In the dialect that forms the basis of the written Evenki language used in the Soviet Union, there are fourteen cases; other Evenki dialects are reported to have an even greater number of case categories.

Oroqen. The Oroqen are very similar to the Evenki, and the languages are so close Oroqen could be considered an Evenki dialect. The name that they go by means 'the reindeer people' or 'the reindeer breeders' (from *oron* 'reindeer' + the possessive suffix). It is usually spelled

"Oroqen" in the PRC, but there are many variants, most commonly "Orochon" in Western-language literature. Since other Tungus groups also keep reindeer, many have been given names that are easy to confuse with the Oroqen.

About 4,000 Oroqen live in China, some ranging over the same territory as the Evenki. However, the majority are found slightly east of the other Northern Tungus group, in the Lesser Khingan Mountain range, near a disputed stretch of the Soviet border along the Amur River (Heilongjiang).

Hezhen. This tiny minority of 1,500 fishing folk is found in the eastern border region of Heilongjiang Province, in the vicinity of Khabarovsk. The Hezhen are called "Nanai" by Soviet scholars, and most of them live in the USSR. The language is as yet little studied in China.

Xibo. The Xibo or (Sibo) are a Southern Tungus people. Most experts classify their language as a dialect of Manchu, but they have traditionally been considered a separate nationality, and that is how they are still classified today. They call themselves "Shivə," not "Manju."

There are some 84,000 Xibo in China, but more than half are almost indistinguishable from the Han. The only large community in which the Xibo dialect is used on a daily basis is that of the 18,000 Xibo living in the Autonomous Xibo County in the Ili River valley on the western border of Xinjiang, where Xibo is written as well as spoken. These Xibo, the descendants of a Manchu border guard posted to Xinjiang in the eighteenth century, are by far the largest group of Manchu speakers in China today.

The Xibo owe their wide dispersion to Manchu military policy during the Qing dynasty. When the Manchus rose to power in China, their cousins the Xibo were a tribe of mounted warriors living in the Nen and Songhua river valleys in central Manchuria. Although they spoke Manchu and were otherwise ethnically almost identical to the Manchus, the Xibo came under the banner of the Khorchin Mongols in the Manchu military alliance. In 1692, fearing that the Xibo were still too cohesive as a military power, the Manchu government reorganized them to reduce the threat of rebellion and redistributed their units among three separate banners. Then, about a decade later, most of these Xibo soldiers were uprooted and dispatched for garrison duty to a number of widely separated places in North China, including Peking and Mukden. This was the first resettlement of the Xibo. A second major resettlement took place a half century later during the reign of the Qianlong Emperor. The Manchu government was fighting a series of campaigns in the northwestern part of the Empire and needed reinforcements to strengthen its military units in Xinjiang. The Xibo troops stationed in Mukden were dispatched en masse in 1764 to fill the breach and were then resettled there permanently as border guards. The Xibo communities now living in Xinjiang are the descendants of those soldiers.

Since the Xibo spoken in Xinjiang is still very much a living language, it is an important source of information about spoken Manchu and earlier stages of Tungus. It is reported to have eight vowel distinctions as compared with the six of Manchu (proper), as well as a complex kind of vowel harmony that works somewhat differently. It is also said to have differences in its morphology. The structure and vocabulary of Xibo have not been affected by Chinese quite as much as Manchu (proper), but there are still a great number of Chinese loanwords, and the intensity of Chinese influence has increased in recent years. Like most of the other languages of China, it has a panoply of social terminology, and words from Chinese like *gungshə* 'commune' and *gəming* 'revolution' have become the vocabulary of everyday life. Because the Autonomous Xibo County is located in a part of Xinjiang with a fairly large Kazakh and Uighur population, the Xibo have borrowed many words from those two languages as well.

Manchu

The 4,300,000 people that the government of China identifies as Manchu should more properly be called the Chinese of Manchu ancestry. Numerous though they may be, the members of this particular minority group are now so thoroughly Sinicized there is virtually nothing to show that they are Manchu. They work in the same professions, live the same lives, and enjoy the same pleasures that the Han do. Nor is there any geographical area where only Manchus live. There is no Manchu region, prefecture, or even county anywhere in Manchuria. In every place where Manchus are found, they live among other groups, especially the Han. Though the Manchus are officially recognized as a minority, they have in fact been Chinese for a long time.

The Manchu language is all but extinct. The only people who speak it on a day-to-day basis are the Xibo minority of Xinjiang, who were discussed in the preceding section. The rest of the Manchus use Chinese as their first language, and most of those among them who still know the old language reportedly speak it with a pronounced Chinese accent. The state of spoken Manchu in Manchuria may be compared to that of Gaelic in the British Isles, an idiom that is also nearing extinction.

Manchu is an important language in East Asia in spite of its present moribund state. For the more than two hundred and fifty years (1644–1911) that the Manchus were in power in China, it was an official language of the Qing dynasty. By the eighteenth century it probably ceased completely to be spoken in the court, even by the Manchus themselves, but all official documents continued to be written bilingually, in Manchu and in Chinese, up until the very end of the dynasty. Even in the first decade of the twentieth century, the great Manchu notices in black print on light yellow paper could still be seen hanging next to the doors of the Yamen.

There is also an extensive translation literature in Manchu. Because it had pledged itself to a state-supported Confucianism, the Qing government had to make the relevant Chinese materials available for the edification and instruction of all its people, and the classical and canonical books were translated on a scale seldom seen before. After the classics and histories came the literature of diversion, beginning with the translation of the famous Chinese novel *The Romance of the Three Kingdoms* in 1650. The ninety-four fascicles of the literary anthology *Guwen Yuanjian* were published in 1685, and the historical compilation *Zizhi tongjian gangmu* began to appear in its 111 translated fascicles in the year 1691. Bilingual editions of all literary genres became available during the Qianlong period (1736–1796), and the care with which these translations were made is seen, for example, in the excellent Manchu edition of *The Golden Lotus*.

In the West, information about China first became available in Manchu, which was the language China used for official diplomatic commerce with Russia from the seventeenth to the nineteenth century. European Sinologists studied Manchu extensively in the eighteenth century and used it for their interpretations and translation of Chinese, a language that was then considerably less well known to them than Manchu. Today Manchu is principally useful—apart from linguistic purposes—as historical source material for the Qing period, especially in places where phonetic transcriptions of place and personal names are needed, and for documents on various minority affairs, which were sometimes composed only in Manchu.

Amost all that is known about the Manchu language comes from this official literature. Direct information from the southern dialect upon which it was based is scant and sometimes conflicting. By the time that the first modern descriptions of the spoken language were made in the nineteenth century, Manchu had for the most part become the artificially cultivated tool of a small number of Chinese officials and intellectuals—a little like Latin in today's Catholic Church. While the descriptions of the structure, grammar, and usage were consistent enough, the reports on the pronunciations were often confusing. One of the six vowels of written Manchu, the one that was used least in the language, was described by a French scholar as a long *o:*, like the *oh* in German *Sohn* 'son'; but a German listening to the language declared the same vowel to be a long *u:*. Later, another German scholar decided that was not long, nor was it either *o* or *u*, but rather a short sound between the two vowels, which he wrote as *ô*. Presumably, this last scholar was closer to the truth, because the vowel patterned in the system as a short sound, and in the eigtheenth century the Korean Translators' Bureau had transcribed it with their alphabetic symbol for *o*. But there is no reliable way to check the pronunciation now, because the Xibo dialect does not have this vowel—in its place we find only an *o* or an *u*. We could imagine having the same kind of problem if we had to describe the sounds of Latin based upon the pronunciations of modern European priests. Whatever the vowel in question may have been, it is customary these days to transliterate its Manchu letter as *û* or *ū* and describe it functionally: it was a back vowel that usually appeared only after postvelar consonants.

The Manchu vowel system was composed of six vowels: the five basic vowels *i, e, a, o, u*, plus this rarer, less well understood *û*. There were in addition some special symbols used in written Manchu to represent the vowels of Chinese loanwords. These sounds imitating Chinese values are believed to have been pronounced as such by Manchus, but they never occurred in native words. The vowel system was very different from the original, Altaic pattern of eight (four front vowels and four back vowels). There was vowel harmony in Manchu, but it was not the regular, predictable kind found in the Turkic or Mongolian languages. As in the other modern Tungus languages, the patterning had been considerably disturbed by historical changes, and the rules had many exceptions. Most parts of the system could be described as little more than the historical relics of true vowel harmony. The relationships that did obtain patterned as follows:

neutral	front	back
i	—	o
u	—	(û)
—	e	a

In this system, the two "neutral" vowels were free to occur with any other vowel or vowels, and the front vowel *e* did not occur with the two regular back vowels *o* and *u*. The vowel *û* usually patterned as a back vowel, but sometimes it was found with the front vowel *e*.

In Manchu, as in the other languages with vowel harmony that were spoken in areas contiguous with China (including Korean), the vowel harmony relationships were traditionally described in terms of the philosophy of the *I Ching*. Syllables with front vowels were called "yin" syllables, and those with back vowels were "yang" syllables. The reason was that the language had a kind of

MANCHU CONSONANTS

	Labial	Denti-labial	Dental	Retro-flex	Alveo-lar	Palatal	Velar	Post-velar	Glottal
Voiceless stop	p		t				k		
Aspirated stop									
Voiced stop	b		d				g		
Voiceless affricate					c[ch]				
Aspirated affricate									
Voiced affricate					j				
Voiceless fricative		f	s		š[sh]		h[x]		
Voiced fricative									
Nasal	m		n				ng		
Voiceless nasal									
Lateral			l						
Voiceless lateral									
Flap or trill			r						
Voiceless flap									
Semivowels	w					y			

sound symbolism in which front vowels represented weak or feminine things, and the back vowels strong or masculine things. In Manchu there were therefore a number of interesting word pairs in which changing the vowels changed the gender.

"yin" (feminine)	*"yang" (masculine)*
hehe 'woman'	haha 'man'
eme 'mother'	ama 'father'
emhe 'mother-in-law'	amha 'father-in-law'
nece 'sister-in-law'	naca 'brother-in-law'
nekcu 'aunt'	nakcu 'uncle'
emile 'hen'	amila 'rooster'
erselen 'lioness'	arsalan 'lion'
hebtehe 'woman's belt'	habtaha 'man's belt'
genggen 'weak'	ganggan 'strong'
huwešen 'Buddisht nun'	hûwašan 'Buddhist monk (from Chinese *héshang* 'monk')

Some of the above examples indicate that this sound symbolism was a mildly productive process. The words for 'lioness' and 'Buddhist nun' were obviously derived from their masculine counterparts.

Manchu had nineteen consonants, given in the table in the usual transcription conventions. The consonant *p* was quite rare and was found principally in loan-words and onomatopoeia, such as *pak pik* 'pow pow! (the sound of many small firecrackers going off).' There had been *p*'s originally in the language, but they had historically changed to *f*. The phoneme *ng* was also found mostly in Chinese loanwords and onomatopoeia, and there was no Manchu letter to represent it;

instead, it was written as a digraph, *nk* (the symbol for *n* plus the symbol for *k*), just as the English phoneme *ng* is written as *n* plus *g*.

Written Manchu was close to being an "open syllable" language. The only consonant that regularly came at the end of native words was *n*—this situation is similar to Japanese. Almost all words ended in a vowel. There were sometimes clusters of two consonants between vowels, such as those in *ilha* 'flower' and *abka* 'heaven,' but in most words the vowels were separated by single consonants. This open-syllable structure may not have been a tendency of all varieties of Manchu, however; it could very well have been an idiosyncrasy of the particular southern dialect that formed the basis of the written language. In the dialect of Manchu heard today among the Xibo (called the "western dialect" by some), many more words are reported to end in consonants. For example, written Manchu *hehe* 'woman' is pronounced *heh* [xəx] in Xibo; written *yasa* 'eye' corresponds to spoken *yas*; written *cimari* 'tomorrow' is spoken *cimar*.

Manchu was remarkable for the number of foreign sounds that were taken into the language from Chinese. Special symbols were devised in the writing system to represent them. Among others, there was the symbol for a high, unrounded back vowel (customarily Romanized with a *y*.) It was found in such words as *sy* 'Buddhist temple' (from Chinese *sì* 'id.') and *Sycuwan* 'Sichuan (Province).' Chinese affricates were represented with consonant symbols not used in native words; for example, *dzengse* 'an orange' (Chinese *chénzi*) and *tsun* 'Chinese inch' (from Chinese *cùn*). A *k* or a *g* in a Chinese loanword was said to have been pronounced differently from a *k* or a *g* in a native word, but the nature of those pronunciation differences has not been adequately described in the linguistic literature.

To govern China the Manchus needed a rich technical vocabulary. Many of the required terms were borrowed directly from Chinese, but others were devised by indirect means using internal resources. In this more circuitous process, the Chinese concept was first taken over, and then the elements of the term were rendered into the most appropriate native roots. For example, the Chinese calligraphic term *kǎishū* 'the standard, model forms of the Chinese characters' was in Chinese composed of the two elements *kǎi* 'model' and *shū* 'writing.' The Manchus translated this term into words of their own language and called it *ginggulere hergen* '(literally) respected writing.' The so-called "ten celestial stems," used in Chinese for sequencing purposes, much as Westerners use alphabetical order "A, B, C, ...," were replaced by the color terms so important in Manchu culture:

	Chinese	Manchu
'A'	jiǎ	niowanggiyan 'green'
'B'	yǐ	niohon 'greenish'
'C'	bǐng	fulgiyan 'red'
'D'	dīng	fulahûn 'reddish'
'E'	wù	suwayan 'yellow'
'F'	jǐ	sohon 'yellowish'
'G'	gēng	šanyan 'white'
'H'	xīn	šahûn 'whitish'
'I'	rén	sahaliyan 'black'
'J'	guǐ	sahahûn 'blackish'

Sometimes new terms were mixtures of Manchu and Chinese. Nurhachi (1559–1626), the founder of the Manchu dynasty, was given the Manchu posthumous title Taizu dergi hûwangdi '(literally) Grand Progenitor First Emperor' to parallel the Chinese title Tàizǔ shàng huángdì. The Chinese word *shàng* that was used in this title had the primary meaning of 'top, above.' Therefore, when the Manchu title was made, this Chinese word was replaced by *dergi*, the Manchu word for 'top, above.' As a result of such Sinicized usage, *dergi* came to have the same implication of 'first' and then, by extension, 'emperor' that the Chinese word *shàng* did, and during the Qing dynasty *dergi* was used in a wide variety of terms and titles having to do with the emperor or the palace.

Besides a voluminous Sinitic vocabulary, Manchu also had many earlier borrowings from other peoples on their borders, especially the Mongols. The words *morin* 'horse' and *temen* 'camel,' for example, were taken from Mongolian. Manchu is also said to have had some Korean vocabulary.

WRITTEN Manchu had a much simpler case system than the other Tungus languages. (Many experts suspect that its grammar was simplified through long, intimate exposure to Chinese.) There were five basic ways of marking a noun or noun phrase to indicate its relationship to the other elements of the sentence:

case	*form*	
absolute	boo	'house'
genitive	boo-i	'of the house'
dative-locative	boo-de	'to the house'
ablative	boo-ci	'from the house'
accusative	boo-be	'[build] the house'

The genitive particle *-i* was also used to mark an "instrumental," e.g., *suhe-i* '[chop it] with an ax.' As in Mongolian, subjects are in the "absolute," that is, they were expressed by the bare noun stem, without any suffixed particles. A great many other noun functions were left in the absolute as well.

Since the functions of the nouns were generally specified by the case particles, the ordering of the elements in the Manchu sentence was fairly free, just as it is in Mongolian. And, again as in Mongolian (or Japanese or Korean), the relative emphasis built toward the end of the sentence. Notice, for example, how the accusative and dative elements in the following sentences can be shifted to draw attention to different things:

Morin-be tere niyalma-de bu-fi,...
horse-ACC that man-to   give-ing
'Having given the horse to that man,...'

Gung-de ere arga-be   we   tacibu-ha?
you-to this   method-ACC who teach-ed
'Who taught you this method?'

The Manchu verb came regularly at the end of each and every sentence and clause. It was composed of a verb stem plus one or more inflectional endings. The set of verb stems in the language was fixed and could not be enlarged by, for example, borrowing verbs from another language. If a noun was to be used as a verb, the verb endings could not be attached to the noun stem, the way case particles could be, so a different process had to be used. In order to make the noun function as a verb, a verbal stem of some kind had first to be suffixed to it. This created a new verb form that could take the endings. For example, the verbal with the meaning of 'to form a crack, to split' was derived as follows:

fiyere(n) 'a crack, a fissure' + (ge)ne- 'to go' ——→ fiyere-ne- 'to crack, to split'

All the many Chinese loanwords in the language were therefore borrowed as nouns only—never as verbs—and when they were to be used as verbals, a dummy verb stem of some sort had to be attached to them. For example, the Chinese verb *hū* 'to call' was borrowed as a noun form and then made into a verb this way:

hû 'a call' + -la- [a postverb] ——→ hû-la- 'to shout, to call'

To illustrate a variety of sentences and how they are used, here is a brief portion of the Manchu version of *The Romance of the Three Kingdoms*:

ILAN GURUN-I   BITHE
three kingdom-'s book

... Hûwang G'ai ubaliya-kai   besergen-ci ebu-fi,
                turn over-EMPH bed-from   get out-ing

hengkile-me baniha bu-he.
kowtow-ing thanks give-ed

K'an Ze hendu-me: "Weile-be elheše-ci   ojorakû. Te uthai
             say-ing   work-ACC slacken-ing won't do now at once

yabu-ci aca-mbi."
act-ing must-s

Hûwang G'ai hendu-me: "Bithe ara-me   waji-habi."
                  say-ing   letter write-ing finish-ed has

   K'an Ze bithe-be   gai-fi,   uthai   tere dobori beye-be nimaha
             letter-ACC take-ing at once that night   self-ACC fish

buta-ra   niyalma obu-fi,   ajige weihu-de te-fi,   emhun šuru-me amargi
catch-ing man   make-ing small boat-in sit-ing alone row-ing north

dalin-i baru   muke eyen-i   dahashûn juraka. Tere dobori
shore-'s toward water current-'s obedient set out that night

šahûrun usiha abka-i jalu   dekde-hebi. Ila-ci ging o-me, muke-i
cold   star sky-'s fullness float-ed has third watch be-ing water-'s

ing-de   isina-fi,   giyang-be bedere-re cooha-i niyalma-de jafa-bu-ha.
camp-to reach-ing river-ACC patrol-ing army-'s men-by   take-give-ed

    K'an Ze hendu-me: "Cenghiyang-de hûdula-me alana! Dergi U
          say-ing   chancellor-to   hurry-ing report east

Gurun-i   K'an Ze-de dalda-ra amba weile bi-fi, cohome acanji-me
kingdom-'s   -by hide-ing big   matter be-ing especially meet-ing

ji-hebi   se-me hendu!"
come-ed has say-ing say

    Tere dobori Z'oo Z'oo olhon-i   ing-de bi-hebi.   Cooha-i
    that night   dry land-'s camp-in be-ed was army-'s

niyalma alana-ra   jakade, Z'oo Z'oo hendu-me: "Jiyansi waka sem-e-o?"
men   report-ing after   say-ing   spy   not call-ing-?

[TRANSLATION]

THE ROMANCE OF THE THREE KINGDOMS

... Turning over, Hûwang G'ai got down out of bed and thanked him with a
kowtow. K'an Ze said: "It won't do to postpone the task. Now I must act
at once." Hûwang G'ai said: "The letter has been written."

Taking the letter, K'an Ze disguised himself as a fisherman and that very
night set out in a small boat, rowing alone toward the north shore following
the current. That night the cold stars floated over the entire sky. It was the
third watch, and when he reached the camp on the water's edge, he was
taken by soldiers patrolling the river.

K'an Ze said: "Report quickly to the chancellor! Say that K'an Ze of the
kingdom of Eastern U has come with an important secret matter especially to
meet with him!"

That night Z'oo Z'oo was in his camp on the land. When the soldiers came
to him with the report, Z'oo Z'oo said: "Is it not a spy?"

Around the turn of the century, there were still some Western scholars
who were not convinced that Manchu was related to the Northern Tungus languages. Part of the reason was that the large Sinitic vocabulary
and the relatively simple structure of Manchu tended to obscure the correspondences that pointed to a truly close relationship. But another
reason for doubting the evidence seems to have been that in an era of
ethnic stereotypes it was still hard to associate the urbane and literate
rulers of China with the simple hunting and fishing folk of Siberia. Yet
that is just what the Manchus had once been. How such a people had
organized so well, learned so much, and then accomplished the subjuga-
tion of a nation at least fifty times more numerous and far more techno-

logically advanced than they is a question that has occasioned endless discussion among experts and need not be gone into here. Nevertheless, the central fact remains that, by whatever means, these Tungusic people conquered China much more completely and ruled it far longer and more successfully than any other outsiders have ever done.

In the end, of course, the Manchus paid the price of success by losing their national identity. Customs, tastes, language—all of these things began to be Sinicized even in the generation before the conquest. The Manchu leaders realized the danger of assimilation and tried to check it through legislation. All Manchus were forbidden by law from intermarrying with Chinese or adopting Chinese customs. The traditional clan systems were protected. Manchu education was made compulsory. The "Willow Palisade," a ditch that was used to mark the northern boundary of where Chinese settlements were allowed, was extended in an attempt to stem the flow of Chinese immigration into Manchuria. Yet, finally, none of these measures proved effective. The Chinese way of life was easier than that of the horseriding warrior, and who would return to a state of barbarism once he had known the sweet taste of civilization? The Manchus were not forced out of China as the Mongols had been, and so they chose to stay. Some traditional formalities were maintained up until the revolution of 1911, but most of the ethnic and linguistic differences between the Manchus and the Han had disappeared long before that. By the eighteenth century the process of assimilation was virtually complete. In the 1930s the Japanese tried to encourage separatist feelings in Manchuria by promoting the study of the Manchu language. The identical policy had worked well among the Mongols, who had welcomed the chance to speak their own language free from Chinese interference. But the Manchus were not interested in speaking Manchu again, much less in seceding from China. Manchu nationalism could not be revived. The twentieth century was far too late for that.

Tungus writing. The oldest Tungus language for which we have written records is that of the Jurchen (or Nǚzhēn, in Chinese). The Jurchen were a confederacy of hunting and fishing tribes who rose to power in northeastern Manchuria around the beginning of the twelfth century. From 1115 to 1234, these Tungusic people ruled over large parts of North China, giving themselves the Chinese-style dynastic name Jin (or 'Golden').

The Jurchen had their own script. It was one that had been adapted from the almost identical writing system of the Khitan, the Inner Asian people whose empire (known as the "Liao" dynasty) the Jurchen had overthrown. We know very little about this original system; for very few examples of Khitan writing have survived, and those that are extant remain almost completely undeciphered. It is not even known with any degree of certainty what kind of language the Khitan spoke. Many experts believe that it was a variety of Mongolian, but that has not been established to everyone's satisfaction. Compared to its Khitan prototype, Jurchen writing is relatively well attested and better understood.

The script that the Jurchen borrowed was very unusual. Only one or two other peoples in East Asia have ever used anything similar. Although it was based upon the Chinese writing system, it was not a set of symbols that had evolved out of Chinese characters, such as the *kana* syllabaries used by the Japanese. Rather, the Jurchen wrote with characters that had only been constructed to look like Chinese. Each character was composed of the same kinds of brush strokes that a Chinese character might be, and it fit into the same space on the page. But the strokes of the character were not combined by the same principles that the Chinese ones were, and the result was a resemblance that was rather superficial. To a Chinese eye, Jurchen characters look odd. Some seem to have a stroke or two in the wrong place, others have a dot that breaks the symmetry. The effect is a little like the pictures that Western artists often produce when they try to imitate Chinese characters.

Jurchen writing has still not been adequately deciphered. Some of the characters of the script can be interpreted with the help of the Sino–Barbarian Glossaries (*Huá-Yí yìyǔ*) that the Chinese compiled much later during the Ming period (1368–1644). But there remains a great deal that is not known about Jurchen writing and the Jurchen language. One important reason for this imperfect understanding is that the early materials are meager. No book written in Jurchen has ever been found. Within the Chinese parts of the Jurchen empire, most writing continued to be done in Chinese, and almost all of the original examples of the Jurchen script are found on a few steles that the Jurchen erected in their ancestral homeland in Manchuria and northeastern Korea.

But even if more Jurchen writing had survived, we still might not know very much more about the Jurchen language. The Jurchen script was not the kind of writing system that reflected the sounds of the words it represented. Like the Chinese characters upon which it was based, the symbols were not tied to any particular pronunciations the way the letters of an alphabet are. The Uighur and Mongolian writing systems, on the other hand, as imperfect as they were in some respects, were nevertheless

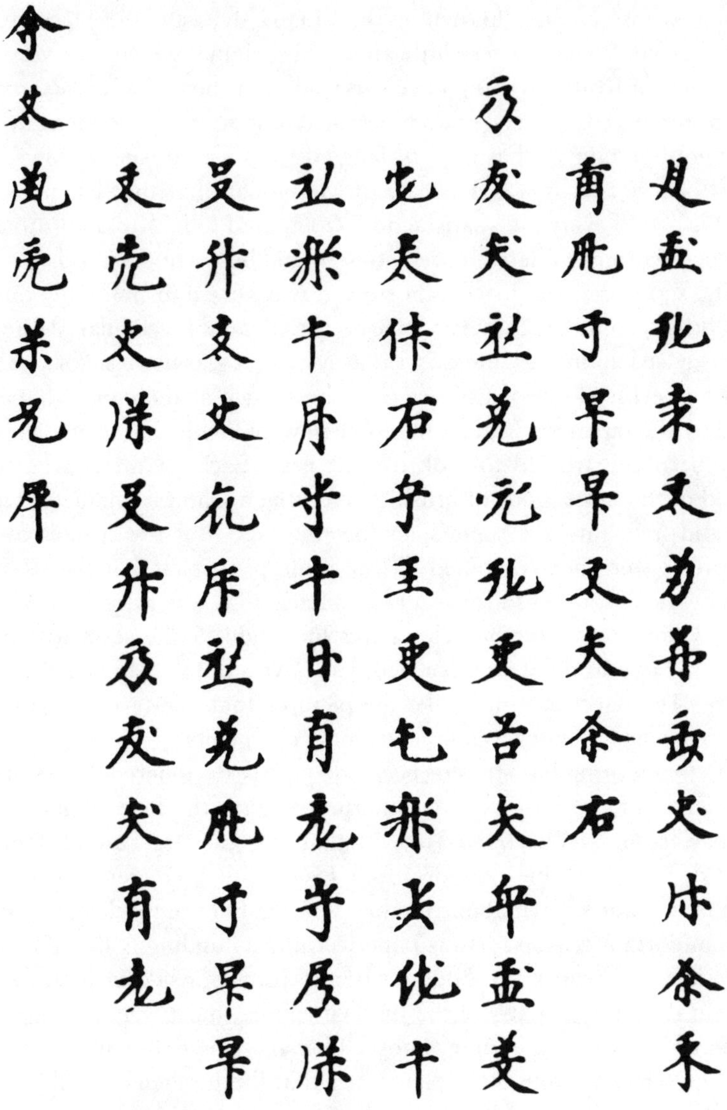

Figure 13. A Memorial written in Jurchen Script, dated A.D. 1520. (from Kiyose 1977)

alphabets, and as a result we know far more of what those languages were like. For the historical study of the Tungus languages, it is unfortunate that alphabetic writing did not reach Manchuria before the rise of the Manchus around the turn of the seventeenth century.

THE Manchus were the descendants of the Jurchen. They began as one of the three branches of the Jurchen nation that existed around the end of the Ming dynasty in China. The word *manju* itself is believed by some experts to come from *mangu*, the Tungus name for the Amur River (Heilongjiang), and to mean nothing more than "the people of the Amur." If this etymology is correct, the name the Manchus took for themselves was nothing more than a toponymic description of their particular branch of the Jurchen. After Nurhachi had united all the other Jurchen tribes under the leadership of the Manchus, his eighth son and successor Abahai (1592–1643) issued an order that the name Jurchen should be banned for all of the tribes, and that from then on, they were all to be called Manchus.

The development of the Manchu writing system was due to Nurhachi's leadership. One of the most important steps in the preparation for the conquest of China was the network of alliances the Manchus built up with the easternmost of the Mongols, and it was not long before Nurhachi had incorporated them into the "banner" system, the Manchu military organization. For administrative purposes, he found that the Mongols' writing system, using their modified version of the old Uighur script, was the most convenient and easy to use, and at first he had all written communication in the Manchu government offices done by Mongol lamas in the Mongolian language. Then in 1599 Nurhachi took the next step and commissioned two of his own banner people, Erdeni and Gagai by name, to construct a "national writing system" for Manchu using the Mongolian script. The script that these two submitted to Nurhachi, later to be known as the *tongki fuka akû hergen* 'writing without dots and circles,' was the first Manchu writing system. Very few examples of this kind of writing still exist today. Since it was an unmodified adaptation of the Mongolian script, it had all of the same orthographic ambiguities that Mongolian writing did. In 1632, six years after the death of Nurhachi, a learned Manchu bannersman named Dahai, the head of the Manchu office of communication with China, Korea, and the Mongols, made an important innovation in this writing system by adding points and circles to certain letters to clarify them. This second version of the Manchu script was therefore called the *tongki fuka sindaha hergen*

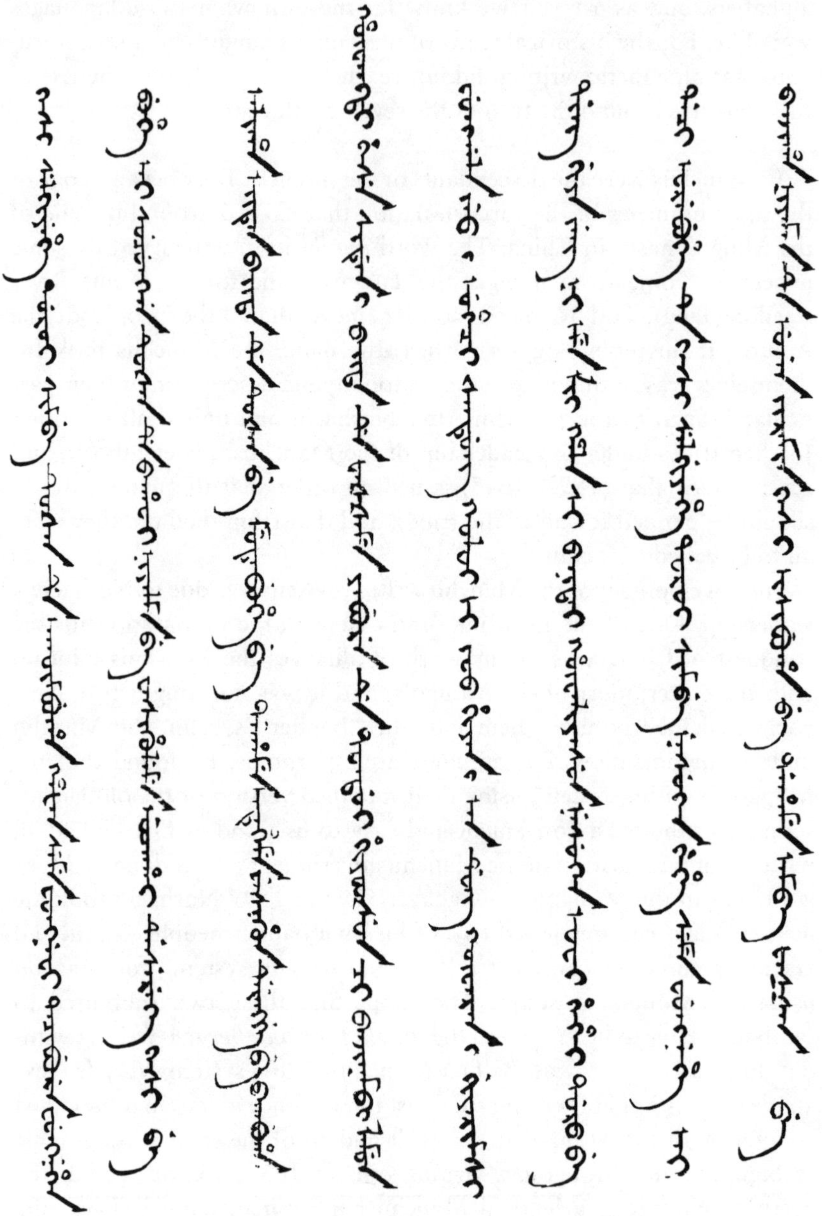

Figure 14. A Manchu Manuscript from the Year 1900.
Note the use of circles and dots as diacritics.

'writing with dots and circles.' This innovation was immediately adopted by the Manchus and became the form of writing that they were to use until the end of the dynasty.

Dahai's innovation with "dots and circles" was simple. For example, in the Mongolian script the same letter was used in many environments to represent both of the vowels *a* and *e*, as well as the consonant *n*. To differentiate the letter, Dahai placed a dot to the left of it if it was to represent *n*, and a dot to the right of it if it was to represent *e*; an unmarked letter represented *a*. These conventions were extremely useful, but they could work only as long as they were rigidly adhered to. The dots and circles did not change the letter shapes, and if they had been left off, the Manchu script would have been no better than the Mongolian. The Mongols had also made partial use of such dots, but only occasionally, in cases where it was essential. In normal circumstances they did not feel obliged to make the extra stroke, and the convention ended up as a rarity that was practically useless. The efficiency of the Manchu script was due entirely to the fact that the Manchus consistently treated the superscripts as integral parts of the letters, much as the French do their accent marks, or the Germans do their umlaut.

Dahai also decided that it was useful to know whether a word was native Manchu or Chinese in origin, and he used dots and circles for this purpose as well. For example, he affixed a dot to the Chinese family name Han to distinguish it from the Manchu word *han* 'emperor, khan.' In addition, as we have mentioned, a variety of superscripts were used to represent pronunciations that were used only for Chinese words.

With the exception of these modifications, the Manchu script remained essentially the same as the Mongolian script. It was written in vertical columns that progressed from left to right across the page, just as Mongolian was. In the early Qing period especially, the appearance was virtually the same. The best early example of Manchu writing is the inscription on a huge stone monument, called the Songp'a pi, that the Manchus forced the Koreans to erect in 1639 to acknowledge their submission to Qing suzerainty. This stele can still be seen standing to the south of the Han River, where it was originally erected, on the outskirts of the city limits of modern Seoul.

Later on in the Qing period, Manchu calligraphy gradually evolved into styles that were distinctly Manchu. But the basic forms of the letters and the ways that they were used stayed the same until the end of the dynasty.

11 THE MINORITIES OF
SOUTH CHINA

Many different languages are spoken in South China and the northern parts of Southeast Asia. In addition to dialects of Chinese, a number of Tibeto-Burman, Tai, Miao-Yao, and Mon-Khmer languages are found in the region as well. There are also several isolated languages that have not been conclusively connected to any of these well-established families.

All of these languages and language families (except Mon-Khmer) are structurally similar to Chinese. Among other things, they have no inflection, and syntactic relationships are expressed by word order or by separate particles.

Because they resemble Chinese so much, these languages are often grouped together into one enormous "Sino-Tibetan," or, sometimes, "Sinitic," family. Such groupings are misleading. These languages do not form a single language family. The fact that they are typologically similar does not necessarily mean that they have a common origin; the structural resemblances are more likely the result of centuries of intimate contact. The names that are used add to the confusion. "Sino-Tibetan" is already the name of a much more specific and viable hypothesis; and to call all of the languages in the area "Sinitic" (meaning "related to Chinese") reinforces all kinds of misconceptions.

The geographical distribution of these languages is intricate and difficult to map with precision. In the highly fragmented environment most ethnic groups live in villages interspersed among those of other groups. Yi, Tai, Miao, Bai, and Han Chinese are often found together, with the Chinese at the top of an elaborate hierarchy. Height up or down a mountainside is usually the most critical factor in determining where an ethnic group will live; seldom does a group have a solid block of territory that belongs to it and it alone. In extremely mountainous areas the cultural variety can range from prosperous Burmese, Siamese, or Vietnamese rice farmers and Chinese tradesmen in the fertile lowlands to migratory slash-and-burn farmers, such as the "Montagnards," traversing the highest slopes. On any given mountain, high above the rice paddies in the valleys, there may be several different villages occupied by as many separate peoples speaking totally unrelated languages. Some groups migrate periodically, complicating the situation still more. At best, boundaries are ill-defined.

For the early histories of these peoples, we depend heavily upon reconstruction and inference through archaeology and linguistic comparison. Written records are scarce. Many groups have learned to write only recently; still others use no writing at all. But even nationalities with old and literate civilizations have difficulty preserving documents from their past because of the warm and humid climate. Perishable materials such as paper, wood, leaves, and bamboo usually last no more than a few years, and records written on them must be continually recopied. Only inscriptions cut into stone have any permanency, and even they often succumb to the combined action of rain and invasive vegetation.

For the past two thousand years this area has been under the influence of India and China (Southeast Asia is still often called "Indochina"). Indian religion and culture began to be important in the western parts of the region when the emperor Aśoka sent a Buddhist mission into what is now modern Burma in the third century B.C. Indian merchants and seamen followed shortly after, greatly expanding commerce in Southeast Asia around the beginning of the Christian era. Within a few centuries Indian civilization had affected the cultures and languages of the greater part of mainland Southeast Asia, including southern Vietnam. Chinese civilization did not penetrate nearly so far south, and the northern half of Vietnam is the only part of the subcontinent that came completely within the Chinese sphere of influence (only the Vietnamese traditionally used Chinese characters, for example, while the other literate peoples wrote with scripts based on Indic alphabets).

The influence from China was of a different kind. What is now South China was at one time ethnographically indistinct from Southeast Asia (see the discussion in Chapter 3); and when this area began to be transformed into Chinese territory, there were repercussions throughout the subcontinent. As the Chinese pushed southward out of North China, their cultural pressure precipitated successive migrations of other peoples still farther south. Some of the most prominent of the modern Southeast Asian nationalities—including the Burmese, the Lao, and the Thai—as well as untold numbers of smaller groups, originated in what is now China. Over two millennia the ethnic currents have been consistently southward, and the migration of some hill tribes from Yunnan into Burma and Laos continues even today, though on a reduced scale since the 1960s. Religion, governmental structure, art, and writing and literature are predominantly Indic. But the basic cultural traits and linguistic connections of many of the peoples living in Southeast Asia had their beginnings in the southern parts of China.

Several thousand years ago, before the Chinese and Indian civilizations began to expand, however, the flow of ideas and culture was very likely in the other direction. Recent archaeological discoveries, though as yet incomplete and uncorrelated with other facts, indicate that in prehistoric times Southeast Asia was an important center of cultural innovation and development. Bronze manufacture in central Thailand has been dated to about 3,000 B.C., a millennium earlier than in China and five hundred years earlier than in India. The same archaeological site has produced a copper implement that is the oldest socketed tool in the world and the oldest metal tool of any kind found in eastern Asia. The imprint of a rice husk has been dated by carbon-14 measurements to 3,500 B.C.—again about a thousand years earlier than rice is known to have been cultivated in India or China—and the remains of other domestic plants, including beans and water chestnuts, suggest that food cultivation in Southeast Asia goes back as far as 10,000 B.C. So far these and other discoveries have not been connected to the early history of either China or India. Nevertheless, many experts are of the opinion that once the archaeological evidence is more complete such connections will be made, and that many of those things now thought of as indigenous Chinese developments, including plant and animal domestication and metal-working, will one day be shown to have been early examples of cultural diffusion from Southeast Asia.

TAI

"Tai," "Thai," and "Dai" are easy to confuse. *Tai* is the standard spelling for the name of the language family. It is also the collective term for the peoples who speak these languages. *Thai* and *Dai*, on the other hand, are the names of two specific Tai groups.

Most of the non-Chinese people in South China are Tai. They are culturally and linguistically related to (but not identical to) the Thai, or Siamese, of Thailand.

The millions of Tai living among the Chinese in South China are an almost invisible presence. The only groups among them who command attention are the colorful Dai of Yunnan, who have been heavily influenced by the Burmese, and the warlike Li of Hainan Island, who are anything but invisible. With these two important exceptions, the Tai all look and act Chinese. They farm the same way; they wear the same clothes. Most are completely bilingual in the local Chinese dialect. About the only significant thing that sets them apart is their home language, which is a variety of Tai instead of one of the similar-sounding Southern dialects of Chinese.

The Tai have long played a large and shadowy role on the edge of the Sinitic world. Around the beginning of the first millennium B.C. they were ensconced in the rice-growing areas of the Yangtze Valley; and, according to some authorities, many of the early Southern states mentioned in Chinese history—including that of Wu, centering around the mouth of the Yangtze near modern Shanghai, and Yue, dominating the area on the South China coast—were actually Tai kingdoms. As these kingdoms were Sinified and gradually swallowed up by expanding Chinese civilization, most of the local Tai peoples became Chinese themselves through cultural and linguistic assimilation. One ethnographer has estimated that at least 60 percent of the Cantonese people must be descended from an aboriginal Tai-speaking population.

But many Tai, especially political and military elite, migrated south before the encroaching Chinese. Petty states grew up in Yunnan and northern Southeast Asia as the centers of Tai control shifted farther south. Eventually these population movements resulted in the present ethnic composition of northern Southeast Asia, where Tai groups from South China, by virtue of their superior organizational strength, dominated and then assimilated more disparate groups. The modern Tai states of Thailand and Laos originated in this way, through migration and conquest.

Thai, or Siamese, is the best-known and most important member of the Tai family of languages. Spoken by around twenty million people, Siamese is the standard language of Thailand. Its written history dates from 1292, when the inscription of King Rama Khamheng of Sukhotai was carved onto a stele in what is now northern Thailand (this inscription is the oldest example of Tai writing). Lao, which is very closely related to standard Thai, is also well-known because it is the language of the independent country of Laos. There are around fifteen million speakers of this language, many of whom live within the borders of Thailand. Smaller numbers of Tai-speaking peoples can also be found in northern Vietnam and Burma.

Tai Languages in China

In the People's Republic of China the Tai family of languages is known as the Zhuàng-Dòng family. *Zhuàng* is the Chinese name for their largest Tai minority, and *Dòng* is the Chinese name for the people who call themselves the Kam. Eight minority languages are classified as members of this family: Zhuang, Buyi, Dai, Kam (or Dong), Sui, Mulam, Maonan, and Li.

This family—Tai, or Zhuang-Dong—is divided into three distinct branches:

1. Zhuang-Dai: The three languages in this branch—Zhuang, Buyi, and Dai—are closely related to each other and to the standard Thai language of Thailand, as well as to standard Lao of Laos.
2. Kam-Sui: The Chinese government recognizes four languages in this branch: Kam, Sui, Mulam, and Maonan. Two other Kam-Sui languages, Mak and Then, have not gained official status in the People's Republic. All of the Kam-Sui languages that are now known to exist are spoken by relatively small groups of Tai in Guizhou and northern Guangxi. These languages are so highly distinctive they are thought to have separated off from the main Tai stem quite early. Fang-Kuei Li, the linguist who is credited with discovering the Kam-Sui languages, has shown them to be only remotely related to the other Tai languages.
3. Li: The several Li "dialects" of Hainan Island are even more distinctive than Kam or Sui. The status of Li as a member of the Tai family is very much open to question.

Be (or Ong-Be), a highly Sinicized language spoken on the northern coast of Hainan Island, also appears to be a member of the Tai family, but it has yet to be definitively classified. It is not an official minority and the number of speakers is unknown.

Zhuang

The Zhuang are China's largest minority by far. According to government figures, there are over 13,300,000 living in South China. The western two-thirds of Guangxi Province and adjacent portions of Guizhou and Yunnan are all predominantly Zhuang territory. There is also a large enclave of Zhuang around Lianshan in northern Guangdong Province.

The Chinese Communists claim a great deal of credit for reviving the fortunes of these people and their language. In the late 1950s, as evidence of its good faith with minorities, the Communist Party decided to create new autonomous regions, including one for the Zhuang in Guangxi Province. The problem with the proposal in this particular case was that it involved making an autonomous region out of a province where the Chinese outnumbered minorities—according to official estimates, the Zhuang comprised only about 33 percent of the population of Guangxi. Moreover, most of the Zhuang themselves professed not to want minority status, preferring instead to be considered Chinese. At a meeting of the provincial assembly Zhou Enlai answered critics of the plan by stressing the need for the Chinese to make amends for past mistreatment of the Zhuang. He suggested that Chinese who did not like the idea of the "repayment of a debt" (*huánqīng*) might prefer to think of it as "apologizing" (*péi bú shì*). In 1958 the Guangxi Zhuang Autonomous Region was formally inaugurated.

At that time Peking seems to have been determined to raise the ethnic consciousness of the Zhuang people. Whereas the Kuomintang had been more than content to let the Zhuang remain anonymous, the Communist Party tried hard to change their attitude. Under the old Nationalist regime, it was now claimed, the Zhuang had hidden their identity out of fear of government suppression. Their language had been "insulted, ridiculed, and even banned by the reactionary ruling classes," the new Chinese leaders maintained, but now the dignity of this people would be restored. Accordingly, in their first surveys of the minorities, Communist researchers found many more millions of Zhuang than had ever been known to exist. Zhuang families and clans were brought protesting out of the Chinese closet. In one study of 152 clans conducted a few years earlier, not a single family admitted to a Southern origin. Those with the surname Zhao claimed Chinese ancestry that stemmed from the palace retinue of the Song court. Those with the surname Wei said that their genealogical lineage went back to the son of the great Han general Han Xing; when the father was executed, they explained, the son had fled south and, in order to conceal his identity, had deleted the left half of the character of his surname *Hán*, leaving a different character pronounced *Wéi*. Yet in spite of such imaginative attempts to conceal their identity, these Southern families were all registered as Zhuang.

In order to restore long-subdued feelings of distinctness, the Communist Party has made special efforts to nurture the Zhuang language. Radio stations throughout the Zhuang Region broadcast in that language. Films that are shown in the movie houses are dubbed into Zhuang. A special Romanized script has been created for the language, and numerous books, mostly translations from Chinese, are published in it. The extent of Peking's emphasis is shown by the fact that Zhuang, along with Tibetan, Mongolian, Uighur, and Korean, has been given official status as one of China's "major" minority languages. The difference between Zhuang and these other four languages is one of need: unlike the other, more distinct nationalities, the bilingual Zhuang can understand and communicate perfectly well in Chinese and are more than happy to do so.

A side benefit of this minority policy has accrued to linguists. The government has invested manpower and money in language studies and dialect surveys, and we now have a fairly substantial body of information on a language that before had been little studied.

What is called "Zhuang" should probably be thought of as two closely related languages. Chinese dialectologists, who have surveyed the speech of some seventy Zhuang-speaking localities, report that the dialects fall into two relatively distinct groups, which they term the "northern dialects" and the "southern dialects." The speech of these two dialect areas is divergent enough to be considered two separate languages, even by the relaxed criteria of mutual intelligibility used in China. The geographical dividing line between these two languages falls roughly along the right branch of the Yu River that flows through southern Guangxi.

Northern Zhuang is more widely spoken than Southern Zhuang, and it is better unified. Thus the standard Zhuang language as designated by the Chinese government is based on Northern Zhuang, especially the dialect that is spoken in Wuming County.

But standard Zhuang should not be thought of as identical to the local speech of any one area. Like most legislated standards—including Received British and standard Japanese—it is intended to transcend regionalisms. Thus there are a number of differences between the sounds that are actually spoken in Wuming, say, and those that are supposed to be standard. Wuming, for example, has a few contrasts between the sounds *qv*- and *v*-, and between the sounds *qy*- and *y*-, but in the standard language these distinctions are ignored.

Standard Zhuang has eighteen consonants. In Wuming the phonemes *b* and *d* are pronounced [qb] and [qd]; in some other localities the glottalization also appears before *m* and *n* in initial position. The consonant *v* patterns as a semivowel (and, according to Fang-Kuei Li's analysis, is actually *w* in Wuming); it appears in initial clusters with velars; *kv*- and *ngv*-. In this standard language the original consonant clusters with liquids (such as *pl- and *kr-), which one sees preserved so well in standard Thai, have been lost; *py*-, *my*-, and *ky*- remain as their trace. The loss of all *r*- and *l*-clusters is undoubtedly the direction in which the Tai dialects of China are progressing (notice that *py*-, *my*-, and *ky*- are sounds commonly heard in the local Chinese dialects). But in a few Zhuang localities (including Wuming) *pl*-, *ml*-, and *kl*- are still preserved.

Standard Zhuang has six basic vowels: *i, e, a, i, u, o*. In addition to these, it has a seventh vowel, *ə*, which appears in loans from Chinese and does not pattern like any of the other vowels. One of the peculiarities of this sound is that it must always be the last element in the syllable.

The tone system is a very characteristic feature of Zhuang. As described by Chinese phonologists, the standard language has eight different tones: (1) low

Zhuang Consonants

	Labial	Denti-labial	Dental	Retro-flex	Alveo-lar	Palatal	Velar	Post-velar	Glottal
Voiceless stop	p		t				k		q
Aspirated stop									
Voiced stop	b		d						
Voiceless affricate									
Aspirated affricate									
Voiced affricate									
Voiceless fricative		f	s			sy	x		
Voiced fricative		v							
Nasal	m		n			ny	ng		
Voiceless nasal									
Lateral			l						
Voiceless lateral									
Flap or trill			r						
Voiceless flap									
Semivowels						y			

rising, (2) low falling, (3) high level, (4) high falling, (5) mid-rising, (6) mid-level, (7) high "checked," and (8) mid-"checked." "Checked" tones are tones found only in syllables that end in -p, -t, or -k. Since the syllable-final stops are never released, the airflow from the mouth is "checked." (Chinese phonologists often use the term "entering tone" to describe such syllables; for a discussion, see Chapter 7.)

This tone system is remarkably similar to ones found in Chinese, especially the Yue (or "Cantonese") dialects spoken in the Guangdong–Guangxi area. It also developed the same way historically. The original Tai language—Proto-Tai—is assumed to have had four tones, A, B, C, and D. Each of these tones later split into two different tones, giving the eight now found in modern Zhuang. This split was conditioned by the phonetic quality of the initial consonants. For example, in Proto-Tai the two words $*pi^A$ 'year' and $*bi^A$ 'fat' had the same tone but different initial consonants. But a voiced initial consonant tended to depress the pitch of the syllable, so that $*bi^A$ 'fat,' with a voiced initial consonant $*b$, came to be pronounced with a slightly lower register than $*pi^A$ 'year.' When the initial $*b$ of 'fat' changed to p, the syllables were left the same except for the pitch. Now the words were distinguished not by initial consonants but by a new tone distinction.

	Proto-Tai	modern Zhuang
'year'	$*pi^A$	pi^1
'fat'	$*bi^A$	pi^2

This is exactly the way that many tone distinctions developed in Chinese.

Most words are just one syllable long, and a syllable is constructed much the same way one is in the Southern dialects of Chinese. The only major difference is that in a few Zhuang dialects (such as Wuming) a syllable can begin with one of the clusters *pl-*, *ml-*, or *kl-*. In the final part of the syllable, a very minor difference is that Zhuang has the vocalic sequences *ai* (e.g., *dai*¹ 'inside') and *ïi* (e.g., *rïi*¹ 'honey'). But otherwise the Zhuang final is the same as that of Cantonese. As in Cantonese, the main vowel can be followed by *-i* or *-u* (these are offglides), or by one of the consonants *-m*, *-n*, *-ng*, *-p*, *-t*, or *-k*. And—again as in Cantonese—when the main vowel is followed by one of the these elements, it can usually be either long or short: *nap*⁷ 'insert,' *na:p*⁷ 'hold under the arm'; *kon*⁵ 'break off,' *ko:n*⁵ 'first'; *rai*² 'be long,' *ra:i*² 'dew.'

A speaker of Zhuang orders the elements of a sentence much the same way that a speaker of Chinese does. The basic arrangement is a "topic" followed by the rest of the sentence, which is often called the "comment." (Compare the discussion of Chinese sentences in Chapter 5.)

> Ta⁴po⁶ da:ng¹ reng²   la:i¹.
> father body   strength is-much
> '(My) father, (his) body strength is great. [= My father is healthy]'

As in Chinese (but not as in Tibeto-Burman languages), the Zhuang verb comes before the object that it governs:

> dam¹ pyak⁷
> plant vegetables
> 'plant vegetables'

> a:ng⁵ syi:ng⁵ fï:n¹
> enjoy sing   Zhuang-songs
> 'enjoy singing Zhuang-style songs'

But this Tai language is conspicuously unlike Chinese in one important aspect of its syntax. Instead of preceding, a modifier follows the element that it modifies. This order is the rule for compound nouns:

> kai⁵-pou⁴   pyak⁷-ha:u¹
> chicken-male   vegetable-white
> 'rooster'   'cabbage'

> dï:n¹-ngu⁴
> month-five
> 'May'

It is the rule for the modification of nouns:

> sai¹   mo⁵ rau²
> book new our
> 'our new book'

And it can be seen in the placement of some adverbs:

sa:ng¹ ra:i⁴sya:i⁴
high   extremely
'extremely high'

Some adverbs also appear *before* what they modify, but when the ordering is changed, they take on a different connotation. The adverb *la:i¹*, which means either 'slightly' or 'very' depending on the syntactic order, is one of these. The normal order is as follows:

ding¹ la:i¹
red   very
'very red'

But the opposite order is also possible:

la:i¹ ding¹
      red
'*slightly* red'

The negative *bou³* is another adverb whose meaning depends on its position. It comes after the verb in a question; it comes before the verb in a statement:

bou³ pai¹   pai¹ bou³
not go   go   not
'not go'   'not going?'

There are also a small number of adverbs that occur exclusively before the verb (and sometimes even before the subject):

Te¹ ha⁴pan⁶ tau³-tang².
he just-now come-arrive
'He just   arrived.'

Measures, or classifiers, of which there is an abundance in Zhuang, come before the noun—as in Chinese:

xa³   tu²   mou¹
three HEAD hogs
'three hogs'

But demonstrative pronouns such as *xan⁴* 'that' are separated from the classifier and follow the noun in the usual modified–modifier order. In the following phrase, *ko¹* is the measure or classifier for 'tree':

ko¹ fai⁴ sa:ng¹ la:i¹ xan⁴
TREE tree high   very that
'that very tall tree'

Directional or locative complements can either precede or follow the verb in patterns roughly analogous to those in modern Chinese:

tok⁸ tang² rok⁷ ti:m³
read until six   o'clock
'read until six'

you⁵ ra:n² tau³
from home come
'come from home'

But the most common way to say that one went somewhere is just a simple verb-object expression:

pai¹ Pak⁷king¹
go   Peking
'go to Peking'

From a Chinese perspective this construction is interesting because the corresponding Putonghua pattern, *qù Běijīng* 'go to Peking,' is the result of influence from the Southern Chinese dialects, which, in turn, were probably influenced by the Tai languages spoken all around them.

Verbs of course do not inflect. But, on the other hand, Zhuang has a complex system of verb compounding and complement formation that gives the language great flexibility of expression. A verb can be followed by another verb functioning as a complement that indicates what takes place as a result of the action of the first verb; for example *kin¹-liu⁴* 'eat (something) all up' is composed of *kin¹* 'eat' plus *liu⁴* 'complete.' If this compound verbal takes an object, the object can either follow the verbal or come immediately after the main verb (in this case 'eat') and before the resultative ending:

kin¹ sa:m¹ va:n³ liu⁴
eat   three bowls complete
'eat three bowls (of rice) all up'

kin¹-liu⁴   sa:m¹ va:n³
eat-complete three bowls
'eat up three bowls (of rice)'

Reduplication adds much to the expressiveness of this verbal system:

Mung² tok⁸-tok⁸ yai³.
you   read-read try
'You try reading it.'

peng⁵ xan¹-xan¹ ne⁶
pull   tight-tight !
'pulled *very* tight.'

There are occasionally some unusual morphological twists to the reduplication. For example, there is the pattern VERB + Xa^1 + VERB + $Xa\ɨ^5$, where "X" stands for the initial consonant of the verb:

sak^8-sa^1-sak^8-saɨ^5
wash   wash
'wash it quickly!'

tok^8-ta^1-tok^8-taɨ^5
read   read
'read it quickly!'

Modality is also expressed by particles, which come after the verb or at the end of the sentence. Some indicate aspect; *tɨk^7*, for example, shows that an act or process is still going on; *dai^3* marks the completion of an act:

nang^6 tɨk^7
sit   -ing
'is sitting'

syai^1 dai^3 syou^6 dam^1
plow -ed then plant
'When (one) finishes plowing, then (one) plants'

Au^1 is used to specify the method by which something is done or made:

Keu^1 pu^6 mɨng^2 myip^8 au^1,   ro^{4}nau^2 syi^1 au^1?
PIECE clothes you   sew   METHOD or   use-machine METHOD
'Is your jacket sewn by hand or is it made by machine?'

Particles can also be used to show the "mood" of a sentence—such things as whether it is a question, an exclamation, or an imperative:

Sou^1 pai^1 rung^6 lɨl^1?
you-all go   valley ?
'Are you going into the mountain valley (to cut firewood)?'

Anyone familiar with Chinese who examines Zhuang will notice immediately how replete it is with loans from that other language. Nouns, verbs, adverbs, measures—even many particles—go back to Chinese antecedents. Such borrowings often bring with them new kinds of grammatical patterns. Zhuang has a "*de*-construction," for example, and it violates the usual Tai syntactic order of modified–modifier:

kung^{6}se^5 ti^6 ra:n^2
commune *de* building
'a commune building'

kou¹ ti⁶ sai¹
I   *de* book
'my book'

But among communities as bilingual as the Zhuang are, it is also easy to import grammatical patterns directly, without the medium of loanwords, and construct them out of native elements. The now-common syntactic order VERB-*Complement* + *Object* must have originated in such a way:

nying²-ta:i¹ so:ng¹ tu²   kuk⁷
hit-die   two   HEAD tiger
'kill two tigers'

Zhuang writing. The Zhuang have no actual script of their own. Until the Communists introduced Romanization in 1957, Chinese characters were the only kind of writing used among the Tai people of Guangxi. Those who were sufficiently literate simply composed and wrote directly in Chinese.

But Chinese characters were also occasionally adapted to transcribe the Zhuang language itself. This transference was accomplished through a tortured combination of methods, much like those of the traditional *chu nom* writing system of Vietnam. Some characters were directly borrowed for their sound or meaning:

Character	Chinese word	Zhuang word represented
鴨	yā 'duck'	pit⁷ 'duck'
古	gǔ 'ancient'	ku¹ 'I'

At other times the Zhuang wrote a word with two Chinese characters—one for the sound and one for the meaning—placed together to form a single, hybrid character:

Chinese words and characters	Zhuang character	Zhuang word represented
那 nà 'that' + 田 tián 'field'	𤬃	na² 'paddy field'
六 luk 'six' + 鳥 niǎo 'bird' (Cantonese)	𪂧	rok⁸ 'bird'

Beyond these basic methods there were many other, even more esoteric ways to transcribe Zhuang words. Chinese characters could be made into Zhuang graphs by deleting or adding strokes; pieces of characters could be lopped off (the side of the character for 'gate' meant 'side' in Zhuang); and totally new characters, somewhat like the *kokuji* of Japan, could be made up, sometimes by principles obscure to us today. And finally, since there was very little common agreement among the Zhuang about the use of these characters, Zhuang texts are often a farrago of nonce creations and individual and regional variations.

A specimen of Zhuang writing has been preserved from the eighteenth century, but the system may have been devised long before that. Yet, in spite of a respectably long history, this method of writing never became widespread. Taoist priests occasionally used it, and ordinary Zhuang merchants sometimes found it convenient for keeping accounts and records. Songs, where the sounds of the Zhuang language itself had to be recorded and preserved, were almost the only things that were ever regularly written down in it. For other purposes the Zhuang found that the Chinese language served them just as well.

Buyi. The Buyi are not clearly distinguishable from the Zhuang either linguistically or culturally, and they are almost as Sinicized. Most speak Chinese, wear Chinese clothes, and think of themselves as close relatives of the Chinese. In some localities other non-Han ethnic groups consider them to be Chinese, especially those Buyi working in towns as tradesmen.

The 2,120,000 members of this minority, except for a few thousand in northern Yunnan, all live in southern Guizhou. They form the northern continuation of the Tai-speaking population of Guangxi.

Linguistic differences between the Buyi and the Zhuang are slight. By Chinese standards, the Buyi language could be called a dialect of Northern Zhuang.

Dai. All of the Tai-speaking population of western Yunnan is classified as "Dai." The term includes groups that have otherwise been known variously as Baiyi, Lü, Nüa, and Chinese Shans. But since these several groups are reasonably well allied culturally and linguistically, and since they all call themselves by some variant of the name Tai, their classification as a single ethnic group is not unreasonable.

The 840,000 Dai are much less Sinicized than the Zhuang and by most cultural criteria belong to Southeast Asia, not China. The majority practice Hinayana Buddhism. They write using variants of the Siamese script. As the name implies, the Dai are closely related to the Thai of Thailand.

Dai belongs together with Thai in the Southwestern group of Tai languages. The various Dai "dialects" are not all mutually intelligible, but they are far less diverse than some of the other languages of Yunnan.

Kam-Sui Branch

The Kam-Sui peoples, and the Kam in particular, are the northernmost Tai-speaking communities. They appear to be aboriginal remnants left unassimilated by the Chinese when they expanded south.

The Kam-Sui languages are structurally like all the other members of the Tai family. But they are separated from the other branches of Tai—and, to a lesser extent, also from each other—by many differences in phonology and vocabulary. Such differences arose as a result of centuries of isolation in the hills of south central China.

Kam. Of all the Tai-speaking peoples, the Kam live farthest to the north and east. They occupy a large block of territory at the intersection of the three provinces, Hunan, Guizhou, and Guangxi. This central mass of speakers is dotted on its northern periphery by several islands of highly Sinicized Kam, who have mixed with Chinese and lost most of their ethnic distinctness. To the south are patches of the other, less numerous Kam-Sui peoples, and these join or are surrounded by Zhuang territory. The Kam are mostly valley-dwelling rice-growers, and the hills throughout much of their range are farmed by the less Sinicized Miao people. Altogether there are about 1,425,000 Kam.

The Kam language is noteworthy for its extraordinarily large number of tone distinctions. Counting six pitch distinctions in "checked" syllables, most dialects of Kam are said to have fifteen different tones. This is surely close to a record. The almost unbelievably large number of tone distinctions seems to have resulted historically from at least two tone splits, both of which happened as a result of changes in the initial consonants, particularly devoicing. Kam now has no voicing contrasts. The other Kam-Sui languages have fewer tones and more vowels and more consonants (Mulam and Maonan also have more vowels).

Sui. Sui is spoken in Guizhou Province, just to the southwest of Kam. About 287,000 people are counted as members of the Sui minority, but not all of that number speak Sui. Those in outlying communities, especially the young, know only Chinese.

Sui has fewer tones than Kam ("only" eight). But it has a very large number of consonants: forty-two, according to Chinese linguists. The system includes palatal stops, postvelar stops, prenasalized stops ($^m b$, $^n d$), "preglottalized" stops and nasals (e.g., $q b$, $q m$), and voiceless nasals. Moreover, for some Sui dialects Chinese linguists describe other consonant distinctions, including a very unusual "nasalized *h*" [ɦ]. The Sui vowel system is almost identical to that of Kam.

Sui writing. The Sui have a system of symbols that is used for divination and geomancy. It is far too simple to have much of a linguistic function and seems to be little more than a set of magic symbols. A few of the 150 or so graphs are real drawings (such as of a bird or fish), and a few others are schematic representations of some characteristic quality ('snail' is indicated by an inward-curving spiral). Most of the rest are borrowings from Chinese and are often written upside-down or backwards, apparently to give the symbol more magical power. For obvious reasons, the Chinese name for Sui writing is "backward writing."

Mulam. In the name Mulam, *mu*⁶ is a classifier for human beings, and *lam*¹ (in some dialects *kyam*¹) is another form of the name used by the Kam, a people to whom the Mulam are related.

The approximately 90,000 Mulam people live in northern Guangxi Province, around the town of Luocheng. This is directly south of the Kam, in Zhuang territory. Most Mulam are fluent in both Chinese and Zhuang.

Like Kam, the Mulam language has no voiced stops. But it does have both voiced and unvoiced nasals and laterals. It also has a more complex system of eleven vowels.

Maonan. The Maonan live in a relatively small, compact community of about 38,000 in northern Guangxi Province, on the Guizhou border, just south of the Sui. The Maonan community is so compact it is said to be completely free of dialect variation. All the Maonan middle-aged and younger speak Chinese, and most know Zhuang as well.

The Maonan language has pre-nasalized stops and "preglottalized" nasals like those of Sui. But the preglottalized stops that existed at an earlier stage of the language (and which have been preserved as *qb* and *qd* in Sui) have in the modern Maonan language lost the glottalization and become *b* and *d*. Maonan has a vowel system virtually identical to that of Mulam; and, like Mulam and Sui, it has eight tones.

Li Branch

Li is spoken by Tai groups in the interior of Hainan, the large Chinese island located about 150 miles due east off the coast of northern

Vietnam. These groups are isolated by rugged terrain and dense, tropical rain forests.

The "wild Li of Hainan" have a long history of resistance against Chinese authority. From the first mention of them in Chinese annals of the Tang period, their name has been associated with revolt. From the Song through the Yuan period, eighteen uprisings were recorded. The insurrections increased in intensity and frequency during the Ming period, when the Li waged campaigns against the Chinese authorities more than thirty different times, the uprising of 1501 being particularly devastating for Ming rule on the island. The turmoil continued throughout the Qing period and into this century.

In July 1943, events connected to the Pacific War precipitated yet another rebellion, but this time one that soon led to a change in the Chinese image of the Li. Up until a few years before, the Kuomintang government had kept hands off the interior of Hainan, confining control to major population centers near the coast. But when the Japanese invaded the island in 1939, the Chinese fled en masse to the interior. The Li resisted these intrusions into their lands and were met with brutal suppression. This finally ignited the bloody insurrection of 1943. In the first rounds of fighting the Li won several stunning victories, but Kuomintang troops finally beat them back and forced the survivors into hiding deep in the interior. At this point, while the rebels were still in hiding, their leader Wang Guoxing managed to link up with the Communist guerrillas who were also active on the island and threw his lot in with them, creating a "Li column" of some 15,000 fighting men devoted to the liberation of Hainan. According to later, romanticized versions of this event, Wang had had a vision of the Red Army in a dream. In the dream he was standing at the top of Five-finger Mountain, Hainan's highest peak, when all at once he saw five red clouds, each of which contained a great, waving red flag. Then he saw that each of the flags was a military banner, being held high by troops of the Red Army, who were singing and beckoning to him to join them. When he woke up he excitedly told his companions about the dream, and they immediately interpreted it as a sign from the god of the mountain that they should join the Red Army in a common cause against the forces of oppression.

However it was the the Li rebels came to fight as an officially recognized unit for the Communist Party, they were the largest (and almost the only) minority group to do so. After the victory of the Communist Revolution, their case was highly publicized by the new regime, and the spirit of the Li column was made into a model for the minorities, much as

Dazhai was at one time made into the model for the agricultural village. The Li and their struggles against the Kuomintang became the plotline for a number of revolutionary stories.

There are an estimated 818,000 of these aboriginal people living on Hainan today. To the Chinese they are all known as "Li," which is the Chinese rendering of the native name "Lhai[1]." But only some of the groups use that name (or dialect variants such as *Tlhai[1]*, *Dai[1]*, *Tsai[1]*, or *T'ai[4]*); others call themselves (among other names) *Ha[3]*, *Gei[4]*, *Mo:i[1]fau[1]*, *Hyɨ:n[1]*, or *Zɨ:n[4]*. And in truth, the Li are not a unified people. They are organized into a number of separate groups.

The Li "language" is really more like a collection of related languages, or so it would seem from the data that have been made available. Chinese sources inform us that there are five different groups of Li "dialects," and that may mean that there are about five different Li languages.

The genetic status of Li has not been definitely established. The languages certainly seem to be Tai, at least in the broad sense of the word. But how closely they are related to the other Tai languages is a matter of some speculation. PRC linguists offer the opinion that, based upon the data they have collected to date, Li seems to be more closely related to the Zhuang-Dai Branch of Tai than to the Kam-Sui Branch. Some scholars, such as Fang-Kuei Li, have cautiously reserved opinion on the matter.

The Li languages have most of the characteristic features expected from members of the Tai family. There are the complex tones, for example, some of which seem to have been produced historically by tonal splits. Some dialects have a few of the old consonant clusters (such as *pl-*); some have what are described as preglottalized initials (*qb-*, *qd-*). The syntactic order is invariably subject, verb, object.

But Li is separated from the rest of Tai enough in both space and time for certain structural differences to have arisen. Unlike any of the other modern Tai languages, the Li languages have the consonant *g*; how it developed is not known, since a source for it has so far not been reconstructed in Proto-Tai. Some Li languages have syllables closed by palatal stops and nasals (as in Vietnamese, but not normally as in Tai). There are also a few particularities in Li grammar.

The greatest difference between Li and the other Tai languages are lexical, however. Some of these have arisen as a result of contrasts in the natural environment. We would not expect, for example, a language spoken on a tropical island to preserve the original Tai words for 'snow,' 'ice,' 'frost,' or the seasons of the year. And, by the same token, we would not expect any of its landlocked relatives to have a basic word for 'sea' (such words in these languages are usually borrowed from Chinese). But even in such basic vocabulary as the terms for parts of the body, Li words are often quite divergent from those found in other Tai languages. These are differences that point to a long separation.

TIBETO-BURMAN

Tibeto-Burman is a family of languages that includes Tibetan, Burmese, and a wide variety of other, less well-known languages. It has more members than any other language family in Southeast Asia. Well over two hundred Tibeto-Burman languages have been recorded so far, making it a family approaching the complexity of Indo-European.

Tibetan and Burmese are both important languages with long literary traditions. As the national language of Burma, Burmese is spoken by a nation of around fifteen million people with a written history dating back to the eleventh century. Most of the early writings in this language are in the form of epigraphs and fragmentary inscriptions. But for the Middle Burmese period—that is, from about the fourteenth to the sixteenth century—the language is fairly well attested; there are even said to be a few original manuscripts from the period, written on palm leaves, kept in Buddhist monasteries.

Tibetan is spoken by a population of something under four million people; but its literature is even older than that of Burmese, and it is better preserved. The Tibetan writing system, which like the Burmese is based on Indic models, was devised in the seventh century, and the orthography was standardized two centuries later in A.D. 816. This form of the written language, known as Classical Tibetan, was the vehicle for a voluminous literature, including the famous Tibetan translation of the Mahayana Buddhist canon and original texts on subjects ranging from medicine to grammar.

The other Tibeto-Burman languages are spoken by fewer people and are far less important politically. They are scattered over a wide area, from western China to eastern India, Nepal, Bangladesh, and beyond, and from Tibet and the Himalayas south to the southernmost parts of mainland Southeast Asia.

The Tibeto-Burman languages are not typologically diverse. The overwhelming majority are characterized by tones and monosyllabic stems, and almost all have a basic syntactic order in which the verb comes at the end of the each clause or sentence. The functions of the phrases in a Tibeto-Burman clause are indicated through the use of postpositions.

And though the original systems have badly decayed in some of the languages spoken in China, most of Tibeto-Burman still preserves traces of earlier prefixes and suffixes (of the kind most clearly seen in Classical Tibetan).

Few language families anywhere are as fragmented as that of Tibeto-Burman. How and why did the Tibeto-Burmans become scattered so widely and into so many small groups? There has been much speculation about this question. Many believe that the ancestors of the Tibeto-Burmans lived somewhere in the western reaches of China, and that cultural or military pressures from the Chinese precipitated a number of early migrations out of China westward. If true, this original dispersion, whenever and however it happened, would have been but the beginning of a process that went on for centuries and to an extent continues even today.

Tibeto-Burman Languages in China

The People's Republic of China recognizes sixteen Tibeto-Burman languages: Tibetan, Monpa, Yi, Lisu, Hani, Lahu, Jino, Naxi, Jingpo, Drung, Qiang, Primi, Lhopa, Nu, Achang, and also Bai. (Although Bai is included on this list because of the official PRC classification, it will be discussed later, in the section on unclassified, or isolated languages.)

The Tibeto-Burman list is easily the longest the Chinese have ever compiled for any group of minority languages, but it is far from exhaustive. Four additional members of this family—Tsaiwa, Gyarung, and two different languages used by the "Deng" people of Tibet—have already been described in recent Chinese publications. Others, including one variety of "Xifan," have been mentioned and are presumably being studied. Moreover, many of the names already placed on the list actually represent groups of related languages instead of single linguistic communities (there are a number of mutually unintelligible "dialects" of Yi, for example).

The Chinese classify their Tibeto-Burman languages into four branches:

1. Tibetan Branch: In Western writings this group is known as "Bodish" (from *Bod*, the Tibetan name for Tibet). It includes Tibetan and Monpa. The Bodish languages are characterized by rich systems of affixation— they have many suffixes and prefixes. If the official Chinese list of minorities were extended, Gyarung would be put into this group. Since Tibet is a linguistic area all of its own, the Bodish languages will not be discussed here. (Cf. the section on linguistic areas in Chapter 9.)
2. Yi Branch: This branch is usually called "Loloish" in most of the linguistic literature. It is more closely related to Burmese than Tibetan. Loloish

includes the many varieties of Yi (or Lolo), as well as Lisu, Hani, Lahu, Jino, and Naxi. The Xifan language mentioned in several Chinese sources is also Loloish, as are three or four other "Xifan" languages spoken in western Sichuan that have been referred to in various Western writings. The Loloish languages are the extreme example in the Tibeto-Burman family of consonantal decay; most have lost the final consonants of the proto-language. But, to make up for these losses, the Loloish languages have developed a variety of additional vowel and tone distinctions.

3. Jingpo Branch: Usually called Kachin in the literature on Southeast Asia, Jingpo is the "linguistic center" of Tibeto-Burman; it provides both a lexical and morphological link between the various branches of the family. Besides Jingpo itself, the Chinese also put the Drung language in this group.

4. Qiang Branch: The Qiang branch includes Qiang and Primi, according to the Chinese system of classification. These languages are genetically close to the Loloish branch.

Lhopa (spoken only in Tibet), Nu, and Achang have not been placed in any of these groups because, according to the Chinese explanations, "their branch affiliations have not yet been determined." Yet Bai, which has not been shown to be related at all to the Tibeto-Burman family, is classified as Loloish by the Chinese. Apparently, the criteria of classification must have varied from case to case.

Yi Branch (Loloish)

Yi. In Western writings the Yi are usually called the "Lolo." "Lolo" is a name with an obscure etymology that comes from a Chinese transcription written around the thirteenth century. "Yi," on the other hand, is a Chinese term that in ancient times was applied to a variety of non-Chinese peoples. But since the Yi themselves have adopted the name, preferring it to "Lolo" in their own usage, that is what they are officially known as in the People's Republic.

One of the most distinctive peoples in all of China, the Yi first caught the imagination of the West when reports of their existence filtered out of China around the turn of the century. In the almost inaccessible wilds of southwestern China, some said, a "blood-proud caste" of tall and noble warriors "fought, rode, herded horses, and ruled ... a stratum of underlings and slaves." Exaggerated descriptions of their "Caucasoid features" and stories of sacred books, written in a strange pictographic script and reportedly containing the arcane secrets of the ruling caste, added to the mystique. In Europe, preparations were made to investigate and expeditions were organized. Unfortunately for such Western ambitions, however, the region was almost impossible to penetrate from the outside since the Yi had still not been pacified by the Chinese. No one—and especially not the Chinese government toward which the Yi were extremely hostile—could guarantee safe passage through the areas controlled by Yi clans. Yet, in spite of the obvious dangers, Western explorers continued to be fascinated by southwestern China. One of these explorers, a British adventurer named Donald Brooke, set out in 1909 to explore the Cool Mountain area of Southern Sichuan, the stronghold of the Independent Yi. No sooner had he and his entourage of a dozen or so crossed into Yi territory than they were attacked. In the battle that ensued, Brooke himself was killed and all of his followers were captured and made into slaves. When word of Brooke's fate reached England, a shocked British government demanded retaliation and justice for the culprits. The Chinese government was forced to act and accordingly dispatched troops to the area. But, short of launching a major and costly military campaign, the Chinese army was virtually helpless in this territory that was theirs in name only. To save face, the government troops hired a native headman-protector to negotiate passage into the Cool Mountain area. With his help, they crossed briefly into Yi territory to the place where Brooke had been attacked. There they burned some houses, killed a few of the local Yi villagers, and then quickly returned to the nearest military post. Inflated reports of this action placated the British government and averted an international incident.

For at least two thousand years the Yi have held their own against domination by the Chinese. Chinese annals since the beginning of the Christian era have described the Yi, under a variety of names, as being masters of the highlands where they still live to this day. In fact, over this time the Yi have actually expanded their range eastward into Guizhou. The center of this region, the Cool Mountain (Liángshān) area of southern Sichuan, is some three hundred miles long by two hundred miles wide. It is protected in its mountain fastness by precipitous terrain, dense forests, and barren wilderness and is accessible only through a few key passes that over the centuries have been easily controlled by the Yi.

Around the beginning of the twentieth century parts of the surrounding countryside were briefly brought under a measure of military protection by Chinese garrisons. But—as Brooke's demise attests—control of the Cool Mountain itself was far from effective. After the fall of the imperial government, even this protection broke down. When the Republic was established in 1912, the Chinese military presence was reduced and the Yi increased their strength to fill the vacuum. Rebellions broke out.

Communication lines between adjacent Chinese towns were cut off. As the Yi clans reassumed control of the entire area, they replenished and modernized their supply of arms. Opium-growing was banned in China in 1935, but since the government had no jurisdiction in the areas controlled by the Yi, opium poppies continued to be the most profitable crop there. Cultivated and processed by hired Chinese laborers and slaves, this drug was not used at all by the Yi themselves. Instead, they sold their produce at great profit on the Chinese black market, accepting only lump silver as payment, and then used this in turn to purchase rifles and ammunition. Around the turn of the century modern firearms were rare in Yi territory. By the Twenties every household had several. Throughout the Thirties and Forties the Yi moved at will over southern Sichuan, terrorizing the Han Chinese populace and even raiding the outskirts of large Chinese towns in order to rob and to take slaves. Observers report that at the first sound of gunfire, terrified Chinese peasants would huddle in their homes, not daring to help their neighbors and hoping only that they would not be attacked next. In some places Yi raids were a nightly occurrence.

Today there are some 5,500,000 Yi living in southern Sichuan, western Guizhou, and mountain areas throughout Yunnan. Traditionally these people were divided into three distinct groups: the Black Yi, the White Yi, and slaves (who have been set free now by the PRC government). The Black Bone (Nosu) aristocracy have been considered the true Yi (or Lolo), and it is they who have long excited curiosity among ethnographers. Many observers have described them as having "oval faces, aquiline noses, and horizontal eyes," but also as having skin that is darker than that of the Chinese. The White Yi, with whom the Black Yi never intermarried, are generally the descendants of Han Chinese slaves who had earned a degree of freedom through faithful service. They are far more numerous than their former Black Yi masters, outnumbering them by perhaps ten to one. (This imbalance may partly explain why the official, posed portraits used to represent this minority do not show the "Caucasoid features" said to be typical of the true Yi, the Black Bone aristocracy.) The White Yi can best be described as serfs, the economic slaves and social inferiors of the Black Yi. But the White Yi traditionally also had certain property rights, among them the right to hold and own their own slaves from the slave class that was below them. Those in the slave class had no actual rights at all. But Yi custom afforded certain expectations even for them. Personal honor among the Black Yi obliged a nobleman, for example, to protect his slaves from injury or predation by members of other clans. His reputation depended on how he treated his slaves, and, among other things, all food in a Black Yi household was shared with the slaves, including their children.

The mainstay of the Yi economy is buckwheat, but the Yi also raise corn, oats, potatoes, green vegetables, and turnips. The Black Yi looked down on farming, and all cultivation was traditionally done by White Yi and slaves. The Black Yi were responsible only for administration and military protection. Even so, however, they usually took great care to tend to their domestic animals themselves, and this custom has given rise to speculation that the Black Yi were originally a pastoral people before they conquered and enslaved the White Yi.

The White Yi are somatically different from the Black Yi, but they have adapted completely to their culture. They wear the same clothing, including the great felt capes that serve both men and women as protection from the rigorous winters and as bedding on the floors at night. Men, both Black and White, swathe their heads with huge turbans, either black, white, or blue in color, through which a braid of hair sometimes protrudes like a horn. The speech of the White Yi, too, is the same as that of the Black Yi.

The great "dialect differences," as they are called in Chinese linguistic sources, are due to geographical dispersion and not to caste distinctions. The Yi of western Guizhou maintain a certain amount of contact with their kinsmen in southern Sichuan, and Guizhou men often journey across the Yangtze to find suitable marriage partners. But the communities of Yi scattered throughout Yunnan to the south are isolated and their languages have consequently diverged. According to these same Chinese sources, there are six of these "dialects" (but one suspects that there are more).

Chinese linguists have published descriptions of at least four different Yi languages, all of which were recorded at various localities in Yunnan. There is as yet almost no published information on the speech of the Independent Yi of the Cool Mountain.

Two of these Yunnan Yi languages, Ahi and Sani, are spoken near Lùnán ('South of the Road'), a town located southeast of the provincial capital of Kunming. Genetically they are closer to Lisu and Hani than they are to the other two Yi languages for which we have descriptions.

The other two Yi languages are called "Nasu" and "Luquan" in the linguistic literature. Nasu was recorded in a village called Hétaojǐng ('Walnut Basket') on the outskirts of Kunming. Luquan is spoken in Lù-quán County, which is located north of Kunming, about halfway to the

NASU CONSONANTS

	Labial	Denti-labial	Dental	Retro-flex	Alveo-lar	Palatal	Velar	Post-velar	Glottal
Voiceless stop	p		t				k		q
Aspirated stop	p'		t'				k'		
Voiced stop	b		d				g		
Voice aspirated stop	b'		d'				g'		
Voiceless affricate			ts	chr		chy			
Aspirated affricate			ts'	ch'r		ch'y			
Voiced affricate			dz	jr		jy			
Voiced aspirated affricate			dz'	j'r		j'y			
Voiceless fricative		f	s	shr		sy	x		
Voiced fricative		v	z	zhr			gh		
Nasal	m		n			ny	ng		
Voiceless nasal	mh		nh						
Lateral			l						
Voiceless lateral			lh						
Semivowels	w					y			

Sichuan border. These two languages are very close to each other. They are separated from the Yi languages spoken to the south by an unusual tonal development in which the pitch values for certain tones seem historically to have been reversed (that is, a high-pitched tone has become low, and a low-pitched tone has become high). In addition, both of these languages have kept distinct the initial consonants of words that originally had a nasal prefix (e.g., *mp-). In other Loloish languages these initials have merged with voiced initials, such as *b-.

		Yi				Lisu
	Cool Mountain (?)	Luquan	Nasu	Ahi	Sani	
*mp-, *mb-	mb-	mp'-	b'-	b-	b-	b-
*b-	b-	b-	b-	b-	b-	b-

Nasu, for which a monograph-length description has been published, is a typical Yi language. The name Nasu means 'black-one.' It is the same word as Nosu, which is what the Black Bone Yi in Southern Sichuan use as the name of their aristocratic class.

The Nasu language has forty-four consonants. The consonants b', d', g', etc. (which developed historically from consonants with nasal prefixes) are described as having "very strong voicing." They are probably like the voiced consonants of the Shanghainese variety of Chinese, which have a kind of aspiration or "murmur" in the following vowel. Nasu also has voiceless nasals, *mh* and *nh*, and a voiceless *lh*, which is like the initial sound of Tibetan *Lhasa* or Welsh *ll* in *Llanelly*; in the part of the world where Yi languages are spoken these are fairly common sounds. None of the consonants, except the glottal stop *q*, can close the syllable. Nasu is typical of the Loloish languages in having radically reduced the consonant distinctions at the end of the syllable. Even the glottal stop, which is the only remnant of all the final stops that Nasu once had, is only a nondistinctive relic since syllables that have it are characterized by a distinctive tone.

The Nasu vowel system is rich, as expected. There are ten basic vowels: *i*, *z* (or *r*), *e*, *a*, *ər*, *ɔ*, *o*, *u*, *ɨ*, *ə*. What we have chosen to write here as *z* (or *r*) is a vowel that occurs only after dental affricates, such as *ts*, or after retroflex affricates, such as *chr*. In either case the tip of the tongue remains at, or very near, the position where the affricate is articulated. Thus, as voicing begins, the vowel is heard after dental affricates (e.g., *ts-*) as the buzzing sound *z*, and after retroflexes (*chr-*, etc.) as a sound much like a Midwestern American *r*. These two different sounds are very nearly the same as those heard in the Peking words *sì* 'four' and *shì* 'persimmon.' The retroflex vowel *ər* is another sound with a Peking Mandarin equivalent, in this case the vowel in *ér* 'child.' The vowels *ɨ* and *ə* in this language are pronounced like *u* and *o*, but without rounding of the lips. Nasu vowels can be pronounced with distinctive nasalization (e.g., *ĩ*), which will be transcribed here as an *-n* after the vowel (*ĩ* is written *in*, for example). This nasalization is the trace that is left of the nasal consonants that once closed the syllable (**-m*, **-n*, **-ng*). Besides all of these vocalic distinctions, Nasu also has a nasal syllable *ng*, which is pronounced like a similar sound in Cantonese.

Nasu has a large number of tones, seven in all: (1) high level, (2) high-mid rising, (3) mid-level, (4) mid-rising, (5) low falling then rising, (6) low falling, (7) "checked" mid-falling. This last tone (tone 7) occurs on syllables that are "checked" by a final glottal stop; these syllables are very short.

The construction of a Nasu word is simple. Most are only one syllable long, and that syllable invariably consists of at most one consonant plus a vowel and a tone. There are no consonant clusters and only a small number of diphthongs.

As in Chinese—and, to an extent, in English as well—the classes to which words belong are not distinguished by their forms. The same word can sometimes function in a sentence as a noun, and other times as a verb. In the following example, the word *ma²* 'dream' appears twice, once as a noun in the meaning 'a dream,' and the other time as a verb in the meaning 'to dream' (in this way its grammatical use parallels that of the English word used to translate it):

Ngu⁶ yi¹,   ma²   tsu²   t'a⁶-də²   ma²-xərq⁷.
I   sleep dream good one-THING dream-succeed
'When I was asleep, I dreamed a good dream.'

Nasu has a relatively large number of measures, or classifiers, that must be used whenever objects are counted. These are used much as in Chinese, except that the number-measure phrase usually follows the noun that it modifies:

pe^{1}te^1 t'a^6-pərq^7
knife one-HANDLE
'one (*or* a) knife'

a^{1}nuq^7 t'a^6-mu^3
bean   one-GRAIN
'one (*or* a) bean'

As the English glosses in these examples imply, Nasu measures are sometimes derived from nouns; occasionally a noun even serves as its own measure word:

(su^3-)pə^6 t'a^6-pə^6
(writing-)book one-BOOK
'a book'

Nasu words are not marked for anything like gender, and only personal pronouns have number. There is nothing that could be called inflection except perhaps for a kind of "pseudo-inflection" of personal pronouns. Here is an example:

ngu^6 'I'   nga^{5}və^3 'my father'
          nga^{6}vi^1 'my older sister'
          nga^5 p'ə^3 'my grandfather'

However, what at first appears to be inflection through vowel and tone change has been better explained as the contraction of two vowels. In the above examples, an initial *a* in the kinship terms *a^{2}və^3* 'father,' *a^{2}vi^3* 'older sister,' *a^{2}p'ə^3* 'grandfather' has been contracted into the syllable vowel of the pronoun, and the tone of the pronoun has changed in compensation.

To make syntactic relationships clear, speakers of Nasu depend upon word order and, to a lesser extent, suffixes. There are a number of caselike markers that can be added after a noun to make its meaning perfectly clear. But these are usually left off whenever the function of that noun can already be determined from the context.

As in almost all other Tibeto-Burman languages, the verb in Nasu always comes after everything else in the clause. Modifiers comes after what they modify, similar to the order in French *vin blanc* 'white wine.'

Real complexity in the Nasu language shows up in the behavior of verbs. Verbs take a variety of endings, which are used to make semantic distinctions that sometimes can only be paraphrased in English. Verbs are compounded by stringing several stems together, and this grammatical device is the usual way to show how, of many possible alternatives, a particular action was accomplished. A common kind of construction is formed, for example, through making potential contructions of the kind found in Mandarin Chinese:

yi^1-gə^5
sleep-finish
'after (someone) had fallen asleep'

t'iq⁷-ma⁶-xərq⁷
grope-not-succeed
'could not find by groping around'

The following story is a Nasu folk tale about a clever troublemaker named Chane. Chane is the hero of many anecdotes. He is a little like the Katzenjammer Kids, a boy who is always causing trouble for those around him.

CHRA³NE¹
Chane

T'a⁶ ni⁶ jrɔ⁵, t'a³ghɨ³   mɔ² t'e² ngu³ t'a⁶-pə²   shrə³-xərq⁷.
one day exist his uncle old they fish one-SOME cut-succeed

U³ xan⁴ch'yi¹ Chra³ne¹ sə⁶   yi⁵ t'e² k'ɨ¹. T'a³ghɨ³   mɔ²
that night   Chane   then go they steal his uncle old

yi¹-gə⁵,   t'i⁶ t'a³ ghɨ³   mɔ² t'e²-bə⁶ lu⁶bu³ t'a⁶ naq⁷
sleep-finish he his uncle old they-'s wall   one hole

kər¹-du⁴,   lə²-gɨ³-yi⁵.   T'a⁶-chrə⁴ t'iq⁷, t'iq⁷-ma⁶-xərq⁷.   T'i³*
dig-through bore-advance-go one-WHILE grope grope-not-succeed he

sə⁶ miɔ¹-miɔ¹   pe²   mər²nər³ sɔ².
then meow-meow make cat   mimic

T'a³ lha¹mɔ² de²: "Ne²   ngu³ veq⁷ k'a²ma¹ tsə²?"
his aunt   say you-all fish take where is-at

T'i⁶ va³ts'ɔ³   t'i⁶ dɔ¹ k'u³: "Veq⁷ u³   po⁶moq⁷-kɨ²
(s)he husband (s)he word answer take   that bowl-inside

tsə², sye⁶ ch'rɔ³ te¹ t'ia⁶ bə⁶, sya² da²dze²-bə⁶
is-at iron pot   hit it-by cover PAUSE ladder-end

tsə²-de³." Chra³ne¹ a⁶ buq⁷ jyu², a²ləq⁷-a²ləq⁷ yi⁵
is-at-ANSWER Chane   by hear   slowly   go

t'e² du² ngu³ yi¹yi⁶   k'ɨ³-duq⁷-le⁴.
they with fish completely steal-exit-come

T'i⁶ du³mɔ² tse²   nyi³bɔ³   t'a⁶-mu⁶   veq⁷, t'ə²
he later   again persimmon ONE-THING take put

t'a³ ghɨ³ mɔ² t'e² chrɔ¹ tsə², t'a⁶-su²   yi¹ ch'yər²,
his uncle old they middle is-at one-SLEEP sleep wake

*The tone is given here as it was recorded (elsewhere in this text the tone of the third person pronoun is 6). This alternation is said to be stylistic variation.

nyi³bɔ³   t'e²   a⁶ yi¹-la⁵.
persimmon they by sleep-mash

T'i⁶ ch'yi² de²: "A⁶mɔ³   lhi³ pe²-wo⁴!" du³mu³
he wife say daughter shit let-go-ed immediately

bə⁶-lu³   g'ɔ⁴-p'i¹, ts'e⁵ Chra³ne¹ ɨ³dɨ³-t'a¹ tsə². Tse²
cover-thing pull-off drop Chane   head-top is-at again

Chra³ne¹ a⁶ k'ɨ³duq⁷-yi⁵.
Chane   by steal-exit-go

Du³mɔ² t'e²   mu³tu² tu²-toq⁷, a⁶mɔ³   lhi³ szq⁷
later   they fire   light-up daughter shit wipe

nyiq⁷ d'ɨ⁴,   t'e² bə⁶-lu³   ma⁶ ngɔ⁵ tse² yi⁵ t'e²
heart think they cover-thing not see   again go they

ngu³ nyi³, ngu³ nyi³ t'i⁶-wər² ma⁶ jrɔ⁵.
fish look fish look it-place not exist

Yi¹yi⁶   sua⁶   k'ɨ³-vi³-wo⁴.
completely person-by steal-AWAY-ed

[TRANSLATION]

ANOTHER ADVENTURE OF CHANE

One day Chane's uncle caught some fish. That night, Chane went to steal them. When his uncle had gone to sleep, he bored a hole through his uncle's wall and crept through. He groped around for a while but he couldn't find the fish. Then, mimicking a cat, he went "meow, meow."

Chane's aunt asked, "Where did you put the fish you caught?" Her husband answered, "I put them in the bowl that's under the pot at the end of the ladder." Chane heard this and quietly went and stole their fish away.

A little later he came back and put a persimmon in his uncle's bed. When they woke up, the persimmon had already been mashed up.

The wife cried, "Oh no! Our baby daughter has shit in the bed!" and immediately jerked off the quilt and dropped it on Chane's head. Chane stole this away, too.

Later Chane's aunt and uncle lit the fire, thinking to wipe up the mess that their daughter had made, and couldn't find their quilt. They they went to look at the fish and discovered that they were gone, too. Somebody had stolen everything away!

Yi writing. For the Yi, writing is not a means of communication. It is associated with divination and magic, and the Yi are content to leave their sacred books and script in the hands of their practitioners of religion, the men called *pimu*.

The *pimu* are simultaneously the chief priests, magicians, diviners, historians, and physicians of the Yi people. Every Yi village has at least one such person (who is always a man, either White or Black but usually White), and with him resides the responsibility for the spiritual life and well-being of the people under his charge. The *pimu* are professionals. They spend their lives training for and practicing their art, which is usually hereditary, being passed down in a *pimu* family from father to son or from uncle to nephew. It demands a long period of training and instruction, and thus it is that the *pimu* are responsible for transmitting and preserving the Yi written language. It is not that the *pimu* guard the sacred books and the Yi script as a secret code. But they are the only people among the Yi who receive anything like a formal education and so are the only ones able to read and write.

Most Yi literature is in the form of ritual and incantation. Here, for example, is a translation of one section of a classic from the Luquan Yi canon, *Performing Rites, Offering Medicine, and Sacrificing Beasts*:

> You, who are among the virtuous dead,
> Did you live in ancient times?
> At the time before you lived,
> Favor and abundance still did not rear sacrificial beasts,
> Prosperity and wealth still did not sow the grain,
> The fate of heaven's gate still had not descended,
> The fate of earth's gate still had not rested.

This particular incantation is part of a ceremony to help the spirit of an ancestor enter paradise.

Yi writing is at least as old as the Ming period—there is frequent mention of it in Chinese chronicles of the time—but some scholars have estimated that it has been in existence for over a thousand years.

The Yi script has been falsely represented as "pictographic." It is a far cry from that. Like Japanese *kana*, the Yi writing system is a kind of syllabary, though a less systematic or standardized one. One arbitrary symbol is used to represent one syllable. Each symbol is fairly simple, most being composed of only three to four strokes. A few characters seem to have been constructed to look like simplified forms of the Chinese seal script, but far and away the majority look like nothing else to be seen in the Chinese world. In some Yi-speaking areas the characters are read from right to left (Middle Eastern-style); in other areas they are

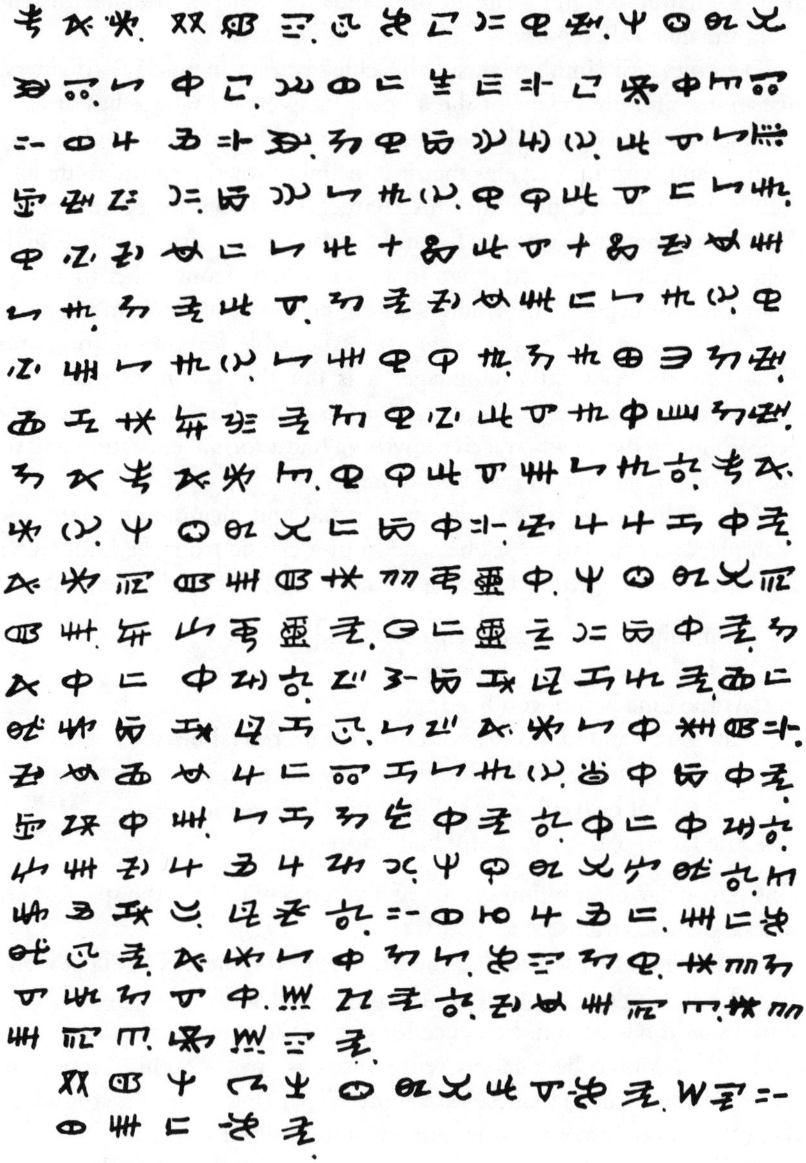

Figure 15. Yi Manuscript, dated 1928.
This particular text is written in horizontal lines that read from left to right.

read from top to bottom (Chinese-style). Styles, traditions, and the characters themselves vary greatly from place to place.

Beyond these few facts little is known about the traditional Yi writing system. No one agrees, for example, on something so basic as how many symbols there were. For the script used in the Sichuan area estimates run around 8,000 characters or so, but this is several factors larger than the total number of distinct syllables in most Yi languages and dialects.

In 1975 the PRC government selected out of these many thousands of symbols 819 graphs and decreed that they be the standard writing system for the Yi. This official syllabary of 819 graphs includes 756 symbols to be used for writing syllables in the Yi language itself, and 63 additional symbols to be used for transcribing loans from Chinese. Information on how widely this standardization is accepted is not readily available.

Lisu. The Lisu are a people culturally and linguistically closely related to the Yi. Most of them live in the rugged mountain ranges of Yunnan, but some Lisu are also found along the Sichuan border north of Kunming. Others, over the past fifty years, have moved south to Thailand. They are now said to be very numerous in Burma as well. Still others were reported in 1979 to have penetrated well into the northeastern parts of India.

About 480,000 Lisu live in China. Those in the upper reaches of the Salween River (Nùjiāng) maintain a fierce independence rivalling that of their cultural cousins, the Yi. Occupying high, easily defended places in the mountains, Lisu clansmen have over the years often preyed upon Chinese caravans passing through the area. The Lisu living farther south—sometimes described as "tame" Lisu—have been heavily influenced by the Han Chinese and are rapidly being acculturated. They raise rice in paddy fields, intermarry with Chinese, and are usually bilingual in the local Chinese dialect.

The Lisu language is not far removed in time from some of the Yunnan varieties of Yi, such as Ahi. We see, for example, the same merger of the prenasalized consonants with voiced consonants—that is, *mb* and *b* are no longer distinguished and both are now pronounced *b*. There is also the extreme phonological poverty at the end of the syllable. The only consonant that can close a syllable in the modern language is a glottal stop -*q*, the last remnant of the old stop distinctions. The nasals that were once at the end of syllables now show their trace only in the form of nasalization left on the vowels.

Lisu syntax is much the same as that of Yi. But one difference is that noun phrases are more commonly marked by particles. Like Lahu, another of its sister languages, Lisu has a complex set of particles used to focus interest, set off topics, and so on. For example, *maq³* sets off a topic very powerfully; it has much the force of a pause after a noun. *Nε⁴* is used in the middle of a long sentence to clarify a subject or a noun that is the focus of interest.

Lisu writing. In the early part of this century there were three different writing systems in use among the various Lisu groups in China. Two of these scripts were alphabets that had been devised by Protestant missionaries. The third was a syllabary invented around 1925 by a Lisu peasant named Wāng Rěnbō.

Wang Renbo grew up in the Lisu area around Weixi in the northwestern corner of Yunnan. According to what is told of his life, Wang is supposed to have been raised by his grandfather, having been left an orphan at a very early age. When Wang Renbo was fifteen, the old man also died, leaving the boy alone with a mortgage to be paid on the small plot of land that they had farmed. By the time the mortgage came due, Wang Renbo discovered that, because he was illiterate and could not read the contract, there was much more interest to be paid on the mortgage than he had thought. He was unable to make the payment and had to forfeit his land. He took a job as a bamboo worker. But since he was still bitter over his inability to read, he spent this period of his life working out a way to represent his own language by carving symbols on bamboo. The result was a syllabary of several hundred characters.

Whatever the truth of this story, Wang Renbo had much in common with the famous Cherokee script-maker Sequoyah. Like Sequoyah, Wang made up his own symbols based on the pattern of a script that he had already seen: just as a number of Sequoyah's Cherokee letters resemble Latin letters, so many of Wang's Lisu letters look vaguely like Chinese characters incised in bamboo. And like Sequoyah's invention, Wang Renbo's script was also a system for writing syllables. But whereas the eighty-five symbols of the Cherokee syllabary have been used efficiently for many years to transcribe spoken Cherokee, the several hundred symbols of the Lisu syllabary were never organized into a single coherent system. By the 1950s the syllabary had come to be used in only three or four counties around Weixi.

Hani. The Hani are one of the southernmost of China's Southwestern peoples. Over a million of them, along with smaller numbers of other minorities, fill the southwestern corner of Yunnan. Several thousand more Hani, under a variety of names, spill over the border into the adjacent regions of Laos and Vietnam. The largest concentrations of this nationality are found around Mòjiāng ('Ink River') near the Yuan River (which farther downstream becomes the Red River that flows through Hanoi). They have been living under a considerable amount of Chinese influence since the Ming period, but, according to older reports, they have maintained a strong ethnic identity. Those Hani living a little farther to the southwest near the Mekong have had closer contacts with Tai groups.

Rainfall is heavy in this part of China, and the climate permits the cultivation of good warm-weather crops. The Hani are known throughout China for the several varieties of tea that they produce, most notably green, and the kind—also grown by other groups in the area—known as "Pu'er tea." Probably the most spectacular accomplishment of the Hani are the terraces for rice paddies that they have constructed over the centuries. Many of these terraces climb from the floor of the river valley up the steep slopes, sometimes all the way to the tops of the mountains. They form literally hundreds of step levels where tiny patches of rice can be planted.

The Hani language is very close to Yi. But the PRC does not classify it as Yi, as it does many of the other Loloish languages of Yunnan, because the Hani are culturally fairly distinct—they know nothing of the Yi script, for example. But the phonological characteristics of Yi are all there: an open syllable structure (except for glottal stops); a rich vocalism (it has ten vowels); nasalized vowels; no offglides; a two-way distinction in "checked" syllables.

Lahu. The Lahu are also a hillfolk of southwestern Yunnan and northern Southeast Asia. The villages of these semi-nomadic people are scattered far and wide throughout the mountain region between the Salween and Mekong rivers (called Nù and Làncāng in China). More than 304,000 Lahu live in China, which is probably more than half of the total population. But many Lahu also live in the northern provinces of Burma, and smaller numbers are found in Thailand and Laos, as well.

The principal cash crop of these slash-and-burn farmers is opium, at least in the Lahu communities in Southeast Asia. The PRC lists tea leaves and tobacco as the main sources of revenue for the Lahu, implying that production of the illicit drug has been completely stopped on Chinese soil. But certainly, at least until recently, the Lahu have been able to maintain a high degree of independence from the Chinese. They are reputed to be excellent hunters, and the crossbow with poison-tipped arrows is still said to be the principal weapon, though firearms are preferred when available.

The Lahu divide themselves into groups with a variety of colorful names: Black Lahu, Yellow Lahu, Red Lahu, and so on. The groupings seem to correlate fairly well with linguistic differences among the Lahu.

Like Hani, Lahu is very close to Yi. Of all the Loloish languages, Lahu is by far the best known, thanks principally to the extensive research done on the language by the American linguist James Matisoff, who, among other things, has published a reference grammar and compiled a bilingual dictionary. Several monographs on Lahu and its dialects have also been published by David Bradley, another American linguist.

Jino. The Jino are a tiny minority of about 12,000 hill farmers living near the Mekong River in the southernmost tip of Yunnan. Much of their way of life resembles that of their Loloish relatives the Hani, whose villages are scattered throughout the same area.

Naxi. The Naxi, who in the past were also known as "Moso," are very nearly unique among the native inhabitants of Yunnan in that they have a fairly old literary tradition of surprising quality. This literature, along with the sacred ceremonies and legends of the Naxi people, is preserved with the aid of an unusual pictographic script of considerable artistic and linguistic interest.

The Naxi are believed to have originated as a pastoral people from much farther north who were forced to migrate south under pressure from the expanding Han Chinese. They prospered in their new homeland in western Yunnan, and around A.D. 1000 they were clearly the dominant people in the area near what is now Lìjiāng, in the loop of the Yangtze. In the fourteenth century the Mongols conquered Yunnan, including the Naxi kingdom, which by then had long been a thriving center of local culture. From that time on the Naxi became subjects of the emperor, and for centuries thereafter their men served loyally in the armies of the Chinese. From the eighteenth century on their fortunes declined, and in the early twentieth century their ruling elite lost what land and power they had left. The last Naxi prince is said to have been executed by the Communists.

Today the subsistence economy of the Naxi people reflects little of their former prosperity and power, but the traditional literature, in the

NAXI CONSONANTS

	Labial	Denti-labial	Dental	Retroflex	Alveolar	Palatal	Velar	Post-velar	Glottal
Voiceless stop	p		t			ty	k		q
Aspirated stop	p'		t'			t'y	k'		
Voiced stop	b		d			dy	g		
Prenasalized stop	ᵐb		ⁿd			ⁿdy	ⁿᵍg		
Voiceless affricate			ts	chr		chy			
Aspirated affricate			ts'	ch'r		ch'y			
Voiced affricate			dz	jr		jy			
Prenasalized affricate			ⁿdz	ⁿjr		ⁿjy			
Voiceless fricative		f	s	shr		sy	x		
Voiced fricative		v	z	zhr		zy	gh		
Nasal	m		n			ny	ng		
Lateral			l						
Flap or trill			r						
Semivowels	w, wy					y			

hands of Bon priests, still sometimes plays a part in their lives. These priests of the Bon religion, a kind of Shamanism that long ago spread to the Naxi from pre-Buddhist Tibet, chant the ancient legends and ceremonies using the pictographic texts as memory aids.

Most of the 245,000 Naxi are still concentrated in their homeland in the loop of the Yangtze, where until recently the deep gorges of the encircling river had kept them isolated from the outside influences of encroaching Chinese settlers. The Naxi have traditionally had close ties with Tibet; in 1949, for example, they joined forces with the Tibetans in the military resistance to the Communists. The alpine nature of much of the environment has also contributed to a Tibetan flavor in the culture of the Naxi: un-Sinicized Naxi still pasture yak and goats on alpine meadows, drink Tibetan-style buttered tea, and practice Lama Buddhism, as well as the older Bon religion.

The Naxi language, with its lack of consonant clusters and its completely open syllable structure, is typologically almost identical to the Yi and other Loloish languages of Yunnan. It is therefore placed in the Yi branch of Tibeto-Burman by Peking linguists. Other experts question this classification, however, and believe instead that the resemblances are superficial. Most historians say that the Naxi were originally a more northern people who migrated into Yunnan centuries ago. If so, there may have been enough close contact with Loloish groups since that migration to result in structural convergence of the languages.

Naxi is described as having two dialects. The western dialect is spoken within the Yangtze loop around Lijiang, and the eastern dialect is spoken in regions across the turbulent Yangtze, outside the loop. The western dialect is relatively uniform, but, according to PRC sources, speakers of the eastern "dialect" often have trouble communicating with each other.

The Naxi language—that is, the "dialect" spoken in and around Lijiang—has forty-eight consonants. There are nine vowels in Naxi: *i, e, a, α, ü, ɿ, ə, o, u*. There are four tones: (1) high level, (2) mid-level, (3) low level, (4) low rising.

Naxi syntactic structure is much the same as that of other Tibeto-Burman languages spoken in Yunnan.

Naxi writing. The Naxi (or Moso) have two separate traditions of "writing," one primarily pictographic and the other syllabic. The pictographic tradition is the older of the two. It is also the more interesting.

A glance at Naxi pictographs is enough to show that they are not the letters of an ordinary writing system. Instead of being arbitrary symbols, most are quite recognizable drawings of real objects. They are a delight to look at. Often flanked by decorative paintings in the margin, these drawings of plants, animals, people, and things are grouped inside rectangular frames arranged comic-book style on the page. The frames are "read" sequentially from left to right. Within each frame the sequence of symbols is generally also from left to right, but that is not invariably so, since there is much backtracking and movement up and down, and sometimes the same drawing is referred to several times as the story unfolds.

In the strictest sense it is wrong to call these pictographs writing, because they do not normally represent the units of a language. They serve, rather, only as mnemonic devices to remind a priest of the details of a story that he already knows by heart. When, as the priest recites the story, his eyes fall upon the picture of a bird with splendid tail feathers, he knows that it is at this point that the mythical white rooster Iyoɨma enters the narrative. But if, on the other hand, the bird has a large black dot on his breast, the priest knows that the bird intended is not Iyoɨma, but his nemesis, the Black Rooster. Moreover, many words of the text— especially those representing abstract concepts—are left completely unrepresented by symbols and must be totally supplied from memory. Sometimes a symbol is inserted into a frame only to elucidate the meaning of another symbol and is itself left unread. At other times a drawing may be "read" two or three times even though it only appears once.

Examples of Rebus Associations Used in Naxi Writing

	Words represented	
Naxi symbol	Basic	Secondary
	myə^3 'eye'	myə^3 'fate'
	xa^2 'food'	xa^2 'sleep'
OR	se^3 'goral'	se^2 [aspect marker]

Obviously this is not writing as we usually know it. The Naxi have never used these pictographs to communicate with each other—they do not exchange letters, write books, or even keep simple accounts and records with them. Anyone can appreciate the graphic beauty of a Naxi text, but only someone well-versed in the mystical lore of Naxi religion can interpret its meaning and translate it into language. It is not enough simply to be able to speak Naxi.

And yet the Naxi pictographs are *almost* writing. Occasionally a picture of a natural object is used secondarily to represent an abstract concept, just in case the Naxi word for this concept *sounds like* the word for the natural object. For example, a drawing of a pair of eyes sometimes means "fate," because the Naxi words for "eye" and "fate" are both pronounced *myə*^{3}. When faced with the problem of how to draw a picture of "fate," some Naxi priests must have decided that a drawing of a homophonous word could serve to remind them of it. Similarly, a drawing of a covered dish can represent "sleep" as well as "food," because both are pronounced *xa*^{2}. Even more to the point, these same kinds of borrowed drawings can be used to represent grammatical markers. The Naxi aspect marker *se*^{2}, which is suffixed to verbs to indicate a change of state, is normally left unspecified in pictographic texts. But if absolutely necessary it can be written using the drawing of a goral (a kind of goat antelope) (usually abbreviated as only the animal's head), because the goral is called *se*^{3} in Naxi. In these rebus-type associations we see the seeds of true writing; for only the relationships within the language itself can be used to make these kinds of connections. (What else besides the Naxi language causes the Naxi to associate "fate" with "eye"?) Once graphs begin to be used this way, they cease to be just drawings and come to represent the units of a language.

It is this writing-but-not-quite-writing nature of Naxi pictographs that makes them so interesting to students of the history of writing. Nothing found in the world today is closer to the earliest forms of Egyptian hieroglyphics, nor does anything resemble more the prototypes of Chinese characters that are found on ancient pottery and bronzes. The drawings themselves are surprisingly similar, as is their primary use as the tools of the practitioners of religion. But more: in both of these early centers of civilization, Egypt and China, the evolution of writing crucially depended upon the discovery of the same principles of word association whose beginnings can just be seen in Naxi.

The genealogical records of the Naxi nobility state that the pictographs were invented by the benevolent king Móubǎo Āzōng in the early part of the thirteenth century. This account is surely apocryphal. The pictographs could never have been the invention of a single man, but must instead have evolved over a long period, most probably in the hands of the priests of Bon Shamanism. Just how and when this happened we do not know. Among the Naxi pictographs are a few tantalizing portrayals of birds and animals found today only in northwestern China and not in Yunnan. But since virtually all of the other flora and fauna that appear in Naxi texts are indigenous to the present home of the Naxi, it seems safe to say that most of the evolution took place there.

The second traditional script of the Naxi is a syllabary, a writing system in which each symbol represents the sounds of a syllable. This script is more linguistically sophisticated and efficient than the pictographs, but it is not a wholly native invention. Many of the symbols were borrowed from the Chinese and others from the nearby Yi (or Lolo). The Tibetan script also provided a visual model. The Naxi often incorporated pictographic symbols into their syllabic writing, but the converse was seldom true. The character of the pictographic writing was generally maintained intact. But occasionally, in some of the texts, syllabic symbols are written next to the drawings of obscure deities to show how their names should be read. (This practice is reminiscent of the way the Japanese elucidate the readings of unfamiliar Chinese characters with their *kana* syllabary.)

ON THE following page is a small portion of a Naxi pictographic text. Two of the three lines of framed drawings in this excerpt are transcribed, with the pictures rearranged and placed over the words associated with them. A vertical line after a phrase or sentence indicates the end of one frame and the beginning of the next.

Line 1

"Ri¹i² wa¹ be²go²   be²go²   zhru³-tyur¹ a³-mə²-nyi³.|
Rii   five brothers brothers hatred-knot hit-not-able

"Tsyi³mi¹ Ch'rwa¹ me²xe³, me²xe³ shrə¹-tyur¹   t'u²-mə²-nyi³.|
Chimi   six   sisters sisters quarrel-knot come-out-not-able

"Be²go² me²xe³ ⁿdzɨ³bo³   chro¹-mə²-nyi³. Gə³   nɨ²   mɨ²-ch'rə¹,
brothers sisters marriage tie-not-able   above come sky-filth

du³-ch'rə¹,| dzɨ²-ch'rə¹,   we²-ch'rə¹,   rər²-ch'rə¹, k'ɨ³-ch'rə¹,|
earth-filth village-filth stockade-filth field-filth raw-land-filth

Line 2

bi²-ch'rə¹, le³-ch'rə¹,   ⁿjyo³-ch'rə¹,   lo³-ch'rə¹
sun-filth¹, moon-filth mountain-filth valley-filth

t'u²-rɨ²-se³. | Xa¹   i² so³   mə² sɨ²,   nyi² i²
come-out-will-CHANGE night at dawn not know day at

xa¹   mə² sɨ²   rɨ²-se³.   Gə²-gə³ sə²-ku² no²
night not know will-CHANGE quickly tree-top wild-grass

tyɨ²lɨ²,   zhrər³ ne³   la²   nɨ²   tsa¹ rɨ¹ tsɑ¹-mə²-t'ɑ¹.|
grow-up leopard with   tiger   come leap all leap-not-receive

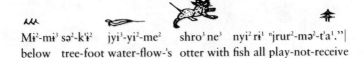

Mi²-mɨ³ sə²-kʼɨ²   jyi³-yi²-me²   shro³ne³   nyi²rɨ¹ ⁿjrur²-mə²-tʼaˈ.ˮ|
below   tree-foot water-flow-'s   otter with fish all play-not-receive

[TRANSLATION]

THE STORY OF THE GREAT FLOOD

[This story is the creation legend of the Naxi people. The central theme of the story is that the disastrous flood was brought about by incest between the first humans. This unclean act, incest, had been strictly proscribed by the gods, but since there were no other people around, the brothers and sisters had little choice if the race was to be continued.

In the brief portion of the story given below, the five brothers and six sisters have just been created. At this point Miꞏꞏroepʼu, the Great God of Light, tells them what they must not do and warns them of the consequences if they break these commandments.]

[Miꞏꞏroepʼu, the Great God of Light, said to them:]
   "Five Rɨɨ Brothers: Brothers must not fight among themselves.
   "Six Chimi Sisters: Sisters must not quarrel.
   "Brothers and sisters: You must not marry each other. For if you do, unclean things will come forth from the sky, from the earth, from the villages, from the stockades, from the fields, from the uncultivated lands, from the sun, from the moon, from the mountains, from the valleys. In the night before the dawn, and in the day before nightfall, it will happen. Tangled grasses will grow quickly to the tops of the high trees, and the leopards and the tigers will be unable to leap. In the dirtied waters at the base of the trees down below the otters and the fish will be unable to play. Above, there will be violent landslides and floodings. Down below, the rising waters will suddenly block the valleys and turn each one into a quagmire."

Jingpo Branch

Jingpo. The Jingpo are primarily a people of northern Burma. At the point where the old Burma Road from Kunming turns sharply north toward Myitkyina, a huge chunk of China projects about eighty miles into the northern Burmese hill country, just lapping over the range of the Jingpo. About 93,000 of these hillfolk—only a small part of the total Jingpo population—live in that corner of Yunnan and are thus Chinese citizens.

The Jingpo are a cultural presence to be reckoned with in northern Burma, where the state of "Kachin," another name for the Jingpo, is a

Jingpo Consonants

	Labial	Denti-labial	Dental	Retro-flex	Alveo-lar	Palatal	Velar	Post-velar	Glottal
Voiceless stop	p		t				k		q
Aspirated stop	p'		t'				k'		
Voiced stop									
Voiceless affricate			ts		ch				
Aspirated affricate									
Voiced affricate									
Voiceless fricative			s		sh				
Voiced fricative					zh				
Nasal	m		n				ng		
Voiceless nasal									
Lateral			l						
Voiceless lateral									
Flap or trill			r						
Voiceless flap									
Semivowels	w					y			

major political unit. In that part of Burma, the Jingpo language is used as a lingua franca by most of the ethnic groups who live there.

At least two of these groups—Tsaiwa (or Atsi) and Lashi—are known to range over the Chinese side of the border. The languages that they speak natively are believed to be closer genetically to Burmese than to Jingpo. But since these tiny ethnic groups use Jingpo in their dealings with outsiders, the Chinese government classes them together and calls their languages "dialects" of Jingpo.

Jingpo (proper) is important linguistically because of the role it plays in linking the Tibeto-Burman family together. It has been described as standing at the "linguistic crossroads of Tibeto-Burman, thus occupying a linguistic position comparable with its geographical setting (northern Burma)." It has lexical and morphological ties to Tibetan in the north and Burmese in the south. It connects these languages in turn to the Loloish (or Yi) languages in China to the east.

The dialect of Jingpo most widely spoken in China can be described as having nineteen consonants. This dialect has several peculiarities in its phonological system that make it different from varieties of the language reported on from Burma. Among other things, it has no *h*-type consonant (although it has a series of aspirated stops *p'*, *t'*, and *k'* that appear to be simple stops plus *h*-type aspiration). Its sister dialects in Burma have a series of voiced consonants (*b, d, g*, etc.), but this dialect, the one spoken in China, has only one consonant with the feature of voicing, *zh*. Also, in other dialects, the liquids *l* and *r* are contrasting sounds. But in the variety of Jingpo spoken in China, the two sounds are in complementary distribution, *r* occurring only in clusters (*pr- k'r-*, etc.) and *l* occurring only initially before a vowel. Therefore, in a true phonemic analysis of this dialect, *l* and *r* would have to be grouped together into a single phoneme and written with the same letter (the choice of *l* or *r* would of course be arbitrary). Using two different symbols is useful as a reminder of actual pronunciations, but it is a graphic luxury that would be rejected by linguistic purists.

Jingpo has a number of initial clusters formed by combinations of consonant plus *r*: *pr-*, *p'r-*, *kr-*, *k'r-*. In all varieties of the language, in both China and Burma, original Tibeto-Burman clusters with **l* (**kl-*, **pl-* etc.) have merged with the *r*-clusters to become *kr- pr-*, and so on. Dental stops, such as *t*, are not found in clusters in Jingpo.

A stop *p, t, k, q*, or a nasal *m, n, ng* can come at the end of a Jingpo syllable. In this respect the language is unlike its Loloish relatives, where most final consonants have been lost or reduced.

The Jingpo dialect described by Chinese linguists has an unusual vocalic distinction. In addition to the five simple vowels *i, e, a, o, u* plus a schwa *ə* that appears in certain restricted places, the dialect also has what Chinese linguists call "tense vowels": *i̬, e̬, a̬, o̬, u̬, ə̬*. According to the descriptions, these tense vowels are articulated with considerable tension in the musculature of the throat and glottis and with a mouth opening slightly smaller than for the corresponding "lax" vowels. It is unclear just what the distinguishing feature of these vowels is and how it developed historically.

Jingpo has three distinctive tones.

The original Tibeto-Burman prefixes, though preserved best in Tibetan, can also to an extent still be found in Jingpo (except for **b-*). There is some evidence in the language for the original suffixes, as well.

In the modern language, suffixation is the principal device for marking grammatical relationships, and Jingpo is remarkable for the complex order in which suffixed elements are arranged. Following a verb stem can come a series of morphemes placed in a definite order and indicating tense, manner, style, person, number, and a variety of nuances, some of which are reminiscent of the endings of Japanese verbs. In the follow example, the morpheme *-aq¹-*, which forms part of the ending for the verb 'to go,' indicates that the action is by a singular, third-person subject, and that it is not in the past:

K'yi³ p'ot²ni²   n² kam³ sa³-yang¹ ko¹,   kə¹loi² sa³-na³-aq¹-k'a³?
he   tomorrow not want go-and   PAUSE when go-will   ?
'If he doesn't want to go tomorrow, then when will he go?'

Drung. The Drung (or in Chinese, the Dúlóng) are an extremely small group of some 5,000 animist farmers, who live in a few villages tucked away in the remote northwestern corner of Yunnan near the Tibetan border. The terrain in this part of China is spectacularly precipitous—peaks reaching upwards of 16,000 feet loom sharply over the gorge of the raging Salween River.

The language that these people speak is classified by Chinese linguists as being close to Jingpo. Most Western linguists, on the other hand, would place it rather in a group together with Nu, a Tibeto-Burman language that is spoken in its immediate vicinity, both to the north and to the south.

Two somewhat divergent varieties of the Drung language have been described, and both are characterized by initial consonant clusters considerably more complex than those found in Jingpo. Drung also has more final consonants, including -*l* and -*r*, and a complex system of suffixes and prefixes. In this way it approaches more closely the typological model of Tibetan, a language to which it is geographically much closer.

Qiang Branch

Qiang. The Chinese have been in contact with Qiang (or K'iang) groups since the beginning of history in that part of the world. References to the Qiang can be found in many of the oracle-bone inscriptions of the second millennium B.C. The character used to write their name is among the oldest of Chinese graphs, and in some of its earliest forms it is still recognizably a drawing of a sheep and a man, the association that most vividly reminded the Chinese of these pastoral people.

At first, the name "Qiang" referred to any number of nomadic herders living in western China. In various shifting alliances they remained on the fringes of civilization until early in the fourth century A.D., when, as one of the "Five Barbarians," they helped overrun all of North China. Later, in the restoration of the Chinese empire that followed during the Sui-Tang period, there was much scattering of the original Qiang. Remnants, however, were left more or less intact in north central Sichuan, sandwiched between the Chinese and Tibetan domains. Those independent and unconquered Qiang who remained in this area are said to be the ancestors of today's Qiang minority.

About 103,000 Qiang now live in north central Sichuan, a little over a hundred miles to the northwest of the modern city of Chengdu. This area has long been the outer edge of Chinese territory, for directly to the west lies the central massif of Asia and the "Roof of the World." In this buffer region between China and Tibet, the Qiang have for many centuries been in close contact with the Chinese on their east and south. Most Qiang are able to speak Chinese, and in some areas the younger generation speak only Chinese. Many are also literate in Chinese.

The Qiang are still herders of sheep, yak, horses, and cattle, but these days they rely increasingly upon agriculture and the sale of mountain herbs to the Chinese to make a living. The mountainous terrain in this part of Sichuan makes for an extremely varied environment, and as a result the Qiang are bound together only loosely. Groups have diverged linguistically, and the Qiang in one area are frequently unable to understand the speech of those in another area.

Until recently, there had been only sketchy and seemingly contradictory descriptions of several different languages that were all called Qiang. In the past few years, however, Chinese experts have conducted surveys and found that there is a basic linguistic division of the Qiang region into northern and southern areas. Now, a representative dialect from each of these two areas has been described in some detail. Although the Chinese call both of them "dialects of Qiang," these two varieties of speech are actually sharply divergent languages. No question of mutual intelligibility could possibly arise here; if groups from the two areas were to come together, it is quite likely that they would have to communicate with each other in Chinese. Relating the languages to each other is a task for the comparative linguist; for the connections between them would certainly not be obvious to the untrained observer.

The typological difference between Southern Qiang and Northern Qiang can generally be described as one of tones versus segmental complexity. Southern Qiang has six tone distinctions. Northern Qiang has no tones at all; but, in compensation, it has many more consonants and vowels. Southern Qiang, the language with tones, has consonant clusters, but its toneless relative Northern Qiang has many more, including some at the end of the syllable. Chinese linguists have attributed this areal difference to the relatively heavy Chinese influence in the southern areas, which they say favored tonality. For similar reasons, the segmental complexity of the northern areas must be due to closer ties with speakers of Tibetan.

The representative dialect of Southern Qiang is that spoken in the village of Táopíng ('Peach Plain'), located about halfway between Lixian and Moxian on the west side of the Min River. Though this tone language has fewer consonants and vowels than Northern Qiang, it nevertheless has a rich segmental structure.

There are forty-three consonants. This language has an unusual four-way distinction: It has "hissing" articulation (such as s), retroflex articulation (such as

SOUTHERN QIANG CONSONANTS

	Labial	Denti- labial	Dental	Retro- flex	Alveo- lar	Palatal	Velar	Post- velar	Glottal
Voiceless stop	p		t				k	K	
Aspirated stop	p'		t'				k'	K'	
Voiced stop	b		d				g	(G)	
Voiceless affricate			ts	chr	ch	chy			
Aspirated affricate			ts'	ch'r	ch'	ch'y			
Voiced affricate			dz	jr	j	jy			
Voiceless fricative		f	s	shr	sh	sy		X	
Voiced fricative			z	zhr	zh	zy		GH	
Nasal	m		n			ny	ng		
Voiceless nasal									
Lateral			l						
Voiceless lateral									
Flap or trill									
Voiceless flap									
Semivowels	w, wy					y			

shr), "hushing" articulation (such as *sh*), and articulation with the blade of the tongue (such as *sy*). The consonant *f* is a distinctive unit, but it appears mostly in loanwords from Chinese and probably became phonemic only in recent years under influence from that neighboring language; older generation speakers of Southern Qiang tend to pronounce this consonant as a bilabial fricative *F*.

Southern Qiang has two kinds of consonant clusters. In the first kind, the post-velar fricative *X* combines with a second consonant: Xtu^5 'embrace (a child),' Xde^1 'cloud,' Xna^5ta^5 'rear,' $Xtsi^5$ 'to complete.' In the other kind of cluster, a labial stop combines with a voiced dental fricative, *z* or *zhr*: $bzia^5$ 'to leak,' $p'zhre^2p'zhre^1$ 'damp.'

The six tones are pronounced as follows: (1) high level, (2) low falling, (3) high-to-low falling, (4) low rising, (5) mid-level, (6) rising then falling.

There are ten vowels: *i, e, a, a, o, u, ə, ü, z, ər*. An unusual vowel by international standards, *z* seems to have been caused by diffusion of the Chinese sound that appears, for example, in the Mandarin word *sì* 'four.'

Máwō ('Hemp Nest'), the village whose speech was chosen as representative of Northern Qiang, lies deep in the mountains, some fifty miles northwest of Taoping. Mawo is on the southern bank of the little Shuǐ River, a tributary that flows west into the Min.

Northern Qiang, a language without tones, has an even richer inventory of consonants than Southern Qiang.

There are forty-seven in all. As can be seen from the table, Northern Qiang not only has a four-way distinction of consonants in the vicinity of the alevolar ridge,

Northern Qiang Consonants

	Labial	Denti-labial	Dental	Retro-flex	Alveo-lar	Palatal	Velar	Post-velar	Glottal
Voiceless stop	p		t				k	K	
Aspirated stop	p'		t'				k'	K'	
Voiced stop	b		d				g		
Voiceless affricate			ts	chr	ch	chy			
Aspirated affricate			ts'	ch'r	ch'	ch'y			
Voiced affricate			dz	jr	j	jy			
Voiceless fricative	F		s	shr		sy	x	X	h
Voiced fricative	V		z	zhr		zy	gh	GH	
Nasal	m		n			ny	ng		
Voiceless nasal									
Lateral			l						
Voiceless lateral			lh						
Flap or trill			ŕ	r					
Voiceless flap			ŕh						
Semivowels	w					y			

it also has an unusually large variety of *l*'s and *r*'s: there are significantly more liquid consonants than the single *l* found in Southern Qiang.

Like Southern Qiang, Northern Qiang has two types of consonant clusters. But in this case the variety within each type is much greater. In the first type, not only X but also *ŕh, ŕ, s, z, shr, x, gh, GH*, and *m* can combine with a second consonant, for a total of sixty-three combinations, for example: *ŕbi* 'cremation,' *slama* 'student,' *spian* 'glue,' *zdα* 'oil,' *xtsəxts* '(a bird name),' *xchyαp* 'pitch dark,' *ghdzə* 'rabbit.' In the second kind of cluster, one of the stops *k', g*, or *K'* combines with one of the consonants *s, z, shr, zhr, sy*, or *zy*: *k'shrəp* 'grass,' *gzə* 'millet,' *K'sər* 'gilding,' *gzyu* 'to look.'

Northern Qiang has eight basic vowels: *i, e, a, α, ɨ, u, ə, ü*. Although this is fewer than the ten vowels in Southern Qiang, Northern Qiang vowels also have two additional dimensions: they can be pronounced long or with distinctive retroflexion, or with a combination of both: *bu* 'plank,' *bu:* 'sugar,' *bu'* 'smallpox,' *Ku:'* 'guest,' *GHu:'Vu* 'swaddling clothes.'

Syllables can end in a vowel, an offglide, or be closed by twenty-two different consonants or twenty-two different consonant clusters.

The phonological systems of all varieties of Qiang, according to Chinese linguists, are now in the process of extremely rapid change. For the most part, this change is toward simplification. In Mawo (Northern Qiang) older speakers make a clear distinction in the articulation of consonants such as *ch-* and *chy-*, but young people today pronounce them the same. Similarly, older and middle-aged people distinguish *K* from *k*, but postvelar consonants like *K* have all become velars for their children and grandchildren. Consonants clusters have especially deteriorated in the speech of the young. Now, in Taoping (Southern Qiang) only the old pronounce the *X* in *Xtə⁵* 'bubble' or *XKe⁵* 'lid'; for the younger generation these words have become *tə⁵* and *Ke⁵*.

All of these changes are related to the equally rapid growth in the size of the vocabulary borrowed from Chinese. Because it is so large and important, this foreign vocabulary has altered the total phonological structure of the Qiang languages. In Taoping, where social and linguistic contacts with Chinese have been relatively greater, the sound *f* has taken firm root, even in native vocabulary. In neighboring dialects with less contact and fewer Chinese loans, the corresponding sound is still the bilabial *F*.

Primi. Altogether there are about 24,000 Primi (called Pǔmǐ in Chinese). Today they are mostly hill farmers, but their ancestors were herders living in the northwest of China, probably near or together with their relatives the Qiang. After the Sui period (seventh century A.D.) the Primi are believed to have fled ever farther south under Chinese pressure, finally ending up around the thirteenth century in the hills of northern Yunnan. The Primi in Yi territory across the Sichuan-Yunnan border are reputed to have once had a literature, which they wrote using a variation of the Tibetan alphabet. But that writing system has long since been abandoned, and today the Primi are a nonliterate people.

The Primi language is classed together with Qiang; and, indeed, there are many similar features. The variety of Primi that has recently been described in Chinese sources has an initial consonant system that could easily be that of a dialect of Qiang. But all that is left of an earlier system of final consonants is the vowel nasalization that occurs in syllables once closed by nasal consonants. This historical loss of final consonants and the proliferation of vowel distinctions—there are thirteen vowels, and they can be followed by offglides—may well be due to the influence of the Loloish languages spoken all around Primi in northern Yunnan. On the other hand, Primi has only two tones, and this is unexpected in a region dominated by the highly tonal Lolish languages.

Other Tibeto-Burman Languages

Nu. The 23,000 Nu usually build their villages on bluffs overlooking the Nu River (which downstream in Burma is called the Salween). The Nu believe that they are the original inhabitants of this long, narrow valley in northwestern Yunnan, but despite this tradition their name is probably not taken from that of the river. More likely, "Nu" is yet another variant of the word for 'black' that comes up so often in the names of the Tibeto-Burman peoples of China (the *na* in Naxi, for example, means 'black,' as does the *no* in Nosu, the Yi word for their "Black Bone" aristocracy).

The Chinese have not classified the language(s) of the Nu within Tibeto-Burman, and the descriptions of the linguistic situation are confusing. No actual data on this language are as yet available from China, but an article about it by the linguist Sun Hongkai is said to be forthcoming. In addition, the Rawang dialect of Burma has already been described in some detail.

Achang. The 20,000 Achang of China live among Jingpo and Dai groups in the westernmost part of Yunnan. There are many more Achang on the Burmese side of the border.

Achang is another language for which almost no information is available. The published Chinese materials say only that it is a member of the Tibeto-Burman family and that it has two different groups of dialects. One Western observer adds that the language seems to be genetically close to Tsaiwa (Atsi) with heavy contact influence from the neighboring Dai.

Most of the Achang of China are fluent in both Chinese and Dai. Many can also read Chinese.

MIAO-YAO

As a language family Miao-Yao is comparatively simple. It consists of only Miao and Yao, and possibly the language of the She, a tiny minority found on the eastern seaboard of South China, in Zhejiang and Fujian provinces. All of the Miao-Yao languages are spoken in China. Dialects of Miao and Yao are also spoken in Southeast Asia and, these days, in Australia, North America, and other places as well. But all of the enclaves outside of China are the result of recent migration. Large-scale population movements of Miao and Yao began to take place across the southern borders of China into Southeast Asia in the nineteenth century; and, in the early 1970s, many of the descendants of these immigrants left Southeast Asia as refugees in the wake of the Vietnam War.

Both the Miao and the Yao are remarkable for their extreme dispersion. Almost all of their settlements, from as far north as Hubei, just below the Yangtze River, to as far south as central Thailand, are found in remote mountain recesses separated from each other by miles of alien territory. None of the peoples of China are more widely scattered.

The major part of the Miao diaspora took place in the relatively recent past. From 1698 to 1855 the Chinese government carried out a series of major military campaigns in Guizhou to suppress these rebellious and restless people. The results were brutal. In the aftermath most of the survivors were scattered, launching the Miao into an era of migration. Many of the population groups known as Black Miao went southwest into Hunan and Guangxi. The Red Miao drifted directly east to Hunan. Some of the White Miao migrated northwest into Sichuan. The Flowery Miao took a southwestern course into Yunnan, some eventually ending up in Vietnam. The Blue Miao dispersed in several directions.

The Yao, who were frequently identified or confused with the Miao, suffered a similar fate, except on a slightly longer timetable. Their dispersion south out of Hunan began in the twelfth and thirteenth centuries, continuing into the nineteenth. Today the various Yao groups are distributed somewhat to the south and to the east of the Miao.

The Miao and the Yao languages are unquestionably related to each other. But they are distinct enough to indicate that the people who spoke the proto-language must very early have separated into two different groups. There is very little way to know where either of those groups was physically located, either before or after separation. But it is commonly taken for granted that the Yao were to the east of the Miao, perhaps in the coastal area of South China, where their own traditions would place them. The Miao, on the other hand, may well have been settled, as some would have it, around the middle course of the Yangtze. (But few historians take seriously the Miao legends that would trace their original homeland to a place somewhere in the Arctic.)

All varieties of Miao-Yao have a typically Southeast Asian linguistic structure. They are typologically close to Tai. The complex tone systems of Miao-Yao have undergone the same kinds of tone splits found in Tai, and they took place historically under much the same conditioning factors. Some initial consonant clusters like those found in Tai are also found in the dialects of these languages. The basic syntactic order is subject, verb, object.

A structural difference between Miao and Yao can be found in the inventory of consonants that can close a syllable. Yao syllables can end in -m, -n, -ng, -p, -t, or -k. But Miao has only a single nasal ending, which is realized phonetically as [-ng] after back vowels and as [-n] after front vowels. In some Miao dialects there is no final consonant at all, but only nasalization of the syllable vowel. An important syntactic difference between Miao and Yao is that in Miao a modifier generally follows what it modifies (as in Tai), while in Yao the modifier precedes (as in Chinese).

Miao

The imperial suppression of the Miao must have seemed at the time to be perfectly justifiable. The territory of Guizhou, where the Miao lived, had been brought into the Empire as a new province in the thirteenth century. From the Chinese perspective, the lands and resources of this province lay untapped; the Miao did not practice Chinese-style agriculture, nor apparently did they know how to exploit the iron, copper, and silver deposits that existed in proven supply there. Chinese settlers quickly began to encroach upon Miao territories, and the Miao, who were either unable or unwilling to adapt, rebelled repeatedly. In one bloody uprising in 1795, Miao warriors overran and sacked frontier towns in three different provinces; hundreds of Chinese settlers were killed and thousands of their homes were burned. Miao determination on such occasions was such that, in at least one rebellion, many men are reported to have killed their own wives and children before going into battle. In the face of what was surely interpreted as unremitting barbarity, it is no wonder that Chinese armies responded with even greater ferocity.

Yet, even so, the Chinese policy of retaliation was not without its humane rationalizations. Here is an excerpt from an eighteenth-century document outlining official reasons why all of the Miao territories had finally to be brought under direct Chinese administration:

> These people are as guileless as suckling pigs and fishes. Their generous virtue is astonishing. The Miao, after all, are human beings; and human beings have similar sentiment; and sentiment is subject to reason. ... How then would they voluntarily desire to remain in their uncivilized state?

The reasoning was plain. Chinese authorities were ready to assimilate anyone who adapted to a Chinese way of life. But anyone who did not do so would be met with scorn and intolerance. In the social hierarchy of late imperial and republican days, the Miao ranked very near the bottom. Even as late as 1941 to 1943, the Kuomintang government was still banning the wearing of Miao dress and the speaking of the Miao language.

Approximately half of the 5,031,000 Miao left in China still live in the hills of Guizhou, the most impoverished province in all of South China. In descending order of concentration, Miao communities are also found in Yunnan, Hunan, Guangxi, Sichuan, and Hubei (the so-called "Miao" of Hainan Island in Guangdong Province are actually Yao). These communities are so scattered and so broken up into groups and subgroups, there are literally dozens of local names for them, most of which refer to something the Chinese found noteworthy about them, their appearance or location, say, or their dress or their hairstyle. Many of the names are indeed memorable. Here are a few examples: the Shrimp Miao, the Short-skirt Miao, the Long-skirt Miao, the Magpie Miao, the Pointed Miao, the Upside-down Miao, the Steep-slope Miao, the Striped Miao, the Big-board Miao, the Cowrie-shell Miao. Only five such names are widely known, however: the Black Miao, the Red Miao, the White Miao, the Blue Miao (Qīng Miáo), and the Flowery Miao (Huá Miáo). These various groups are often referred to loosely—and mistakenly—as the "Miao tribes." It may well be that the Miao once had some kind of kin-based organization that could have been called "tribe," but today there is no political organization above the level of the village, and the use of such a term in reference to the Miao is simply not appropriate.

The authorities of the People's Republic do not use the term "tribe." Nor do they refer to the Miao by those colorful epithets of the past, holding such names to be degrading. Instead, the designations they use are either native names or village locations. They classify the people by the dialect that they speak.

There are many varieties of Miao and they are not all mutually intelligible. But they have not diverged greatly, especially considering how widely separated they are. (The Miao people have not been in their present, dispersed state long enough yet for that to have happened.) Chinese linguists classify the dialects into three large groups.

One of the peculiarities of Miao is that it has a very small number of distinctions at the end of a syllable. The number of initial consonants, on the other hand, is especially rich. The dialect spoken in Dànánshān (Big South Mountain), Huanjie County, Guizhou Province, is representative of the most widely spoken of the three major dialect groups. It has forty-nine consonants. As can be seen from the table of consonants, the greatest complexity in the system is prenasalization, in which a consonant is pronounced with a short nasal onset. The semivowel *w* only occurs in loanwords from Chinese. There are a few initial clusters.

The vowels of Miao are few. In the Dananshan dialect there are but six: *i, e, a, u, o, (ər)*. The retroflexed ("r-like") vowel *ər* is only found in Chinese loanwords. Altogether there are only twenty-five possible finals in this dialect (not counting tone distinctions), and twelve of them only occur in words borrowed from Chinese (in the following list, the twelve Chinese finals are given in parentheses):

Miao Consonants

	Labial	Denti-labial	Dental	Retro-flex	Alveo-lar	Palatal	Velar	Post-velar	Glottal
Voiceless stop	p		t			ty	k	K	
Aspirated stop	p'		t'			t'y	k'	K'	
Prenasalized stop	^{m}p		^{n}t			^{n}ty	^{ng}k	^{N}K	
Prenasalized aspirated stop	^{m}p'		^{n}t'			^{n}t'y	^{ng}k'	^{N}K'	
Voiceless affricate			ts	chr		chy			
Aspirated affricate			ts'	ch'r		ch'y			
Prenasalized affricate			^{n}ts	^{n}chr		^{n}ch'y			
Prenasalized aspirated affricate			^{n}ts'	^{n}ch'r		^{n}ch'y			
Voiceless fricative		f	s	shr		sy			
Voiced fricative		v		zhr		zy			
Nasal	m		n			ny	ng		
Voiceless nasal	mh		nh			nyh			
Lateral			l						
Voiceless lateral			lh						
Semivowels	(w)								

```
     e   a  o  (ər)  (ei)   ai  eu      au     ou   en      ang  ong
  i  (ie)                           (iau) (iou) (ien) (iang)
  u  (ue)  ua    (uei)  (uai)                  (uen) (uang)
```

The Miao system of finals has an unusually small set of vocalic distinctions.

There are eight tones: (1) high falling, (2) mid-falling, (3) high level, (4) low falling, (5) high mid-level, (6) low rising, (7) mid-level, (8) mid-rising. These tones developed from an original system of four tones through much the same kind of historical process as that which produced the modern Tai and Chinese systems.

The Miao have borrowed many words from the Chinese, and such borrowing has become especially common in recent decades. The newest loans are overwhelmingly the terms of politics, economics, and modern Chinese (or world) culture. Alongside loanwords in the humble terminology of everyday life—such as 'soap,' 'matches,' 'socks,' 'school,' 'middle school,' 'club,' and 'radio'—there is the ever-present, politicized jargon of today's China: 'land reform,' 'cooperative,' 'industrialization,' 'progress,' 'commune,' and the like. These words stand out sharply from native vocabulary. They are usually dissyllabic forms borrowed from Southwestern Mandarin, and the sounds are often different from native Miao words.

But Miao also has many ancient words in common with Chinese. Unlike modern borrowings, these older loans are monosyllabic and difficult to tell apart from native words because they fit the same phonological patterns. Not only do such things as the tone categories match, but the mutual restrictions between tones and initials work the same way. Many of these words have to do with early culture—

the names of metals, domestic animals, 'chopsticks,' 'ink,' 'lacquer,' and the like. There are also more abstract terms that belong to the basic vocabulary of the language, things like 'broken,' 'embrace,' 'strength,' 'air,' 'stop.' Such words show that there was early, intimate contact between the ancestors of the Miao and the Chinese. This contact must have had an effect upon the structures as well as the vocabularies of the languages.

Miao words are constructed much like Chinese words. But there are occasionally some interesting differences. In some of the dialects, measures (or classifiers), many of which are borrowed from Chinese, regularly inflect. In the dialect of Shimenkan, for example, each measure has five forms, the choice of which indicates the size, appearance, and definiteness of an object ("definiteness" refers here to a semantic difference that can be approximated in English by the use of the definite article "the" versus the indefinite article "a"). To illustrate, here are the five forms of lu^1, the measure for round or hollow objects:

lu^1 (definite or indefinite, large, attractive)
lai^1 (definite, ordinary)
la^1 (definite, tiny)
lai^2 (indefinite, ordinary)
la^2 (indefinite, tiny)

Miao syntax is probably most similar to Tai. However, the majority of patterns would not be exotic to speakers of Chinese.

The normal order in a sentence is subject, verb, object:

$Ko^3 lai^2$ la^2.
I   plow field
'I plow the fields.'

A modifier generally follows what it modifies:

$^NKai^2 nyo^2$ $pang^2$ la^1
meat ox   flower red
'beef'   'red flower'

But a number phrase or a personal pronoun precedes what it modifies, as in Chinese:

$plou^1 pua^5$ ki^3 mi^5mau^6
four hundred CATTY wheat
'four hundred catties of wheat'

$nyi^4 ti^2$
he   brother
'his brother'

Some of the grammatical resemblances to Chinese are the result of obvious, and recent, borrowings. One such conspicuous intrusion is that of the important

Chinese function word *de*; it has made its way into many Miao dialects, including that of Dananshan:

Lo¹   na³ zyau⁶ ch'ra¹le⁷.
THING this is   new-*de*
'This is new.' (Cf. Chinese *xīnde* 'new.')

Ni⁴ zyau⁶ pe¹le⁷ lau¹si¹.
he is   we-*de* teacher
'He is our teacher.'

But sometimes the borrowing is more subtle. One less obvious way the Miao have borrowed is by loan translation. Using native words, the Miao say (literally) 'to eat white' when they mean that someone ate without paying for it. This locution is borrowed from colloquial Chinese, where the color term *bái* 'white' has the extended meaning of 'free of charge.' This kind of loan translation is comparable to the importation into English of such Gallicisms as *a marriage of convenience, art object, it goes without saying, I've told him I don't know how many times*, which are word-for-word imitations of French idioms. But loan translation from Chinese into Miao is often more systematic and has penetrated the structure of the language much more thoroughly. In Miao, for example, the native word meaning 'to beat, knock' has come to appear in a wide variety of constructions that parallel the uses of the Chinese verb *dǎ* 'to beat, hit.' Thus in Miao one now says (literally) 'to beat the telephone' to mean 'to phone'; 'to beat a wager' means 'to bet'; 'to beat a needle' means 'to give an injection'; 'to beat wine' means 'to buy wine.' In this and other ways the expressive range of the language comes to conform in many of its details to that of Chinese.

Miao writing. The Miao have no writing system of their own invention. However, around the turn of the century Western missionaries introduced a system of Romanization that seems to have gained favor among many of the Miao groups. The popularity of this alphabet may have been enhanced by the extraodinary amount of success the Christian missions had had in proselytizing the Miao. Despised by the Chinese and exploited by their landlords (both Chinese and non-Chinese) the Miao were receptive to such imported ideas. The Romanization took root and was in general use in some areas up until the time of the Communist Revolution.

In 1956 the new Chinese government held a scientific seminar on the problems of the Miao language and its writing system. The missionary-devised Romanization was criticized as an "imperfect alphabetic system," and a resolution was adopted calling for a writing system that conformed as closely as possible to the Pinyin system used for Chinese. Pinyin-based Romanization was accordingly devised for Miao to fit that requirement.

She. Some 369,000 people in southeastern China are classified as Shē. They are highly Sinified, and many—perhaps most—speak only Hakka or Min dialects of Chinese. The majority live in mountain villages in Zhejiang, Fujian, and Guangdong provinces. But a few tiny communities can also be found farther inland in Jiangxi and Anhui.

Until recently nothing was known about the She language outside of China. In 1982, however, Chinese researchers published some of the results of their studies of the 1950s, supplemented by new data gathered in the Seventies. This work reveals a language with some of the typological features of Yao (e.g., syllables closed by -*p*, -*t*, or -*k*; modifiers preceding what they modify) but a language that nevertheless seems to be genetically closer to Miao.

Yao

"Yao" is one of the most confused ethnic classifications in China. The many groups known by that name are scattered widely and have been influenced by many diverse peoples; there is very little in all of their cultures that is invariably and unmistakably the same. The "Yao" call themselves by more than twenty different names.

The authorities in the People's Republic classify 1,403,000 people as members of the Yao minority. However, only about 44 percent of these people speak the language normally referred to as Yao (the native name for this language is Myen). Another 32 percent of the "Yao" speak Punu, which is a variety of Miao, while yet another 1 percent or so speak Lakkya, a language that has been classified by PRC linguists as a variety of Kam (that is, it belongs to the Tai family). And, of the rest of the "Yao," 11 percent are said to speak "a type of Chinese that differs from the regular Chinese spoken in those areas." What language the remaining 12 percent of this minority speak we are not told. Finally, to add to the confusion, the "Miao" of Hainan Island are linguistically Yao. The ancestors of these "Hainan Miao" were brought to the island in the sixteenth century by Chinese forces to help fight in their military campaigns against the Li. At that time the Chinese called them "Miao" and that is what they still call them today.

The Yao language—that is, Myen—is reasonably homogeneous, however. All of its dialects are not necessarily mutually intelligible; there are probably many that are not. But all of the known varieties are enough alike to be quickly and easily recognized as Yao.

Yao (or Myen) is in general phonologically richer than Miao. It does not have so many initial consonants, but it does have far more distinctions in the final part of the syllable. In this respect the sound system of Yao typologically resembles Cantonese, which is the dominant idiom in most of the areas where the Yao live. Like Cantonese, Yao has the endings -*m*, -*n*, -*ng*, -*p*, -*t*, -*k* (-*k*, however, is said to occur in only one or two words). It also has distinctive vowel length, though in some dialects, notably those spoken in Hunan, this distinction "tends to disappear." In such areas Hakka, not Cantonese, may perhaps be the Chinese with whom the Yao most frequently come into contact (Hakka dialects do not have vowel length). Yao usually has from six to eight tones, but there are some dialects that have more than ten.

As do many of the other minority languages of China, Yao has a number of sounds that only appear in loanwords from Chinese. The aspiration of consonants is one such feature. Several vowels also do not appear in native words.

MON-KHMER

Most of the Mon-Khmer live well to the south of China. The most important and best known of these are the Khmer, the national majority of Kampuchea, the country that used to be called Cambodia. There are perhaps eight million Khmer altogether, counting those in northeastern Thailand and the displaced Khmer in refugee camps or overseas. The Mon are a minority of southern Burma and Thailand. Other Mon-Khmer peoples make up what are believed to be older ethnic strata in more northern parts of Southeast Asia; they are generally described as darker and shorter than the peoples originally from farther north, such as the Lao.

Three Mon-Khmer minorities are found in China, all on the extreme southwestern edge of Yunnan. Two of these groups are very small: there are only 12,300 Benglong and 59,000 Blang. The third Mon-Khmer group in China, the Wa, are more numerous and politically more important.

Wa

The 300,000 Wa of Yunnan are part of a more extensive population that is centered in northern Burma. The history of these people is not known, but most groups appear to have been in their present range for a long time. The Wa have resisted intrusions into their territory, and those who are not Buddhists have had little contact with other groups. They live in relative seclusion on high mountain slopes.

The long isolation of the Wa has been enhanced by their well-deserved reputation as headhunters. In headhunting country a collection of skulls was always kept in a grove outside each village to ensure the well-being of the people who lived there. According to the religion of the Wa, the possession of these skulls prevented the ghosts of the former owners from wandering too far away, and instead, their spirits remained nearby, driving off all the evil banes that could strike the village and cause sickness or crop failure. The planting and harvest seasons were especially important, and each year around those times a small band of Wa would set out from the village in search of fresh heads. Ambush was preferred, and the unwary traveler was often the victim. Up until a few decades ago, Wa country was carefully avoided by Burmese, British, and Chinese alike.

The Wa are at most on the fringe of the Sinitic world. The structure of their language is relatively unlike Chinese. Wa is said to have no tones, though in some dialects syllables with "tense" vowels are automatically pronounced with high pitches. There are many consonant clusters, as well as voiced "aspirated" consonants, such has *b'*, contrasting with plain voiced consonants like *b*. The syntactic order is also quite different; in many constructions, for example, the verb can come before the subject. In recent years the Yunnan Wa have begun to absorb such Chinese loanwords as 'telephone,' 'factory,' 'worker,' 'tractor,' and 'commune.' But the basic vocabulary is still relatively free of Chinese influence.

Unclassified or Isolated Languages

Gin

The Gin are a group of 12,000 Vietnamese fishermen living just over the Chinese side of the border. "Gin" is what the Vietnamese call themselves, just as "Han" is the name the Chinese use for their ethnic group.

Tujia

The Tujia are a highly Sinified group of farmers living in north-western Hunan and adjacent parts of Hubei and Guizhou. There are about 2,833,000 Tujia, but their existence as a minority was not discovered until the nationwide language surveys of the 1950s.

Little is known of their language, and it has not yet been officially classified in the People's Republic. From the fragmentary evidence that is available, however, some linguists believe that it is Tibeto-Burman. If so, Tujia would be by far the most northeasterly language in that family.

Gelao

The Gelao are a very small minority of some 54,000 located mostly in the hill areas of northwestern Guizhou, but a few tiny communities also exist in Hunan, Yunnan, and Guangxi. Gelao are found in Vietnam as well, just across the border from China. In all of these places, including Guizhou, the Gelao are rapidly being assimilated by neighboring Chinese or Tai populations.

Information about this language is scanty. The American comparativist Paul Benedict would class it as a peripheral member of the Tai family, most closely related to the Li languages. Chinese linguists have not accepted this classification, however, preferring to leave the question of its linguistic affinities open.

Bai

The origin of the Bai—or Minjia, as they were formerly called—has been the subject of much curiosity and speculation. But their history, insofar as it is known from Chinese records, begins with the Mongol invasion of the Nanzhao kingdom of Yunnan.

In the middle of the thirteenth century Chinggis Khan's grandson Khubilai led his Mongol armies past cloudy and misty southern Sichuan and entered what the Chinese called Yúnnán—literally, the land "South of the Clouds." It was non-Chinese territory. The entire region south of Sichuan was geologically a high shelf that extended out several hundred miles to the southeast off the end of the Himalayan Range. Ribbing the top of this shelf were rugged mountains cut by narrow river valleys that only occasionally broadened out into inhabitable lake plateaus. Few Chinese had ever lived there, and the greatest power in the region was a kingdom called Nanzhao, where a few elite families of uncertain origin ruled over a great amalgam of peoples. The unstoppable Mongol forces quickly took the capital at Dali in 1253, causing the ruling families to flee south. This turn of events left a power vacuum, and when Khubilai consolidated his conquests he made the entire land "South of the Clouds" a province of the Chinese Empire. From this time on, Yunnan was to be a permanent part of China.

When the Mongols and the Chinese moved in to occupy Dali, they found that the most important people living there were the Bai. The Bai had not been the rulers of Nanzhao, but they had produced the wealth that had sustained it because they knew how to grow rice. As a large and well-established population of farmers who cultivated rice in much the same way that the Chinese did, the Bai were a relatively distinct nationality in Yunnan. Skill in the methods of intensive agriculture was a commodity that set the Bai apart from the other peoples in the area.

After the conquest of Yunnan, Chinese immigrants quickly took over all the arable land on the other large lake plateaus, but around Dali the older inhabitants remained in place to become the mainstay of the local economy. To the Chinese, for whom economic considerations were more important than ethnic ones, these hard-working peasants were known simply as Mínjiā, the "Common People," to distinguish them from all the Chinese officials, soldiers, and merchants who by now had settled in the area. The Bai themselves, however, continued to use their own name $P\varepsilon^2tsi^1$, the "White People," (or other dialect variants), and in 1956 the Peking government officially changed the Chinese name of this group from Mínjiā to Bái 'White,' which fit the local term well in both sound and meaning.

Today, the 1,131,000 members of the Bai minority occupy a solid block of territory in northern Yunnan. They have not been displaced by the Chinese and still farm all of the choice rice-growing lands on the plain around Dali. The great height of this plain, some 6,000 feet, combines with a latitude of just above the Tropic of Cancer to make an invigorating climate with a long growing season. Water is plentiful, and, unlike the red clay found in most of the rest of Yunnan, the soil is heavy and black. The Bai are not herders by profession, but at the bases of the mountains they have enough space to graze cattle, which they milk in order to make cheese. One of the kinds of "milk cake" that the Bai make has become a delicacy among the Han Chinese of Yunnan and is regularly shipped to the provincial capital at Kunming (most Chinese outside of the province, of course, still consider such milk products disgusting and unfit for human consumption). The large lake in the middle of the Dali

Plateau—called Ěrhǎi, or 'Ear Lake'—is also well exploited by the Bai; and large catches of fish, taken either with tame cormorants in the shallows or with nets in deep waters, are consistently available on the Dali markets. All told, the position of the Bai among the Southwestern minorities is an enviable one. No other non-Han group in northern Yunnan has been so successful.

THE enigma of the Bai is in essence a linguistic question: The language that they speak has not been shown to be related to any other. It has elements that look like Tibeto-Burman; others that look like Tai or Mon-Khmer; and some tantalizing ones that look like Chinese on several levels. But none of these prove a genetic affinity. Who then are the Bai? They are among the oldest inhabitants of Yunnan, but we do not know where they came from.

In the PRC the Bai are classed as a Tibeto-Burman people, and their language is put into the Yi branch of that language family. This classification is premature. It is still not known what, if any, language family Bai belongs to, much less which branch.

An interesting hypothesis is that Bai is an ancient branch of Sinitic—that is, that it separated from the Chinese stock some time before the Old Chinese period some 2,500 years ago. The idea has been around for a long time, but so little was previously known about the Bai language that the hypothesis was never systematically explored. Recently, however, several works on Bai have been published, and interest in the idea has revived. For advocates of this hypothesis, evidence from the various Bai dialects has come to be of increased importance.

On a superficial level, Bai is much like the Loloish languages. With its many tones, vowels, and open syllables, it sounds very similar.

The standard Dali dialect has a simple system of twenty consonants. It has twelve vowels: *i, e, ɛ, a, ü, ö, ɔ, ə, ɨ, u, o, v*. The vowel *ɨ* is a high, mid-back vowel; after the consonants *ts, ts', s,* or *z*, the tip of the tongue moves little in the pronunciation of this vowel, and so in this position it sounds like the minimal vowel heard in Mandarin *sì* 'four' or *zì* 'word, character.' The phoneme *v* usually serves as a consonant, but in this language it can also function as a vowel. There are eight tones: (1) high mid-level, (2) mid-level, (3) low mid-level, (4) low falling, (5) high falling, (6) low rising, (7) low falling-rising, (8) high-level "checked."

In its grammar, too, Bai resembles Tibeto-Burman: Modifiers follow modified; verbs compound and take endings to indicate mood, aspect, and the like. But, curiously, the most consistent typological feature of Tibeto-Burman is not found in Bai; for instead of preceding, objects follow verbs in this language:

Bai Consonants

	Labial	Denti-labial	Dental	Retro-flex	Alveo-lar	Palatal	Velar	Post-velar	Glottal
Voiceless stop	p		t				k		
Aspirated stop	p'		t'				k'		
Voiced stop									
Voiceless affricate			ts						
Aspirated affricate			ts'						
Voiced affricate									
Voiceless fricative		f	s				x		
Voiced fricative		v	z						
Nasal	m		n				ng		
Voiceless nasal									
Lateral			l						
Voiceless lateral									
Flap or trill									
Voiceless flap									
Semivowels	w, wy					y			

Ngɔ³ ε² ngv⁶.
I   like fish
'I like fish.'

The Chinese have had considerable influence upon the Bai for a very
long time. Beneath layers of modern loans, the Bai language has a large
stock of words that can be directly compared to Middle Chinese, the
literary standard of the seventh century. These ancient borrowings are
extensive and systematic. Beyond these loans, there are probably still
older and less systematic layers of borrowings.

What remains to be shown is whether or not there are common elements in Bai and Chinese (or some other language) that are older than all
such loans and would point to a shared ancestry. These are the connections that the comparative linguist is ultimately looking for.

APPENDIX A

Chinese Sounds and the Pinyin Romanization System

b	Initial *b-*, as in *bèi* 'to memorize,' is pronounced much like the *b* in English *bay*, except that it is not voiced. An even closer approximation of this sound is the *p* that occurs in English *spay* (with the pronunciation of the *s* suppressed).
p	Initial *p-*, as in *pèi* 'to match,' is pronounced much like the *p* in English *pay*, except that it is more strongly aspirated.
m	Initial *m-*, as in *mèi* 'to embezzle,' is pronounced like the *m* in English *may*.
f	Initial *f-*, as in *fèi* 'to waste,' is pronounced like the *f* in English *Fay*.
d	Initial *d-*, as in *dòu* 'beans,' is pronounced much like the *d* in English *dough*, except that it is not voiced. A closer approximation is the *t* that occurs in English *stow* (with the *s* suppressed).
t	Initial *t-*, as in *tòu* 'to penetrate,' is pronounced much like the *t* in English *tow*, except that it is more strongly aspirated.
n	Initial *n-*, as in *nèi* 'inside,' is pronounced like the *n* in English *nay*.
l	Initial *l-*, as in *lòu* 'to leak,' is pronounced like the *l* in English *low*.
g	Initial *g-*, as in *gòu* 'to be enough,' is pronounced much like the *g* in English *go*, except that it is not voiced. A closer approximation is the *c* that occurs in English *scone* (with the *s* suppressed).
k	Initial *k-*, as in *kòu* 'to button,' is pronounced much like the *c* in English *Coe*, except that it is more strongly aspirated.
h	Initial *h-*, as in *hòu* 'behind,' is sometimes pronounced like the *h* in English *hoe*, and sometimes with velar friction, as in German *ach*.
j	Initial *j-*, as in *jì* 'to remember,' is pronounced similarly to the *j* in English *jeep*, but the tip of the tongue is held down behind the lower front teeth and the sound articulated with the blade of the tongue against the front part of the palate. The lips are not rounded (before nonrounded vowels). Also, unlike the English sound, Chinese *j-* is not voiced.
q	Initial *q-*, as in *qì* 'air,' is pronounced similarly to the *ch* in English *cheap*, but the place of articulation is the same as that of *j-*. It is also more heavily aspirated than the English sound.
x	Initial *x-*, as in *xì* 'to be thin,' is pronounced similarly to the *sh* in English *she*. But, like initial *j-*, it has palatal articulation and the lips are not rounded.
z	Initial *z-*, as in *zài* 'again,' is pronounced much like the *ts* in English *it's I* (with the initial *i* left off).

c	Initial *c*-, as in *cài* 'vegetable,' is pronounced much like the *ts-h* in English *it's high* (with the initial *i* left off).
s	Initial *s*-, as in *sài* 'to compete,' is pronounced much like the *s* in English *sigh*.
zh	Initial *zh*-, as in *zhào* 'to shine,' is pronounced similarly to the *j* in English *joust*, but the tip of the tongue is curled up to a place just behind the alveolar ridge. The lips are not rounded. Also, unlike the English sound, *zh*- is not voiced.
ch	Initial *ch*-, as in *chǎo* 'to be noisy,' is pronounced similarly to the *ch* in English *chow*, but the place of articulation is the same as that of *zh*-. It is also more heavily aspirated than the English sound.
sh	Initial *sh*-, as in *shǎo* 'to be few,' is pronounced similarly to the *sh* in English *shout*, but the place of articulation is the same as that of *zh*-.
r	Initial *r*-, as in *rào* 'to go around,' is pronounced similarly to the *r* in Midwestern American English *rowel*, but the lips are not rounded.
a	Final -*a*, as in *mǎ* 'horse,' sounds like the *a* in English *ma*.
ai	Final -*ai*, as in *ǎi* 'short,' sounds like the *ai* in English *aisle*.
ao	Final -*ao*, as in *sǎo* 'to sweep,' sounds like the *au* in *sauerkraut*.
an	Final -*an*, as in *ān* 'tranquil,' sounds like German *an*. It resembles English *(c)on*, except that the tongue is held a little farther toward the front of the mouth.
ang	Final -*ang*, as in *máng* 'busy,' sounds like English *ma* plus an *ng* sound.
e	Final -*e*, as in *hē* 'to drink,' sounds similar to the *u* in English *huh*, except that the back of the tongue is drawn up higher and slightly farther toward the rear of the mouth.
er	Final -*er*, as in *ěr(duo)* 'ear,' sounds like the *er* in American English *her*, except that the corners of the mouth are spread more.
ei	Final -*ei*, as in *hēi* 'black,' sounds like the *ei* in English *heinous* or *eight*.
en	Final -*en*, as in *bèn* 'stupid,' sounds like the *un* in English *bun*.
eng	Final -*eng*, as in *rēng* 'to throw,' sounds like the *ung* in English *rung*.
o	[see *uo*]
ou	Final -*ou*, as in *(ké)sòu* 'cough,' sounds like the *ou* in English *soul*.
ong	Final -*ong*, as in *róng* 'to melt,' has a vowel with a value between the *u* in *rue* and the *o* in *roe*. [NOTE: This final never occurs without an initial; cf. *weng*.]
yi, -*i*	Final -*i* is pronounced three different ways. (1) After the consonants *z*-, *c*-, and *s*-, as in *zì* 'word, character,' *cì* 'to stab,' or *sì* 'four,' it is a weakly buzzing, syllabic *z*. (2) After the consonants *zh*-, *ch*-, *sh*-, and *r*-, as in *zhǐ* 'paper,' *chī* 'eat,' *shì* 'business,' or *Rì(běn)* 'Japan,' it is a syllabic American *r*. (3) After other consonants,

such as in *lín* 'forest,' or in syllables without an initial, such as *yī* 'one,' it sounds much like the vowel in English *lean* or *ye*.

ya,
-ia
Final *-ia*, as in *liǎ* 'two,' sounds like the *ya* in *Ilya*.

ye,
-ie
Final *-ie*, as in *yě* 'also,' sounds like the *ye* in *yet*.

yao,
-iao
Final *-iao*, as in *qiáo* 'bridge,' sounds like the *iao* in Italian *ciao* ('bye!') or the *yow* in English *yowl*.

you,
-iu
Final *-iou*, as in *yǒu* 'to exist,' sounds like the *yo* in *yoke*. In a syllable with an initial, such as *jiǔ* 'wine,' final *-iou* is abbreviated to *-iu*.

yan,
-ian
Final *-ian*, as in *yān* 'smoke, tobacco,' sounds like the *yan* in *Yancey*.

yin,
-in
Final *-in*, as in *bīn* 'shore,' sounds like the *in* in *carbine*.

yang,
-iang
Final *-iang*, as in *yáng* 'sheep,' sounds like German *ja* plus an *ng* sound.

ying,
-ing
Final *-ing*, as in *píng* 'flat,' sounds like the *ing* of English *ping* except that the vowel is closer to the *i* of *machine*.

yong,
-iong
Final *-iong*, as in *yòng* 'to use,' has a main vowel with a value between the *u* of German *jung* and the *o* of English *tone*. Medial *i-* has some lip rounding in this final and sounds a little like medial *ü-*.

wu,
-u
Final *-u*, as in *shū* 'book,' sounds like the vowel in English *shrew*, except that the tongue is a little higher and farther back. The rounding of the lips is kept the same throughout the syllable.

wa,
-ua
Final *-ua*, as in *wā* 'to dig,' sounds like the *wa* of *water*.

wo,
-uo
Final *-uo*, as in *wǒ* 'I,' has a main vowel like that of the final *-e*, except that it has some lip rounding carried over from the medial *u-*. During the articulation of this *o*, however, the lips unround somewhat.

wai,
-uai
Final *-uai*, as in *wài* 'outside,' sounds like the *wi* of *wide*.

wei,
-ui
Final *-uei*, as in *wèi* 'for the sake of,' sounds like the *wei* of *weigh*. In a syllable with an initial, such as *duì* 'to be right,' final *-uei* is abbreviated to *-ui*.

wan,
-uan
Final *-uan*, as in *wán* 'to be finished,' sounds like the English word *wan*.

wen,
-un
Final *-uen*, as in *wèn* 'to ask,' sounds a little like English *won*, but the vowel sound is shorter and the *n* longer. In a syllable without an initial, such as *lún* 'take turns,' final *-uen* is abbreviated to *-un*. [NOTE: Since this is only an orthographic device, *-un* is NOT pronounced like the *oon* of English *loon*; in spite of the spelling,

the pronunciation still has the vowel sound of English *won* even in a syllable with an initial.]

wang,
-uang Final *-uang*, as in *wáng* 'king,' sounds like the Chinese-American surname "Wong," though this Anglicized spelling was made up on the basis of the sounds of a Southern dialect.

weng Final *-ueng*, as in *wēng* 'old man,' has a main vowel like the *u* of English *sung*. This final NEVER occurs with an initial, just as the final *-ong* never occurs without one; hence, the two can be thought of as the same final, even though their vowel sounds are different.

yu,
-ü Final *-ü*, as in *qù* 'to go' or *lǜ* 'green,' is pronounced like the *u* in French *lu* or the *ü* in German *lügen*. English speakers can approximate this sound by saying *Lee* with the lips pursed.

yue,
-üe Final *-ue*, as in *yuè* 'moon,' *xuě* 'blood,' or *lüè* 'omit,' sounds like the *ye* of English *yet* with the lips strongly rounded during the articulation of the *y*.

yuan,
-üan Final *-üan*, as in *yuán* 'round' or *quàn* 'advise,' sounds like the final *-ian* with the lips strongly rounded during the articulation of the medial *i-*.

yun,
-ün Final *-ün*, as in *yūn* 'to be dizzy' or *jūn* 'to be equal,' sounds like the *un* of French *uni*, except that the lips becomes slightly unrounded during the articulation of the vowel.

APPENDIX B

A Comparative Table of the Pinyin and Wade-Giles Romanizations

Pinyin	Wade-Giles	Pinyin	Wade-Giles	Pinyin	Wade-Giles
a	a	cheng	ch'êng	du	tu
ai	ai	chi	ch'ih	duan	tuan
an	an	chong	ch'ung	dui	tui
ang	ang	chou	ch'ou	dun	tun
ao	ao	chu	ch'u	duo	to
ba	pa	chua	ch'ua	e	ê
bai	pai	chuai	ch'uai	ei	ei
ban	pan	chuan	ch'uan	en	ên
bang	pang	chuang	ch'uang	eng	êng
bao	pao	chui	ch'ui	er	êrh
bei	pei	chun	ch'un	fa	fa
ben	pên	chuo	cho	fan	fan
beng	pêng	ci	tz'ŭ (ts'ŭ)	fang	fang
bi	pi	cong	ts'ung	fei	fei
bian	pien	cou	ts'ou	fen	fen
biao	piao	cu	ts'u	feng	feng
bie	pieh	cuan	ts'uan	fo	fo
bin	pin	cui	ts'ui	fou	fou
bing	ping	cun	ts'un	fu	fu
bo	po	cuo	ts'o	ga	ka
bu	pu	da	ta	gai	kai
ca	ts'a	dai	tai	gan	kan
cai	ts'ai	dan	tan	gang	kang
can	ts'an	dang	tang	gao	kao
cang	ts'ang	dao	tao	ge	kê, ko
cao	ts'ao	de	tê	gei	kei
ce	ts'ê	dei	tei	gen	kên
cen	ts'ên	deng	têng	geng	kêng
ceng	ts'êng	di	ti	gong	kung
cha	ch'a	dian	tien	gou	kou
chai	ch'ai	diao	tiao	gu	ku
chan	ch'an	die	tieh	gua	kua
chang	ch'ang	ding	ting	guai	kuai
chao	ch'ao	diu	tiu	guan	kuan
che	ch'ê	dong	tung	guang	kuang
chen	ch'ên	dou	tou	gui	kui

Pinyin	Wade-Giles	Pinyin	Wade-Giles	Pinyin	Wade-Giles
gun	kun	ku	k'u	ming	ming
guo	kuo	kua	k'ua	miu	miu
ha	ha	kuai	k'uai	mo	mo
hai	hai	kuan	k'uan	mou	mou
han	han	kuang	k'uang	mu	mu
hang	hang	kui	k'ui	na	na
hao	hao	kun	k'un	nai	nai
he	hê, ho	kuo	k'uo	nan	nan
hei	hei	la	la	nang	nang
hen	hên	lai	lai	nao	nao
heng	hêng	lan	lan	ne	nê
hong	hung	lang	lang	nei	nei
hou	hou	lao	lao	nen	nên
hu	hu	le	lê, lo	neng	nêng
hua	hua	lei	lei	ni	ni
huai	huai	leng	lêng	nian	nien
huan	huan	li	li	niang	niang
huang	huang	lia	lia	niao	niao
hui	hui	lian	lien	nie	nieh
hun	hun	liang	liang	nin	nin
huo	huo	liao	liao	ning	ning
ji	chi	lie	lieh	niu	niu
jia	chia	lin	lin	nong	nung
jian	chien	ling	ling	nou	nou
jiang	chiang	liu	liu	nu	nu
jiao	chiao	long	lung	nü	nü
jie	chieh	lou	lou	nuan	nuan
jin	chin	lu	lu	nüe	nüeh
jing	ching	lü	lü	nuo	no
jiong	chiung	luan	luan	o	o
jiu	chiu	lüe	lüeh	ou	ou
ju	chü	lun	lun	pa	p'a
juan	chüan	luo	luo	pai	p'ai
jue	chüeh	ma	ma	pan	p'an
jun	chün	mai	mai	pang	p'ang
ka	k'a	man	man	pao	p'ao
kai	k'ai	mang	mang	pei	p'ei
kan	k'an	mao	mao	pen	p'ên
kang	k'ang	mei	mei	peng	p'êng
kao	k'ao	men	mên	pi	p'i
ke	k'ê, k'o	meng	mêng	pian	p'ien
kei	k'ei	mi	mi	piao	p'iao
ken	k'ên	mian	mien	pie	p'ieh
keng	k'êng	miao	miao	pin	p'in
kong	k'ong	mie	mieh	ping	p'ing
kou	k'ou	min	min	po	p'o

Pinyin	Wade-Giles	Pinyin	Wade-Giles	Pinyin	Wade-Giles
pou	p'ou	shen	shên	wo	wo
pu	p'u	sheng	shêng	wu	wu
qi	ch'i	shi	shih	xi	hsi
qia	ch'ia	shou	shou	xia	hsia
qian	ch'ien	shu	shu	xian	hsien
qiang	ch'iang	shua	shua	xiang	hsiang
qiao	ch'iao	shuai	shuai	xiao	hsiao
qie	ch'ieh	shuan	shuan	xie	hsieh
qin	ch'in	shuang	shuang	xin	hsin
qing	ch'ing	shui	shui	xing	hsing
qiong	ch'iung	shun	shun	xiong	hsiung
qiu	ch'iu	shuo	sho	xiu	hsiu
qu	ch'ü	si	szŭ, ssŭ	xu	hsü
quan	ch'üan	song	sung	xuan	hsüan
que	ch'üeh	sou	sou	xue	hsüeh
qun	ch'ün	su	su	xun	hsün
ran	jan	suan	suan	ya	ya
rang	jang	sui	sui	yan	yen
rao	jao	sun	sun	yang	yang
re	jê	suo	so	yao	yao
ren	jên	ta	t'a	ye	yeh
reng	jêng	tai	t'ai	yi	yi
ri	jih	tan	t'an	yin	yin
rong	jung	tang	t'ang	ying	ying
rou	jou	tao	t'ao	yong	yung
ru	ju	te	t'ê	you	yu
rua	jua	teng	t'êng	yu	yü
ruan	juan	ti	t'i	yuan	yüen
rui	jui	tian	t'ien	yue	yüeh
run	jun	tiao	t'iao	yun	yün
ruo	jo	tie	t'ieh	za	tsa
sa	sa	ting	t'ing	zai	tsai
sai	sai	tong	t'ung	zan	tsan
san	san	tou	t'ou	zang	tsang
sang	sang	tu	t'u	zao	tsao
sao	sao	tuan	t'uan	ze	tsê
se	sê	tui	t'ui	zei	tsei
sen	sên	tun	t'un	zen	tsên
seng	sêng	tuo	t'o	zeng	tsêng
sha	sha	wa	wa	zha	cha
shai	shai	wai	wai	zhai	chai
shan	shan	wan	wan	zhan	chan
shang	shang	wang	wang	zhang	chang
shao	shao	wei	wei	zhao	chao
she	shê	wen	wên	zhe	chê
shei	shei	weng	wêng	zhei	chei

Pinyin	Wade-Giles	Pinyin	Wade-Giles	Pinyin	Wade-Giles
zhen	chên	zhuai	chuai	zong	tsung
zheng	chêng	zhuan	chuan	zou	tsou
zhi	chih	zhuang	chuang	zu	tsu
zhong	chung	zhui	chui	zuan	tsuan
zhou	chou	zhun	chun	zui	tsui
zhu	chu	zhuo	cho	zun	tsun
zhua	chua	zi	tzŭ (tsŭ)	zuo	tso

NOTES

There are a number of general works on the Chinese language, each with different emphases. Karlgren's popular books on Chinese (1926, 1929, and 1949) are still among the best and most entertaining introductions to be found, though the style and the views of the language that these works express are of a different era. Forrest's *The Chinese Language* (1948) is intended as a more comprehensive and scholarly treatment, and it devotes a chapter to related and contiguous languages; but it also shows its age now, and the prose is dry and demanding. Newnham's *About Chinese* (1971) is a small paperback with a lively style intended for people who know absolutely no Chinese at all. Kratochvil's *The Chinese Language Today* (1968) is a serious work that focuses principally on the structure of the modern language; it is accurate and highly respected by most specialists. John DeFrancis's recently published *The Chinese Language: Fact and Fantasy* (1984) is an essay on the nature of Chinese characters and Chinese efforts at script reform; it goes a long way toward demolishing the myths that have grown up around Chinese writing. The most comprehensive and detailed description of Chinese, both modern and historical, is Jerry Norman's *Chinese* (1988).

A few general bibliographies of Chinese linguistics have been published; the most recent and extensive of these is Yang 1974.

Two short articles, Chang 1967 and Luo and Fu 1954, have been written on the non-Han languages of China. Other general overviews can be found in various surveys of the languages of the world (e.g., Meillet and Cohen 1952, Voegelin and Voegelin 1977).

Chapter 1. "A Language for All of China"

The excerpt from Qian Xuantong's letter, Qian 1918. Further details of the exchange between Qian, Chen, and other Chinese intellectuals are found in Zhao 1963. The atmosphere of the early Republican period is described briefly and vividly in DeBary et al. 1960. Chinese students in Japan, Jansen 1975. DeFrancis 1950 is the best single source for the history of this period, and the story as told here draws heavily upon it and its bibliography. Barnes 1982 is another useful work. Anecdotes about the early years of the National Language Movement can be found in Li Jinxi 1934. For more details, see Fang 1965. The description of the language situation around the turn of the century is largely taken from Chao 1976c. The slight disdain some Southerners felt toward Mandarin is also described in that source. Y. R. Chao is reported to have once said that, all his younger life, he could never totally wipe out the feeling that Northern speech (especially Pekinese) was a language of servants and maids (Mantaro Hashimoto, personal communication). The tasks and details of the conference, DeFrancis 1950. The problems associated with defining "language" and "dialect" are explained in Hockett 1958. The romantic historian was Jules Michelet, and the quote was supplied by Robert Somers (personal communication). On the Guoyin dictionary and Wang Pu, Chao 1976b, 1976c, 1976d. Hu Shih and literary reform, C. T. Hsia 1961. Language policy in the USSR, Austerlitz 1982, DeFrancis 1950, Dreyer 1976. Language policy after the Communist Revolution, DeFrancis 1967, Chen 1973. The quote from the PRC document on language policy is a slightly altered version of the translation given in Chen 1973. The anecdote about the destruction of telegraph lines, Lehmann 1975.

CHAPTER 2. "CHINA, NORTH AND SOUTH"

An overview of Chinese geography and climate is given at the beginning of Reischauer and Fairbank 1958. A somewhat longer and more technical account is Hsieh 1973. A marvelously clear introduction to the subject can be found in Wiens's high school textbook *China*, but the reader has to ignore the juvenile format and style. The best detailed description is Cressey 1955. The term "Inner China" as a concise description of the area where the Han Chinese have traditionally been concentrated was suggested by Adele Rickett.

CHAPTER 3. "THE SPREAD OF NORTHERN INFLUENCE"

Mao Dun's attitude in the 1930s and his activism on behalf of separate standards are described in detail in DeFrancis 1950. The recent pronouncement on Putonghua, Mao Dun 1978. The quote from Zhou Enlai's speech is an excerpt from Zhou Enlai 1979. The remarks on the linguistic behavior of refugees in Hong Kong come from the Introduction to Seybolt and Chiang 1979, and the facts about teacher training in the 1950s are also from that source. Cantonese schoolroom behavior is discussed in Light 1980. M. Hashimoto 1978a ascribes special importance to substrata in the formation of Chinese; this work and a number of other recent books and papers have generated considerable interest among East Asian linguists in the spread of areal features. For additional references on the subject, see the notes to Chapter 9. Ballard 1981 contains an interesting and detailed description of various linguistic substrata in South China, but the interpretation of those elements is somewhat different from the more orthodox one given here. The early Sinification of Yue, Bielenstein 1947, 1959. Migrations and the policies of the Qin emperor, Lee 1978. The official Chinese glossaries of various foreign languages were known as the *Huá-Yí yìyǔ* [Sino-Barbarian glossaries]. The historical process through which the South was Sinified has been documented most carefully in Hartwell 1982; some details concerning Sichuan were supplied by Robert Hartwell in personal communication. Ho 1959 gives a somewhat different interpretation of the history of population movements in China. The mixing of immigrants and natives in South China, Lee 1978. The sixteenth-century travel guide to the Southwest is described in Lee 1977. The results of language transference are explained in Bloomfield 1933. Mencken 1979 supplies a list of words taken from American Indian languages into English. The examples of Chilean Spanish and Indo-Aryan, Bloomfield 1933. The observation that the number of tones in Chinese increases toward the south comes from Norman 1970; M. Hashimoto 1976 and 1978a elaborate on the meaning of this phenomenon. The Cantonese examples and the descriptions of their use are taken from O. Y. Hashimoto 1972. The dialect forms for the perfective suffix come from M. Hashimoto 1976. "The mystic version of the substratum theory," Bloomfield 1933. The giving way of the Wu dialects before Mandarin, and in particular the situation in Danyang and Jingjiang, is described in Chao 1976b.

Chapter 4. "The Standard" (Pronunciation)

The 1956 pamphlet is cited and quoted at length in DeFrancis 1967. The background of Pinyin and Latinxua is discussed extensively in DeFrancis 1950 and the sources given in its bibliography; a succinct and informative summary can be found in Kratochvil 1968. The 405 syllables are listed, among other places, in the Beijing Language Institute text, *Elementary Chinese* (1971). Light 1980 contains specific examples of how the Chinese spelling system is used in the elementary school classroom. Technically speaking, Chinese names for the Pinyin letters do exist because names were coined when Pinyin was adopted as the official Romanization; however, few people today—including linguists—remember what they are. Still fewer actually use them. The Peking Mandarin palatals (*j, q, x*) once attracted a great deal of attention, and there is a considerable amount of technical literature dealing with them. Because of certain historical developments, described in the section "From Middle Chinese to Peking Mandarin" at the end of Chapter 7, these consonants occur in complementary distribution with each of three other series of consonants: the velars (*g, k, h*), the dental sibilants (*z, c, s*), and the retroflexes (*zh, ch, sh, r*). In a phonemic analysis of the Mandarin system, economy of description demands that the palatals be identified with one of these other three series of consonants, but the choice is fairly arbitrary. Many of the writings on Chinese phonemics from the 1930s through the 1950s deal with how the choice should be made; see especially Chao 1934 and 1968, Hartman 1944, Hockett 1947, Martin 1957. In later, postphonemic treatments of Mandarin phonology, concern has shifted away from the curious distribution of the palatals to other kinds of problems; cf. Cheng 1973. The retroflex is discussed in more detail in the section "Word Formation" in Chapter 5. The table of finals is adapted from the one given in Chao 1968. Cheng 1973 shows how the many phonetic values of main vowels in Mandarin can be derived from a simple, underlying, two-way contrast between *a* and *e*. Mandarin tones are a perennial favorite of linguists and phoneticians; see the bibliography on the subject in Yang 1974. On Mandarin tone *sandhi*, see Chao 1948a, Hockett 1950, Martin 1957, Cheng 1973. Cheng 1973 also has an extensive discussion of toneless syllables. Long lists of examples of neutral tones, including a separate list of ones now considered nonstandard in the PRC, can be found in Tai 1978. The analogy of ripples and waves was used to explain the relationship between tones and intonation in both Chao 1968 and Boyle 1970. The intonation used by Chinese radio announcers, Tai 1978. The table of sounds in the Peking dialect is taken from the Beijing Language Institute's *Elementary Chinese* (1971). In Appendix A, the description of standard Mandarin sounds through comparisons to English was inspired in part by the Yale dictionary (Institute of Far Eastern Languages 1966), and some of the examples are taken from that source. There are also a few examples borrowed from Walton 1978 and two or three from Huang and Stimson 1975. The comparative Romanization table in Appendix B is an emended version of the one found in Wu et al. 1979.

CHAPTER 5. "THE STANDARD (GRAMMAR)"

The story of James Burnett and the linguistic prejudices of his day comes from R. H. Robins's chapter "The Eve of Modern Times" in his *A Short History of Linguistics* (1968). Holger Pedersen's classic history of nineteenth-century linguistics, *The Discovery of Language* (1959), is also useful for understanding the intellectual background of earlier periods. For discussion of von Humboldt and his typology, as well as for what Max Müller made of the classification, see Anttila 1972. For perspective on typology, see Austerlitz 1974. Schleicher's Darwinian view is propounded in Schleicher 1863. Schleicher's evolutionary model of language types penetrated deeply into the Western mind and remains there today, as an abundance of popular writing on the subject shows; see, for example, the remark in Seward 1983 that "Japanese ... is now in what is called the agglutinative stage of its development" (noted in McCawley's 1984 review). For Whitney's response to Schleicher, Whitney 1872. The examples showing how the Chinese normally use the third-person pronoun *tā* only in reference to humans are modeled on those given in Li and Thompson 1981. The graphic distinctions in the use of *de*, Chao 1968. A discussion of the contributions of Boas and Sapir, Robins 1968. In his popular book *Language* (1921), Sapir leveled vitriolic criticism at the indexing of languages according to some preconceived notion of developmental level:

> There is a ... reason why the classification of languages has generally proved a fruitless undertaking. It is probably the most powerful deterrent of all to clear thinking. This is the evolutionary prejudice which instilled itself into the social sciences towards the middle of the last century and which is only now beginning to abate its tyrranical hold on our mind. Intermingled with this scientific prejudice and largely anticipating it was another, a more human one. The vast majority of linguistic theorists themselves spoke languages of a certain type, of which the most fully developed varieties were the Latin and Greek that they had learned in their childhood. It was not difficult for them to be persuaded that these familiar languages represented the "highest" development that speech had yet attained and that all other types were but steps on the way to this beloved "inflective" type ... (p. 123).

The American ambassador's question about the lack of an abstract 'it' in Chinese comes from Chao 1976e. Needham's remark is on p. 199 of the second volume of his *Science and Civilisation in China* (1956). The glowing review of Bloom 1981 is Elman 1983. The Chinese example of a conditional clause with three English translations comes from the treatment of the topic in Li and Thompson 1981. The question about the triangle is on p. 31 of Bloom's book. The example sentence with tenseless *qù* 'go, went, gone'; Huang and Stimson 1975. The colloquial examples of Chinese counterfactuals were supplied by Eugene Liu, Loretta Pan, and Victor Mair. Loretta Pan suggested the contextual interpretations of the sentence involving skill with chopsticks. Chao's reference to Bertrand Russell, Chao 1976e.

The examples *fingerprint* and *finger mark*, Chao 1968. Some of the examples illustrating the look of printed words, Fowler 1965. The spellings *for ever* and *forever* were in competition for centuries in the British Isles, as several citations in *The Oxford Dictionary of Quotations* show; today, however, *for ever* is firmly established as the correct form (cf. Fowler 1965). The relevance of the Biblical passage was suggested by Robert Austerlitz. Chao (1968) calls the *zì* "the sociological word," because it is what the general Chinese public "is conscious of, talks about, has an everyday term for, and is practically concerned with in various ways" (p. 136). Some of the examples of polysyllabic morphemes, Kratochvil 1968. *Làngmàn* 'romantic' and *jùlèbù* 'club' are actually Japanese coinages, pronounced *rōman* and *kurabu* in Japan. They were picked up quickly in China because they were written with Chinese characters in a way that had meaning for speakers of Chinese; see the discussion in Miller 1967, pp. 259–62. More documentation and examples of Japanese loans into Chinese can be found in Gao and Liu 1958, Wang Lifa 1958, Zheng Dian 1958. The story of the Shanghai contest to name Coca-Cola comes from Loretta Pan in personal communication.

The example *kānménde*, Chao 1968. The discussion of word formation largely follows Chao 1968, which is the most detailed analysis of Chinese words that we have. Another useful treatment of word morphology can be found in Y. C. Li et al. 1984. The history of suffixes, Ōta 1958. A detailed and informative discussion of the suffix *-r* can be found in Tai 1978, and some of the examples given here come from that source. The suffix *-r* is written with the character for *ér* 'child,' suggesting that it is identical to that morpheme. But Chao (1968, p. 46) says that the suffix is not derived from one morpheme alone; in origin, *-r* represents rather the conflation of three different but homophonous suffixes, each derived respectively from *-lǐ* 'therein,' *rì* 'day,' and *ér* 'child.' The complex changes in the pronunciation of *-r*, Chao 1968. The modern suffixes, *-xue*, *-xing*, and many others come from written Japanese usage; see Gao and Liu 1958. In addition to prefixes and suffixes, says Chao (1968), Mandarin Chinese also has infixes, namely, the potential-marking elements *-de-* and *-bu-*, as in *kàn-de-jiàn* 'can see' and *kàn-bu-jiàn* 'can't see.' These elements are also called infixes in many other grammars; e.g., Y. C. Li et al. 1984. The infix treatment is avoided here for two reasons. First, calling *-de-* and *-bu-* infixes means that the term "infix" must be slightly redefined; in conventional usage, only elements that are inserted *within* a morpheme qualify to be called "infixes." That is the way the process of infixation works in languages such as Tagalog. The Mandarin elements *-de-* and *-bu-*, by contrast, only go *between* morphemes. Secondly, treating *-de-* and *-bu-* as infixes, even in the sense that Chao uses the word, makes them the only two productive elements of this kind in the whole language. In order to keep *-de-* and *-bu-* from seeming a structural anomaly, they are treated here, under the section on "Verbs," as integral parts of suffixed verbal complements. The ancient dictionary with a listing of the number of syllable types was the *Qièyùn* dictionary of A.D. 601; more precisely, this work contained a total of 3,612 distinct syllables; see M. Hashimoto 1978b, pp. 29ff.

The starting point for grammatical analysis is Y. R. Chao's classic *A Grammar of Spoken Chinese* (1968). This work focuses principally upon the classification of word types and morphological processes, an area in which it sets the standard; almost all works on Mandarin structure begin with the categories that it contains.

More detailed coverages of Chinese syntax can be found in Li and Thompson's reference grammar *Mandarin Chinese* (1981), and in Y. C. Li et al. 1984, which is the first of a projected two volumes. Both books have good bibliographies. Helen Lin's *Essential Grammar for Modern Chinese* (1981) is pedagogically oriented. The description of Chinese grammatical structure given here is modeled, in part, on treatments in the above works (especially Chao 1968); ideas and examples are also drawn from a variety of textbooks and dictionaries, including DeFrancis 1976, Tewksbury 1948, Fenn and Tewsbury 1967, Huang and Stimson 1975, Hsu and Brown 1983, Beijing Language Institute 1971, 1980, Walton 1978, Institute of Far Eastern Languages 1966, F. F. Wang 1967, Wu et al. 1979. The examples of verbless predicates, O. Y. Hashimoto 1971. For historical information the principal source is Ōta 1958. Jerry Norman points out that the use of the adjective *mǎn* 'full' as an adverb meaning 'really' is now considered nonstandard—it is a borrowing from the Wu dialects. Reduplicated adjectives such as *hǎohāorde* (from *hǎo* 'good') often have a retroflex suffix -*r*, and usually the subordinative -*de* (cf. Chao 1968, pp. 205ff); also, the second syllable is normally pronounced with the first tone, even though it is conventionally written in the PRC as if the tone did not change: *hǎohǎorde*. The use of sentence-particle *le* as summarized briefly here largely follows Walton 1978.

Chapter 6. "Today's Dialects"

The dialect population percentages, Yuan et al. 1960. Yuan et al. 1960 is the standard source of information about Chinese dialects; like almost all other modern works, it is based on the classification originally proposed in F. K. Li 1937. F. K. Li 1973 is an update and a summary of how the dialects are classified. Egerod 1967 describes the general dialect situation. For a fairly complete bibliography of Chinese dialectology, see Yang 1981.

The classification of Mandarin, Yuan et al. 1960, Stimson 1966, Norman 1988.

For a description of Shanghai and its history, see Pan 1983. The Shanghai dialect as a "metropolitan hodge-podge," George Kennedy, quoted in Sherard 1972, p. 7. The principal sources for the description of the Shanghai dialect are Sherard 1972 and 1982. The slight revision of the vowel system was suggested by Robert Austerlitz. Other sources of Wu dialect information include Yuan et al. 1960, Chao 1928, 1976b, Ballard 1969, Walton 1976. Chao's anecdote about the Shanghai stereotype, Chao 1976b, p. 42.

The descriptions of Gan and Xiang, as well as the quote concerning "New Xiang" and "Old Xiang," Yuan et al. 1960.

The principal source of information about Yue dialects and Cantonese is O. Y. Hashimoto 1972. Additional sources, Chao 1947, Boyle 1970, Yuan et al. 1960, Huang 1965. Lau 1977 is a Cantonese-English dictionary; Rao et al. 1981 is a dictionary of idiomatic Cantonese arranged by pronunciation, and Zhonghua Shuju 1976 gives the Cantonese pronunciation of characters. South Chinese cooking, Anderson and Anderson 1977. The ethnic sensitivity of Cantonese speakers versus Wu speakers, Sherard 1972. Some descriptions of pronunciations, Boyle 1970. The z-like pronunciation prized by certain Cantonese families, Chao 1947, p. 18. The descriptions of tones, especially the "changed tones," are in places almost verbatim from Chao 1947. The examples of changed tones are mostly from Yuan et al. 1960. The description of grammar, Yuan et al. 1960 and O. Y. Hashimoto 1972. The basic text of "The North Wind and the Sun" is taken from Yuan et al. 1960, but the story has been retold and slightly altered by Irene Liu.

Min history, Norman 1970. The general characterization and many examples, Yuan et al. 1960. The Chinese linguist who divides Fujian Min into nine groups is Ye Guoqing, mentioned on p. 239 of Yuan et al. 1960. The classification of Min into inland versus coastal, Norman 1970 and Norman 1988. Amoy phonology, Yuan et al. 1960; Taiwanese, Zheng and Zheng 1977. Li Yongming 1959 is a monograph on the Cháozhōu dialect. An Amoy-English dictionary (1976) and other Amoy (or Taiwanese) language materials have been published by the Maryknoll Language School of Taiwan. Older and more comprehensive dictionaries of Taiwanese were published by the Taiwan Sōtokufu in the 1930s. Literary and colloquial strata in Min, Norman 1979, Sung 1973.

The distribution of Hakka, M. Hashimoto 1973. Hakka history and cultural background, Cohen 1968, Hsieh 1929. Arguments why Hakka should be treated as linguistically Southern can be found in Norman 1988. The phonological system of Meixian, Yuan et al. 1960. Examples are taken from M. Hashimoto 1973, Yuan et al. 1960; 'hair' is from Norman 1988. The Taiwan Sōtokufu Kantongo jiten (1932b) is actually a dictionary of Hakka. The transcribed folk tale, Yuan et al. 1960.

CHAPTER 7. "HISTORY"

The text of the Qieyun preface upon which the translation is based comes from Dong 1974, p. 79; the lines omitted in that source are taken from Long 1968, a Hong Kong photocopy of Wang Renxu's Tang period redaction of Qieyun. The translation has been abridged in the following places: "Furthermore, some authors make single rhymes...." Here the text contains specific examples of rhymes and finals that had been put together. "Lü Jing's Yun ji [and other works of its kind]...." The names of six authors and titles are mentioned. The passage about jade and gold is an elaboration of two literary allusions that appear in parallel phrases. A more literal translation would be, "Why bother crying over jade? One can never get the hanging gold." The allusions were found by P. Y. Wu, who also helped with other parts of the text. Still other passages were interpreted by Gari Ledyard and C. T. Hsia. Qieyun itself has 193 rhymes, but the Song redaction Guǎngyùn, which Karlgren used for his reconstructions, has 206. Fǎnqiè are traditionally attributed to Sūn Yán, who used them in his third-century Eryǎ yīnyì (cf. Martin 1953, p. 1); philologists, however, have recently found fǎnqiè in earlier works dating from the late Han. Gopal Sukhu supplied the information about Indian influence. Much of the background information on traditional Chinese philology comes from Dong 1974 and Wang Li 1957. The account of Karlgren's life and career is based almost entirely upon Søren Egerod's beautiful and moving tribute (1979). The description of Karlgren's early months in China, Egerod

1979, p. 4. The display of Middle Chinese vowels as reconstructed by Karlgren, Martin 1953, p. 20. Karlgren's explanation for the large number of vowel distinctions in *Qieyun* is on p. 690 of *Études*. The information on what copies of *Qieyun* are extant and when they were discovered, Dong 1974, pp. 80–81. Karlgren's statement about the "phonemic principle," Karlgren 1954, pp. 366–67. Pulleyblank's suggestions, Pulleyblank 1962, 1963. Karlgren's retort, Karlgren 1963. There is now a truly voluminous literature on the reconstruction of Middle Chinese; see Bodman 1967, Yang 1974. The transcription of the poem by Du Fu is patterned upon materials used by Hugh Stimson in a poetics seminar; the translation also comes from that seminar.

Dating Old Chinese is problematic. The rhymes and the character constructions reflect the same phonological system; but when that system actually existed is a matter that has not been resolved. Tradition assigns the compilation of *The Book of Odes* to the time of Confucius, and from this has come the conventional date of 550 B.C. for Old Chinese. A succinct history of Chinese writing can be found in Ch'en 1966 (but the book should not to be relied upon for its discussion of the relationship of writing to language). Oracle bones, Keightley 1978, Shima 1967. For a perspective on the early stages of Chinese writing, see the section on Naxi writing in Chapter 11. The nature of Chinese writing is described in Martin 1972, Miller 1967, and DeFrancis 1984; note especially DeFrancis's history of the controversies surrounding this subject. On the figure 90 percent, see Martin 1972, p. 84, and the references cited there. Scholars who believe that all Middle Chinese tones were derived from segmental distinctions in Old Chinese include, among others, Edwin Pulleyblank and Tsu-lin Mei; scholars who oppose this view include Wang Li and F. K. Li.

CHAPTER 8. "CHINESE WRITING TODAY"

The opening quote, Karlgren 1929, p. 41. Hu Shih on the inevitability of phonetic writing, Zhao 1963, p, 174. On the subject of Chinese writing, Lu Xun is reported to have said, among other things, "If the characters are not destroyed, China is sure to die" (DeFrancis 1950, p. 219; also cf. pp. 113–16). Alphabetic writing as the revolutionary ideal, Chen 1973, p. 708. The supporter of the Latinization Movement was Ni Haishu; his prediction is on p. 570 of Ni 1949. The story of the post-1950 script reform movement, DeFrancis 1967, 1984. The objections to character simplification, Wang Kang 1956, pp. 18–19; quoted in DeFrancis 1967. In 1951 Mao Zedong said, "Our written language must be reformed; it should take the direction of phonetization common to all the languages of the world" (quoted in Lehmann 1975, p. 51; also cf. Chen 1973, p. 710, fn. 16). Mao's suggestion, Chen 1973, p. 710. Guo Moruo's 1955 speech is translated, in part, in T. Hsia 1956. Zhou Enlai 1979 is a complete translation of Zhou's 1958 report. The origins of simplified characters, Liu 1930, Yi 1955. The comparison of eye movements for vertical versus horizontal writing, Gibson and Levin 1975, Martin 1972. Different type fonts, upper-case versus lower-case letters, and the confusability of letters, Gibson and Levin 1975. Japanese language reform, Miller 1967, Kodansha 1983. The alliance of writing reformers and computer specialists, DeFrancis 1984.

CHAPTER 9. "THE CHINESE AND THEIR NEIGHBORS"

The quote from Sun Yat-sen comes from his first lecture on the doctrine of nationalism, 27 January 1924. The PRC government quote, in several variations, appears in many publications; in this case it is taken from Ma et al. 1981. The expansion of China in the Qianlong period to unprecedented size, Wakeman 1975, pp. 101–102 (but note that the figure given on the top of p. 102, "six million square miles," which Wakeman says is the area added to the realm by the conquest of Ili and Turkestan, is high by about a factor of ten). Dreyer 1976 is the standard source of information on minority politics in the PRC, and its bibliography is excellent. The Soviet model for minority policy, Austerlitz 1975. Historical perspective on Chinese minorities, Eberhard 1982, Pulleyblank 1983. The policy today on birth control, June Dreyer in personal communication. Education in minority schools, David Bradley in personal correspondence. Minority classification, Fei and Lin 1956 and, in English, the more recent summary in Fei 1980. The Sanya and Hans Stübel, Paul Benedict in personal communication. Bynon 1977 contains an introduction to the concept of linguistic areas, and its bibliography can be used for more detailed references. The spread of grammatical features in China, Hashimoto 1976, 1978. A comprehensive, general source of information about the Chinese national minorities is Ma et al. 1981. The 1982 population figures, Beijing Review 1983 (this article was brought to my attention by David Bradley).

CHAPTER 10. "THE MINORITIES OF NORTH CHINA"

Sinor 1969 is an excellent introduction to the history of Inner Asia. Borrowings, Poppe 1965. The descriptive outline of Altaic largely follows Poppe 1965; some of the perspective derives from Austerlitz 1980. Mongolian examples, Poppe 1970. Much of the general discussion of Altaic comes out of conversations with Robert Austerlitz.

Background and history of the Turkic peoples, Sinor 1969, Menges 1968a. The absorption of non-Turkic elements, Menges 1968a; the "Iranization" of Turkic languages around Xinjiang, Menges 1968a, Comrie 1983. The story of Chuvash, Poppe 1965; more detailed references can be found in its bibliography. An important source of information about individual Turkic languages is Deny et al. 1959, and many of the references cited here are contained in that volume. The classification of Turkic languages, Benzing and Menges, 1959. Chiang Kai-shek's statement about "racial stock," Dreyer 1976. The description of Tatar, Thomsen 1959a. Kazakh, Menges 1959. Kirghiz, Comrie 1983. The figures on Uzbek, Comrie 1983; some of the linguistic information on Uzbek, Wurm 1959. A description of the phonology of Uzbek, Sjoberg 1962. Yellow Uighur and Salar, Thomsen 1959b. The background and history of the Uighurs are described in readable fashion in Sinor 1969; Pritsak 1959b adds detail. The description of Uighur given here is from Pritsak 1959b supplemented with some details and examples from Jarring 1933. Turkic runes and writing and the Uighur alphabet are described briefly in Poppe 1965 and in more detail, with examples and texts, in Gabain 1950.

The closeness of the Mongolian family, Austerlitz 1980. Poppe 1970 provides a clear, concise overview of the family. The classification of Mongolian into Mongolian proper versus the "archaic" varieties, Rona-Taš 1960. Moghol, Pritsak 1959a, 1964. The classification of the Mongolian languages in China and the existence of the Yunnan Mongols, Todaeva 1957, 1959a, 1959b. The principal source for Dagur is Martin 1961; some additional information comes from Poppe 1964a. Santa (Dongxiang), Todaeva 1959a; Liu 1981. Bao'an, Todaeva 1959a; Liu and Lin 1980. The history of the Monguor and the Chinese custom of calling them Tǔrén, Mostaert 1931. Schröder 1964 discusses the ethnographic background information, but it is not a source of linguistic information. The information on Monguor clusters and how they developed comes from Rona-Taš 1960. The term "Mongolian proper" comes from Comrie 1983, and the classification given here was in some senses inspired by the one used in that source. On mutual intelligibility, see Austerlitz 1980. The "agricultural Mongols" versus the "herding Mongols," Dreyer 1976. Some information on the life of the agricultural Mongols can be found in Bosson and Unenseĉen 1962; there are some oral texts transcribed in this work. The historical sketches given here are from Poppe 1970 and Sinor 1969. The analysis of the Khalkha dialect comes from Poppe 1970, but it has been modified along the lines of Martin 1961. Poppe 1970 lists an eighth vowel, schwa; but this minimal vowel only occurs, in unstressed positions, as a phonetic reduction of other vowels. Mongolian writing, Poppe 1964b, 1970, Chen 1981. Some information on hP'ags-pa comes from Gari Ledyard.

Northern Tungus versus Southern Tungus, Benzing 1956. The Evenki meeting with Cossacks in 1607 at the Yenisei is discussed in Lopatin 1958. The idea that the Northern Tungus made an important technological or social innovation belongs to Robert Austerlitz; he suggests that the innovation may possibly have been the domestication of reindeer. The Evenki and the Solon, Lie 1978. The meaning of "Evenki," Menges 1968b. The name "Solon," Benzing 1956. The ethnological description of the Evenki, Hiekisch 1879. Evenki vowel harmony, Comrie 1983. Manchu has the fewest cases of any Tungus language, and Evenki has the most, according to Lopatin 1958. The etymology of "Oroqen," Menges 1968b. Oroqen vocabulary, Li Shulan 1981. The identification of the Hezhen with the Nanai, Jerry Norman (personal communication). History of the Xibo people, Wu and Zhao 1981. Xibo language, Li Shulan 1979. The principal source for Manchu is Haenisch 1961. Other sources include Möllendorf 1892, Austin 1962, Sinor 1968, Kiyose 1977, Norman 1978. The description by a French scholar, Harlez 1884; that of the first German scholar, Möllendorf 1892; the second German scholar, Haenisch 1961. The description of vowel harmony and the yin–yang examples are taken from Haenisch 1961; a few examples are also from Möllendorf 1892. The historical change of p's, Benzing 1956. The Xibo examples, Li Shulan 1979. Examples of Manchu vocabulary, Norman 1978. Examples of an "instrumental," Sinor 1968. Loans, cases, derivation, etc., Haenisch 1961. The example text, Haenisch 1961. The failure of Japanese language policy in Manchuria, Dreyer 1976. The Jurchen script, Kiyose 1977. The etymology of "Manchu" was suggested by Cincius, as quoted in Benzing 1961, p. 12; Lopatin 1958 also suggests this etymology. The history of Manchu writing closely follows Haenisch 1961.

CHAPTER 11. "THE MINORITIES OF SOUTH CHINA"

The best general reference on the ethnic groups of Southeast Asia is LeBar et al. 1964. The description here, especially concerning prehistoric cultural influence, owes much to discussions with Paul Benedict. On the possibility of cultural flow out of the area, see Solheim 1972.

Sixty percent of the Cantonese descended from Tai, see Wiens 1954, p. 274. Tai words in Chinese, You 1982. The population estimates of Tai-speaking nationalities comes from David Bradley in personal correspondence. The names Tai, Thai, Siamese, etc., Briggs 1949. Be is described in M. Hashimoto 1980 and the references given there. The anecdote about Zhou Enlai and the Zhuang, Dreyer 1976. The Zhuang language being "insulted, ridiculed, and even banned ... ," the introduction to Wei and Tan 1980. The attempts to hide Zhuang surnames, Wiens 1954, p. 34. This description of Zhuang is taken from the PRC handbook on the language, Wei and Tan 1980. The Wuming dialect, F. K. Li 1956. The tone development in Tai, F. K. Li 1977. Zhuang writing, F. K. Li 1956 and the PRC handbook. Zhuang songs are given in Chinese translation in F. K. Li 1956, and their structure is explained in F. K. Li 1936. Buyi, Yu 1980. Dai, Yu and Luo 1980. The work that establishes the Kam-Sui Branch of Tai is F. K. Li 1965. The Kam (Dong) language, Liang 1980a. Sui, Zhang 1980. Maonan, Liang 1980b. The Li languages, Ouyang and Zheng, 1980, Fu Zhennan 1983. The recent history of the Li, Dreyer 1976.

General characteristics of Tibeto-Burman, Benedict 1972. On the homeland of the Tibeto-Burmans, see Meillet and Cohen 1952, pp. 530–31. The PRC classification, Ma Yin et al. 1981. On the languages of minority groups in Tibet, including the "Deng" people, the Monpa, and the Lhopa, see Sun et al. 1980. "Xifan," K. Chang 1967. Jingpo as the "linguistic center" of Tibeto-Burman, Benedict 1972. Much of the ethnographic information about individual Tibeto-Burman groups is taken from Ma Yin et al. 1981. The terms "Yi" and "Lolo," LeBar et al. 1964. The quote about a "blood-proud caste," Wiens 1954, p. 94. The incident involving Donald Brooke, Wiens 1954, p. 290, and Yueh-hua Lin 1961, p. 10 (but in this translation of Lin's original Chinese work, "Brooke" is called "Burk" by mistake). The Yi involvement in opium and terror is described in Lin 1961; this book contains a number of terrifying stories about contacts between the Yi and the Chinese. For another perspective, see Winnington 1959. The ethnic characterization of the Yi comes largely from LeBar et al. 1964 and Lin 1961. The Ahi variety of Yi is described in Yuan 1953; Sani is described in Ma 1951; and information on Luquan can be found in Ma 1948. James Matisoff and David Bradley inform me that Fu Maoji's 1950 Ph.D. thesis at Cambridge was written on Liangshan (Cool Mountain) Yi. The historical development of Loloish, Matisoff 1972, Bradley 1978. The description of Nasu, the examples, and the story about "Chane," are all taken from Gao 1958. The *pimu*, Lin 1961. The lines from the Yi classic are taken from Ma 1948. Yi writing, Li Min 1979. The recent standardization of Yi writing, DeFrancis 1984. Lisu and Lisu writing, Minority Language Bureau 1959. Hani, Li Yongsui 1979. Lahu, Matisoff 1972, 1973, forthcoming; Bradley 1979. Jino, Gai 1981. Naxi, Jiang 1980. The information on Naxi writing comes principally from Li Lincan et al. 1953, 1957.

Fu Maoji 1981, 1984 are also useful sources. Rock 1963–1972 represents the most extensive compilation of Naxi texts that is available and it contains excellent reproductions, some of them in color; but the discussion of linguistic facts is often misleading. The sample of a Naxi text given here is from Li Lincan et al. 1957. Jingpo, Minority Language Bureau 1958; Liu 1964. David Bradley (personal communication) says that the Jingpo vowels described in Chinese sources as "tense" seem to be vowels followed by glottal stops. Tsaiwa, Cheng 1956. Drung, Lo 1945; Sun 1979. The two Qiang languages discussed here, Sun 1981; for other varieties of Qiang, see K. Chang 1957, *Zhongguo yuwen* 1962. Primi, Lu 1980. The characterization of the Nu nationality is taken from LeBar et al. 1964. The Rawang dialect of Nu, Morse 1963. The Achang nationality, LeBar et al. 1964; the Achang language, Dai and Cui 1983.

The story of Miao struggle and rebellion against the Chinese, Wiens 1954. Miao and Yao being related, Downer 1961. Miao and Yao legends of their origins, Wiens 1954. The linguistic descriptions and information and data on Miao and Yao are taken from the various articles collected in Purnell 1972. Also see Wang Lianqing 1983. The quote about the Miao and their virtue, Wiens 1954, p. 235. The Kuomintang ban on Miao language and dress, Gjessing 1956. The designations of the Miao in the PRC, the introduction to Purnell 1972. Miao loans from Chinese, Miao Language Team 1972, Lin Ying 1972. The She language, Mao and Meng 1982. The three languages used by the Yao, Purnell 1972, p. 239; K. Chang 1967. The "Yao language" (Myen), Mao and Zhou 1962.

The ethnographic information on the Mon-Khmer peoples, LeBar et al. 1964. The Benglong language, Yan 1983. The Wa language, Qiu et al. 1980.

Information about the Vietnamese living in South China, the "Gin," comes from Paul Benedict and David Bradley in personal communication. The language of the Gin, Wang Lianqing 1983. Gelao, Wang and Deng 1980. Much of the ethographic and historical information about the Bai comes from Fitzgerald 1941. Information on the Bai language, Xu and Zhao 1964, Zhao Yansun 1981. The data from the Dali dialect of Bai, Dell 1981. Recent arguments that Bai is Sinitic, Benedict 1982.

BIBLIOGRAPHIC ABBREVIATIONS

BIHP	*Bulletin of the Institute of History and Philology, Academia Sinica*
BMFEA	*Bulletin of the Museum of Far Eastern Antiquities*
CAAAL	*Computational Analyses of Asian & African Languages*
HJAS	*Harvard Journal of Asiatic Studies*
HRAF	Human Relations Area Files
JAOS	*Journal of the American Oriental Society*
JAS	*Journal of Asian Studies*
JCL	*Journal of Chinese Linguistics*
JCLTA	*Journal of the Chinese Language Teachers Association*
LTBA	*Linguistics of the Tibeto-Burman Area*

GENERAL BIBLIOGRAPHY

Anderson, E. N. and Marja L. Anderson. 1977. "Modern China: South." In Chang 1977, pp. 317–82.

Anttila, Raimo. 1972. *An introduction to historical and comparative linguistics.* New York: Macmillan.

Arisaka Hideyo. 1957. *Kokugo on'in-shi no kenkyū* [Studies on Japanese historical phonology]. Tokyo: Sanseido.

Austerlitz, Robert. 1974. "The frustrations of linguistic typology: Limitations or stimulants?" *Acta Universitatis Carolinae* [Prague]: 101–106.

——. 1976. "Bilingualism: The context beyond linguistics." *General Linguistics* 16.2–3: 68–71.

——. 1982. "Three thoughts on Dr. Kreindler's thoughts." *The International Journal of the Sociology of Language* 33: 53–56.

Ballard, William L. 1969. "Phonological history of Wu." Ph.D. diss., University of California, Berkeley.

——. 1981. "The linguistic history of South China: Miao-Yao and Southern dialects." Typescript.

Barnes, Dayle. 1982. "Nationalism and the Mandarin movement: The first half-century." In Cooper 1982, pp. 260–90.

Beijing Language Institute. 1971. *Elementary Chinese.* Peking: Shangwu Press.

——. 1980. *Elementary Chinese readers.* Peking: Foreign Language Press.

Bielenstein, Hans. 1947. "The census of China during the period 2–742 A.D." *BMFEA* 19:125–63.

——. 1959. "The Chinese colonization of Fukien until the end of T'ang." *Studia Serica Bernhard Karlgren Dedicata*, ed. Søren Egerod, pp. 98–122. Copenhagen: E. Munksgaard.

Bloom, Alfred. 1981. *The linguistic shaping of thought: A study in the impact of language on thinking in China and the West.* Hillsdale, N.J.: Lawrence Erlbaum Associates.

Bloomfield, Leonard. 1933. *Language.* New York: Holt, Rinehart, and Winston.

Bodman, Nicholas Cleaveland. 1967. "Historical linguistics." In Sebeok 1967, pp. 3–58.

Bolinger, Dwight. 1975. *Aspects of language.* 2d ed. New York: Harcourt Brace Jovanovich.

Boltz, William G. 1967–1968. "Canton: The Seville of China." *Romance Philology* 21: 171–74.

Boyle, Elizabeth. 1970. *Cantonese Basic Course.* Washington, D.C.: FSI.

Cao Bohan. 1949. "The Chinese language movement since the May Fourth period." In Seybolt and Chiang 1979, pp. 26–41.

Catford, J. C. 1977. *Fundamental problems in phonetics.* Bloomington: Indiana University Press.

Chang, K. C., ed. 1977. *Food in chinese culture.* New Haven: Yale University Press.

Chao, Yuen Ren. 1928. *Xiandai Wu-yu de yanjiu* [Studies on the modern Wu dialects]. Peking: Qinghua xuexiao yanjiuyuan.

―――. 1934. "The non-uniqueness of phonemic solutions of phonetic systems." *BIHP* 4.4: 363–97. Reprinted in *Readings in linguistics*, ed. Martin Joos, pp. 38–54. Washington, D.C.: ACLS.

―――. 1941. "Distinctions within Ancient Chinese," *HJAS* 5: 223–27.

―――. 1947. *Cantonese primer*, Cambridge, Mass.: Harvard University Press.

―――. 1948a. *Mandarin primer*, Cambridge, Mass.: Harvard University Press

―――. 1948b. *Hubei fangyan diaocha baogao* [Report on a survey of the dialects of Hubei]. Shanghai: Shangwu Yinshu-guan.

―――. 1968. *A grammar of spoken Chinese*. Berkeley: University of California Press.

―――. 1970. *Language and symbolic systems*. Cambridge: Cambridge University Press.

―――. 1976a. *Aspects of Chinese sociolinguistics*. Stanford: Stanford University Press.

―――. 1976b. "Contrasting aspects of the Wu dialects." In Chao 1976a, pp. 34–47.

―――. 1976c. "What is correct Chinese?" In Chao 1976a, pp. 72–83.

―――. 1976d. "Some contrastive aspects of the Chinese National Language Movement." In Chao 1976a, pp. 97–105.

―――. 1976e. "Notes on Chinese grammar and logic." In Chao 1976a, pp. 237–49.

Ch'en Chih-mai. 1966. *Chinese calligraphers and their art*. Melbourne: Melbourne University Press.

Chen, S. H. 1973. "Language and literature under Communism." in Wu 1973, pp. 705–35.

Cheng, Chin-chuan. 1973. *A synchronic phonology of Mandarin*. The Hague: Mouton.

Chiang Yee. 1973. *Chinese calligraphy*. Cambridge, Mass.: Harvard University Press.

Cohen, Myron L. 1968. "The Hakka or 'Guest People': Dialect as a sociocultural variable in southeastern China." *Ethnohistory* 15: 237–92.

Cooper, Robert L., ed. 1982. *Language spread: Studies in diffusion and social change*. Bloomington: Indiana University Press.

Cressey, George B. 1955. *Land of the 500 million*. New York: McGraw-Hill.

DeBary, Wm. Theodore, Wing-Tsit Chan and Chester Tan. 1960. *Sources of Chinese tradition II*. New York: Columbia University Press.

DeFrancis, John. 1950. *Nationalism and language reform in China*. Princeton: Princeton University Press.

―――. 1967. "Language and script reform." In Sebeok 1967, pp. 130–50.

―――. 1976. *Beginning Chinese*. 2d. rev. ed. New Haven: Yale University Press.

―――. 1984. *The Chinese language: Fact and fantasy*. Honolulu: University of Hawaii Press.

Dobson, W.A.C.H. 1959. *Late Archaic Chinese: A grammatical study*. Toronto: University of Toronto Press.

―――. 1962. *Early Archaic Chinese: A descriptive grammar*. Toronto: University of Toronto Press.

———. 1964. *Late Han Chinese: A study of the Archaic Han shift.* Toronto: University of Toronto Press.

Dong Tonghe. 1954. *Zhongguo yuyin-shi* [The history of Chinese phonology]. Taipei: China Cultural Publication Foundation.

———. 1974. *Hanyu yinyun-xue* [The study of Chinese phonology]. Taipei: Yingyu Publishing Company.

Downer, G. B. 1959. "Derivation by tone-change in Classical Chinese." *BSOAS* 22: 258–90.

Dreyer, June Teufel. 1976. *China's forty millions.* Cambridge, Mass.: Harvard University Press.

Egerod, Søren. 1967. "Dialectology." In Sebeok 1967, pp. 91–129.

———. 1979. Obituary for Bernhard Karlgren. In *Annual Newsletter of the Scandinavian Institute of Asian Studies* 13: 1–24.

Elman, Benjamin A. 1983. Review of Bloom 1981. *JAS* 42.3 (May): 611–14.

Emeneau, Murray B. 1980. *Language and linguistic area,* Stanford: Stanford University Press

Fang Shiduo. 1965. *Wushi-nian lai Zhongguo guoyu yundong-shi* [The history of China's National Language Movement over the past fifty years]. Taipei: Guoyu Ribao-she.

Feifel, Eugen. 1967. *Geschichte der chinesischen Literatur.* Hildesheim: Georg Olms Verlagsbuchhandlung.

Fenn, Henry C. and M. Gardner Tewksbury. 1967. *Speak Mandarin.* New Haven: Yale University Press.

Forrest, R.A.D. 1948. *The Chinese language.* London: Faber and Faber.

Fowler, H. W. 1965. *A dictionary of modern English usage.* Oxford: Oxford University Press.

Fromkin, Victoria, ed. 1978. *Tone: A linguistic survey.* New York: Academic Press.

Gao Mingkai and Liu Zhengtan. 1958. *Xiandai Hanyu wailai-ci yanjiu* [A study of foreign words in modern Chinese]. Peking: Wenzi Gaige Chuban-she.

Gibson, Eleanor J. and Harry Levin. 1975. *The psychology of reading.* Cambridge, Mass.: MIT Press.

Hansen, Chad. 1983. *Language and logic in ancient China.* Ann Arbor: University of Michigan Press.

Hartman, Lawton M. 1944. "The segmental phonemes of the Peiping dialect." *Language* 20: 28–42.

Hartwell, Robert M. 1982. "Demographic, political, and social transformations of China, 750–1550." *HJAS* 42.2: 365–442.

Hashimoto, Mantaro J. 1973. *The Hakka dialect: A linguistic study of its phonology, syntax, and lexicon.* Cambridge: Cambridge University Press.

———. 1976. "The agrarian and pastoral diffusion of languages." In *Genetic relationship, diffusion and typological similarities of East & Southeast Asian languages.* Tokyo: Japan Society for the Promotion of Science.

———. 1978a. *Gengo ruikei chiri-ron* [Linguistic typogeography]. Tokyo: Kōbun-dō.

———. 1978b. *Phonology of Ancient Chinese: Volume I.* Study of Languages &

Cultures of Asia & Africa Monograph Series, no. 10. Tokyo.

———. 1979. *Phonology of Ancient Chinese: Volume II*. Study of Languages & Cultures of Asia & Africa Monograph Series, no. 11. Tokyo.

———. 1980. "Typogeography of phonotactics and suprasegmentals in languages of the East Asian continent." *CAAAL* 13: 153–64.

Hashimoto, Oi-kan Yue. 1971. "Mandarian syntactic structures." *Unicorn* 8: 1–149.

———. 1972. *Studies in Yue dialects 1: Phonology of Cantonese*. Cambridge: Cambridge University Press.

Ho, Ping-ti. 1959. *Studies on the population of China, 1368–1953*. Cambridge, Mass.: Harvard University Press.

Hockett, Charles F. 1947. "Peiping phonology." *JAOS* 67: 253–67.

———. 1950. "Peiping morphophemics." *Language* 26: 63–85.

———. 1958. *A course in modern linguistics*. New York: Macmillan.

Hsia, C. T. 1961. *A history of modern Chinese fiction, 1917–1957*. New Haven: Yale University Press.

Hsia, Tao-tai. 1956. *China's language reform*. Mirror Series, no. 21. New Haven: Yale University Press.

Hsieh, Chiao-min. 1973. "Physical geography." In Wu 1973, pp. 29–43.

Hsieh, T'ing-yu. 1929. "Origin and migration of the Hakkas." *Chinese Social and Political Science Review* 13.3: 202–27.

Hsu Ying and J. Marvin Brown. 1983. *Speaking Chinese in China*. New Haven: Yale University Press.

Huang, Parker Po-fei. 1965. *Cantonese sounds and tones*. New Haven: Far Eastern Publications.

Huang, Parker Po-fei and Hugh M. Stimson. 1975. *Standard spoken Chinese*. New Haven: Far Eastern Publications.

Iakhontov, S. E. 1968. "Chinese phonology of the first millennium B.C., Part I." Trans. Jerry Norman. *Unicorn* 1: 47–65.

———. 1970. "Chinese phonology of the first millennium B.C., Part II." Trans. Jerry Norman. *Unicorn* 6: 52–75.

Institute of Far Eastern Languages. 1966. *Dictionary of spoken Chinese*. New Haven: Yale University Press.

Jansen, Marius. 1975. *Japan and China: From war to peace, 1874–1972*. Chicago: Rand McNally.

Kao, Diana L. 1971. *Structure of the syllable in Cantonese*. The Hague: Mouton.

Karlgren, Bernhard. 1915–1926. *Études sur la phonologie chinoise*. 4 vols, Uppsala: K. W. Appelberg.

———. 1923. *Analytic dictionary of Chinese and Sino-Japanese*. Paris: Librairie orientaliste Paul Geuthner.

———. 1926. *Philology and Ancient China*. Oslo: H. Aschehoug.

———. 1929. *Sound and symbol in Chinese*. London: Oxford University Press.

———. 1949. *The Chinese language*. New York: Ronald Press.

———. 1954. "Compendium of phonetics in Ancient and Archaic Chinese." *BMFEA* 22: 211–367.

———. 1957. "Grammata Serica Recensa." *BMFEA* 32: 1–332.

———. 1962. *Zhongguo yinyun-xue yanjiu* (Karlgren 1915–1926, trans., ed., and expanded by Y. R. Chao, F. K. Li, and Luo Changpei). Taipei: Shangwu Press.

––––––. 1963. "Loan characters in pre-Han texts." *BMFEA* 35: 1–128.

Kavanagh, James F. and Ignatius G. Mattingly. 1972. *Language by ear and by eye: The relationships between speech and reading*. Cambridge, Mass.: MIT Press.

Keightley, David N. 1978. *Sources of Shang history: The oracle bone Inscriptions of Bronze Age China*. Berkeley: University of California Press.

––––––. ed. 1983. *The origins of Chinese civilization*. Berkeley: University of California Press.

Kodansha, Ltd. 1983. *Kodansha encyclopedia of Japan*. Tokyo: Kodansha.

Kratochvil, Paul. 1968. *The Chinese language today*. London: Hutchinson.

Kurath, Hans. 1972. *Studies in area linguistics*. Bloomington: Indiana University Press.

Lau, Sidney. 1977. *A practical Cantonese-English Dictionary*. Hong Kong: Government Printer.

Lee, James. 1977. "China's southwestern frontier: Comparative patterns of migration and economic development, 1250–1850." Typescript.

––––––. 1978. "Migration and expansion in Chinese history." In *Human Migration*, ed. William McNeill and Ruth Adams, pp. 20–47. Bloomington: Indiana University Press.

Lehmann, Winfred P., ed. 1975. *Language and linguistics in the People's Republic of China*. Austin: University of Texas Press.

Li, Charles N. and Sandra A. Thompson. 1974. "Co-verbs in Mandarin Chinese: Verbs or prepositions?" *JCL* 2: 224–57.

––––––. 1981. *Mandarin Chinese: A functional reference grammar*. Berkeley: University of California Press.

Li, Chi. 1957. *The Communist term 'The Common Language' and related terms*. Studies in Chinese Communist Terminology Series, no. 4, pt. I. Berkeley: University of California Press.

Li, Fang-Kuei. 1937. "Languages and dialects of China." In *The Chinese Yearbook*, pp. 59–65. Shanghai: Commercial Press.

––––––. 1971. "Shangguyin yanjiu." *Qinghua xuebao*, n.s. 9.1–2: 1–61.

––––––. 1973. "Languages and dialects." *JCL* 1: 1–13.

––––––. 1974. "Studies on Archaic Chinese phonology" (F. K. Li 1971, trans. G. L. Mattos). *University of Hawaii Working Papers in Linguistics* 6.1: 171–282.

––––––. 1983. "Archaic Chinese." In Keightley 1983, pp. 393–408.

Li Jinxi. 1934. *Guoyu yundong shigang* [A brief history of the National Language Movement]. Shanghai: Shangwu yinshu-guan.

Li Rong. 1956. *Qieyun yinxi* [The phonological system of *Qieyun*]. Peking: Kexue chuban-she.

Li, Y. C., Robert L. Cheng, Larry Foster, Shang H. Ho, John Y. Hou, and Moira Yip. 1984. *Mandarin Chinese: A practical reference grammar for students and teachers* (Vol. 1). Taipei: The Crane Publishing Co.

Li Yongming. 1959. *Chaozhou fangyan* [The Chaozhou dialect]. Peking: Zhonghua shuju. Reprinted 1978. Hong Kong: Sun Chau.

Light, Timothy. 1980. "Bilingualism and standard language in the People's Republic of China." *Georgetown University Round Table on Languages and Linguistics*, pp. 259–79.

———.1983. "Variation studies: The current need in Chinese linguistics." *CAAAL* 21: 83–92.

Lin, Helen T. 1981. *Essential grammar for modern Chinese*. Boston: Cheng & Tsui.

Liu Fu. 1930. *Song-Yuan yilai suzi pu* [A catalogue of vulgar characters used since the Song and Yuan dynasties]. Peking: Academia Sinica.

Long Yucun. 1968. *Tangxie quanben Wang Renxu kanmiu buque Qieyun jiaoqian* [A corrected and annotated edition of the Tang Copy of the Complete *Wang Renxu kanmiu buque Qieyun*]. Hong Kong: Tuhong zhiban.

Lotz, John. 1972. "How language is conveyed by script." In Kavanagh and Mattingly 1972, pp. 117–24.

Luo Changpei. 1930. *Xiamen yinxi* [The phonetic system of the Amoy dialect]. Peking: Academic Sinica.

———. 1934. *Guoyin zimu yanjin-shi* [A history of the evolution of the National Phonetic Alphabet]. Reprinted 1968. Hong Kong: Zhongguo yuwenxue-she.

Ma Jianzhong. 1899. *Ma Shi wentong*. Reprinted 1954. Peking: Zhonghua shuju.

Mabuchi Kazuo. 1954. *Inkyō kōhon to Kōin sakuin* [An index to the *Yunjing jiaoben* and the *Guangyun*]. Tokyo: Ennan-dō.

McCawley, James D. 1984. Book notice of Seward 1983. *Language* 60.4: 994–95.

McCoy, William John, Jr. 1966. "Szeyap data for a first approximation of Proto-Cantonese." Ph.D. diss. Cornell University.

Mao Dun. 1978. "Writing reform takes another big stride forward." In Seybolt and Chiang 1979, pp. 380–82.

Martin, Samuel E. 1953. "The phonemes of Ancient Chinese." Supplement to *JAOS* 16.

———. 1957. "Problems of hierarchy and indeterminacy in Mandarin phonology." *BIHP* 29: 209–29.

———. 1972. "Nonalphabetic writing systems: Some observations." In Kavanagh and Mattingly 1972, pp. 81–102.

Maryknoll Language School. 1976. *Amoy-English dictionary*. Taizhong: Maryknoll Language Service Center.

Mathews, R. H. 1967. *Chinese-English dictionary*. Rev. American ed. Cambridge, Mass.: Harvard University Press.

Mei, Tsu-Lin. 1970. "Tones and prosody in Middle Chinese and the origin of the rising tone." *HJAS* 30: 86–110.

Mencken, H. L. 1979. *The American language*. 4th ed. New York: Knopf.

Miller, Roy Andrew. 1967. *The Japanese language*. Chicago: University of Chicago Press.

Mills, Harriet. 1956. "Language reform in China: Some recent developments." *The Far Eastern Quarterly* 15.4: 517–40.

Needham, Joseph. 1956. *Science and civilisation in China*. Vol. 2. Oxford: Oxford University Press.

Newnham, Richard. 1971. *About Chinese*. Harmondsworth: Penguin.

Ni Haishu. 1949. *Zhongguo yuwen de xinsheng* [Rebirth of the Chinese language]. Shanghai: Shidai chuban-she.

Norman, Jerry. 1970. "A characterization of the Min dialects." *Unicorn* 6: 19–34.

———. 1971. "Tonal development in Min." *Unicorn* 7: 1–32.

———. 1972. "A preliminary report on the dialects on Mintung." *Unicorn* 10: 20–35.

———. 1974. "The initials of Proto-Min." *JCL* 2.1: 27–36.

———. 1979. "Chronological strata in the Min dialects." *Fangyan* 4: 268–74.

———. 1988. *Chinese*. Cambridge: Cambridge University Press.

Ōta Tatsuo. 1958. *Chūgokugo rekishi bunpō* [A historical grammar of modern Chinese]. Tokyo: Kōnan shoin.

Pan Ling. 1983. *In search of old Shanghai*. Hong Kong: Joint Publishing Co.

Pedersen, Holger. 1959. *The Discovery of language*. Bloomington: Indiana University Press.

Pulleyblank, E. G. 1962. "The consonantal system of Old Chinese." *Asia Major* 9: 54–144.

———. 1963. "The consonantal system of Old Chinese (cont.)." *Asia Major* 9: 206–265.

———. 1972. "Some new hypotheses concerning word families in Chinese." *Unicorn* 9: 1–19.

Qian Xuantong. 1918. "Zhongguo jinhou zhi wenzi wenti" [The problems of China's present and future script]. In Zhao 1963, pp. 169–74.

Rao Bingcai, Ouyang Jueya, and Zhou Wuji. 1981. *Guangzhouhua fangyan cidian* [A dictionary of the Cantonese dialect]. Hong Kong: Shangwu Yinshuguan.

Reischauer, Edwin O. and John K. Fairbank. 1958. *East Asia: The great tradition*. Boston: Houghton Mifflin.

Robins, R. H. 1968. *A short history of linguistics*. Bloomington: Indiana University Press.

Schleicher, August. 1863. *Die darwinische Theorie und die Sprachwissenschaft*. Weimar: Hermann Böhlau.

Sebeok, Thomas A., ed. 1967. *Current trends in linguistics II: Linguistics in East and South East Asia*. The Hague: Mouton.

Serruys, Paul L.-M. 1962. *Survey of the Chinese language reform and anti-illiteracy movement in Communist China*. Studies in Chinese Communist Terminology Series, no. 8. Berkeley: University of California Press.

Seward, Jack. 1983. *Japanese in action*. 2d ed. New York: Weatherhill.

Seybolt, Peter J. and Gregory Kuei-ke Chiang, eds. 1979. *Language reform in China*. White Plains, N.Y.: M. E. Sharpe.

Shadick, Harold. 1968. *A first course in literary Chinese*. Ithaca: Cornell University Press.

Sherard, Michael. 1972. *Shanghai phonology*. Ph.D. diss., Cornell University.

———. 1982. *A lexical survey of the Shanghai dialect*. CAAAL Monograph Series, no. 8. Tokyo.

Shima Kunio. 1967. *Inkyo bokuji sōrui* [A comprehensive classification of the oracle bone inscriptions]. Tokyo. Taian.

Skinner, G. William, ed. 1977. *The city in Late Imperial China*. Stanford: Stanford University Press.

Somers, Robert M. 1979. "The end of the T'ang." In *Sui and T'ang China 589–906, Part I*. Vol. 3 of *The Cambridge History of China*, ed. Denis Twitchett, pp. 727–55. Cambridge: Cambridge University Press.

Stimson, Hugh M. 1962. "Ancient Chinese *-p, -t, -k* endings in the Peking dialect." *Language* 38: 376–84.

———. 1963. *The Jong Yuan Yin Yunn*. New Haven: Yale University Press.

———. 1966. "Mandarin dialects: A problem in classification." *JCLTA* 1.3: 92–98.

Sung, Margaret M. Y. 1973. "A study of literary and colloquial Amoy Chinese." *JCL* 1.3: 416–36.

———. 1979. "Chinese language and culture: A study of homonyms, lucky words, and taboos." *JCL* 7: 15–28.

Tai, James H–Y. 1976. *Lexical changes in Modern Standard Chinese in the People's Republic of China since 1949*. Washington, D.C.: USIA.

———. 1977. *Syntactic and stylistic changes in Modern Standard Chinese in the People's Republic of China since 1949*. Washington, D.C.: USIA.

———. 1978. *Phonological changes in Modern Standard Chinese in the People's Republic of China since 1949*. Washington, D.C.: USIA.

Taiwan Sōtokufu. 1932a. *Tai-Nichi dai jiten* [A comprehensive Taiwanese-Japanese dictionary]. Taipei: Taiwan sōtokufu.

———. 1932b. *Kantongo jiten* [A Japanese-Hakka dictionary]. Taipei: Taiwan sōtokufu.

———. 1938. *Shintei Nichi-Tai dai jiten* [A new comprehensive Japanese-Taiwanese dictionary]. Taipei: Taiwan sotokufu.

Tewksbury, M. Gardner. 1948. *Speak Chinese*. New Haven: Far Eastern Publications.

Tōdō Akiyasu. 1956. *Chūgokugo bunpō no kenkyū* [A study of Chinese grammar]. Tokyo: Kōnan shoin.

———. 1957. *Chūgokugo on'inron* [Chinese phonology]. Tokyo: Kōnan shoin.

Walton, A. Ronald. 1976. *Phonological redundancy in Shanghai*. Cornell University East Asia Papers, no. 11. Ithaca: China-Japan Program, Cornell University.

———. 1978. "Students' guide to elementary Chinese." Typescript.

———. 1983. *Tone, segment, and syllable in Chinese: A polydimensional approach to surface phonetic structure*. Cornell University East Asia Papers, no. 32.

Wang, Fred Fang-yu. 1958. *Introduction to Chinese cursive script*. Mirror Series A, no. 28. New Haven: Yale University Press.

———. 1967. *Mandarin Chinese Dictionary*. South Orange, N.J.: Seton Hall.

Wang Kang. 1956. *Zenyang shixing wenzi gaige* [How to carry out writing reform]. Wuhan: Hubei Renmin Chuban-she.

Wang Li. 1947. *Zhongguo xiandai yufa* [The grammar of modern Chinese]. Shanghai: Zhonghua shuju.

———. 1957. *Hanyu yinyun-xue* [The study of Chinese phonology]. Peking: Zhonghua shuju.

————. 1957–1958. *Hanyu shigao* [A draft history of the Chinese language]. Peking: Zhonghua shuju.

————. 1979a. "The present state of Chinese linguistics and its problems." In Seybolt and Chiang 1979, pp. 78–90.

————. 1979b. "A criticism of the beourgeois thought in my linguistic work." In Seybolt and Chiang 1979, pp. 272–87.

Wang Lifa. 1958. *"Xiandai Hanyu zhong cong Riyu jielai de cihui" [Vocabulary in modern Chinese borrowed from Japanese]. Zhongguo yuwen* 68 (Feb.): 90–94.

Wang, William S. -Y. and Anatole Lyovin. 1970. *CLIBOC: Chinese linguistics bibliography on computer.* Cambridge: Cambridge University Press.

Whitney, William Dwight. 1872. "Strictures on the views of August Schleicher respecting the nature of language and kindred subjects." *Transactions of the American Philological Association* (1871): 35–64.

Wiens, Herold J. 1962. *China.* Grand Rapids: Fideler.

Wu Jingrong, et al., eds. 1979. *The Chinese-English dictionary.* Hong Kong: Commercial Press.

Wu, Yuan-li, ed. 1973. *China: A handbook.* New York: Praeger.

Yang, Paul Fu-mien. 1974. *Chinese linguistics: A selected and classified bibliography.* Hong Kong: The Chinese University Press.

————. 1981. *Chinese dialectology: A selected and classified bibliography.* Hong Kong: The Chinese University Press.

Yi Xiwu. 1955. *Jianti zi yuan* [The etymologies of simplified characters]. Peking: Zhonghua shuju.

Young, Linda Wailing. 1982. "Inscrutability revisited." In *Language and social identity*, ed. John J. Gumperz, pp. 72–84. Cambridge: Cambridge University Press.

Yuan Jiahua, et al. 1960. *Hanyu fangyan gaiyao* [An outline of the Chinese dialects]. Peking: Wenzi gaige chuban-she.

Zhao Jiabi, ed. 1963. *Zhongguo xin wenxue daxi* [The new literature of China series]. Hong Kong: Xianggang wenxue yanjiu-she.

Zheng Dian. 1958. "Tan xiandai Hanyu zhong de Riyu yuhui" [A discussion of Japanese vocabulary in modern Chinese]. *Zhongguo yuwen* 68 (Feb.): 90–94.

Zheng Liangwei and Zheng Xie Shujuan. 1977. *Taiwan Fujianhua de yuyin jiegou ji biaoyin-fa* [The structure and an orthography for the sounds of the Taiwan variety of Fukienese]. Taipei: Student Book Company.

Zheng Linxi. 1959. *Hanzi gaige* [The reform of Chinese characters]. Shanghai: Jiaoyu chuban-she.

Zheng Linxi, et al. 1952. *Zhongguo wenzi gaige wenti* [The problems of Chinese script reform]. Peking: Xin jianshe zazhi-she.

Zhongguo Yuwen Zazhi-she, ed. 1954. *Zhongguo wenzi pinyin-hua wenti* [Problems with the alphabetization of Chinese writing]. Shanghai: Zhonghua shuju.

Zhonghua Shuju. 1976. *Putonghua-Yueyin Zhonghua xin zidian* [The new Zhonghua dictionary of Putonghua and Cantonese]. Hong Kong: Zhonghua Shuju.

Zhou Enlai. 1958. "Dangqian wenzi gaige de renwu." *Wenzi gaige* [Feb.]: 1–6.

———. 1979. "The immediate tasks in writing reform" (trans. by Gregory Kuei-ke Chiang of Zhou Enlai 1958). In Seybolt and Chiang 1979, pp. 228–43.

Zhou Fagao. 1955. *Zhongguo yuwen yanjiu* [Studies on Chinese language and literature]. Taipei: Zhonghua wenhua.

———. 1962. *Zhongguo gudai yufa* [A historical grammar of ancient Chinese]. Part II, Special Publication no. 39 of the Institute of History and Philology of the Academia Sinica, Taiwan.

Zhou Zumo. 1957. *Hanyu yinyun lunwen ji* [Collected essays on Chinese phonology]. Shanghai: Shangwu yinshu-guan.

BIBLIOGRAPHY FOR CHINA'S MINORITY LANGUAGES

GENERAL

Austerlitz, Robert. 1975. "Folklore, nationality, and the twentieth century in Siberia and the Soviet Far East." *Journal of the Folklore Institute* 12: 203–10.

Beijing Review. 1983. "China's national minorities." *Beijing Review* 27.2 (25 May): 19–20.

Bynon, Theodora. 1977. *Historical linguistics*. Cambridge: Cambridge University Press.

Chang, Kun. 1967. "National languages." In Sebeok 1967, pp. 151–87.

Chang, Kwang-chih. 1977. *The archeology of Ancient China*. New Haven: Yale University Press.

Dreyer, June Teufel. 1976. *China's forty millions*. Cambridge, Mass.: Harvard University Press.

Eberhard, Wolfram. 1942. "Kultur und Siedlung der Randvölker Chinas." *T'oung Pao* 38, supplement.

———. 1971. *A history of China*. Berkeley: University of California Press.

———. 1982. *China's minorities: Yesterday and today*. Belmont, Calf.: Wadsworth Publishers.

Fei, Hsiao-tung. 1980. "Ethnic identity in China." *Social Sciences in China* 1.1: 94–107.

Fei Xiaotong [Hsiao-tung Fei] and Lin Yuehua. 1956. "On the question of national distinctions among the minority nationalities of China." *Renmin ribao* (10 Aug.): 7.

Hashimoto, Mantaro J. 1976. "Language diffusion on the Asian continent." *CAAAL* 3: 49–66.

———. 1978. *Gengo ruikei chiri-ron* [Linguistic typogeography]. Tokyo: Kōbun-dō.

Hu, C. T. 1970. *The education of national minorities in Communist China*. Washington, D.C.: Government Printing Office OE-14146.

Lehmann, Winfred P., ed. 1975. *Language and linguistics in the People's Republic of China*, Austin: University of Texas Press.

Luo Changpei and Fu Maoji. 1954. "Guonei shaoshu minzu yuyan wenzi de gaikuang" [A survey of the languages and scripts of the minority peoples in China]. *Zhongguo yuwen* 3: 21–26.

Ma Yin et al., ed. 1981. *Zhongguo shaoshu minzu* [The minority peoples of China]. Peking: Renmin chuban-she.

Meillet, Antoine and Marcel Cohen. 1952. *Les langues du monde*. New ed. Paris: Centre National de la Recherche Scientifique.

Pulleyblank, E. G. 1983. "The Chinese and their neighbors in prehistoric and early historic times." in *The origins of Chinese civilization*, ed. David Keightley, pp. 411–66. Berkeley: University of California Press.

Schwarz, Henry G. 1962. "Language policies toward ethnic minorities. *The China Quarterly* 16: 170–82.

Sebeok, Thomas A., ed. 1967. *Current trends in linguistics II: Linguistics in East Asia and South East Asia*. The Hague: Mouton.

Wakeman, Frederic, Jr. 1975. *The fall of Imperial China*. New York: The Free Press.

THE MINORITIES OF NORTH CHINA

Austerlitz, Robert. 1970. "Agglutination in northern Eurasia in perspective." In *Studies in general and oriental linguistics presented to Shiro Hattori on the occasion of his sixtieth birthday*, ed. Roman Jakobson and Shigeo Kawamoto, pp. 1–5. Tokyo: TEC Company.

———. 1980. "Ural-Altaic languages." In *The academic American encyclopedia*, vol. 19, pp. 474–76. Danbury, Conn.: Grolier.

Austin, William M. 1962. "The phonemics and morphophonemics of Manchu." In *American studies in Altaic linguistics*, ed. Nicholas Poppe, pp. 15–22. Bloomington: Indiana University Press.

Benzing, Johannes. 1956. *Die tungusischen Sprachen*. Wiesbaden: Franz Steiner Verlag.

Benzing, Johannes and Karl Heinrich Menges. 1959. "Classification of the Turkic languages." In Deny 1959, pp. 1–10.

Bosson, James and B. Unensečen. 1962. "Some notes on the dialect of the Khorchin Mongols." In *American Studies in Altaic Linguistics*, ed. Nicholas Poppe, pp. 23–44.

Chen Naixiong. 1981. "Menggu-wen zhong de tongxingci" [Word forms that are the same in the Mongolian script]. In *Minzu yuwen lunji* [Collection of essays on nationality languages], pp. 345–58. Peking: Minzu yinshua-chang.

Comrie, Bernard. 1983. *The languages of the Soviet Union*. Cambridge: Cambridge University Press.

Deny, Jean, Kaare Grønbech, Helmuth Scheel, and Zeki Velidi Togan, eds. 1959. *Philologiae Turcicae Fundamenta*. Wiesbaden: Franz Steiner Verlag.

Gabain, A. von. 1950. *Alttürkische Grammatik*. Leipzig: Harrassowitz.

Haenisch, Erich. 1961. *Mandschu-Grammatik*. Leipzig: Veb Verlag Enzyklopadie.

Harlez, Charles Joseph de. 1884. *Manuel de la langue Mandchoue: Grammaire, anthologie et lexique*. Paris: Maisonneuve Frères & C. Leclerc

Hiekisch, Carl. 1879. *Die Tungusen*. St. Petersburg: Buchdruckerei der kaiserlichen Akademie der Wissenschaft. Reprinted 1966. Oosterhout: Anthropological Publications.

Jarring, Gunnar. 1933. *Studien zu einer osttürkischen Lautlehre*. Lund: Borelius.

Kiyose, Gisaburo N. 1977. *A Study of the Jurchen language and script: Reconstruction and decipherment*. Tokyo: Hōritsubunka-sha.

Li Shulan. 1979. "Xibo-yu gaikuang" [A brief description of the Xibo language].

Minzu yuwen 1979.3: 221–32.

———. 1981. "Elunchun-yu cihui shulüe" [A brief description of the vocabulary of Oroqen]. In *Minzu yuwen lunji* [Collection of essays on nationality languages], pp. 405–26. Peking: Minzu yinshua-chang.

Lie, Hiu. 1978. "Solonisches Material aus dem Huin-gol," In *Tungusica*, ed. Michael Weiers, vol. I. pp. 126–78. Wiesbaden: Otto Harrassowitz.

Liu Zhaoxiong. 1981. *Dongxiang-yu jianzhi* [A handbook of the Dongxiang (Santa) language]. Peking: Minzu chuban-she.

Liu Zhaoxiong and Lin Lianyun. 1980. "Bao'an-yu he Sala-yu li de queding yu fei-queding yuqi" [Definite and indefinite intonation in the Bao'an and Salar languages]. *Minzu yuwen* 3: 23–28.

Lopatin, Ivan A. 1958. "The Tungus languages." *Anthropos* 53: 427–40.

Martin, Samuel E. 1961. *Dagur Mongolian grammar, texts, and lexicon based on the speech of Peter Onon*. Bloomington: Indiana University Press.

Menges, Karl Heinrich. 1959. "Die aralo-kaspische Gruppe." In Deny 1959, pp. 434–88.

———. 1968a. *The Turkic languages and peoples*. Wiesbaden: Otto Harrassowitz.

———. 1968b. "Die tungusischen Sprachen." In *Altaistik*, vol. 3: *Tungusologie*, ed. B. Spuler, pp. 21–256. Leiden: E. J. Brill.

Möllendorf, Paul Georg von. 1892. *A Manchu grammar, with analyzed texts*. Shanghai: American Presbyterian Mission Press.

Mostaert, Antoine. 1931. "The Mongols of Kansu and their language." *Bulletin of the Catholic University of Peking* 8: 75–89.

———. and A. de Smedt. 1945. *Le dialecte monguor parlé par les mongols du Kansou occidental*, pt. 2: *Grammaire*. Peking: Catholic University.

Norman, Jerry. 1978. *A concise Manchu-English lexicon*. Seattle: University of Washington Press.

Poppe, Nikolaus. 1960. *Vergleichende Grammatik der altaischen Sprachen*. Wiesbaden: Otto Harrassowitz.

———. 1964a. "Die dagurische Sprache." In *Altaistik, vol. 2: Mongolistik*. ed. B. Spuler, pp. 137–42. Leiden: E. J. Brill.

———. 1964b. *Grammar of written Mongolian*. Wiesbaden: Otto Harrassowitz.

———. 1965. *Introduction to Altaic linguistics*. Wiesbaden: Otto Harrassowitz.

———. 1970. *Mongolian language handbook*. Washington, D.C.: Center for Applied Linguistics.

Pritsak, Omeljan. 1959a. "Das Mogholische." In Deny 1959, pp. 159–84.

———. 1959b. "Das Neuuigurische." In Deny 1959, pp. 525–63.

———. 1964. "Das Mogholische." *Altaistik, Vol. 2: Mongolistik*, pp. 159–84.

Ramstedt, G. J. 1952. *Einführung in die altaische Sprachwissenschaft*. Helsinki: Suomalais-ugrilainen Seura.

Reischauer, Edwin O. and John K. Fairbank. 1958. *East Asia: The Great Tradition*. Boston: Houghton Mifflin.

Rona-Taš, A. 1960. "Remarks on the phonology of the Monguor language." *Acta Orientalia Academiae Scientiarum Hungaricae* 10.3: 263–67.

Schröder, Dominik. 1964. "Der Dialekt der Monguor." *Altaistik, Vol. 2: Mongolistik*, pp. 143–58.

Sinor, Denis. 1968. "La langue mandjoue." *Tungusologie*, pp. 257–80.

———. 1969. *Inner Asia*. Bloomington: Indiana University Press.

Sjoberg, Andrée F. 1962. "The phonology of standard Uzbek." In *American studies in Altaic linguistics*, ed. Nikolaus Poppe, pp. 237–61. Bloomington: Indiana University Press.

Street, John. 1962. "Kalmyk schwa." In *American studies in Altaic linguistics*, pp. 263–91.

Thomsen, Kaare. 1959a. "Das kasantatarische und die westsibirischen Dialekte." In Deny 1959, pp. 407–34.

———. 1959b. "Die Sprache der Gelben Uiguren und das Salarische." In Deny 1959, pp. 564–67.

Todaeva, B. H. 1957. "Yanjiu Zhongguo ge Menggu-yu he fangyan de chubu zongjie" [A preliminary summary of a study of the Mongolian languages and dialects of China]. *Zhongguo yuwen* 9: 32–40.

———. 1959a. "Über die Sprache der Tung-Hsiang." *Acta Orientalia Academiae Scientiorum Hungarica* 9: 273–310.

———. 1959b. "Mongolische Dialekte in China." *Acta Orientalia Academiae Scientiorum Hungarica* 10: 141–69.

Tucci, Giuseppe. 1949. *Tibetan painted scrolls*. 3 vols. Rome: La Libreria dello Stato.

Underhill, Robert. 1976. *Turkish grammar*. Cambridge, Mass.: MIT Press.

Wurm, Stefan. 1959. "Das Özbekische." In Deny 1959, pp. 489–524.

Wu Yuanfen and Zhao Zhiqiang. 1981. "Xibozu xiqian gaishu" [A general account of the westward migration of the Xibo]. *Minzu yanjiu* 2: 22–29.

THE MINORITIES OF SOUTH CHINA

Benedict, Paul K. 1942. "Thai, Kadai, and Indonesian: A new alignment in southeastern Asia." *American Anthropologist* 44: 576–601.

———. 1972. *Sino-Tibetan: A conspectus*. Edited by James Matisoff. Cambridge: Cambridge University Press.

———. 1975. *Austro-Thai language and culture*. New Haven: HRAF Press.

———. 1982. "Sinitic and Proto-Chinese." Paper presented at the Fifteenth Annual Sino-Tibetan Conference, August 1982, Peking.

Bradley, David. 1975. "Nahsi and Proto-Burmese Lolo." *LTBA* 2.1: 93–150.

———. 1978. *Proto-Loloish*. Scandinavian Institute of Asian Studies Monograph Series, no. 39. Copenhagen.

———. 1979. *Lahu Dialects*. Canberra: Australian National University Press.

Briggs, Lawrence Palmer. 1949. "The appearance and historical usage of the terms Tai, Thai, Siamese, and Lao." *JAOS* 69: 60–73.

Chang, Kun. 1957. "The phonemic system of the Yi Miao dialect." *BIHP, Academia Sinica* 29: 11–19.

———. 1967. "A comparative study of the southern Ch'iang dialects." *Monumenta Serica* 26: 422–44.

Cheng Mo. 1956. "Zaiwa-yu jianjie" [A brief introduction to the Tsaiwa language]. *Zhongguo yuwen* 53: 41–44.

Clarke, Samuel R. 1911. *Among the tribes in Southwest China*. London: Morgan and Scott.

Dai Qingxia and Cui Zhichao. 1983. "Achang-yu gaiyao" [A brief description of the Achang language]. *Minzu yuwen* 3: 69–80.

DeFrancis, John. 1984. *The Chinese language: Fact and fantasy.* Honolulu: University of Hawaii Press.

Dell, François. 1981. *La langue bai: Phonologie et lexique.* Paris: Editions de l'École des Hautes Études en Sciences Sociales.

Downer, G. B. 1961. "Phonology of the word in Highland Yao." *Bulletin of the School of Oriental and African Studies* 24: 531–41.

Egerod, Søren. 1981. "Sino-Tibetan languages." *Encyclopaedia Britannica Macropaedia* 16, pp. 796–806.

Fitzgerald, C. P. 1941. *The tower of five glories.* London: The Cresset Press.

Fu Maoji. 1981. *Naxi-yu tuhua-wenzi "Bai bianfu qu jing ji" yanjiu* [A study of a Naxi pictographic manuscript, "White Bat's Search for Sacred Books"], Vol. I. CAAAL Monograph Series, no. 6. Tokyo: CAAAL.

———. 1984. *Naxi-yu tuhua-wenzi "Bai bianfu qu jing ji" yanjiu,* Vol. II. CAAAL Monograph Series, no. 9. Tokyo.

Fu Zhennan. 1983. "Hainan-dao xi-haian de 'cunhua'" ["Cun speech" on the west coast of Hainan Island]. *Minzu yuwen* 4: 68–71.

Gai Xingzhi. 1981. "Jinuo-yu gaikuang" [A brief description of the Jino language]. *Minzu yuwen* 1: 65–78.

Gao Huanian. 1958. *Yiyu yufa yanjiu* [A study of the grammar of the Yi (Nasu) language]. Peking: Kexue chuban.

Gjessing, Gutorm. 1956. "Chinese anthropology and New China's policy toward her minorities." *Acta Sociologica* 2: 45–66.

Hashimoto, Mantaro J. 1980. *The Be language.* Tokyo: Japan Society for the Promotion of Science.

He Qixiang. 1981. "Gelao-yu gaikuang" [A brief description of the Gelao language]. *Minzu yuwen* 4: 67–76.

Jiang Zhuyi. 1980. "Naxi-yu gaikuang" [A brief description of the Naxi language]. *Minzu yuwen* 3: 59–73.

LeBar, Frank M., Gerald C. Hickey, and John K. Musgrave. 1964. *Ethnic groups of Mainland Southeast Asia.* New Haven: HRAF Press.

Li, Fang-Kuei [Li Fanggui]. 1936. "Wuming tuge" [The native songs of Wuming]. *Annals of Academia Sinica (Zhongguo yanjiu-yuan yuankan)* 3: 215–20.

———. 1956. *The Tai dialect of Wuming.* BIHP, Academia Sinica Series A, no. 19. Taipei: Academia Sinica.

———. 1965. "The Tai and Kam-Sui languages." *Lingua* 14: 148–79.

———. 1981. "Tai languages." *Encyclopaedia Britannica: Macropaedia* 17, pp. 989–92.

———. 1977. *A handbook of comparative Tai.* Honolulu: University of Hawaii Press.

Li Lincan, Zhang Kun [Kun Chang], and He Cai. 1953. *Mosuo xiangxing wenzi zidian* [A dictionary of Moso (Naxi) pictographs]. Hong Kong: Shuowenshe.

———. 1957. *Mosuo jingdian yizhu liuzhong* [Translations and annotations of Moso (Naxi) classics]. Taipei: China Series Publishing Committee.

Li Min. 1979. "Yi wen" [Yi writing]. *Minzu yuwen* 4: 304–306.

Li Yongsui. 1979. "Hani-yu gaikuang" [A brief description of the Hani language]. *Minzu yuwen* 2: 134–51.

Liang Mei. 1980a. *Dong-yu jianzhi* [A handbook of the Dong (Kam) language]. Peking: Minzu chuban-she.

———. 1980b. *Maonan-yu jianzhi* [A handbook of the Maonan language]. Peking: Minzu chuban-she.

Lin Ying. 1972. "Chinese loanwords in Miao." In Purnell 1972, pp. 55–81.

Lin, Yueh-hua. 1961. *The Lolo of Liang Shan*. Trans. Ju-shan Pan; ed. Wu-chi Lin. New Haven: HRAF Press.

Liu Lu. 1964. "Jingpo-yu gaikuang" [A brief description of the Jingpo language]. *Zhongguo yuwen* 132: 407–17.

Lo, Ch'ang-P'ei [Luo Changpei]. 1945. "A preliminary study of the Trung language of Kung Shan." *HJAS* 8.3–4: 343–48.

Lu Zhaozun. 1980. "Pumi-yu gaikuang" [A brief description of the Primi language]. *Minzu yuwen* 4: 58–72.

Luo Changpei [Ch'ang-P'ei Luo] and Fu Maoji. 1954. "Guonei shaoshu minzu yuyan wenzi de gaikuang" [A survey of the languages and scripts of the minority peoples in China]. *Zhongguo yuwen* 3: 21–26.

Ma Xueliang. 1948. *Luowen "Zuoji, xianyao, gongsheng jing" yizhu* [Annotated translation of the Lolo sacred book "Performing Rites, Offering Medicines, and Sacrificing Beasts"]. BIHP, Academia Sinica Publications no. 20. Peking.

———. 1951. *Sani yiyu yanjiu* [A study of Sani, a Yi dialect]. Peking: Advanced Studies Publishing House.

Mao Zongwu and Meng Zhaoji. 1982. "Boluo She-yu gaishu" [A brief description of the She language of Boluo District]. *Minzu yuwen* 1: 64–80.

Mao Zongwu and Zhou Zuyao. 1962. "Yaozu yuyen gaikuang" [A brief description of the languages of the Yao Nationality]. *Zhongguo yuwen* 3: 141–48.

Maspero, Henri. 1952. "Les langues tibeto-birmanes." in Meillet and Cohen 1952, pp. 529–70.

Matisoff, James A. 1972. *The Loloish tonal split revisited*. Center for South and Southeast Asia Studies, Research Monograph no. 7. Berkeley: University of California Press.

———. 1973. *The grammar of Lahu*. Berkeley: University of California Press.

———. 1978. *Variational semantics in Tibeto-Burman: The 'organic' approach to linguistic comparison*. Philadelphia: Institute for the Study of Human Issues.

———. 1980. "Stars, moon, and spirits: Bright beings of the night in Sino-Tibetan." *Gengo kenkyu* 77: 1–45.

———. forthcoming. *Lahu-English dictionary*. Philadelphia: Institute for the Study of Human Issues.

Miao Language Team. 1972. "A brief description of the Miao language." In Purnell 1972, pp. 1–25.

Miller, Roy Andrew. 1969. "The Tibeto-Burman languages of South Asia." In *Current trends in linguistics V: South Asia*, ed, Thomas A. Sebeok, The Hague: Mouton. pp. 431–49.

Minority Language Bureau. 1958. *Jingpo-yu yufa gangyao* [An outline of Jingpo grammar]. Peking: Minority Language Bureau, Academia Sinica.

———. 1959. *Lisu-yu yufa gangyao* [An outline of Lisu grammar]. Peking: Minority Language Bureau, Academia Sinica.

Morse, Robert H. 1963. "Phonology of Rawang." *Anthropological Linguistics* 5.5: 17–41.

Mu Yuzhang and Duan Ling. 1983. "Lisu-yu gaikuang" [A brief description of the Lisu language]. *Minzu yuwen* 4: 72–81.

Nishida Tatsuo. 1967. *Seika moji* [Xixia writing]. Tokyo: Kinokuniya.

Ouyang Jueya and Zheng Yiqing. 1980. *Li-yu jianzhi* [A handbook of the Li language]. Peking: Minzu chuban-she.

———. 1983. "Hainan-dao Yaxian Huizu de Huihui-hua" [The Huihui speech of the Hui nationality in Yaxian, Hainan]. *Minzu yuwen* 1: 30–40.

Purnell, Herbert C., Jr., ed. 1972. *Miao and Yao linguistic studies: Selected articles in Chinese, translated by Chang Yu-hung and Chu Kuo-ray.* Cornell University Southeast Asia Program, Linguistics Series V, Data Paper #88. Ithaca: Southeast Asia Program, Cornell University.

Qiu Efang, Li Daoyong, and Nie Xizhen. 1980. "Wa-yu gaikuang" [A brief description of the Wa language]. *Minzu yuwen* 1: 58–69.

Rock, Joseph F. C. 1963–1972. *A Na-Khi–English encyclopedic dictionary.* Serie Orientale Roma, no. 28. Rome: Instituto Italiano per il Medio ed Estremo Oriente.

Shirokogoroff, S. M. 1930. "Phonetic notes on a Lolo dialect and consonant L." *BIHP, Academia Sinica* 1.2: 183–225.

Solheim, Wilhelm G. 1972. "The 'new look' of Southeast Asian prehistory." *Siam Society Journal* 60.1: 1–20.

Sun Hongkai. 1979. "Dulong-yu gaikuang" [A brief description of the Drung language]. *Minzu yuwen* 4: 292–303.

———. 1981. *Qiang-yu jianzhi* [A handbook of the Qiang language]. Peking: Minzu chuban-she.

Sun Hongkai, Lu Zhaozun, Zhang Jichuan, and Ouyang Jueya. 1980. *Menba, Luoba, Deng ren de yuyan* [The languages of the Monpa, Lhopa, and Deng peoples]. Peking: Zhongguo shehui kexue chuban-she.

Voegelin, C. F. and F. M. Voegelin. 1977. *Classification and index of the world's languages.* New York: Elsevier.

Wang Chunde. 1981. "Tantan Miao-yu goucifa [A discussion of word structure in Miao]. In *Minzu yuwen lunji* [Collection of essays on nationality languages], pp. 372–89. Peking: Minzu yinshua-chang.

Wang Jun and Deng Guoqiao. 1980. *Gelao-yu jianzhi* [A handbook of the Gelao language]. Peking: Minzu chuban-she.

Wang Lianqing. 1983. "Jing-yu gaiyao" [A brief description of the Jing (Gin) language]. *Minzu yuwen* 1: 65–80.

Wei Qingwen and Tan Guosheng. 1980. *Zhuang-yu jianzhi* [A handbook of the Zhuang language]. Peking: Minzu chuban-she.

Wiens, Herold J. 1954. *China's march to the tropics.* Hamden, Conn.: Shoe String Press.

Winnington, Alan. 1959. *The Slaves of the Cool Mountain.* London: Lawrence and Wishart.

Xu Lin and Zhao Yansun. 1964. "Bai-yu gaikuang" [A brief description of the

Bai language]. *Zhongguo yuwen* 131: 321–35.

Yan Qixiang. 1983. "Benglong-yu gaiyao" [A brief description of the Benglong language]. *Minzu yuwen* 5: 67–80.

You Rujie. 1982. "Lun Tai-yu liangci zai Han-yu nanfang fangyan zhong de diceng yicun" [On the substratal traces of Tai measure words in the Southern Han Chinese dialects]. *Minzu yuwen* 2: 33–45.

Yu Cuirong. 1980. *Buyi-yu jianzhi* [A handbook of the Buyi language]. Peking: Minzu chuban-she.

Yu Cuirong and Luo Mizhen. 1980. *Dai-yu jianzhi* [A handbook of the Dai language]. Peking: Minzu chuban-she.

Yuan Jiahua. 1953. *Axi minzu ge ji qi yuyan* [The folk songs of the Ahi people and their language]. Peking: Minzu chuban-she.

Zhang Junru. 1980. *Shui-yu jianzhi* [A handbook of the Sui language]. Peking: Minzu chuban-she.

Zhao Yansun. 1981. "Bai-yu he Han-yu Putonghua de duibi yanjiu" [A comparative study of Bai and Han Chinese Putonghua]. In *Minzu yuwen lunji* [Collection of essays on nationality languages], pp. 47–110. Peking: Minzu yinshua-chang.

Zhongguo yuwen, ed. 1962. "Qiang-yu gaiyao" [A brief description of the Qiang language]. *Zhongguo yuwen* 121: 561–71.

Zhou Zhizhi and Yan Qixiang. 1983. "Bulang-yu gaiyao" [A brief description of the Blang language]. *Minzu yuwen* 2: 71–81.

INDEX

Principal page numbers for particular entries appear in italics.

LIBRARY OF CONGRESS CATALOGING-IN-PUBLICATION DATA

Ramsey, S. Robert, 1941–
  The languages of China.

  Bibliography: p.
  Includes index.
  1. Chinese language. 2. China—Languages. I. Title.
PL1071.R34 1986   409'.51   86-12212
ISBN 0-691-06694-9 (alk. paper)

S. ROBERT RAMSEY is Associate Professor in the
Department of Hebrew and East Asian Languages and
Literatures at the University of Maryland.